NARRATING THE LANDSCAPE

The Charles M. Russell Center Series
on Art and Photography of the American West

B. Byron Price, General Editor

NARRATING THE LANDSCAPE

Print Culture and American Expansion in the Nineteenth Century

MATTHEW N. JOHNSTON

UNIVERSITY OF OKLAHOMA PRESS : NORMAN

Library of Congress Cataloging-in-Publication Data

Names: Johnston, Matt, 1970– author.
Title: Narrating the landscape : print culture and American expansion in the nineteenth century / Matt Johnston.
Description: First [edition]. | Norman : University of Oklahoma Press, 2016. | Series: The Charles M. Russell Center series on art and photography of the American West ; Volume 24 | Includes bibliographical references and index.
Identifiers: LCCN 2015037905 | ISBN 978-0-8061-5223-3 (hardcover : alk. paper)
Subjects: LCSH: Landscapes in art. | Landscape prints, American—19th century. | Art and society—United States—History—19th century. | United States—In art. | United States—In popular culture.
Classification: LCC NE954.2 .J65 2016 | DDC 700/.46—dc23
LC record available at http://lccn.loc.gov/2015037905

Narrating the Landscape: Print Culture and American Expansion in the Nineteenth Century is Volume 24 in the The Charles M. Russell Center Series on Art and Photography of the American West.

The paper in this book meets the guidelines for permanence and durability of the Committee on Production Guidelines for Book Longevity of the Council on Library Resources, Inc. ∞

1 2 3 4 5 6 7 8 9 10

Contents

NARRATING THE LANDSCAPE

Introduction

Landscape and Narrative in Nineteenth-Century American Visual Culture

IN 1847, WILLIAM GUILD of Boston published a railroad guidebook that described the sights along the newly constructed Boston and Worcester line, connecting the Massachusetts capital and chief port with the commercial corridor of the Hudson River.[1] For the nineteenth-century traveler, the guidebook might have punctuated a trip with moments of interest and afterward served as a personal souvenir of the excursion, but for the modern reader, not actually involved in that trip, its value may seem slight. In essence, the travel guide mediates or augments another experience; in and of itself it is incomplete. Similarly, the basic components of Guild's railroad guidebook are not especially remarkable. Its dimensions are modest (it is about five by eight inches in size and some sixty-four pages in length). Its tiny electrotype illustrations, mostly of houses, road crossings, and bridges, quickly become monotonous, as does the overblown text pointing out the aesthetic merits of the landscape and the engineering achievements of the different viaducts and tunnels encountered on the route (plate 1 and figure 13). Even the vertical route line that appears on every verso page seems to signal an overriding uniformity that ensures the discovery of more or less the same thing from page to page. Guild's *Chart and Description* certainly has considerable historical value, especially in terms of the onset of industrialization and urbanization in American society at midcentury, with a wealth of information pertaining to the construction of the Boston and Worcester line, the kinds of commercial goods produced and shipped in the area, and the growth of suburban enclaves outside Boston. More than a snapshot of development at this time, the guide also testifies to a belief in economic, technological, and social progress, a faith presumably shared by Guild's audience. Still, the book's own character as an experience, as a particular kind of narration and picturing of the world, seems easy to ignore, as the modern reader familiar with nineteenth-century American history in some sense anticipates the gist of its "content" ahead of time.

Despite being a sightseeing guide, the *Chart and Description* is also notably self-reflexive, inasmuch as it repeatedly draws attention to the railroad itself (instead of the surrounding countryside), and railroad companies were typically the financial backers of these kinds of guidebooks. Guild concludes his declaration of purpose in publishing his book by assuring the reader that it contains "much information of value, especially much knowledge in regard to the peculiarities, cost, and construction of the Western Railroad," and in keeping with this objective, the railroad is a recurring feature of the landscape prints that illustrate it.[2] Rather than viewing this self-reflexiveness as yet another proof of the guidebook's banality, I want to use it as a starting point for accessing its peculiar novelty, as if it were calling attention not just to the railroad as a technological marvel but also to itself as a new kind of imaging device. Guild's brief introduction is followed by a short paragraph and a chart instructing the reader how to use the guidebook (plate 1, left side). The text is explicit as to where the rider should sit on the train (facing toward or away from the engine depending on whether one is traveling to or from Boston), a directionality that applies to the order of the text itself (so one is asked to read either "upward"—somehow—or "downward"). In addition, the "Explanation of the Chart" carefully specifies how noteworthy sights visible outside the passenger car window are identified in abbreviated form on either side of the vertical route line on the guide's lefthand pages, sights that are then explicated in the textual descriptions and landscape prints located on its righthand pages. The route line, divided into evenly spaced mile markings, furthermore helps to translate the speed of the swiftly moving train into an equally accelerated reading and viewing pace (at the train's reported velocity of forty miles per hour, there are about eight minutes' reading time per two-page spread). Thus, Guild's *Chart and Description* precisely coordinates a fairly rapidly shifting visual, textual, and pictorial experience, mediating the rider's perception and understanding of the passing landscape more substantively than might be expected in an inexpensive mass-market booklet.

One of the most celebrated and defining aspects of this period of American history was the nation's rapid growth from a sparsely populated and mostly agrarian group of states along the eastern seaboard to a transcontinental entity with increasingly dense industrial metropolises. Guild's work is both a symptom and an instrument of key social and economic changes taking place at this time, but scholars have, perhaps not surprisingly, concentrated on the role of literature and the fine arts in developing themes of the progress of civilization.[3] In particular, art historians have, until recently at least, focused on landscape painting as the preeminent pictorial locus for disseminating the widespread belief in the country's Manifest Destiny to settle and develop the continent.[4] Paintings in this genre were viewed by large urban audiences in annual group shows, like those held after 1825 by the National Academy of Design, or occasionally in blockbuster exhibits of single works, like Frederic Edwin Church's display of *The Heart of the Andes* in 1859. Earlier in the century especially, landscape and genre paintings were often promoted as a "democratic" art, and early art institutions, such as the American Art-Union, were more egalitarian in their membership and exhibition practices than the traditional European academy system was, but a privileged status was implicitly ascribed to fine art, and this distinction would become increasingly conspicuous after the Civil War.[5] The more commonplace versions of landscape art (such as Guild's little book), and the part they played in the physical and cultural development of the nation, have only lately begun to receive direct attention as a central subject themselves.

This is not to say that scholarship on landscape painting denies the importance of print materials in shaping nineteenth-century society; to the contrary, an examination of such work over the past few decades reveals an increasing appreciation for this component of the nation's visual culture. More to the point, studies of American print materials are experiencing a period of growth, and print ephemera such as political cartoons, popular prints, and advertising cards are receiving sustained, focused attention as opposed to being merely enlisted as ancillary visual evidence in works addressing some other American historical topic.[6] The present study seeks to expand on this recent enthusiasm, looking specifically at illustrated books that privileged landscape imagery and investigating practices of orchestrating text and image as an object of study in its own right. Nonetheless, existing print scholarship remains somewhat restricted to a specialist audience; as Georgia Barnhill, director of the Center for Historic American Visual Culture at the American Antiquarian Society, wrote in a recent book review: "There is a rich body of literature on American print and periodical illustration, not to mention works on American prints of all types. . . . Unhappily, most of the literature seems to be consumed by a small universe of curators and collectors."[7] To a certain extent as well, though, scholarship on landscape prints in particular remains beholden to models of interpretation developed for landscape paintings, as earlier art historians sought to extend those models outward to embrace more popular cultural art forms.

Thus, in Angela Miller's landmark study, *The Empire of the Eye: Landscape Representation and American Cultural Politics, 1825–1875,* her choice of "representation" over "painting" in the title highlighted her intent to incorporate visual forms other than the fine arts (such as print imagery) into her larger argument.[8] Indeed, territorial and industrial expansion spurred a remarkable proliferation of new types of publications, not only addressing novel subjects resulting from exploration and economic development, but also presenting these subjects in innovative ways through recent printing inventions such as wood engraving, electrotype, and high-speed rotary presses. While landscape painting dramatically increased in popularity and prestige during this time, perhaps more striking is the variety of means by which images of landscape were made available to different kinds of audiences through the medium of print. Although Miller's book reveals a profound familiarity with nineteenth-century print culture, this characteristically takes the form of printed texts, not images, that describe or discuss landscape; besides a limited selection of Currier and Ives and *Harper's Weekly* prints (to be sure, among the most widespread of American print images), almost all the illustrations in her book are reproductions of paintings.

The tendency to acknowledge but not closely examine print images in a work such as Miller's, one that aspired to move beyond an emphasis on painting to address "representation" as a whole, arguably proceeds from an assumption about the derivative nature of print illustrations in relation to paintings. In her introduction, Miller seems to agree with Benedict Anderson's famous equation of a national with a specifically print audience, but she simultaneously seems to assert the adequacy of painting as a representative vehicle in a democratic "image-language" that also includes print images:

> In realizing what Benedict Anderson has termed the "imagined community" underlying a sense of nationalism, Americans, like their European counterparts, relied on a "print-language." To Anderson's crucial definition, I would add the essential role played in the American context by visual images in creating a community transcending bonds of clan, caste, or religion, and working across space and time. Like the written word, images were circulated through prints and periodicals with a national readership or in oil paintings available to more limited, metropolitan audiences. They developed their own national audience, engendering a set of common experiences and creating a set of reference points shared by people otherwise unconnected. . . . Images were thus central to the formation of American nationalism.[9]

"Visual images" are correlated with the "written word" and are found in both "prints and periodicals" and "oil paintings." This initial differentiation as to medium (and audience) then gives way to an affirmation of joint effectiveness: "They developed their own national audience" (however "limited" the "metropolitan audiences" of painting might be). At the very least, prints and paintings appear here as equivalent and allied agents, with the result that Miller's subsequent analysis of painting alone is offered as an adequately comprehensive treatment of a democratic "image-language."

In many ways, this subsuming of analyzing print images within an exploration of the expressive models generated in painting marks later scholarship as well, even when more explicitly directed at a mass culture subject. For example, Richard Gassan's *The Birth of American Tourism: New York, the Hudson Valley, and American Culture, 1790–1830* details the growing touristic development of the Hudson River by closely examining each of the region's first scenic guidebooks.[10] One of Gassan's major arguments, in the early chapter "The Revolution of Seeing: Tourism and the Founding of the Hudson River School," concerns the leading part played by such guidebooks in shaping the demand for, and more importantly an eye for, "picturesque" scenery in the newly formed United States. Even before the emergence of a native landscape painting school, such works are seen as the "first attempt[s] to present America with an image of itself that moved away from the 'beautiful' toward the picturesque."[11] Nonetheless, as Gassan shows, these initial forays themselves imitated an already established British picturesque tradition. If they make it possible for the artist Thomas Cole to focus on landscape subjects alone, they do so primarily by transferring that tradition to an American setting, not by generating ways of seeing that are particular to the structure of the guidebook.[12]

There are many reasons for privileging painting in an examination of images as a whole produced at this time. Most nineteenth-century artists produced engravings, lithographs, and other print versions of their work; after all, a print is (by definition) a copy of something else, and that something else was often a painting. As a copy, the print is often regarded as at best a diminished echo of the real thing: smaller, devoid of color, without texture. Conversely, American art history teems with printmakers who later became successful painters, from Asher B. Durand to Winslow Homer. Some scholars discuss these artists' printmaking background as a significant influence on their painting technique. Even in these cases, however, there is often a tendency to see the shift to painting as a progressive development, a movement toward a more fully formed artistic expression.[13] Within broader studies of American book illustration, this bias has arguably fostered a more traditional, connoisseur-like approach, which is only lately being superseded; historically, such studies often took the form of comprehensive catalogs describing the evolution of drawing and mark-making styles in woodblock, lithography, and intaglio.[14] Finally, and more subtly, prints of landscapes are often found within texts (as in Guild's railroad guidebook); embedded in another order of representation, they seem to lose their own representational autonomy or force. Or rather, their force in conjunction with the accompanying text is characteristically ignored in favor of a more familiar, supplemental role as "illustration," a term that frequently implies a subordinate relationship to the text.[15] In this book I turn upside down such assumptions (however tacit or implicit they may be) and the kind of analysis that accompanies them. Instead of treating the embedding of print imagery in text as an enervating process, I concentrate on how this embedding opens up new (and unrecognized) expressive possibilities for both print images and text.

This tendency of art historical scholarship on landscape painting to reach out to encompass other visual media while still upholding the primacy of the painting medium is comparable to how nineteenth-century American literary studies has frequently recognized the importance of "mass culture" while refraining from fully engaging it. Even work that proposes to treat the "encounter between literary culture and mass culture as . . . an event in social history that inaugurates a 'postliterary' era when literary culture could no longer presume to be the implicit model of the public sphere" is often still committed to the canonical text.[16] Thus, in *Frantic Panoramas: American Literature and Mass Culture, 1870–1920,* Nancy Bentley examines in detail "mass culture" documents like the autobiography of P. T. Barnum, but her focus remains "understanding the high literary culture that emerged at the turn of the century"; the separate "public sphere" of mass culture remains principally significant in terms of its effects on traditional literature and less as an object of analysis itself (even though Bentley notably expands this corpus to include nonwhite, nonmale writers who have been just as traditionally excluded).[17] Literary historians acknowledge that an increasingly industrial, increasingly consumerist popular culture was affecting, modifying, even transforming "high literary culture," yet the productions of the latter are still consistently seen as the fullest explication of this process. In terms of the print material considered in this study, William Dean Howells's 1890 *Hazard of New Fortunes* comes to mind, in particular the condescending discussion of graphic design, illustration styles, and page layout for the new bi-weekly *Every Other Week* by the magazine's principals. Basil March, the novel's hero and the journal's editor, explains his distaste for illustrations by saying, "I find that I look at the pictures in an illustrated article, but I don't read the article very much. . . . You've got to doing them so prettily that you take our eyes off the literature, if you don't take our minds off."[18] As Bill Brown observes in *A Sense of Things: The Object Matter of American Literature,* analyses addressed squarely at the "things" of a nascent "mass culture" might paradoxically "[leave] things behind, never quite asking how they become recognizable, representable, and exchangeable to begin with."[19] My view, however, is that among those "things" are print materials, illustrated books, that are indeed "fashioning" their own "object-based historiography and anthropology," and that such documents (across a range of discourses outside literature proper) were in the vanguard of processes redefining the object world of nineteenth-century American society.[20]

The present study undertakes to advance the current understanding of print culture within American art history and American literary studies by extending scholarship that has recognized how different kinds of "narrativity" (forms of structure and engagement that appear intrinsically textual) inform and inhabit many aspects of nineteenth-century visual culture. Of particular interest is scholarship on landscape painting, which has already explored how many of these works characteristically programmed different stories about the nation's expansion and development—different versions of past and future history—into the organization of represented space.[21] These studies explain how the perception of history in paintings by Cole and Durand, founding figures of a dominant paradigm for the genre throughout most of the century (the so-called Hudson River school), hinges on establishing a parallel between the movement of the viewer's eye through represented space and the unfolding over time of a narrative of civilization.[22] Thus, in Durand's 1853 *Progress,* "specific temporal correlates were assigned to the organizing planes within the image, embedding historical meaning in the very structure of space itself": as the eye moves back into space, it also moves forward in time, enacting and normalizing the progress of civilization. This progression is most apparent on the righthand side of the painting, which contains a succession of both habitations and transportation technologies: farmstead, town, busy seaport; wagon, canal boat, train (plate 2).[23] But this type of correlation between pictorial space and some schematization of history is necessarily limited by the kind of historical narrative it makes available to the viewer. American landscape painters generally operated within a set of constraints that determined the expressive possibilities of the medium, most notably the hierarchy of genres inherited from English and French painting traditions.[24] Although individual artists contrived to elevate their work by incorporating aspects of history painting within their pictures, the hierarchical order was a determining logic in the selection and conception of painting subjects. This in turn meant that landscape imagery was conditioned to express a certain idealized version of history as this term (history) was understood within the genre hierarchy. As a result, interpretation tends to remain on the level of allegory: reading narratively becomes synonymous with reading allegorically.

Returning to Guild's railroad guidebook, if we regard it as derivative of painting in its presentation of landscape imagery, we might go on to note that the artist, Merrill Wheelock, was an aspiring watercolorist and an architect (he designed the Masonic Temple in Boston). In other words, Wheelock was a person who might have wanted to be an artist on a par with Durand, but his abilities or professional opportunities kept him from devoting himself exclusively to painting. If we look at the landscape prints themselves, we might note that they at best contain prosaic and abbreviated versions of picturesque conventions found in painting, such as a kind of foreground platform for the viewer and a clearly indicated path into depth, a way of guiding the eye into the background (plate 1 and figure 13). But if landscape painting at this time was organizing vision, or the viewing of depicted space, along narrative lines in order to convey ideologically loaded conceptions of national history, is Guild's work still to be regarded as essentially derivative? Admittedly, as in Durand's painting, there is a similar fascination with social and technological progress, registered primarily through the material evidence of railroad engineering that Guild's work returns to again and again. Yet Durand's painting relied on a static spectator and an act of viewing that moved slowly from point to point in the depicted landscape in order to enact or reify progress, whereas the rapidity of train travel precluded such extended acts of spectatorship. Instead, as described in more detail in the following chapter, "progress" is realized in Guild's book in that quickly shifting interplay between visual, textual, and pictorial orders of experience so carefully laid out in the "Explanation of the Chart." The viewer experiences parallel movements in three different visual and representational senses: progress through the visibly passing landscape, progress through the text as it is read, and progress through the images as they are viewed.

Guild's synthesizing, or "syncretic," organization of the visual, the textual, and the pictorial is clearly related to but just as clearly *not* merely derivative of strategies for narratively organizing vision in painting. Is the notion of progress conveyed by Guild's book then fundamentally the same as that found in Durand's painting? Do the differences in their experiential components, especially those having to do with time—rapid and shifting in Guild, extended and continuous in Durand—shape correspondingly discrete perceptions of national history? Furthermore, would such differences reflect on important social distinctions (that is, between the viewers of either work) or important discursive distinctions (that is, between an illustrated book and a painting)? In chapter 1, I return to these questions as they apply to transportation guides. The basic premise informing the present study, however, is that a unique kind of rhetoric, specifically one involving a syncretic textual and pictorial presentation of landscape, was a key persuasive aspect of illustrated books across a range of discourses at this time, and that it was not merely an extension or adoption of "narrative" effects in painting. In addition, I argue that the evolution of this rhetoric went hand in hand with the growth and differentiation of disciplines, institutions, and social practices critical in promoting, normalizing, and effecting the nation's territorial expansion and its industrial development. In an era of film we may easily forget the visceral potential offered by conjunctions of words and pictures. In the present day, we may generally regard pictures in these circumstances as "illustrations," parallel pictorial versions of what we read in a text. But in that earlier era, the nineteenth century, illustrated texts offered commensurately vivid possibilities for combining narrative with imagery.

Rethinking the Use of Landscape Imagery in Nineteenth-Century American Illustrated Books

The types of books that foregrounded landscape imagery in this period (roughly the years 1825–1875) can be divided into four prominent groups, which are the subjects of the following four chapters, each of which is instrumentally connected to the project of national expansion and commercial growth. First, geological survey reports, produced by the U.S. Topographical Corps of Engineers and its successors, were part of an initiative to map new territories and locate a suitable route for a transcontinental railroad. Second, ethnographic studies, many of them mandated and funded by the federal government, facilitated management of Native populations as white settlement moved west of the Appalachian Mountains and then the Mississippi River. Third, gift books, scenic guides, and treatises celebrating the unique merits of American landscape scenery articulated a normalizing aesthetic analog to the economic consumption involved in the development of natural resources. Finally, transportation guides (especially those produced for steamboat and railroad routes) explicitly mediated access to areas opened for settlement or developed as destinations in an emerging tourist industry. All these kinds of books relied on a hybrid textual and pictorial mode of presenting landscape as these various disciplines and industries came into being and evolved over the course of the century.

More specifically, just as the viewer's experience of time is an important difference in the way Durand's *Progress* and Guild's book conditioned landscape perception, each of the following chapters explores how illustrated books establish new kinds of knowledge and models of consumption, principally by demonstrating or simulating new temporal frameworks through their presentation of landscape. I use the term "temporal framework" to denote different discursive characteristics having to do with time. One such characteristic is the pace or tempo that structures various social practices (protracted enjoyment versus instant gratification as models of consumption, for example). Also important, though, is the span of time encompassed by a field of inquiry (thus, geological eras are much vaster than human history, which itself subdivides broadly into prehistoric archaeological and historical ethnographic pasts). In this regard, the model of historical narrative and spectatorship found in contemporary landscape painting was initially influential, specifically landscape painting that evolved from the picturesque tradition originating in England in the eighteenth century. As each of the next four chapters shows, however, the formation of key discourses connected with territorial and commercial growth involved shifts away from picturesque strategies for pairing imagery and narrative.

At this point, I want to address some of the wider historical reasons for regarding syncretic textual and pictorial practices in illustrated books as an especially important and compelling rhetoric in its own right, as something more than an uncomplicated juxtaposition of words and pictures, and then foreground some aspects of the methodology employed here to analyze that rhetoric. Overall, it is striking how advances in print illustration paralleled the development of other media that sought to combine narrative with visual imagery over the course of the century. New print technologies not only served an expanding audience, they also enabled publishers to imitate and enlarge on the syncretic techniques for combining pictures and stories found in more exclusively visual media. The nineteenth century produced a whole array of new imaging technologies and visual media, and it has been the task of art history to develop ways of assessing their representational strategies and impact on various audiences. Scholarship has steadily moved from its traditional emphasis on painting and sculpture to address first printmaking and photography, and then other forms, by turns increasingly exotic (such as the stereoscope and the phenakistoscope) or increasingly familiar (such as newspaper illustrations). Within the field of American art history, studies of painting persistently influenced the assessment and interpretation not only of print images but of many other, more recent visual media as well.[25] Thus, for example, treatments of the panorama have typically appeared within discussions of viewing models derived from or serviceable for painting; which is to say, panoramas are also often treated somewhat like a variant dialect of the "image-language" spoken by painting.[26]

One notable characteristic shared by many of the imaging technologies developed in the nineteenth century (as well as painting) is that they often involved or allowed the incorporation of narration to create a composite form of representation. Visitors to panoramas and dioramas were often informed about the significance of specific details contained within views through a voice-over narration given by a guide. Although landscape was the dominant subject of panoramic views, themes highly suitable for narrative treatment were also common, such as famous battles, in which important episodes and turning points were mapped out in space as striking features within the depicted view and were also enumerated in their proper order over time through the script spoken by the guide. In the United States, moving panoramas were especially popular. In this version, the 360-degree panoramic landscape is replaced by a running band of terrain viewed over the course of a fictional journey (simulated by a long screen of painted canvas moving in one direction between two spools) and again accompanied by a voice-over narration, so that space is even further transformed into time.[27] Other narrative-based imaging technologies popular in the nineteenth century include the illustrated lecture and the magic lantern show. Stereoscopic photographic views, perhaps the most commercially successful form of photography at this time, were typically sold as numbered sets so that they too could be experienced as a temporal sequence of images. The oddest nineteenth-century imaging inventions—the phenakistoscopes, thaumatropes, and zoetropes—depended on knowledge of the temporal mechanisms of vision itself, specifically the phenomenon of persistence of vision.[28]

Moreover, the incorporation of narrative in these different media could take the form of vocal accompaniment or a key containing text and print illustrations. For example, printed guidebooks to panoramas (containing reproductions of panoramic views and textual explanations of them) were a frequent substitute for voice-over narration, making them quite similar in many respects to Guild's publication. Such guidebooks—for panoramas, but also for illustrated lectures and magic lantern shows—are often the only surviving artifacts of inherently ephemeral events.[29] They benefit the historian, but they also gave contemporaries who could not attend these events the opportunity to experience them vicariously; in other words, they also acted as substitutes for the events. Guidebooks such as Robert Burford's *Description of a View of the Falls of Niagara* enabled American audiences to participate in England's panorama craze, even as those panoramas depicted sites more readily accessible to Americans.[30] George Harvey's *Illustrations of the Scenery, Resources, and Progress of Our Country* duplicated in print his illustrated lecture, which (echoing the work of Durand and others) supposedly chronicled the process by which "a wilderness of gloom and desolation [was made] into a land teeming with the fruits of civilization and happiness."[31] In general terms, one of the most entrenched methods for interpreting and making sense of art in the nineteenth century was to educe a story that was the perceived expressive content of a painting or sculpture. Harvey was a landscape painter, but his work was conceived in terms of narration, not merely exhibition, and his guidebook attempts to reproduce this juxtaposition of image and narrative. In a related manner, reviews of landscape paintings frequently "walked" the viewer through depicted space, explicating its significance within a larger narrative framework.[32] In short, the books examined in this study are part of a larger continuum of technologies and practices that connect images with stories, in many cases playing a constitutive role in them. Understanding the different relations of reference between words and pictures in these illustrated books gives concrete form to the often implicit or inferential processes of association, matching events and places, found in so many media forms in the nineteenth century.

Finally, developments in print technology were not geared exclusively to lowering cost or increasing volume; many of them also enabled experimentation with the size, positioning, and frequency of illustrations in relation to text. In particular, the wood engraving and its more durable mass-production analogs (the stereotype and later the electrotype) allowed for the possibility of printing type and illustration together, making it substantially easier to lay these elements out on the page in more complex arrangements. Lower printing costs also made it possible to increase the number of illustrations in a given publication, likewise resulting in more elaborate illustration schemes. Moreover, if the new printing technologies of the first half of the nineteenth century were primarily industrial in character, allowing for more efficient mass production, they also spurred the exploration (or creation) of new consumer audiences and new print products to satisfy them. Steam-powered presses and steel-faced printing plates contributed to a multiplication of production and consumer demand in a kind of industrial-era version of Johannes Gutenberg's print revolution. The most conspicuous examples of the cultivation of new print markets and concomitant experimentation with page layout were the illustrated newspapers and magazines, such as *Harper's Weekly, Leslie's Illustrated,* and *Putnam's Magazine* (to name a few), but a similar exploration of audience interest and a similar variety of illustration schemes can be associated with the books, pamphlets, and other print materials published by the transportation and tourist industries and by the emerging disciplines of ethnography and geology.

In the chapters that follow, I work out from the books themselves to investigate their strategies for combining landscape prints with textual narrative. My close-reading approach brings with it some methodological advantages and disadvantages. On the one hand, I bring a level and intensity of attention to the artistry behind materials that may have been effective participants in important social and economic changes but have typically not been examined in this way before. On the other hand, the eventual plausibility of my interpretations often depends primarily on the books themselves. For example, I can only speculate how a railroad guidebook such as Guild's was used; I have no direct evidence of its experiential impact, such as a diary entry. I can and do take note of what the author intended, in the form of instructions to the reader, like Guild's "Explanation of the Chart," and I can and do support the significance of changes in illustration schemes by assessing how broadly they are adopted across what types of print materials. I also assess the impact of these books on social practices, such as scenic tourism, by comparing the kinds of activity they seem to promote with period observations of touristic behavior. Above all, though, it has been difficult to characterize how such a syncretic textual and pictorial rhetoric functions, how these books align the very act of reading them with a visceral experience of the kinds of time that structure the disciplines and industries these books both belong to and assist in creating. While scholarship on landscape painting has shed light on the connections between viewing and historical narrative that made works by Cole and Durand especially effective, historians of both material culture and literature have also approached the question of the temporal experience of viewers or readers in ways that help clarify the kinds of temporal operations occurring in illustrated books. Building on my initial view of Guild's book as a new imaging technology, a hybrid text/image machine, taking it apart requires a textual, pictorial, and mechanical perspective.

The first key operation has to do with how these books bridge the seemingly alien signifying modes of text and image.[33] Yet the control exercised over what the eye does over time also parallels, in a general way, many of the nineteenth century's newest imaging devices, such as the phenakistoscope, the thaumatrope, and the zoetrope.[34] The illustrated books examined here may be thought of as occupying a kind of intermediate position between painting and optical toy, between fine art and mass culture. To capture the orchestration of movements between text and image, I have adopted an equally split perspective. One point of comparison is how these various optical devices required the isolation and subjection of the viewer in relation to visual stimuli. Thus, in using the stereoscope, spectators were compelled to precisely position their eyes in front of a viewing device that blocked out a visual awareness of their surroundings. As a railroad guidebook, Guild's work seems singularly unobtrusive and was doubtless often employed in a correspondingly casual manner—taken up and discarded at one's whim—but as I have begun to show, his "Explanation of the Chart" points to a rather more meticulous orchestration of both looking and reading, as do other kinds of illustrated books that are likewise prefaced by instructions, however gently phrased. I want to propose that, while Durand's painting used compositional devices to guide the viewer's eye through the depicted landscape, the passing scenery viewed through the train car window was in some more potent sense beyond the passenger's control, and that the organization of Guild's book reflects this greater subjection of the viewer/reader. What is more, many optical toys depended on controlling specifically the rate of speed at which viewers were exposed to visual stimuli. Here again there is a parallel in Guild's railroad guide: the measured route line helps facilitate the reader's rapid movement between text and image, while the length of text segments and the amount of detail within images correlates a reading and viewing pace with the speed of the moving train. These phenomenological aspects of illustrated books are explored more fully in chapter 1, but at this point I want at least to acknowledge that the approach I bring to my material has been shaped by attending to how temporal experience is controlled in imaging devices (including precinematic technologies) that might seem far removed from illustrated books.

The second key operation concerns how illustrated books condition transitions or transformations between not texts and images, but different kinds of time. The encounter with place made available to the reader operates within two primary temporal registers: the active chronology in which landscape and its incidents are presented (the time of the reader), and the larger, more abstract spans of time that the features of landscape are intended to convey (the history of nations or races, but also more recently introduced time frames, such as evolutionary or geological time). In addressing how illustrated books manage transitions between temporal registers, this book has been influenced not only by art historical analyses of narrative in landscape painting but also by literary studies directed at understanding movements between the time of the reader and the time of the text.[35] In *Time and Narrative,* Paul Ricoeur undertakes to demonstrate that both historical and fictional narrative offer a "reply," a kind of resolution, to a related dilemma, "the aporias of temporality."[36] For Ricoeur, the notions of referentiality behind the "real" past uncovered by historical research and the "unreal" world of the imagination described in fiction appear as complementary facets of an ongoing human project to reconcile the individual, internal experience of time with the recognition of its essentially alien, external nature.[37] Whether history or fiction, texts are templates through which external "worlds" (or more precisely, external manifestations of time) are experienced through individual, internal acts of reading. The relevance of Ricoeur's work can be seen in the way my objects of study present landscapes (or "worlds") as being at once indicative of and structured by different timespans (required by the evolving disciplines of geology and ethnography as well as the transportation and tourist industries). I have not embraced Ricoeur's "poetics of narrative" (his theory that narrative provides an answer to the "aporias of temporality"); instead I have focused on ascertaining how the temporal aspects of reading and viewing are oriented by these books as similar to characteristics of the larger timespans that underlie their various intentions and purposes in describing and picturing landscape. In other words, the activities of reading and viewing enact, on a smaller but proportional scale, the shape and contour of history. In a sense, this small-scale enactment parallels the equation between eye and historical movement in Durand's *Progress,* but I particularly want to emphasize the specificity by which texts paired with images might effect this enactment, if only because the "text" in Durand's painting is purely inferable, not a concrete variable as it is in Guild's book.

The present book is not an attempt to catalog what is after all a broadly defined set of cultural productions—popular landscape prints wherever they appear in texts. Within the four groupings of geological, ethnographic, scenic, and transportation literature, I highlight works that deploy narrative text and landscape prints in particularly rich ways—not representative works per se, but works that more fully develop practices found in less ambitious illustrated books. The subject matter is also confined to the United States; parallel developments in European tourism and science are noted where they arise, but I advance no claim of a global phenomenon in the practices of juxtaposing text and illustrations in print materials in this period. Instead I concentrate on the work accomplished by these practices in relation to these discourses in the United States, to avoid obscuring what is unique to this country's pattern of territorial expansion and industrial development.[38] Last, I have pointedly chosen works within the period 1825–1875, so that my time frame corresponds with the period frequently demarcated by traditional art historical studies of landscape painting, but my primary motivation in selecting this time frame is to trace not a rise-and-fall pattern but something more akin to a fall-and-rise.[39] American landscape painting is often understood to decline in popularity just as the frontier is being closed and the centripetal forces of Reconstruction are casting doubt on national unity; in some sense the genre's purpose is superseded by events. Instead, this study charts the "fall" of visual narrative forms associated with painting and the "rise" of new forms connected with tourism and science; visual narrative remains a potent form of expression, but it both serves other purposes and is primarily found in other media, namely print media.

Tourism and science are the larger subject categories here because they are both major players in the nation's territorial and commercial growth in this period and because landscape imagery is a conspicuously important aspect of print publications connected with them. I am not insisting that these newer methods for syncretically deploying text and illustration became a dominant paradigm in all print materials at this time, just that they are highly influential within tourism and (ethnographic and geological) science. The search for a unitary "spectator" is a problematic aspect of much writing on nineteenth-century landscape painting and visual culture generally over the past several decades. Thus Jonathan Crary's work, for example, has been criticized for endowing models of vision with an unjustified force in driving and shaping history.[40] In contrast, the approach taken in this study proceeds from the bottom up, through close readings of primary texts, in an effort to understand the development and operation of a specialized form of textual and visual rhetoric and its relationship to expansionist ideologies within tourism and science. In a general way, though, the features of that rhetoric as it evolves within later illustrated books prove somewhat similar for both tourism and science. In either case, picturesque viewing models are replaced at some point by a visual narrative form characterized by fragmentation, speed, and superficiality—what I call a "railroad narrative." From one point of view, this coincidence is largely circumstantial. Many of the artists involved in the production of these illustrated books provided sketches or photographs that found their way into both tourism and science, opening a conduit whereby their construction of space (and its amenability to narrative viewing) can carry over from one arena to the other. Ethnography and geology played prominent roles in the surveys that opened up the West for settlement and commercial development, including scenic tourism. It stands to reason that some of the terms by which landscape was rendered meaningful in the earlier survey reports might influence those terms in the later touristic literature; after all, the first national parks were often those places of particular significance for ethnographers and geologists (for example, Yosemite and Yellowstone).

In pursuing a deeper correspondence between the enterprises of tourism and science, I concentrate on how visual narrative forms function similarly in tourism and science on the level of persuasion, of giving readers what they are encouraged to think they want. In the books discussed in this volume, the production of knowledge and the production of commodities are linked by shared efforts to establish and then satisfy a desire for possession (the reality and substance of knowledge and commodities). I specifically connect this persuasive function with the instantiation and validation of new "temporal frameworks" (the pace or tempo structuring a social practice or the range of time covered by a field of inquiry). Industrial book production thus facilitates a parallel sort of specialization within scientific disciplines and the tourist market, one that involves not just new economies of scale but also new ways of activating desire and imagination. But while these enterprises are linked in employing ways of orchestrating text and image to convey the kinds of time in some sense underwriting them, those temporalities are also in an important sense essentially distinct.

In older art historical scholarship, the relationship between art and society is characteristically analyzed as symbolic with regard to time. Thus, Cole is seen to use the landscape genre to depict cyclical models of history as a cautionary corrective to the dangers of an uncomplicated belief in unchecked progress. Later scholarship goes further, noting how time is thematized in the very organization of viewing. For example, in "The Iconology of Wrecked or Stranded Boats in Mid to Late Nineteenth-Century American Culture," David C. Miller discusses how the "neutral and visually rhythmic forms" of later, so-called luminist landscape paintings function as "equaliz[ing]" factors that he persuasively associates with many of the conditions of postbellum American life.[41] In particular, "The painting's design heightens the demand on the viewer to respond to a visual spate of insistent visual stimuli that compete for attention," which Miller connects with a sober awareness of the atomizing potential of democratic individualism as attested by the experience of the Civil War.[42] Furthermore, he links the effect of this lack of clear visual hierarchies with the beginnings of a modernist self-conscious sensibility: "As things equalize, the mind struggles to reimpose hierarchy. In doing so it is thrown back upon itself, becoming self-consciously aware of its ongoing effort to apprehend the unfamiliar."[43] Studies of "modernity" often connect aspects of sameness, fragmentation, and instantaneity, as deployed in a work of art or a work of fiction, with some essential quality of modern experience. In Bentley's *Frantic Panoramas,* discussed above in relation to literary studies and approaches to mass culture, the crash of the colliding locomotives in staged train collisions is also a kind of "insistent visual stimul[us]," which is emblematic of the shock effect that she shows is a shared source of alarm and also possibility for early twentieth-century writers' engagement with modern life.[44] In both cases, the artist or writer is seen to represent what is broadly characteristic of modern life by enabling the viewer or reader to share in that experience as well as to present that experience as a threat to a formerly established order in the process of being dismantled. In contrast, this study attempts to shift the discussion of the significance of new notions of time to the actual temporal experiences—conditioned by objects like illustrated books—that structured many of the activities constitutive of modern life. Their possible significance relative to contemporary social and economic concerns—including changing notions of class and racial identity, evolving understandings of consumption, choice, and taste—are explored individually in the chapters that follow. In privileging the view of the historical artistic or literary witness, we risk mistaking a response to what is a perceived overall condition for what is in fact being actively produced in all its multiplicity as new modes of engagement with the world. More than this, though, we risk missing what made those modes of engagement especially compelling to begin with.

1

Reading the Past outside the Window

Competing Visions of History in Paintings and Railroad Guidebooks

ALAN WALLACH explains in "Thomas Cole's *River in the Catskills* as Anti-Pastoral" how this 1843 painting (plate 3) registers the artist's anxiety about the destructive potential of modern improvements represented by the railroad, arguably the most potent symbol and agent of change in the nineteenth century.[1] As Wallach observes, this work of Cole has been recognized as an important milestone by generations of scholars who have charted the evolution of American landscape painting. Most of these scholars have focused on how the genre represented concerns about the nation's future development at the outset of the most intense period of American territorial expansion and settlement.[2] Their dominant interpretation sees Cole as normalizing the appearance of the train by concealing it within a traditional picturesque view of natural scenery. Such picturesque elements include the gazing foreground figure who encourages protracted contemplation across an expanse of natural and manmade elements, as well as a viewing path that proceeds slowly along a pristine watercourse to the rail crossing, and thence to the farming community and other clearings beyond. What is suggested is an easy transition to a pastoral idyll that industry does not disturb, an unproblematic narrative of historical progress. Such an alignment of the viewer's pathway into space with a sunny allegorical narrative mirrors, although less explicitly, the organization of Durand's nearly contemporary *Progress* (plate 2) as well as numerous later works of the Hudson River school. But as Wallach argues, "What would a landscape painting look like if it embodied a critical or negative representation of the railroad? . . . Given the artistic means at Cole's disposal . . . it is difficult to believe that he would have painted a close-up view of a fire-breathing, mechanical behemoth."[3] Instead, according to Wallach, Cole manifests his displeasure subtly, evoking a specialized and mostly pleasurable genre known as the pastoral landscape and then eliminating certain of its constitutive details, thereby suggesting

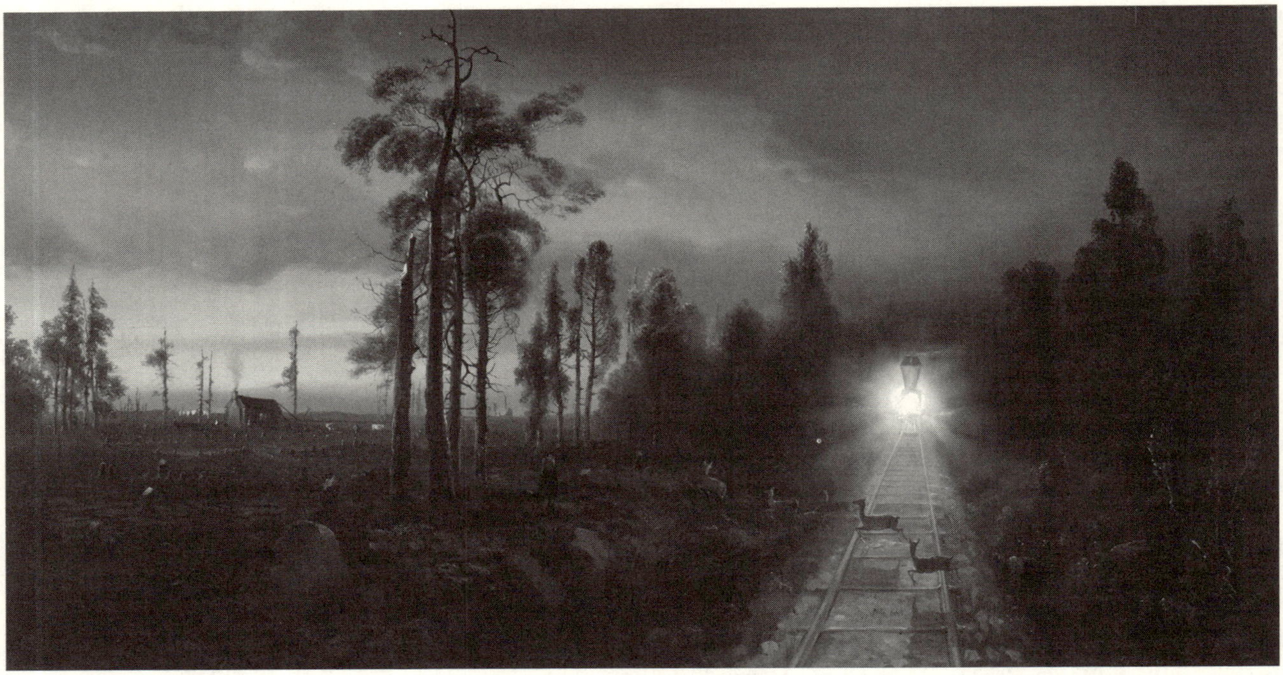

FIGURE 1. Andrew Melrose, *Westward the Star of Empire Takes Its Way*, c. 1865. Oil on canvas; 29½ × 46 in. Courtesy Autry National Center of the American West, Los Angeles, California.

a darker vision (for example, in the foreground, where we would expect to find sheltering trees for the red-jacketed onlooker, we instead find blasted tree stumps).[4]

Wallach's argument hinges on an inertia of aesthetic conventions, the incapability of paintings to represent critical views of historical progress that involved radical changes to existing pictorial norms and habits.[5] Although more visceral "close-up view[s] of . . . fire-breathing, mechanical behemoth[s]" did occasionally appear, as in Andrew Melrose's *Westward the Star of Empire Takes Its Way* (1865; figure 1), American landscape painting typically avoided getting too close to the train. Unlike paintings, however, railroad publications from the same period frequently highlighted the unusual sights available to riders. In an image from Henry T. Williams's *Pacific Tourist,* a guidebook produced shortly after the opening of the transcontinental railroad, in 1869, the endangered deer of Melrose's painting are shown grazing happily, undisturbed by the passing train (figure 2).[6] This almost bucolic scene has the effect of minimizing an even more basic difference between the print and Melrose's work (and landscape painting in general)—namely, the way the illustration replicates the tangential, shearing perspective of a seated passenger in a moving train. The advances in print technology of the first half of the century—notably wood engraving and electrotyping—as well as the appeal of new sights for a growing and largely expansionist reading public, encouraged an inventiveness in print illustrations generally. Most visibly, the new illustrated journals that came

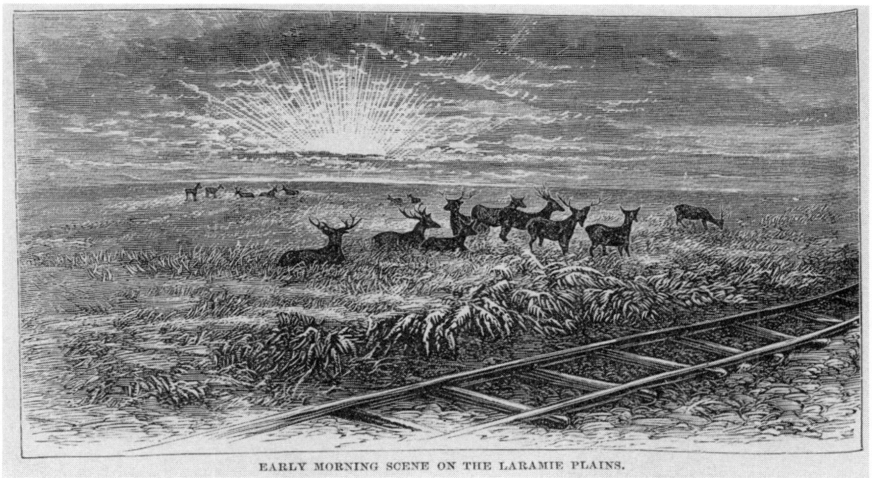

FIGURE 2. Unknown artist, *Early Morning Scene on the Laramie Plains*. Illustration from Henry T. Williams, *The Pacific Tourist: Williams' Illustrated Trans-Continental Guide of Travel, from the Atlantic to the Pacific Ocean,* 2nd ed. (New York: Williams, 1876). RB 2676. Courtesy the Huntington Library, San Marino, California.

on the market in the 1840s and 1850s, such as *Harper's Weekly,* aimed to distinguish themselves from their competitors through the frequent and clever use of pictures.[7] In terms of landscape imagery, paintings did provide familiar compositional models, but just as often views of landscape in print illustrations could evoke other imaging technologies, such as the Claude glass or some other viewing device, and present sequential aspects of spectatorship or other visual phenomena that were not easily captured in painting (figures 3 and 4).[8]

If Cole's critique of the nation's development hinged on a careful manipulation of picturesque conventions, what views of progress were offered in print images that deviated more dramatically from the constraints of landscape painting, and how did this deviation impinge on a viewer's apprehension of time? This chapter explores this question by examining illustration schemes in transportation guidebooks in the years 1825–1875, a period spanning the introduction and integration of the steamboat and the train as prevalent means of travel that dramatically increased the ability of Americans to move around their country. The function of such guides was primarily practical, but what interests me is their insistent experimentation with representing progress or history as a key component of the sites they described, as well as the notion that such an abstract or intangible notion as "history" could be experienced phenomenally in different ways, in the here and now, via the guidebooks' mediation of travelers' exposure to the landscape. If painting represents history or an idealized projection of future development through a correlation of real/visual and imagined/physical movement (as in Cole's and Durand's works), transportation guidebooks rework this equation, drawing its terms together more closely, by mediating the experience of actual travel. Instead of an imagined traversal of pictured space vested in the

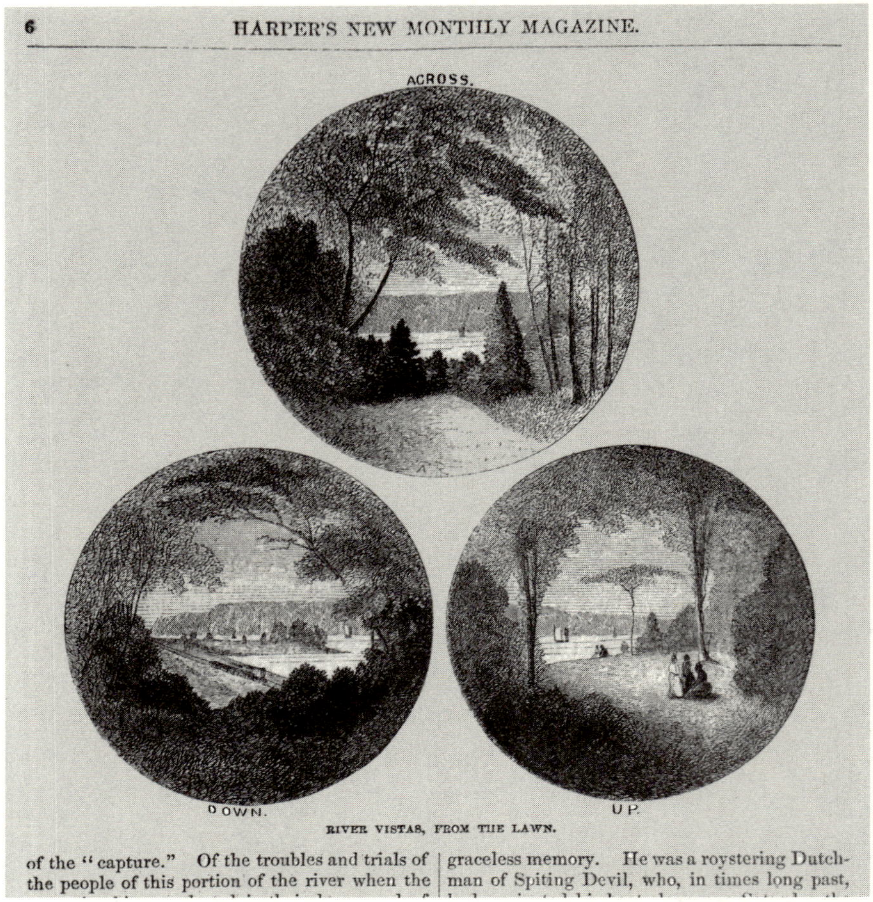

6 HARPER'S NEW MONTHLY MAGAZINE.

ACROSS.

DOWN.

UP.

RIVER VISTAS, FROM THE LAWN.

of the "capture." Of the troubles and trials of the people of this portion of the river when the

graceless memory. He was a roystering Dutchman of Spiting Devil, who, in times long past,

FIGURE 3. Unknown artist, *River Vistas, from the Lawn*. Illustration from "Sunnyside, The Home of Washington Irving," *Harper's New Monthly Magazine* 14, no. 79. Courtesy Reed College Library.

eye's movement, the real progress of the viewer's body itself is charged with larger historical significance.[9] My basic contention in this chapter is that while landscape painting generally retains the same basic viewing patterns and corresponding constructions of historical meaning found in the works of Cole and Durand from the period 1825–1875, the evolution of illustration schemes in transportation guidebooks moves away from this ensemble of spectatorship and historical significance in the direction of something else.[10] Specifically, I show how railroad guidebooks develop an altogether different form of narrative viewing—a "railroad narrative"—to evoke an altogether different notion of the nation's historical progress, largely because this new narrative order has a closer kinship with a new world of commercial goods—as opposed to a world, a nation, shaped by history—than the picturesque viewing models from which it emerged.

The railroad is a major protagonist in the myth of Manifest Destiny and a powerful symbol of a new era in the United States, entailing expansion, industrialization, and commercial culture—if not modernity by many definitions, then its immediate prehistory. To explore the possibilities and

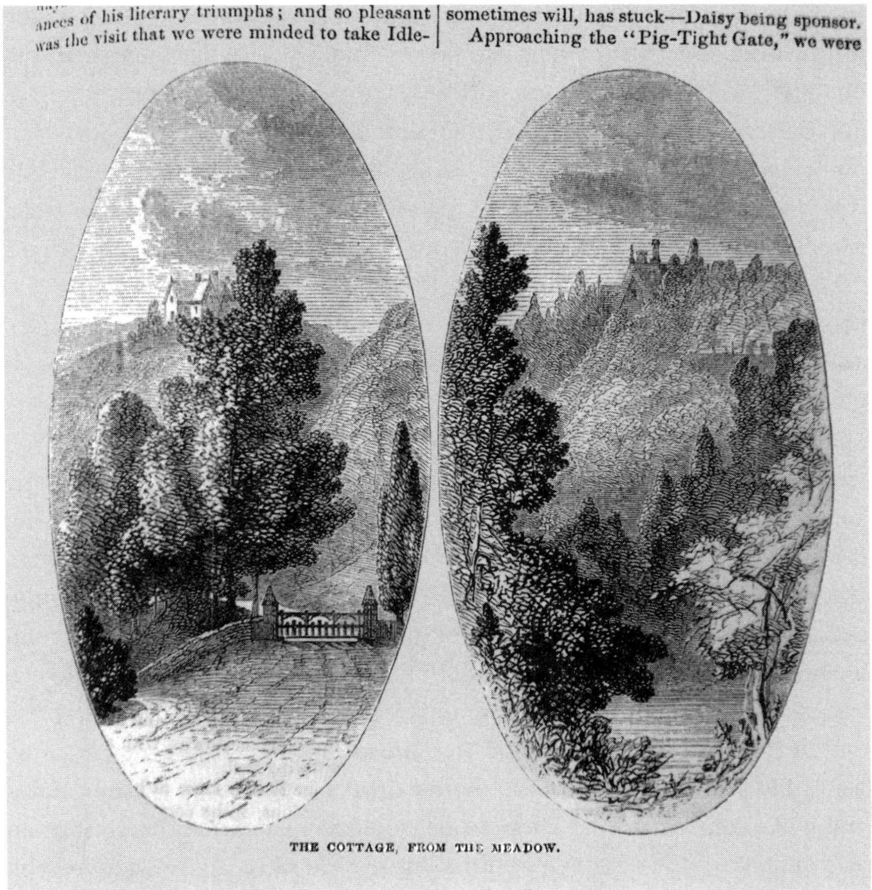

FIGURE 4. Unknown artist, *The Cottage, from the Meadow.* Illustration from T. Addison Richards, "Idlewild, The Home of N. P. Willis," *Harper's New Monthly Magazine* 16, no. 92. Courtesy Reed College Library.

issues of representing history through the sights associated with train travel, and how contemporary scenic guides either obscure or promote that perspective, it is helpful to review the different ways in which the railroad has been understood to represent progress in painting. Particularly striking is how landscape painting avoids or suppresses the novel visual possibilities of railroad travel, or at least contains them within the conventions of the European picturesque tradition. The railroad is primarily conceived iconographically, as an allegorical symbol of progress, or used as a compositional device within established picturesque conventions, even though it could serve as a technology of representation in its own right, not just alluding to progress indirectly or abstractly, but impressing on the rider an emphatically vivid experience of it. The machines themselves were formidable examples of modern technology and engineering, and riders were taken up and swept along by them, literally and dramatically "progressing," with sensations altogether distinct from previous experience: passengers visually (and acoustically) isolated from the landscape outside and traveling along a geometrically precise path that did not conform to the prevailing topography. From the window of a moving train, the outside terrain dramatically separates into three distinct mobile planes: foreground imagery flits by, objects in the middle ground seem to curve or peel away, and background landscape features seem to move imperceptibly, so that one can look away for a time and still see them when one looks back.[11] It is this visceral dimension that painting avoided and that railroad guidebooks would eventually draw on to shape a new perspective toward the landscape.

Beginning with Leo Marx's *The Machine in the Garden,* art historical scholarship has long remarked on the ambivalence with which writers and artists of the period greeted the possibilities for material and social change enabled by a connecting network of rail lines across the country.[12] Many such writers and artists describe the immediate experience of train travel as a removal of possibilities, a kind of imprisonment within or subordination to the order of the machine.[13] Cole describes how "the body is made to be merely a sort of Tender to a Locomotive Car; its appetites & functions wait on a Machine which is merciless & tyrannical," while according to the English critic John Ruskin, the train "transmutes a man from a traveller into a living parcel."[14] Henry David Thoreau alludes to a similar objectification in his famous meditation on train travel at the end of the chapter on "Sounds" in *Walden* (1854), comparing trains to "invisible bolts" that are "shot," squeezing the body even further into a bullet-like compartment.[15] Thoreau also speculates on what this revolution in transport bodes for the nation's future. He both acknowledges the promise of a new era figured by the train and questions whether that promise can be made good: "When I hear the iron horse make the hills echo with his snort like thunder, shaking the earth with his feet, and breathing fire and smoke from his nostrils . . . it seems as if the earth had got a race now worthy to inhabit it. If all were as it seems, and men made the elements their servants for noble ends!"[16] In seeking a vantage point from which to gauge this harbinger of a new history, however, Thoreau tends to situate himself outside the train. He vividly describes how the train condenses distance and enforces its own time schedule like a discharged bullet—instantaneous, linear, undeviating—reconfiguring the relationship between national space and its accessibility over time. But he advocates a perspective removed from such effects, a view not *from* the train but *of* the train: "Men are advertised that at a certain hour and minute these bolts will be shot toward particular points of the compass. . . . Every path but your own is the path of fate. Keep on your own track, then. . . . Now that the cars are gone by and all the restless world with them, and the fishes in the pond no longer feel their rumbling, I am more alone than ever."[17] It seems possible to explain Thoreau's sense of loneliness in terms of a perspective that is increasingly not shared; if Americans are

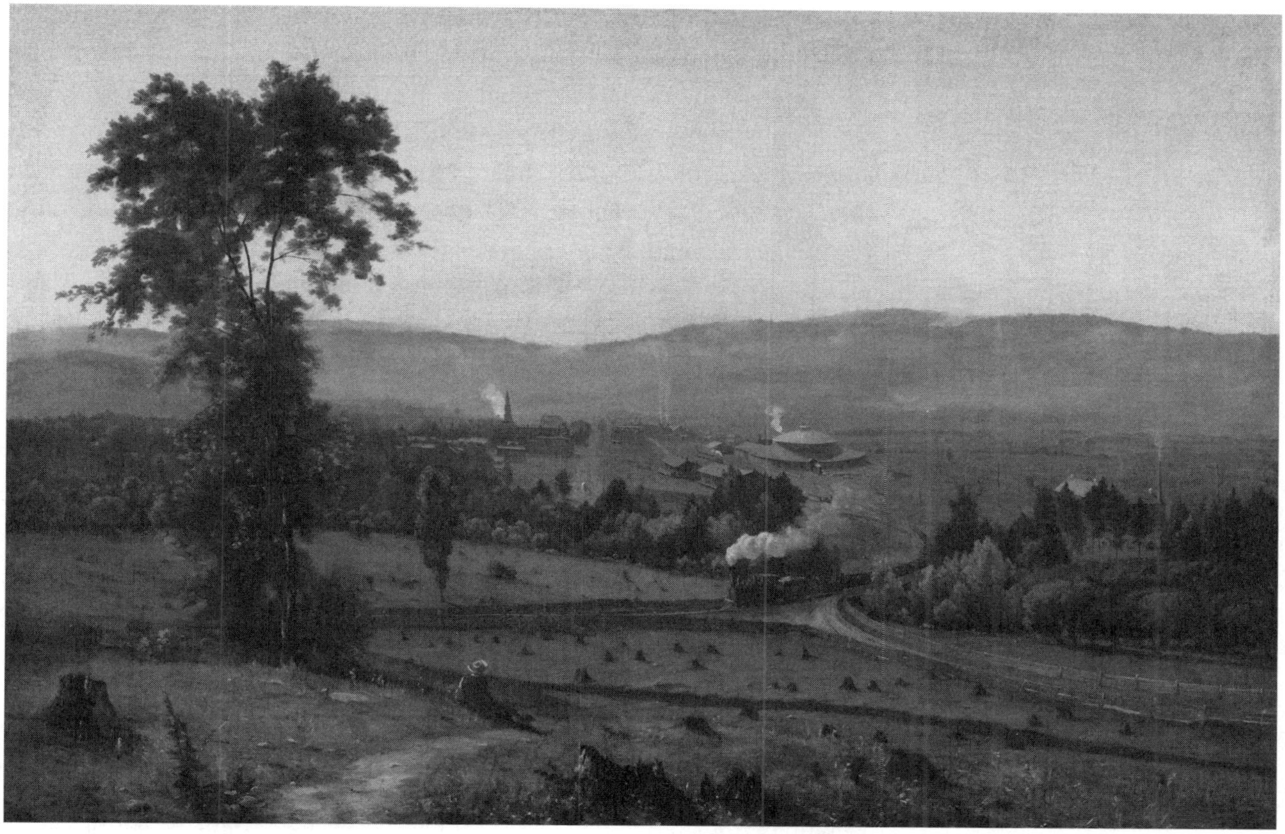

FIGURE 5. George Inness, *The Lackawanna Valley*, c. 1856. Oil on canvas; 33⅞ × 50³⁄₁₆ in. Courtesy National Gallery of Art, Washington, DC. Gift of Mrs. Huttleston Rogers.

organizing their lives according to the routes and schedules of the train, then Thoreau's point of view is even more his own.

Such an outside viewpoint, which could be identified with an unshared sightline (one's "own track"), connoting a resistance toward being captured by the "fate" of a new "restless world," is replicated time and again by painters who incorporated the train into their compositions. Whether the train is represented positively (as in Durand's *Progress*) or more ambivalently (as in Cole's *River in the Catskills* or George Inness's *The Lackawanna Valley*, 1856; figure 5), these paintings follow the picturesque convention of depicting a substitute spectator for the viewer in the foreground, who gazes across an expanse of pastoral scenery along an unhurried viewing path defined by winding watercourses and gradually diminishing natural features. Also typical is the generalized historical narrative organized by the movement of the viewer's eye into depth, usually moving from earlier to later stages of civilization. The consistent positioning of the train toward the back of depicted space (well removed from the vantage point of the viewer) is partly necessitated by the fact that it signifies progress or an advanced stage in this narrative. Moreover, in these paintings the train almost always crosses the viewer's line of sight; rarely is the viewer offered a sightline aligned with the trajectory of the train. Compositionally, the sightline indicated by the railroad (obliquely crossing the gaze of the viewer) is a kind of coulisse, channeling the viewer's eye along a characteristically serpentine path into depth. The railroad's association with rapid movement, the sharp pull of its tracks' more geometrically precise lines, and its effectiveness as a sign or symbol of the future (confirming the pull of the implied historical narrative) all function as compelling stage directions for the viewer's optical perusal of the painting.

Given these conventions that distance and dissociate the viewer from the train, American art historical scholarship, following the work of Marx, has often occupied itself with parsing the subtle visual cues that tell us just where a particular painter could be positioned on the spectrum of approval or disapproval of the train and its attendant associations. Although the consensus has been that most painters reduced the size of the train and obscured its presence to accommodate it within traditional picturesque views, producing a "landscape of reconciliation," other scholars, in addition to Wallach, have teased out more impassioned responses in slight departures from those conventions.[18] Even though artists received commissions from patrons connected with the railroad and were even invited to take tours on specific rail lines for the purpose of promoting them, what seems most striking about their work, again, is that the view from the train remains largely absent.[19] Signs of an apparently compulsive suppression have spurred an abundance of art historical interpretations that gesture toward larger social and cultural concerns. Yet the varying attitudes of painters toward the process of industrialization that the train epitomized only partly explain its capacity to figure a new phase in national history through its iconographical significance and compositional properties alone, but never through any new perspectives on landscape that it offered.

Following Wallach's lead (and underscoring what is radically different in print views from the train, such as in Williams's guidebook), I suggest that what is also involved here is a basic incompatibility between the sights of train travel and the customary means by which painting guided the viewer's eye through depictions of landscape. Scholars have noted how Melrose's anomalous painting, *Westward the Star of Empire Takes Its Way* (figure 1), depicts a dramatic and violent intrusion of industrial mechanization into the natural environment (the graveyard of stumps on the left, the fleeing deer threatened by the onrushing train), but it is also possible to read the painting as dramatizing this incompatibility, portraying a "landscape of irreconciliation."[20] The negative effect of the picture derives significantly from the threatening manner by which it stages stark deviations from the pictorial norms of the picturesque tradition. Gone is the gently curving serpentine path into depth, which nudged the viewer's eye from point to point but still fostered an impression of freedom of movement. Replacing it are the rigid, locked-in tracks of the railroad, framed by a constraining avenue of trees, forcing the viewer's eye into a head-on collision with the approaching locomotive. The emphasis on distance and the prolonged temporality of painting are also absent, with a view into the background cut off by the train, and a sense of urgency called forth by the fleeing deer and imminent disaster.[21] Finally, in brutally bald terms, Melrose portrays the merging of the vantage points of painting and train as unavoidably lethal, perhaps even suggesting that the train, in its capacity to mediate views of landscape, will soon overpower and destroy painting—or at least the imagined painter, standing before the easel with *his* eyes locked in the headlights.

Williams's "sunny" print of deer on the prairie (figure 2) contains many of the same departures from picturesque practice; instead of a sense of self-directed perusal of landscape features, there is an unproblematic sensation of being carried past the deer. What had been a nightmare inability to move (under one's own volition) in Melrose's painting is here a pleasant conveyance past sights that require no sustained examination. The visual rhetoric of landscape painting was compelling: it did not simply evoke an experience of progress or history; it also intimated a kind of control or mastery over that history on the part of the viewer. What I want to propose here is that the reluctance of painters to represent the view from the train speaks to a threatened way of rationalizing both place and history in visual and narrative terms. It is not just that values important to these writers and artists were endangered by the train and its attendant associations of industrialization; rather, one of the ways by which writers and artists understood and articulated those values was likewise somehow "at risk" in relation to a new set of values and a new way of picturing and writing—in effect, a new narrative order—suggested by the phenomenal experiences of train travel.

Imitating Painting in Print Albums and Steamboat Guidebooks

The transportation guidebooks that evolved over the course of the nineteenth century took a variety of forms, from small, cheaply printed pamphlets to larger, more elaborate bound books. The narrative texts they contained likewise varied, from brief notices of sites to more extended expositions, as did their illustrations, in terms of size, frequency, positioning on the page, and number of color plates. Different audiences were also targeted, especially in terms of class and education, a differentiation that became more pronounced as the century progressed and touristic travel became a more affordable form of recreation. Like many of the print materials examined in this book, these transportation guidebooks resist familiar means of assessing creative intention by reference to an individual author or artist. They are often corporate productions whose contributing artists and authors may not even be identified; the author is often the publisher, which in the case of large-scale publishing firms like Appleton's may reflect a pool of company ghostwriters or the fact that texts are often an amalgamation of extracts from previous editions.

In their presentation of landscape scenery, the first guidebooks—especially those intended for steamboat travel—stressed a continuity of scenic representation with the dominant tradition of landscape views at that time, instead of promoting visual experiences that were unique to developing modes of transportation. This tradition was the picturesque mode of landscape representation, which ultimately descended from the topographical views, or *vedute,* of famous sites, both natural and manmade, encountered on various versions of the Grand Tour in Europe.[22] Originally a rite of passage for young aristocrats in the eighteenth century, this early form of touristic travel became an increasingly widespread phenomenon among the emerging middle and upper classes of the growing industrial and capitalist economies, including the United States. It also provided a means to aspire to, as well as reinforce, a sense of class identity, because it presupposed a set of touristic interests, including an aesthetic appreciation of landscape scenery, that required a level of cultural education and disposable time and income previously available only to the aristocracy.[23] Landscape painting was intimately involved in this social phenomenon, as were prints based on paintings or on drawings produced by artists specializing in landscape scenes.[24] Just as John Robert Cozens and Thomas Girtin in England and Hubert Robert in France were critical in shaping the romantic picturesque aesthetic underlying scenic tourism in Europe, so American landscape painters were pivotal in translating that aesthetic into a form suitable for the version of scenic tourism taking root in the United States.[25]

To a certain degree, the influence of painting in molding the rituals of scenic tourism was consonant with the latter's initial restriction to social elites, since both painting and recreational travel were luxury items. Exclusivity of aesthetic vision was also one of the ways through which early landscape painters conceptualized the value of their work. In his diaries, Cole describes his searching out of views for his first landscape works in the Catskills region of New York as a process of discovery, almost entitling him to sole ownership of those views.[26] Elsewhere, as he admires another view in the Catskills, he distinguishes sharply between what he sees and the experience of a nearby group of vacationers who happen to be sharing the prospect: "We loitered a short time about the cliffs in front of the house[,] gazing on the vast landscape below—ever charming[,] ever new. There was much company & as usual in such places few that enjoyed the magnificence that nature spread around them. They seemed to have no object, no project for enjoyment. . . . What a desecration of the place where nature offers a feast of higher holier enjoyment!"[27] The ability to discern historical significance (or "associations") in landscape scenery was an important aspect of aesthetic exclusivity, although it was a problematic aspect in the context of the widespread perception that the United States lacked any considerable remains of past human events, a handicap that supposedly detracted from the picturesque qualities of the nation's sites of natural beauty.[28] This perception may explain the zeal with which scenic guides identified sites of incidents from colonial history and the Revolutionary War. The absence of visible traces of the past supplied an extra incentive to borrow or recreate pictorial devices from paintings or prints of sites with recognized picturesque value—not the specific features of known monuments, but characteristic conventions used in their presentation. Instead of emerging from a visible physical trace, history often resided purely in an act of vision, the movement of the eye across terrain in a specific way, for which the only available models were earlier representations of acknowledged picturesque locations.

As scenic tourism took on the character of a business in conjunction with developing steamboat and railroad routes, its exclusive association with wealth and privilege weakened; recreation and travel became profitable activities for entrepreneurs to market to a wider social and economic range of consumers. By the 1820s and 1830s, steamboats and canalboats offered fairly affordable transportation to a network of "watering places" and recreational destinations; for example, the American Grand Tour traveled up the Hudson River to Saratoga Springs and thence to Buffalo and Niagara Falls.[29] The production of guidebooks describing these sites facilitated their touristic development, paralleling the role of Baedeker's guides and Murray's handbooks in Europe.[30] Moreover, when more numerous railroad connections were being built between principal cities and towns in the East in the 1850s and 1860s, entrepreneurs took advantage of the successes and failures of earlier scenic tourism, so that train and stage routes, hotels, and various entertainments were developed in conjunction with one another, and market expansion jumped to an even larger scale, a process culminating in the construction of railroad routes in the Trans-Mississippi West.[31] Concurrently, during the second quarter of the nineteenth century, landscape painting enjoyed its widest appeal, as democratically minded art institutions like the American Art-Union, which also favored landscape works in its exhibitions, came into being.[32] It makes sense, then, that the viewing conventions and received meanings of painting not only exerted an influence on guidebooks at the outset of steamboat travel, but continued to exert a shaping force on this discourse over the next several decades.

I want to track this influence more concretely by looking first at early collections of printed landscape views produced by prominent artists, to examine how these collections pair narrative text with scenic illustrations and thereby offer a model for steamboat guidebooks.[33] *American Landscape* was the first issue of an intended, but abandoned, series illustrating famous landscape sites in the United States; its coeditors were William Cullen Bryant and Asher B. Durand.[34] This first volume featured engravings based on landscapes painted by several artists in the early stages of their careers, such as Cole, Durand, and Robert W. Weir, before landscape painting coalesced as a dominant genre in American art. This publication promoted their work by pointing out and explaining the nation's scenic beauty, using prints of their work with short textual descriptions of the sites' unique natural charms and the major historical incidents that occurred there. Bryant declares, "The object of the work is to give a series of views of the more remarkable scenes in our country, faithfully and accurately copied; views which shall convey to him by whom these scenes have never been visited, a just image of their characteristic features, and retouch and brighten it in the memory of him who has seen them . . . and to furnish the descriptions and illustrations necessary for understanding the views."[35] The guide was conceived, in fact, as a substitute for visiting the actual places it represented or as a memento that rendered return visits to the sites unnecessary. The location of the sites' picturesque beauty is thereby transferred jointly to the engravings and their textual explications—the printed "views" and "the descriptions and illustrations necessary for understanding" them. This bridge between text and illustrations is a major factor in the process by which the guide incorporates the basic viewing conditions of distance and duration used in contemporary landscape painting to construct an image of history in the landscape.

The text sections begin with an overview of the site and progressively narrow their focus down to specific details, in the manner of an extended visual engagement that first brackets an overall view and then moves from point to point into the distance. The effect is to concentrate the viewer's attention on the signs of past events and to steadily build up a composite narrative history. The text provides both the associational details necessary for the viewer to decode the landscape depicted in the engraving and a model for looking. It prompts the viewer to move through the image along a set narrative path, covering a certain distance over time, a path reinforced by familiar picturesque compositional devices in the print. Moreover, the sections of text are relatively short, never more than a couple of pages, so the reader can easily keep them in mind when examining the print. In a sense, image and textual description reflect each other as mnemonic aids indefinitely, yielding more general effects of distance and duration that give the sites' history an additional palpability that neither visual nor verbal representation could provide alone. The historical ensemble or array of events explicated by the text clearly coheres in the form of a picture, confirmed by the engraving that follows, namely an object contemplated at a certain distance rather than a succession of events experienced as a movement through the text. Conversely, because the text precedes the engraving, the print presents a view that cannot be only traversed imaginatively; rather, the viewer is held back, distanced or suspended, as the historical incidents associated with each point of the topography claim their share of attention.[36] The juxtaposition of verbal and visual representation produces a perceptible sense of prolongation, a delay that corresponds with "history" inasmuch as the recognition of history is the primary object in both the verbal and the visual representation of the landscape.

Put another way, just as history covers a long interval of time, this delay felt on the part of the reader or viewer is also perceptibly a "long time" relative to a movement through the picture that only superficially identifies objects; it is not the same length of time as the history described but a smaller-scale version of a long time nonetheless. More precisely characterizing the experience of time was a prominent goal in early structuralist studies of literature, especially Gérard Genette's *Narrative Discourse*. Genette's approach has since been superseded, to the extent that this topic is investigated at all, by a turn principally to effects of accelerated speed alone as a recurring condition of modern literature, but applying it to illustrated books helps to bring out some of the distinctive features and effects involved in moving between text and image.[37] In analyzing the experience of time in works of fiction, Genette identifies three key aspects of "narrative time" versus "story time," understood as ways of organizing the experiential time of the reader in relation to the time reported by the text: order, or "anachrony"; duration, or "anisochrony"; and frequency. Genette's scheme seems applicable to the relationship between text and image in *American Landscape* at least in terms of the first two aspects—"anachrony" and "anisochrony"—inasmuch as the textual descriptions of *American Landscape* provide a model for perusing the illustrations in terms of a specific sequence of notable sights and a protracted form of engagement with them. However, the relationship between text and image is clearly not unidirectional, because the picture supplements what has been asserted by the description. Moreover, this reciprocal relation produces a second-order dimension of experienced time, as noted above. Overall, one could say that the movement between text and image in *American Landscape* both complicates and partially resolves what is a principal obstacle in Genette's analysis: namely, the ambiguity of "narrative time" as a notion itself. As Genette notes, "reading time varies according to particular circumstances" so that "nothing here allows us to determine a 'normal' speed of execution," a dilemma he only partly solves by "measuring" the former in terms of page count.[38] Introducing a pictorial dimension not only complicates the "speed of execution" to include both reading and viewing, on the side of "narrative time," but—as is the case with *American Landscape* and many transportation guidebooks—the traversal of space is additionally tied to some imagined "movement" through history, on the side of "story time." However, one notable feature of later transportation guidebooks is precisely that "narrative time" becomes more controlled, as the length of a text and the amount of detail in a picture are circumscribed by real travel time, providing something like Genette's nonexistent "isochronous narrative, our hypothetical reference zero . . . where the relationship duration-of-story/length-of-narrative would remain always steady."[39]

In *American Landscape,* the interplay of reading and viewing is sustained in the guide's presentation of its sites, whether they are primarily natural or clearly marked by human occupation, as in *Fort Putnam* and *Winnipiseogee Lake* (figures 6 and 7). The illustration of Fort Putnam, based on a painting of the same site by Weir, situates the viewer behind the ruins of the fort, looking out over the boat-dotted Hudson toward a distant range of mountains, its left portion obscured by a passing shower. A contrast emerges between the foreground, the more or less arrested past (the ruins), and the background, the ongoing present (the boats plying back and forth across the river, the transient rain). This pattern of looking, moving back and forth between the immediate vicinity of the fort and the distant horizon, between the past and the present, is anticipated by the preceding section of text. After first describing the site's general location and historical significance, the text then draws attention to its current dated appearance and its strategic position as an observation post in the Revolutionary War (the view replicated in the engraving): "Since the peace of 1783, Fort Putnam . . . has been gradually dismantled, and at last suffered to fall into decay, so that it now appears a venerable ruin of massive military architecture, crowning the woody steep of a mountain. . . . From its dilapidated bastions, the eye wanders over a wide sea of mountain ridges." This establishment of a past vantage point is followed by a listing of the contemporary sights visible from it: "the rich plains of Duchess and Orange counties, filled with farms and villages" and the Hudson itself, "covered with the white sails of sloops and with steamboats."[40] The text then finally "returns" to the fort, to the "ruins rich with the most hallowed associations," and recites the principal events of the Revolutionary War that occurred in its vicinity, prompting the viewer to picture their reenactment: "As we muse over this magnificent scene of great events, the imagination insensibly kindles, and the plain below, and the forts, and rocks, become peopled again with the soldiers and the

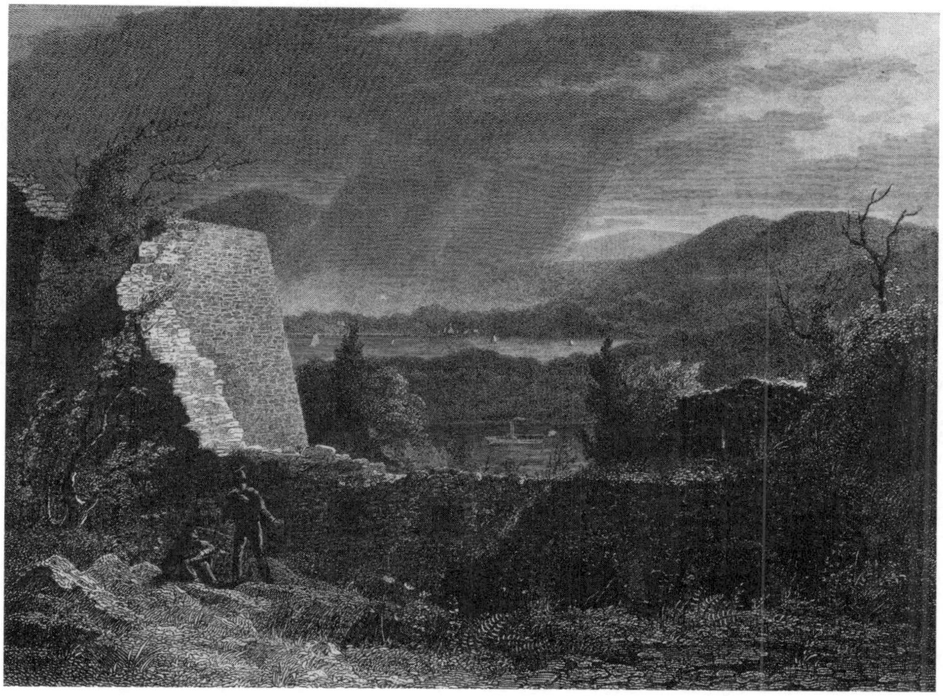

FIGURE 6. Robert W. Weir, *Fort Putnam*. Illustration from William Cullen Bryant and Asher B. Durand, *American Landscape*, no. 1 (New York: E. Bliss, 1830). Courtesy the Metropolitan Museum of Art. Gift of Mrs. Frederic F. Durand, 1930.

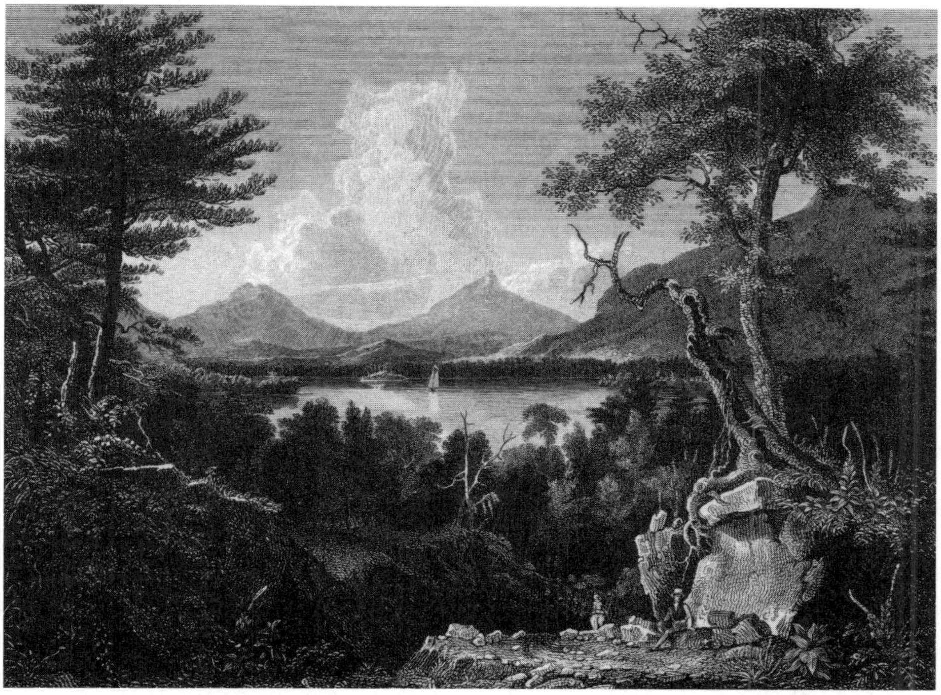

FIGURE 7. Thomas Cole, *Winnipiseogee Lake*. Illustration from William Cullen Bryant and Asher B. Durand, *American Landscape*, no. 1 (New York: E. Bliss, 1830). Courtesy the Metropolitan Museum of Art. Gift of Mrs. Frederic F. Durand, 1930.

chiefs of the revolution."[41] This back-and-forth movement between past and present echoes a reciprocal movement between text and image, as the fort's history is legible both as text and as the physical features of its depicted ruined state. Verbal and visual history illuminate each other.

Incidents from the Revolutionary War were a staple of historical content in the views presented in *American Landscape,* as well as in transportation guidebooks. Although these incidents were not directly assimilable to the transitions from wilderness to farmstead to town typical of the progress of civilization depicted in many landscape paintings, they nonetheless comport with its progressive trajectory. Thus, what was a battlefield is now "the rich plains of Duchess and Orange counties, filled with farms and villages." As actual places, they do not correlate with the generalized significance of landscape features in paintings such as Cole's *River in the Catskills,* where the depicted town becomes every town. But in *American Landscape* and the earlier transportation guides especially, actual places are typically described through features—the wilderness, American Indian habitation, a bustling town, a thriving farming community—that figure in that allegorical construction of history.

The section of text on Winnipiseogee, which is accompanied by an engraving based on a painting by Cole, partially reverses this movement from past to present. Unlike Fort Putnam, the site lacked any conspicuous ruins. In his preface, Bryant addressed the contemporary concern with America's lack of visible traces of the past by noting that their absence had the effect of "abstracting the mind from the associations of human agency" and "carry[ing] it up to the idea of a mightier power, and to the great mystery of the origin of things."[42] Rather than evoking thoughts of the deity, or of manmade structures of the future (Cole's answer to this deficiency in his 1836 "Essay on American Scenery"), the text here begins with a foreground of closely observed natural detail and then moves into the distance as it seeks for "traces of the red men," aligning physical distance with antiquity.[43] Ultimately, this section of text conjures up past remains by transforming the scene's natural features into elements of Native architecture and social practice: "This lake and the neighboring waters were favourite resorts of the Indians; they spent their summers fishing in them, and basked away on their banks their hours of ease in the months when they rested from the chase. The children of the forest had the most exquisite taste for rural scenery."[44] This conflation of the natural and the social is further extended by the survival of putative Native names for nearby rivers and mountains. Winnipiseogee, translated as "the smile of the Great Father," has a poetic quality that harmonizes with the aesthetic merits of the site.[45] In other words, despite the absence of crumbling ruins, Bryant's text constructs a viewing trajectory that shares many of the structural traits of associational contemplation, if not its typical historical content. What is more, the absence of visible signs of the past heightens the engraving's dependence on the text to complete the picturesque ensemble. This dependence is emphasized by the fact that the only specifically identifiable features in the printed view (beyond the lake itself) are the peaks of Mounts Washington and Chocorua, which mark the endpoints of visual movement into the distance and into the past: their historical significance lies purely in their nomenclature, the stories associated with their names.

The text and illustrations of *American Landscape* thus work together to imitate the view of history cultivated in contemporary landscape paintings, such as those produced by the artists who provided the sketches and paintings on which the illustrations were based: Cole, Weir, and Durand. (Durand was also responsible for "finishing," or touching up, the plates.) This view is neither forceful nor prescriptive, in the same way that such paintings suggested progress and history in a direction of vision that was essentially unobtrusive, that maintained the viewer's sense of freedom. Indeed there is a certain correspondence to be noted between the view of history so often represented in painting (generally untroubled narratives of steadily advancing civilization) and the experience of viewing as a kind of leisure.[46] In *The Magisterial Gaze,* Albert Boime argued that the point of view typically established in antebellum landscape painting was a visual analog for mastery or ownership of the land, internalizing and normalizing the avarice driving national expansion and development within an aesthetic experience.[47] As Boime points out, many of the patrons of these works were closely involved in this enterprise as businessmen, so that their business activities would apparently comport in a positive way with this depiction of progress.[48] Effects of distance and duration also speak to a project of cultural legitimation shared by many writers and artists at this time, in which emphasizing historical extension heightens the impression of a cultural pedigree in what was still a recently formed nation. Even here, though, Boime's analysis is applicable in the sense of viewing as an analog for mastery or ownership of not land, but cultural capital. Like the picturesque discoveries described by Cole in his diary, and despite the fact that *American Landscape* was targeted toward a broad audience, effects of distance and duration help establish cultural worth while also suggesting the viewer's exclusive relation to it.

Steamboat guidebooks largely replicate this pattern of coordinating textual descriptions and printed landscape views, but they additionally begin to integrate an attentiveness to sequential sights visible from the moving steamboat. *Nelson's Illustrated Guide to the Hudson* (1860) is particularly suggestive because it exerts more effort than most guides to reconcile what might seem to be contradictory methods for narratively organizing the viewing of landscape imagery in order to convey a sense of history: namely, using both axial (depth-seeking) and lateral (breadth-seeking) paths of vision.[49] Nelson guides were one of the most highly regarded travel aids at midcentury, covering a number of scenic routes in the Northeast, not all of which were steamboat trips.[50] Their value lay in identifying and locating culturally significant landmarks, attractions, buildings, and so forth as well as supplying relatively detailed background information, although they left out prices of tickets, admittance fees, and advertisements. Other steamboat guidebooks shared general structural characteristics with the Nelson guides but were less elaborate and more mundane in their content.[51]

The Nelson guide to the Hudson River traces a journey upriver from New York to Albany, interspersing short textual descriptions with prints of picturesque sights, which are wood engravings based on photographs, printed in black and the primary colors to more closely replicate views of the passing scenery on a sunlit balmy day. As in Bryant's and Durand's work, the text illuminates and interprets the view: "In fulfilling the office of guide to these beauteous scenes, it has been our endeavour to cull their 'faint traditions' from every available source, and so to inweave them with the description of the scenery."[52] Also like *American Landscape,* the Nelson guide purports to stand in for an actual trip: "For those who, with all man's nomadic disposition, lack the opportunity to carry out their wanderings, it will spread before their mind's eye Nature in her most varied aspects, and transport them in spirit far from their own fireside to grand and glorious scenes, rendered more dear to each free-born American as the theatre of the most thrilling episodes of that glorious war that made him so."[53] Here, however, there is an implication of easy mobility or moving-between (pairing travel with narrative, "nomadi[sm]" and "wandering" with "episodes") that contrasts with Bryant's "series of views," each of which commanded independence and exclusivity in relation to one another. Moreover, the Nelson guide likens itself to "a cheerful companion, who can tell [the traveler] all about what he sees—the name of each place, and its history, real and legendary" but who also "knows when to hold his tongue."[54] It suggests ongoing intermittent use and refers outside itself, to the passing landscape, to the user's waning interest, again in contrast to the more closed world of Bryant's scenic journal. A latent opposition arises between a self-contained and closed image of landscape and a perspective that moves between images, which in turn could be equated with an opposition between axial and lateral spectatorship: the one sustained and depth penetrating, the other brief and surface oriented. Overall, the Nelson guide tries to incorporate both to a certain degree.

The Nelson guide contains numerous instances of short text sections paired with engraved illustrations to produce the sustained, distanced view of landscape found in *American Landscape*. *Peekskill from Verplanck's Point* (plate 4) reprises many of Bryant's and Durand's picturesque pictorial devices, such as the elevated viewpoint and the jutting landmasses that direct the eye in a long curve toward the distant hills. That the vantage point in this image is not on the river itself, but on a hill on the eastern side of the river, frees these devices to operate with greatest effect, even though the text is explicitly addressed to a passenger on a steamboat. As in the print of *Fort Putnam* (figure 6), this vantage point is identified with the past, with a British encampment early in the war and, later, with the former base camp of Washington's army, while here too the present is indicated by the moving traffic of boats on the Hudson. The paired text begins with a lengthy account of General "Mad Anthony" Wayne's assault on Fort Stony Point (to the left in the print), notes that a false attack was made on Verplanck's Point as a diversion, goes on to explain the Dutch origin of the name and Washington's use of the point as a base of operations, and concludes by rehearsing the many stories of betrayal and treason connected with Peekskill. The text provides both the associative details and the viewing path for the engraving, with the eye moving back and forth between historically significant sites in the foreground and background.

Peekskill from Verplanck's Point is one of several episodes in which the reader is held up in an examination of landscape and its historical associations, which corresponds with the elevated, distant view of paintings, but the guidebook also encourages a different awareness of history, which aligns the forward movement of the steamboat with the progression of a historical narrative. This correlation between narrative and physical movement is a feature of contemporary moving panoramas (a fad for moving panoramas of specifically rivers began in the previous decade, following the successful tour of John Banvard's 1847 *Panorama of the Mississippi River*). Such simulated journeys likewise organized discrete incidents within larger narrative arcs: for example, general movements from civilization to wilderness are traced in the specific sights one sees as one moves from cities to unsettled areas.[55] In Nelson's guide, the recounting of the Revolutionary War focuses on a limited number of parallel, interrelated stories, and as the reader passes by sites connected with these stories, the narratives move forward. In other words, the traveler vicariously reenacts these dramas of the war, and this effect is heightened by the text's emphasis on causality, how certain events inevitably lead to other events. After its discussion of Peekskill, the text notes how the bombardment of the British ship the *Vulture* in this area led to the capture of the British spy Major Andre—an action that took place in another location. A developing network of events is tied to a network of sites; just as the steamboat passenger is compelled to pass by those sites, so those events are bound together in a chain of inevitability. It further becomes possible to relate the guidebook's fascination with stories of betrayal and treason to this connection between location and narrative episode. Control of different stretches of the Hudson passed back and forth between the British and the Americans several times. With enemy territory often as close as the other side of the river, "switching sides" could be a short trip, both morally and geographically, and the movement of the traveler's eye from west bank to east bank retraces this vacillation.[56]

Such efforts at aligning the boat's movement with a larger narrative trajectory promote a briefer, more superficial engagement with individual landscape views. The focus here on a larger series of linked events tied to a sequence of views works against the sustained, distance-seeking form of spectatorship encouraged elsewhere by the guidebook. An unavoidable degree of confusion is also involved in keeping up with the threads of numerous stories, which would probably be unsustainable except for the relatively slow movement of the steamboat. Although the Nelson guide does experiment with this lateral form of spectatorship, it typically returns to the axial form in its textual framing of engravings and the kind of view represented in them. Something resembling the view from the steamboat does appear, such as the *Entrance to the Highlands opposite Peekskill* (figure 8), which follows *Peekskill from Verplanck's Point.* Scenes like these are usually chosen to show a distinctive profile of hills not viewable from a land-based perspective, but overall images of this kind are the exception rather than the rule. The recognition of an ephemeral or passing sequence of scenes is more forcefully demonstrated by a common mapping apparatus that functions as a kind of table of contents, as in Charles Taintor's *The Hudson River Route,* published in 1869 (figure 9).[57] Here a verso map of the river marked with major towns and geographical features faces a recto page with double columns of text describing the principal points of interest on the west and east banks of the river. This preliminary mapping apparatus is followed by the extended textual descriptions and isolated landscape views that are found in the Nelson guide, but Taintor's presentation allows the passenger to correlate that picturesque mode of viewing the landscape with the actual sequence of passing scenes that take place on the steamboat journey.

History and Landscape in Railroad Guidebooks

With the development of the railroad in the 1830s and 1840s, the kind of sights available to the traveler shifted away from a stable picturesque model in step with the increasing velocities made possible by advances in engineering. As Thoreau observed in "Sounds," two of the most noticeable effects of train

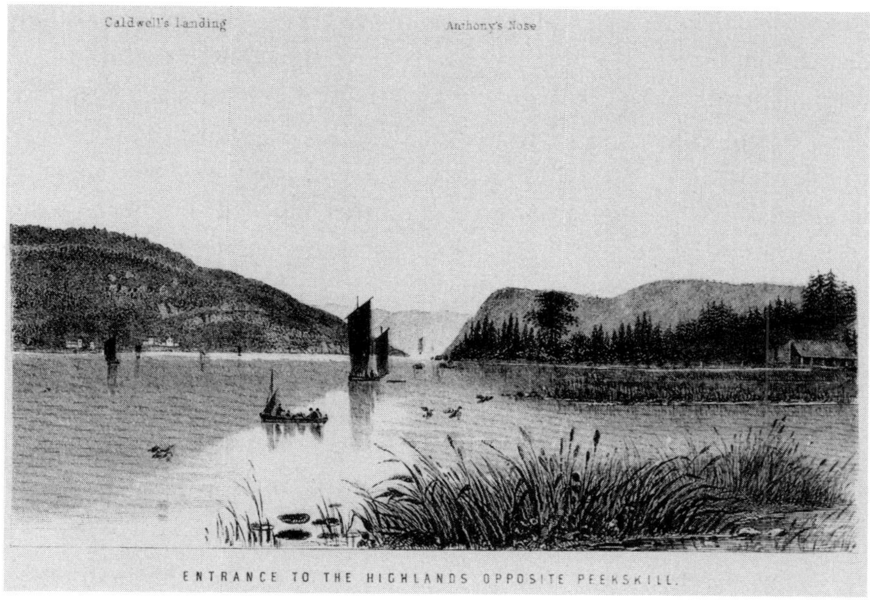

FIGURE 8. Unknown artist, *Entrance to the Highlands opposite Peekskill.* Illustration from Thomas Nelson, *Nelson's Illustrated Guide to the Hudson and Its Tributaries* (New York: Nelson and Sons, 1860). Courtesy the University of Chicago Library.

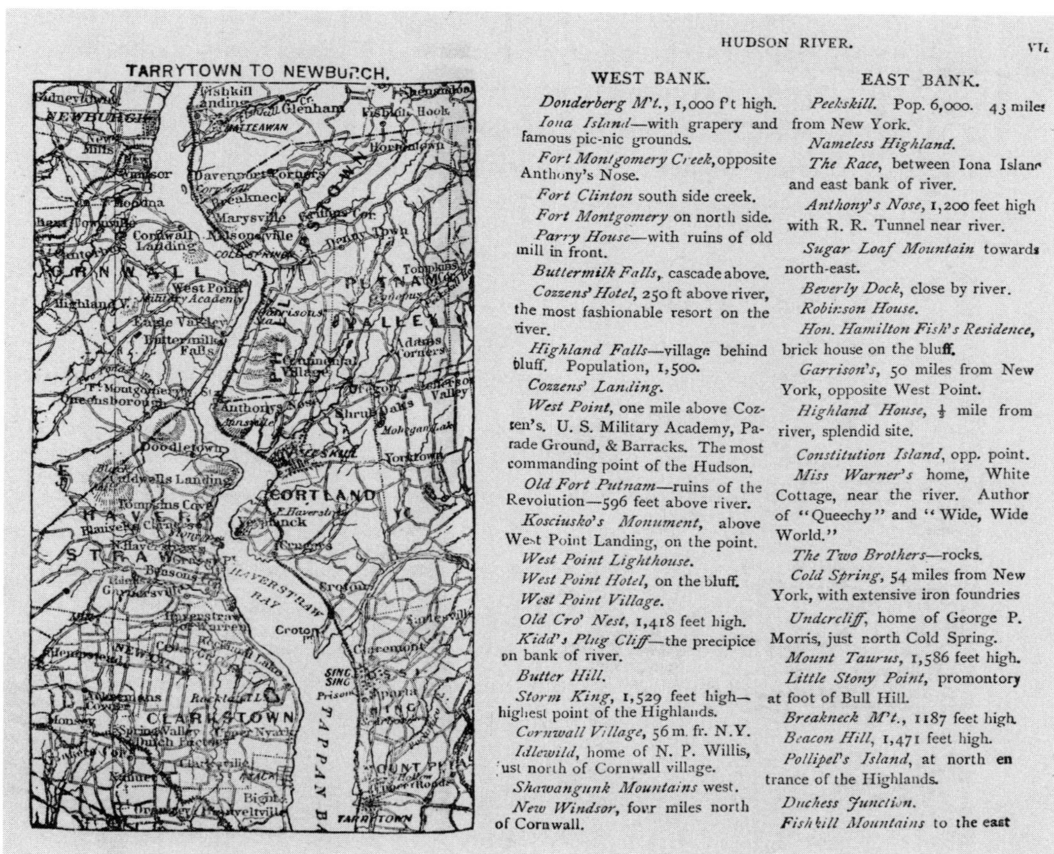

HUDSON RIVER.

TARRYTOWN TO NEWBURGH.

WEST BANK.

Donderberg M't., 1,000 f't high.

Iona Island—with grapery and famous pic-nic grounds.

Fort Montgomery Creek, opposite Anthony's Nose.

Fort Clinton south side creek.

Fort Montgomery on north side.

Parry House—with ruins of old mill in front.

Buttermilk Falls, cascade above.

Cozzens' Hotel, 250 ft above river, the most fashionable resort on the river.

Highland Falls—village behind bluff. Population, 1,500.

Cozzens' Landing.

West Point, one mile above Cozzen's. U. S. Military Academy, Parade Ground, & Barracks. The most commanding point of the Hudson.

Old Fort Putnam—ruins of the Revolution—596 feet above river.

Kosciusko's Monument, above West Point Landing, on the point.

West Point Lighthouse.

West Point Hotel, on the bluff.

West Point Village.

Old Cro' Nest, 1,418 feet high.

Kidd's Plug Cliff—the precipice on bank of river.

Butter Hill.

Storm King, 1,529 feet high—highest point of the Highlands.

Cornwall Village, 56 m. fr. N.Y.

Idlewild, home of N. P. Willis, just north of Cornwall village.

Shawangunk Mountains west.

New Windsor, four miles north of Cornwall.

EAST BANK.

Peekskill. Pop. 6,000. 43 miles from New York.

Nameless Highland.

The Race, between Iona Island and east bank of river.

Anthony's Nose, 1,200 feet high with R. R. Tunnel near river.

Sugar Loaf Mountain towards north-east.

Beverly Dock, close by river.

Robinson House.

Hon. Hamilton Fish's Residence, brick house on the bluff.

Garrison's, 50 miles from New York, opposite West Point.

Highland House, ½ mile from river, splendid site.

Constitution Island, opp. point.

Miss Warner's home, White Cottage, near the river. Author of "Queechy" and "Wide, Wide World."

The Two Brothers—rocks.

Cold Spring, 54 miles from New York, with extensive iron foundries

Undercliff, home of George P. Morris, just north Cold Spring.

Mount Taurus, 1,586 feet high.

Little Stony Point, promontory at foot of Bull Hill.

Breakneck M't., 1187 feet high.

Beacon Hill, 1,471 feet high.

Pollipel's Island, at north entrance of the Highlands.

Duchess Junction.

Fishkill Mountains to the east

FIGURE 9. Unknown artist, *Tarrytown to Newburgh.* Illustration from Charles Taintor, *The Hudson River Route: New York to Albany* (New York: Taintor Brothers, Merrill, 1869). Courtesy Library of Congress.

travel were the collapse of distance between previously remote locations and the imposition of a time schedule alien to the natural rhythms of the rotating planet. In *The Railway Journey,* Wolfgang Schivelbusch describes how the train seemingly replaced traditional space and its traversal over time with what he characterizes as a "machine ensemble," a new spatial awareness comprising tracks and engines that imposed an artificial order on the natural landscape.[58] This new spatial awareness deprived individual communities of their unique identity: "As the space between the points—the traditional traveling space—was destroyed, those points moved into each other's immediate vicinity: one might say they collided. They lost their old sense of local identity, formerly determined by the spaces between them."[59] This reorganization of basic phenomenal categories was paralleled by the visual experience to be had from the train car window, which critically involved the destruction of both distance and duration:

> Unlike the driver, the travelers had a very limited chance to look ahead: thus all they saw was an evanescent landscape. . . .
>
> The recommendation to look at things "from a certain distance" does not seem entirely realistic, in view of the traveler's situation in the train compartment: enclosed in it, the traveler has no way of distancing himself from the objects. . . . Increased velocity calls forth a greater number of visual impressions for the sense of sight to deal with.[60]

In sum, railroad travel impeded key components of the picturesque view of landscape. Although the train could be a potent symbol of historical progress within a traditional oil painting (or print) that supported that picturesque observer, train travel itself enforced a fundamentally different mode of perception.

In general, passengers were required to recalibrate how their senses positioned themselves in relation to an exterior (the landscape outside) and an interior (their immediate surroundings in the car). They had to switch from a sustained and axial view into distance to a rapidly shifting, lateral sequence of views perceived as shallow. Steamboat guidebooks engaged this switch from axial to lateral perception to some degree, but in train travel it was a much more forceful sensation. Even so, railroad guidebooks continued to highlight the historical significance of landscape by using familiar picturesque constructions of space. Williams's *Pacific Tourist* (featuring the unusual, tangential view of unharmed deer, figure 2, which I contrasted earlier with Melrose's painting) prominently advertised the involvement of such well-known landscape painters as Thomas Moran and featured a frontispiece (figure 10) that shares many of the compositional features of Durand's *Progress* (plate 2). In *America's*

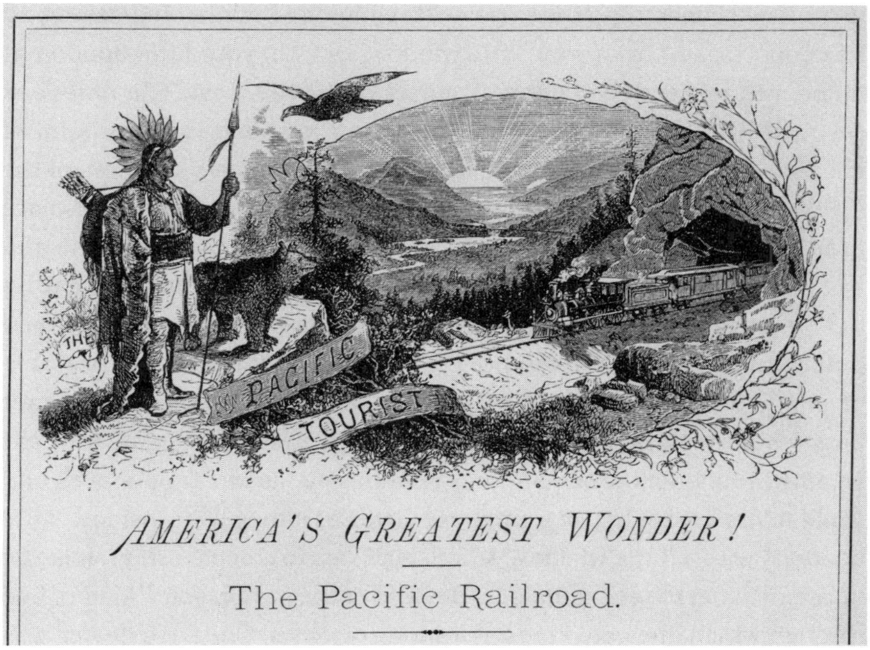

FIGURE 10. Unknown artist, *America's Greatest Wonder!* Illustration from Henry T. Williams, *The Pacific Tourist: Williams' Illustrated Trans-Continental Guide of Travel, from the Atlantic to the Pacific Ocean,* 2nd ed. (New York: Williams, 1876). RB 2676.
Courtesy the Huntington Library, San Marino, California.

Greatest Wonder! an Indian gazes admiringly at a landscape vignette from which he is visually separated; a sightline winds along a watercourse and terminates in a florid sunset or sunrise, while two trains crisscross this sightline. In Durand's painting, two Indian hunters are hidden in a group of trees and shrubs on the left, visually separated from a sightline that proceeds toward a setting sun, while in the middle distance a train moves at an angle across the dominant viewing path.

Nonetheless, while a substantial number of illustrations in the *Pacific Tourist* exhibit this stable picturesque composition, the text also refers to an alternative visual engagement with landscape available to riders on the Union Pacific Railroad. In an early section describing the comfort of the new Pullman cars, Williams writes:

> On some lovely, balmy, summer day, when the fresh breezes across the prairies induce us to open our doors and windows, there may often be seen curious and pleasant sights. Standing at the rear of the train, and with all doors open, there is an unobstructed view along the aisles throughout the entire length. On either side of the train, are the prairies, where the eye sees but wildness, and even desolation, then looking back upon this long aisle or avenue, he sees civilization.[61]

Williams stresses the physical separation of the car occupants from the landscape through which they travel: "As our train moves on, it introduces us to new scenes. . . . You carry with you your Pullman house and all its comforts, and from your little window, as from your little boudoir at home, you will see the mighty wonders of the Far West."[62] In *America's Greatest Wonder!* the train is viewed from the stable vantage point of contemporary landscape painting, but here "the mighty wonders of the Far West," the view of the terrain available from the train itself, takes place in an oddly enclosed and mobile compartment. Its oddity is underscored by the shuffling of interiority and exteriority: Williams invites the rider to take a position at the rear of the train in order to see both inside and outside, while the "Pullman house" is less a building than a portable object ("You carry [it] with you"). Meanwhile, the sustained and distant picturesque view is replaced by a series of "new scenes" outside the car window, which follow one another relentlessly "as our train moves on," while riders are sealed off from those vistas as if they were inside a "little boudoir" with a "little window." It is a small step to compare this miniature house or room to recent imaging devices of the parlor, some kind of box through which one could look at a series of views. One such device was the stereoscope, which merged two views into one like the simultaneous views inside and outside the train that Williams describes.[63] At the same time, though, Williams is imposing a historical allegory on the landscape by looking at it through this viewing apparatus—the train—telescoping the multiple stages of Durand's narrative of Manifest Destiny into a flickering alternation of "desolation" and "civilization." What I think makes this allegorical view so strange is its presentation of historical allegory as a visual novelty—not the product of sustained and informed contemplation but an immediate and thrilling experience.

Williams's guide provides an introduction to some of the ways by which railroad travel modified the perception of landscape and history, but I want to focus in this section on a midcentury railroad guidebook that amplifies the characteristics of subsequent publications, William Guild's *A Chart and Description of the Boston and Worcester and Western Railroads* (1847).[64] Tracks were first laid in the United States in the 1830s, and the route covered by Guild was one of the earliest important rail links, connecting Boston with Albany on the Hudson River. Although it is a relatively early railroad guide (or perhaps because of this fact), Guild's work was already sensitive to the novel sights made possible by a train moving quickly through the countryside, and the guide seems surprisingly complacent about how these sights compromised then-prevalent picturesque viewing conventions.[65] As in Williams's *Pacific Tourist* (figure 2), there are prints of the shearing, tangential view outside the train compartment, as well as multiple views aligned with the course of the track itself (figures 11 and 12). There is a marked contrast between the view *At Newton Corner*, with its almost serene perspectival pull into a quiet countryside, and Melrose's alarming *Westward the Star of Empire Takes Its Way* (figure 1). The prosaic character of these scenes derives largely from the utilitarian function of the railroad. The location of rail lines was a matter of cost efficiency, of selecting easy grades and inexpensive land, so views that correspond with prevailing conventions of landscape beauty are accidental.[66] Industrial development followed the extension of rail lines. It was advantageous for factories and mills to be close to the tracks, further obscuring open views of the countryside. Although railroad guides, like steamboat guides, attempted to make the trip interesting or entertaining, the brevity of a train trip tended to focus attention more on the destination than the

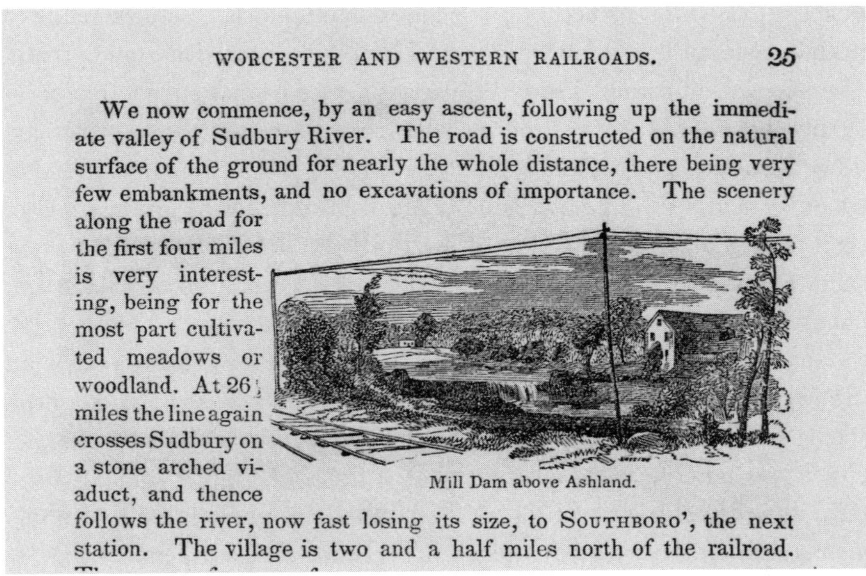

WORCESTER AND WESTERN RAILROADS. 25

We now commence, by an easy ascent, following up the immediate valley of Sudbury River. The road is constructed on the natural surface of the ground for nearly the whole distance, there being very few embankments, and no excavations of importance. The scenery along the road for the first four miles is very interesting, being for the most part cultivated meadows or woodland. At 26½ miles the line again crosses Sudbury on a stone arched viaduct, and thence follows the river, now fast losing its size, to SOUTHBORO', the next station. The village is two and a half miles north of the railroad.

Mill Dam above Ashland.

FIGURE 11. Unknown artist, *Mill Dam above Ashland.* Illustration from William Guild, *A Chart and Description of the Boston and Worcester and Western Railroads* (Boston, MA: Bradbury and Guild, 1847). Courtesy the University of Chicago Library.

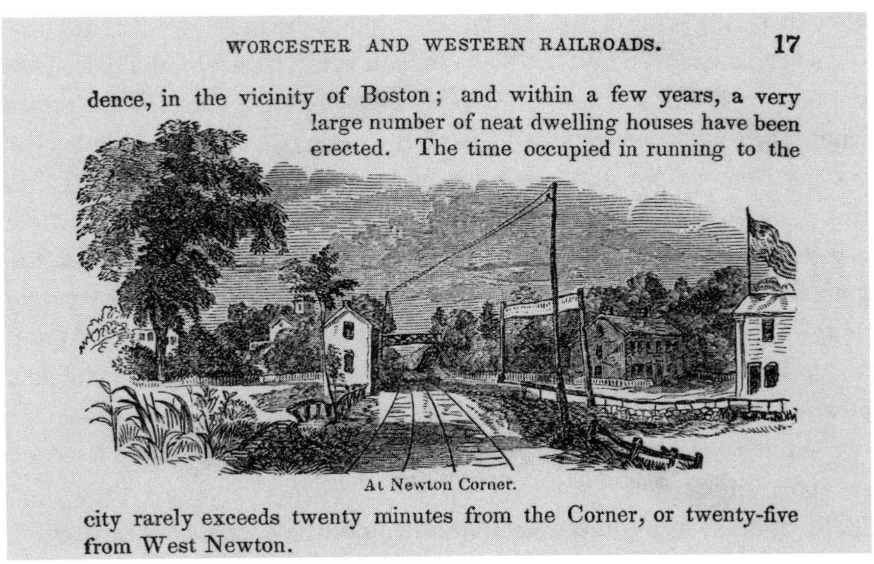

WORCESTER AND WESTERN RAILROADS. 17

dence, in the vicinity of Boston; and within a few years, a very large number of neat dwelling houses have been erected. The time occupied in running to the city rarely exceeds twenty minutes from the Corner, or twenty-five from West Newton.

At Newton Corner.

FIGURE 12. Unknown artist, *At Newton Corner.* Illustration from William Guild, *A Chart and Description of the Boston and Worcester and Western Railroads* (Boston, MA: Bradbury and Guild, 1847). Courtesy the University of Chicago Library.

route.[67] To the extent that the prints in Guild's guidebook compete for the viewer's attention, one of their recurring fallback tactics is to direct the reader to the railroad itself (the engineering "marvels" of cuttings, bridges, and roundhouses).

Guild's guidebook, like Williams's *Pacific Tourist,* does contain a number of vistas reminiscent of the stable, distanced observer (plate 1 and figure 13), but these views are noticeably panoramic in format, with a strong lateral composition. Accompanying textual descriptions stress the imminent, transitory nature of these landscapes: "Upon emerging from the brick walls of the city, a pleasing panorama [of Boston] meets our view" and "very soon one of the most lovely and charming views [of Quinsigamond Pond] . . . bursts upon our view."[68] The active tense of these descriptions is intensified by the slight diagonal foreground baseline in both images, a tilt that tends to impel a lateral movement in front of them. The absence of frames around these vignettes is also suggestive of an evanescent view. Moreover, the lateral orientation discourages a prolonged movement into depth, just as Schivelbusch notes that the rapid speed of trains "call[ed] forth a greater number of visual impressions for the sense of sight to deal with." The absence of lengthy historical narratives in the text sections enhances this rapid, lateral orientation; compared with *American Landscape,* there is less to look for in the images as supplied by the text.

Registration of the novel sights afforded by train travel is not restricted to the engraved illustrations alone. Rather, the entire assemblage of the scenic guide—its correlation of text, printed images, and actual scenery—engenders and mediates a new model of railroad spectatorship, what I term a "railroad narrative." This mediation is foregrounded by Guild's instructions to the reader on the use of his book (as discussed in the introduction). The "Explanation of the Chart" instructs riders how to orient their viewing position in relation to the direction of the moving train and how to use the measured vertical route line on verso pages to identify sights outside the train car window. This information also in a sense determines where the reader/viewer should be on the recto page, which contains the textual descriptions and printed views of those sights. Compared with the example of steamboat guides, though, Guild's guidebook as a whole is essentially a more rigorous version of Taintor's mapping apparatus, the map now more actively determining the size and positioning of text and image elements (see figure 9 and plate 1), bringing together the text and image sections that were separated in earlier guides. This suturing also clearly juxtaposes a tempo predicated on the rate of travel with the pace of reading the scenic guide itself—that eight-minute time frame for each two-page spread determined by the train's reported velocity.[69] Altogether, Guild's guidebook requires a constantly mobile eye, capable of switching

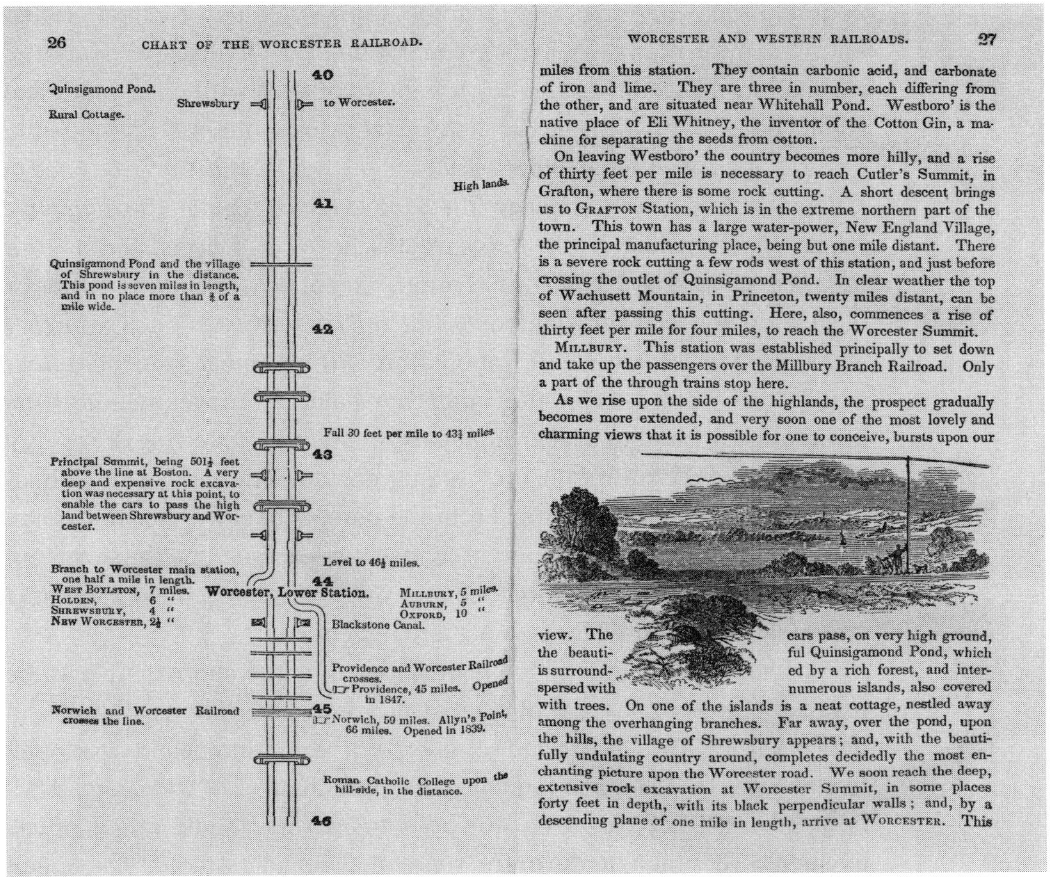

26 CHART OF THE WORCESTER RAILROAD.

40

Quinsigamond Pond.

Shrewsbury — to Worcester.

Rural Cottage.

High lands.

41

Quinsigamond Pond and the village of Shrewsbury in the distance. This pond is seven miles in length, and in no place more than ¾ of a mile wide.

42

Fall 30 feet per mile to 43¾ miles.

43

Principal Summit, being 501½ feet above the line at Boston. A very deep and expensive rock excavation was necessary at this point, to enable the cars to pass the high land between Shrewsbury and Worcester.

Level to 46½ miles.

Branch to Worcester main station, one half a mile in length.

44

Worcester, Lower Station.

West Boylston, 7 miles.
Holden, 6 "
Shrewsbury, 4 "
New Worcester, 2½ "

Millbury, 5 miles.
Auburn, 5 "
Oxford, 10 "

Blackstone Canal.

Providence and Worcester Railroad crosses.
Providence, 45 miles. Opened in 1847.

Norwich and Worcester Railroad crosses the line.

45

Norwich, 59 miles. Allyn's Point, 66 miles. Opened in 1839.

Roman Catholic College upon the hill-side, in the distance.

46

WORCESTER AND WESTERN RAILROADS. 27

miles from this station. They contain carbonic acid, and carbonate of iron and lime. They are three in number, each differing from the other, and are situated near Whitehall Pond. Westboro' is the native place of Eli Whitney, the inventor of the Cotton Gin, a machine for separating the seeds from cotton.

On leaving Westboro' the country becomes more hilly, and a rise of thirty feet per mile is necessary to reach Cutler's Summit, in Grafton, where there is some rock cutting. A short descent brings us to Grafton Station, which is in the extreme northern part of the town. This town has a large water-power, New England Village, the principal manufacturing place, being but one mile distant. There is a severe rock cutting a few rods west of this station, and just before crossing the outlet of Quinsigamond Pond. In clear weather the top of Wachusett Mountain, in Princeton, twenty miles distant, can be seen after passing this cutting. Here, also, commences a rise of thirty feet per mile for four miles, to reach the Worcester Summit.

Millbury. This station was established principally to set down and take up the passengers over the Millbury Branch Railroad. Only a part of the through trains stop here.

As we rise upon the side of the highlands, the prospect gradually becomes more extended, and very soon one of the most lovely and charming views that it is possible for one to conceive, bursts upon our view. The cars pass, on very high ground, the beautiful Quinsigamond Pond, which is surrounded by a rich forest, and interspersed with numerous islands, also covered with trees. On one of the islands is a neat cottage, nestled away among the overhanging branches. Far away, over the pond, upon the hills, the village of Shrewsbury appears; and, with the beautifully undulating country around, completes decidedly the most enchanting picture upon the Worcester road. We soon reach the deep, extensive rock excavation at Worcester Summit, in some places forty feet in depth, with its black perpendicular walls; and, by a descending plane of one mile in length, arrive at Worcester. This

FIGURE 13. Unknown artist, *Quinsigamond Pond.* Illustration from William Guild, *A Chart and Description of the Boston and Worcester and Western Railroads* (Boston, MA: Bradbury and Guild, 1847). Courtesy the University of Chicago Library.

from one order of representation to another, at a rate in keeping with the shifting scenes outside the train, and then assimilating them into some composite narrative form.[70] Reading on the train, as Schivelbusch notes, quickly became a common topic in the discourse surrounding the unique visual experiences of railroad travel: "The effects of reading while traveling were discussed generally in medical circles in the 1860s. The debate as to whether it was harmful or beneficial related the practice to the special stresses put on the optical sense by rail travel, and to visual perception in general."[71] The Guild guidebook thus represents an effort to integrate three different orders of "rhythmic representation": textual narrative, "moving pictures" (resonating with other imaging technologies predicated on passing images, such as the recently popular moving panorama), and the "evanescent landscape" offered by the train.[72]

Just as the railroad guide engendered a model of spectatorship that differed significantly from the picturesque tradition that structured contemporary paintings and steamboat guides, it also elicited a different perception of history in its presentation of the landscape. Scattered throughout the Guild guidebook are views of sites with clear historical significance, often locations of major past events, but just as frequently general signs of either an older social order (the *Old Mill*, the *Rude Shed at Palmer*) or a new industrial age (the *State Lunatic Hospital*, the *Clappville Factories*). These historically redolent sites, however, succeed one another in no readily apparent narrative order, except as a recurring either/or vacillation between agrarian/past and industrial/present. Their arbitrary sequencing resists any steady rationalization into a linear sequence either in depth (as when the viewer of landscape paintings moves steadily from foreground present to background past) or laterally, following the overall movement of the train (like the broader narrative threads of steamboat guidebooks such as Nelson's). From the perspective of a viewer expecting a picturesque organization of landscape features, the arrangement of text and illustration in Guild shapes an experience of history that is comparatively fragmentary, rapid, and ephemeral.

The sense of fragmentation is heightened by the clipped style of the text, which resembles that of condensed route descriptions. As railroad networks increased in size and complexity, a verbal shorthand developed to efficiently describe the sequence of stops, changes of train, and directions involved in getting from one point to another.[73] Guild's book opens by succinctly breaking down the route in a similar fashion: "The line of railroad extending from the city of Boston to Greenbush, in the Hudson River, opposite the city of Albany, consists of the Boston and Worcester Railroad, which begins in Worcester, and extends to the Massachusetts state line, at West Stockbridge, and the Albany and West Stockbridge Railroad, which terminates at Greenbush."[74] This choppy, condensed syntax characterizes Guild's descriptions as a whole, in their brevity and, more broadly, in the constant movement among various objects of scenic interest. The style reflects the stress laid on the efficient presentation of information in more commercialized forms of tourism, both in the United States and Europe.[75] Other railroad guidebooks that forego the large quantity of illustrations found in Guild's book otherwise resemble it in the use of this condensed syntax and compressed treatment (and what landscape prints they do contain are often of the same panoramic unframed vignette format).

Overall, the recurrent visibility of history typical of steamboat guides to the Hudson River is reduced here; instead the emphasis is on tracking the speed and variety of social and technological progress. Guild nowhere states that his aim is to explicate the signs of the past.[76] Instead he writes, "The great object of the work is to increase the pleasures of railroad traveling, and the number of railroad travellers, by directing attention to the great variety of natural and artificial objects with which our railroads are skirted."[77] This attention to "artificial objects" (any manmade inventions or products) tends to level the historical depth that had been stressed in picturesque guidebooks. Where something like history is addressed in Guild's book, it takes the form of recounting developments in the construction of the railroad line, which are technological and belong to the recent past. This interest in the train carries over into what is considered most notable in the passing landscape, namely engineering wonders like viaducts and bridges. The constant shifting between briefly noted landscape features, combined with the reader's constant shifting between orders of representation, translates into a persistent oscillation between "natural and artificial objects" that resembles the flickering view between wilderness and civilization described by Williams (there also the train itself was somehow incorporated into the view from the train), but more clearly here as a new and distinct visual narrative form that is sustained throughout the work.

The Railroad Narrative and Commercial Culture

If there is any narrative continuity in this fragmentary, flickering sequencing of scenes, it clearly does not inhere in any protracted, leisurely movement between points in an overall structure. Rather, Guild's perfectly straight and omnipresent route line evokes a continuity that is insistently enforced, in the rapid and unremitting subjection of the viewer to an apparently "artificial" ordering of views over time. "Fragmentation," "mobility," and "shallowness" have been associated with a whole host of late nineteenth-century American social ills connected with industrialization: urban alienation, social disconnection, and the superficiality of commercial culture.[78] But in "'What Ought to Be Seen': Tourists' Guidebooks and National Identity in Modern Germany and Europe," Rudy Koshar argues against a purely negative assessment of the commercialization of tourism in the nineteenth century: "This point of view invites one to rethink an older scholarship's tendency to see consumption as passive and superficial."[79] As he notes, scenic guidebooks (such as Guild's) served a real purpose in facilitating and enabling social mobility, a topic I return to in chapter 2. Here, though, in order to situate the railroad narrative more generally in relation to a growing industrial and commercial culture, I want to concentrate on how the shift from picturesque viewing to railroad narrative involved a parallel shift in a fantasy of control or ownership.[80] If railroad guides like Guild's emphasize a distinctive experience of progress, they do so through a visual narrative form that is ultimately best suited to marketing products and that can be found in some of the new print publications being created at midcentury to encourage consumer demand.

In *Parallel Tracks,* Lynne Kirby draws an analogy between the visual experiences of railroad travel and early silent cinema and characterizes spectatorship in both as essentially dreamlike:

> The train is a mechanical double for the cinema and for the transport of the spectator into fiction, fantasy, and dream. . . . In both cases, passengers sit still as they rush through space and time, whether physically and visually, as on the train, or merely visually, as in the cinema. The train would then be cinema's mirror image in the sequential unfolding of a chain of essentially still images and the rapid shifts of point of view that the train and cinema experiences entail.[81]

Both the train and the movie theater isolate viewers from their immediate surroundings and facilitate an experience of detached, enclosed spectatorship, but perhaps the most dreamlike aspect common to both is the passivity of the viewer. The sense of train travel as dreamlike is suggested by riders' accounts cited by Schivelbusch. Although he does not emphasize this aspect, many accounts point in this direction—for example, in a journal entry by Joseph von Eichendorff: "These travels by steam keep on shaking the world . . . like a kaleidoscope, incessantly, the landscapes speeding by in ever-changing grimaces."[82] The "kaleidoscop[ic]" sequence of views (like the alteration of past and present in Guild's guidebook) is an imposition of irrational juxtaposition (because the train "keep[s] on shaking the world") that is suggestive of the suspension of the conscious mind in sleep.[83] Sometimes such dreamlike accounts are quite explicit:

> The beauties of England being those of a dream, should be as fleeting. They never appear so charming as when dashing on after a locomotive at forty miles an hour. Nothing by the way requires study, or demands mediation. . . . Everything is so quiet, so fresh, so full of home, and destitute of prominent objects to detain the eye . . . that I love to dream through these placid beauties whilst sailing in the air, quick, as if astride a tornado.[84]

Oscillations between delicacy and force, floating inactivity and hurried movement ("dream[ing] through those placid beauties . . . as if astride a tornado"), arise from the simultaneity of sitting still in the train compartment and rushing past the scenery outside, provoking an almost surreal sensation. Notably, though, the author of this passage submits happily to this dreamlike experience, "in which nothing by the way requires study, or demands mediation."

By contrast, the picturesque landscape view "worked" in part because it simulated an experience of mastery and ownership, through the viewer's depicted elevated position and how the viewer's eye seemed to direct the historical narrative attached to the landscape's features. Vestiges of this arrangement emerge in Williams's *Pacific Tourist*, in his comparison of the visual experience of train travel to being in one's home and viewing scenes at will through some kind of imaging device. Guild's book (in conjunction with the unique viewing possibilities of train travel) deprives the viewer of that specific illusion of owning the land and its history by negating the impressions of distance and duration that constituted the sleight of hand in the picturesque mode of viewing. Instead, it fosters the viewer's impression of being enclosed and contained within a dreamlike, random flux of history. Rather than conclude that the result is a world suddenly without historical order, though, I want to claim that the railroad narrative elicits a different kind of imaginative projection from the viewer, and makes a different appeal to the viewer's desires for agency—namely, one that is comfortable with the excitement of rapidly shifting points of view. The fundamental change is one from a fantasy of protracted enjoyment to a fantasy of instant access, so that agency takes a form akin to consumer choice, and the perception of instant access opens up the widest possible field for its exercise.[85]

The connection between new forms of commercial desire and new ways of narratively organizing the viewing of landscape scenery becomes clearer in examining the development of pictorial city guides—a genre that likewise experienced significant growth and diversification at midcentury. Such books were often, basically, commercial directories that posed as quasi-artistic mappings of specifically urban space. Occupying a kind of middle ground between art and commerce, they guided the user through the urban environment, offering textual and pictorial commentary on what they identified as significant landmarks of the city similar to the mediation of scenic views offered by transportation guidebooks. Besides the urban context, an essential difference is that these guides associated immediate access and consumer desire much more rapidly and explicitly in some of their later forms. That being said, their early forms included print versions of panoramas, which were produced in the United States not long after the first painted versions and were, initially at least, more historical in orientation. John Vanderlyn's *Palace and Gardens of Versailles* (1819), installed behind New York City Hall, is generally considered the first successful painted panorama in this country.[86] Print panoramas of cities initially consisted of a foldout view (or a composite view comprising several sheets), with numbers identifying significant sites within the image, followed by extended textual commentary on those sites (a presentation reminiscent of the pairing of map and text in the Taintor steamboat guide).

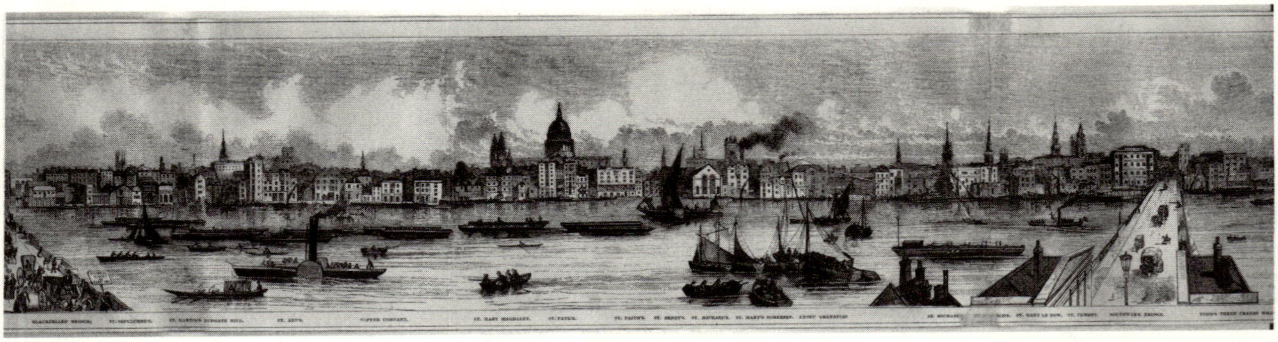

FIGURE 14. Henry Vizetelly, engraver, *Grand Panorama of London and the River Thames,* c. 1844 (detail). © Trustees of the British Museum.

By midcentury, however, several panoramic city guides had dispensed with the elevated viewpoint of traditional painted panoramas and had instead adopted the format of the moving panorama. Some of these later guides employed accordion-fold sheets containing an expansive, lateral view of the city organized along a major thoroughfare or river, as in the *Grand Panorama of London and the River Thames* (1844; figure 14). The forward, or rather sideways, movement of the reader is prompted by how the passing scenes correspond with the pages of a book; one "reads" from left to right, encountering prominent structures like St. Paul's and quasi-genre incidents involving groups of boats (the water even gets choppier as one gets closer to the tidewater in subsequent illustrations). There is no textual supplement at all, though, and so no reason to linger beyond the interest of the images themselves. Whatever narrative prolongation there was in the explication of sites in such transportation guidebooks as the Taintor guide has been sharply reduced here, but at the cost of articulating their (cultural, historical) significance. I want to suggest that this elimination of any prolonged consideration of sites parallels the rapid and brief treatment of scenery in railroad guidebooks. In both cases, the elimination of the configurations of space and temporality found in the earlier steamboat guidebooks opens the way for a new configuration, one that lends itself here to a more commercial reading of the city.

Many American versions of the foldout city panorama were explicitly conceived as business directories, such as Julio Rae's *Philadelphia Pictorial Directory and Panoramic Advertiser* (1851) and DeWitt Clinton Baxter's *Panoramic Business Directory,* which was printed intermittently from 1859 into the 1880s.[87] Rae's *Panoramic Advertiser* consisted of sheets containing outline prints of buildings on the north and south sides of important commercial thoroughfares, such as Chestnut Street, each accompanied by a sheet containing detachable business cards and advertisements (figures 15 and 16). Businesses would pay a fee to have their names inscribed on the depicted buildings and to receive business cards on the opposite sheet; in return, they would also get a limited number of sheets to pass out to

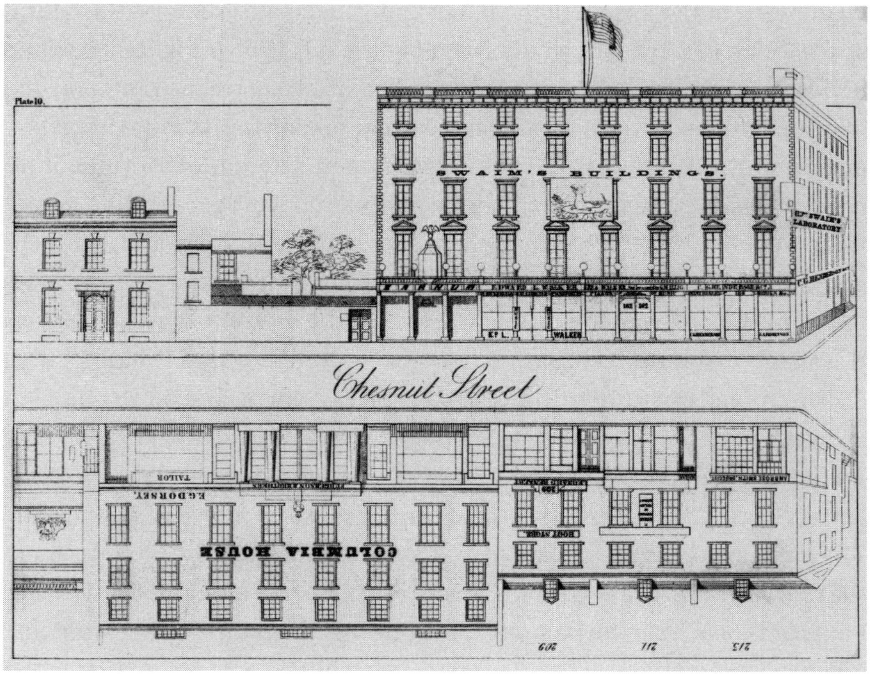

FIGURE 15. Unknown artist, profile view of Chestnut Street showing Barnum's American Museum. Illustration from Julio H. Rae, *Rae's Philadelphia Pictorial Directory and Panoramic Advertiser* (Philadelphia, PA: Rae, 1851). Courtesy the Library Company of Philadelphia.

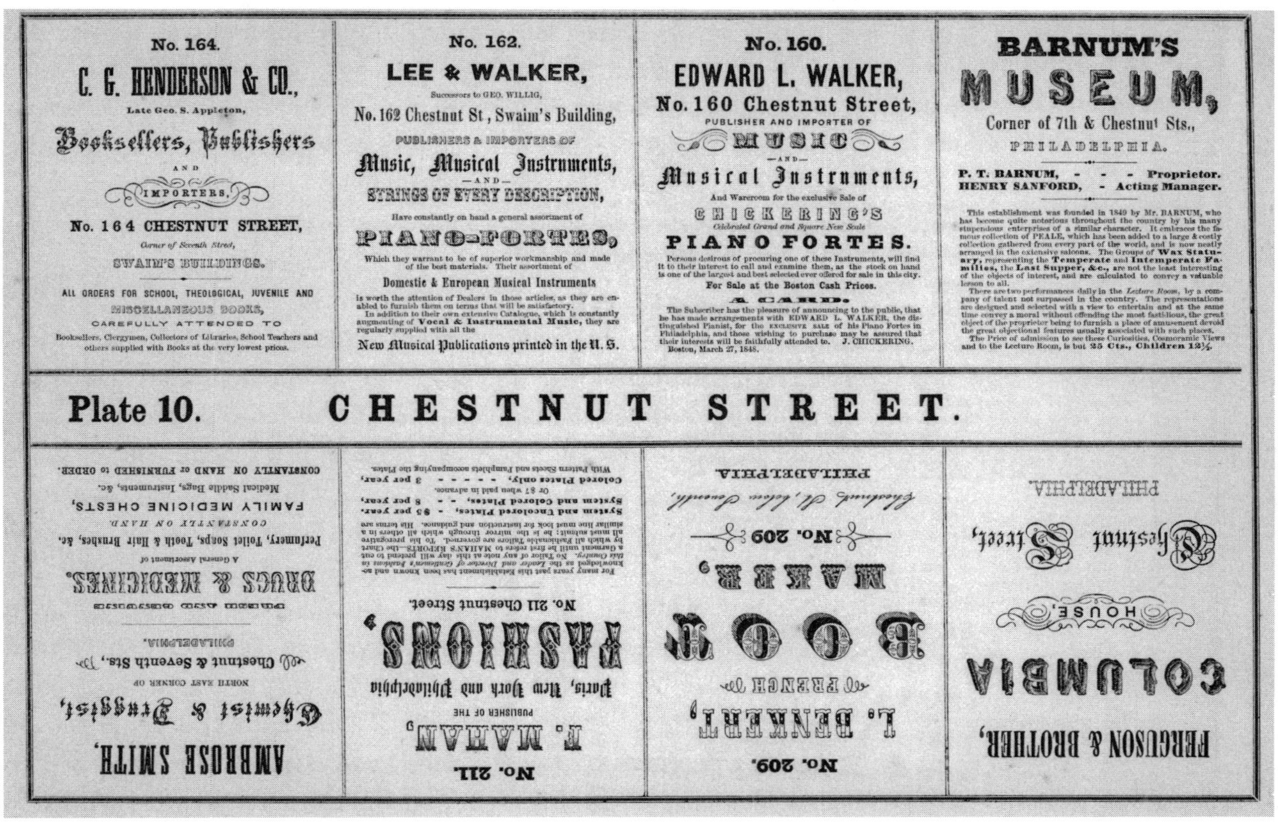

FIGURE 16. Unknown artist, accompanying advertisements for the profile view of Chestnut Street. From Julio H. Rae, *Rae's Philadelphia Pictorial Directory and Panoramic Advertiser* (Philadelphia, PA: Rae, 1851). Courtesy the Library Company of Philadelphia.

customers. In the format of the panoramic business directory, the lateral space found in the London panorama (figure 14) is further flattened, while indications of a third dimension, like the cross-street on the right, intrude like vertiginous tunnels. At the same time, these streets are completely empty; they do not provide a setting for human interactions as miniature narrative moments, as in the London panorama. Moreover, unlike steamboat guidebooks, which often attempted to align lateral movement with some kind of inclusive narrative that connected individual points on the route, in the panoramic business directory the viewer's eye slips across the sheet, instantly confronting the facade of this or that building, with no directional cues other than the street numbers printed at the top and no sense of beginning or end that could be compared to a book. The only arresting force comes from the viewer's exercise of choice in relation to the variety of commercial products and services displayed by the storefronts. The absence of depth, duration, and an evolving storyline—the traits of the railroad narrative—is driven home by the correspondence between the kinds of sheets, as if the pictures of storefronts are really not substantially fuller representations of the commercial establishments advertised in the business cards.[88] The business cards are also arranged on the north and south sides of the street, while the distinguishing traits of flatness and focus on type are used in both advertisement and street view, suggesting their basic equivalence.[89] The sense of proximity and immediate access to the commercial establishment suggested by Rae's pictorial directory translates into business cards literally in hand. Users of the directory are thus not merely encouraged to visit a commercial establishment of their choosing but are given a further means to act on their choice.[90]

I do not want to imply that Rae or Baxter conceived of their works as wholly lacking historical value. Rae writes that part of his intention was to "keep the public notified of" changes to the buildings and businesses, "showing the progress of improvements." Baxter reflects more verbosely: "It is within recollection of the present generation that a store in any block of Chestnut Street . . . was a rare exception, while the broad front, substantially built mansions of some of our most opulent citizens were the prevailing feature of that thoroughfare, but which has given way to the inexorable demands of trade." Baxter's reference to the former residences of prominent citizens resonates with a sense of history reconstructed through the architectural remains of past inhabitants, but he goes on to replace any such notion of history with the inevitability of progress, the "inexorable demands of trade."[91] This sense of ongoing progress within a single category of activity—not a qualitative shift, from residence to business, but developments within business alone—echoes the shallower notion of history in Guild's guidebook, its focus on engineering improvements to the train itself, a flickering of old and new. One of Baxter's editions refers to Rae's earlier project as a prior record that can be compared with his own set of views, and a comparison of the same street sections in their directories does confirm the rapid pace of commercial development in these decades (plates 5 and 6). The buildings in Baxter's prints have slightly more depth, a surface texture of moldings and doorways, and a patriotic color palette of light red and blue; he also includes figures. Yet the controlling narrative concern is shopping, producing a repetitiveness that precludes any hierarchical or directional ordering of scenes. A comparable sameness characterizes the replacement of one business by another; the businesses are surface entities almost reducible to the type announcing their names, and they are located in an undifferentiated historical continuum. Interchangeability across the buildings is matched by a certain interchangeability in spatial and historical depth. What I have tried to arrest in this discussion, though, is the transition from historical narrative to spatial mapping as the conceptual framework that organizes and validates the image of the city. As storefronts replace the venerable houses of the city's principal families, accounting for the appearance of the city in terms of historical narratives becomes increasingly difficult; not only have the signs of hallowed occupation been erased, but the new markers reference no history, only commercial transactions.[92] Although sensitive to the changes transforming Philadelphia, Rae and Baxter offer not an image of the city composed of historically significant features that can be arranged into a coherent narrative, but rather an efficient spatial mapping that facilitates the satisfaction of material desire.

Other midcentury pictorial city guides pursued the same strategy of spatial mapping rather than visualizing a historical trajectory, such as directories produced in conjunction with world's fairs and city expositions. Solyman Brown's *The Citizen and Strangers' Pictorial and Business Directory* (1853) was produced on the occasion of New York's World's Fair of that year and, like the directories of Rae and Baxter, consisted of illustrations of businesses that paid for inclusion in the guide.[93] Brown's guide was not a foldout version of the moving panorama but a book containing business cards arranged according to the amount and timing of advertising fees, with a scanty, discontinuous narrative text appearing every few pages and an index at the end. Brown's work replicates the aspiration of the exposition to situate New York as a modern metropolis. It dwells on engineering marvels like the Erie Canal and the Croton Aqueduct, while also frankly acquiescing to the driving force of commercial culture: "The master passion of New-York city is the love of wealth."[94] Greed is the organizing principle of the city, and as the guide maintains, it extends its tentacles of commerce to encompass the world itself. The streets of New York, in their total length, reach far beyond the confines of Manhattan Island, a range articulated in an image that recalls the foldout city panorama: "It appears . . . that the streets of the city . . . equal in the aggregate 261 miles—and therefore the buildings occupying both sides of the streets, if placed side by side in a single row, would extend from Manhattan Island to Buffalo."[95] The city is also imagined as a commercial leviathan: "Its enterprise spans the earth, traverses the air, and fathoms the sea. New-York is the business-heart of the nation; the vital centre of its commercial organism. Canals, rivers, railroads, ships, electric wires, are the vascular conduits of its circulating system."[96] *The Citizen and Strangers' Pictorial and Business Directory* offers itself as a mapping of this mercantile giant, a containment of the driving force of greed, but its apparatus of reading and viewing, of coordinating text with print illustrations, privileges access to material goods over the perception of history to account for the social world it describes. The format of Brown's guidebook has its origins in a quasi-artistic visualization of the city, the stationary panorama, that employed the elevated viewpoint and comprehensive, carefully measured space of landscape painting, the familiar picturesque compositional devices used by the Hudson River school to present a historical image of the nation. To a modern observer, though, it looks just like a series of advertisements, a kind of nineteenth-century version of the Yellow Pages (itself now almost obsolete in print form). This dramatic shift in the organization of text and illustration reflects but also participates in the ascendancy of a commercial perspective in the way urban environments were understood—but understood by whom exactly? The following chapter looks more closely at how such changes related to evolving audiences for scenic and tourist print publications, particularly in terms of class.

2

The Anatomy of Greed

Newport Tourist Literature and the Luminist Works of William Trost Richards and John Frederick Kensett

IN THE PRECEDING CHAPTER I show how transportation guidebooks, while initially dependent on the picturesque traditions of landscape representation, gradually engaged ways of looking and reading that critically involved the negation of those traditions. More precisely, what I have called a railroad narrative entailed the cancellation of effects of distance and duration that had previously enabled viewers of landscape paintings and prints to experience different constructions of national history as they viewed depicted sites. I also associated this new narrative order with a new perception of the immediacy of progress as well as new forms of commercial desire. The development of pictorial city guides like those produced in Philadelphia by Rae and Baxter, though not transportation guidebooks per se, shared many of the traits of this new narrative order and pointedly revealed a shift toward a fantasy of immediate access directed toward the acquisition of material goods. Baxter's "directory" emphasizes this kind of economic activity in its default narrative moment of shopping, but his figures also look at each other (plate 6). Their appraisal of the commercial goods on display appears to be coordinated with their appraisal of each other in a prefiguring of Thorstein Veblen's notion of conspicuous consumption, articulated in his *Theory of the Leisure Class.*[1] In some instances, as in the store at 727 Chestnut Street, one can discern dummies modeling clothes, ghostlike alter egos of the pedestrians outside. Baxter's guidebook thus not only structures economic activity but aligns it with behaviors of display and assessment that organize the social sphere.

The present chapter pursues these implications further by situating the railroad narrative in relation to emerging class identities, to the meaning and visibility of class and social status, at the dawn of the Gilded Age. While chapter 1 is broadly directed at print culture in the Northeast, here I focus on visual materials, both illustrated books and landscape paintings, devoted primarily to Newport, Rhode Island. Beginning in the 1850s and extending into the 1880s, this site witnessed intense development as a tourist destination and was a major locus for debating and enforcing class differences in the years just before and after the Civil War.[2] In this chapter, I show how middle-class, or lower-middle-class, Newport guidebooks evolved along the same lines as transportation guides in their organization of narrative text and landscape illustration, with a similar effect of evoking an experience of instantaneous access to commercial goods.[3] By contrast, genteel guidebooks enlisted the protocols of picturesque viewing more forcefully in fostering a socially exclusive engagement with landscape. Pushing beyond my earlier dissociation of landscape painting practice from developments in transportation print materials, though, I want to complicate an overly reductive series of oppositions: middle class versus upper class, print versus painting. Not only do I discuss print culture as an important aspect of upper-class self-definition and social exclusion, I also relate the development of landscape painting practice, particularly that of the so-called luminist painters John Frederick Kensett and William Trost Richards, to illustration schemes in both genteel and mainstream scenic guides.[4] Paintings and prints stand in a dynamic relationship to each other in a way that mirrors the dynamic construction of class identity in this rapidly changing coastal tourist destination.

George William Curtis's *Lotus-Eating,* a collection of short essays describing prominent watering places and summer resorts in the Northeast, was one of the more literary guidebooks published early in this period, and it will serve in this chapter as the primary example of guides intended for a wealthier audience.[5] Curtis, a contributing editor to several East Coast newspapers and literary journals, whose books tended to consist of observations of polite society and recountings of tours to foreign (especially European) places, was just becoming a well-known travel writer and arbiter of taste when *Lotus-Eating* was published.[6] Although it covered most of the resorts' principal attractions, *Lotus-Eating* was akin to a gift book, the nineteenth-century equivalent of a coffee table book, with decorative stamping on the cover, gilded letters on the spine, and small wood engravings of sketches made by Kensett. When the book appeared in 1853, the business of scenic tourism had already developed to the point where picturesque conventions of viewing were being adjusted, in works intended for a privileged audience like *Lotus-Eating,* to maintain class distinctions more forcefully. In general, the intention of these adjustments, which critically involve the relation of Curtis's text to Kensett's illustrations, is to stress a point of view that is fugitive or difficult to attain—that is to say, exclusive.[7]

After vignettes describing the Catskill Mountains, Niagara Falls, Saratoga Springs, and Lake George, the final chapters on Newport offer a culminating evocation of the ideal destination for the midcentury tourist of means who was unwilling to travel outside the country. The tone of the whole book is openly exclusive, and a recurrent subject of comment is the perceived incapacity of most Americans to properly enjoy their nation's finest spots of natural beauty, identified as the resorts that Curtis describes. As he notes early in the first chapter, in what becomes a refrain for him, and for many other genteel travel writers as the century progresses, "None more than the Americans make it a principle to desert the city, and none less than Americans know how to dispense with it. So we compromise by taking the city with us, and the country gently laughs us to scorn."[8] By the time Curtis reaches Newport, his disdain for the uneducated city dweller has mounted to the point where he interrupts his description of the town to vent his scorn at such length that he takes up the rest of the chapter, requiring him to resume the description in the following one. Curtis regarded the middle-class aspirations for the trappings of affluence as a gross affront to the art of gracious living: "Society is as much a sphere of art as any of the more recognized spheres. . . . I doubt if in any country in which wealth is not hereditary, so that a permanent and large class is secure from the necessity of some kind of gold digging, whereby man becomes of the earth, earthy, there can ever be the simplest and finest tone of society."[9] Contemptuous of the growing number of urban visitors to Newport, Curtis baldly aligns taste and aesthetic sensitivity with class status and proceeds to associate an elevated social position with the past (in the form of hereditary wealth). For him, there are two Newports: a historical place in which taste prevailed, and a vulgar modern version driven by New York fashion: "This whirl of fashionable equipages, these hats and coats, this confused din of dancing music, scandal, flirtation, serenades, and supreme voice of the sea breaking through the fog and dust; this singing, dancing, and dawdling incessantly; this crushing into a month in the country that which crowds six months in town—these are the foot-prints of Fashion upon the sea-shore."[10] One of Curtis's conceits, in fact, is to compare himself to Rip Van Winkle, waking up in a present that transforms his memories of the historical Newport into nostalgic reminiscences.[11]

Because Newport was a more socially exclusive destination in the first half of the century, the extensive investment, advertising, and construction targeted toward less affluent tourists, beginning in the 1840s and 1850s, made it possible to identify the past with the vestiges of occupation by an earlier and wealthier group of visitors.[12] All the Newport guidebooks stress (though for different reasons) that one distinctive characteristic of the town was its attractiveness to successive generations of social elites, whose pedigree seemingly diminishes with time. Newport was first the largest and most culturally sophisticated of the early colonial ports, then one of the last refuges for loyal Tories during the Revolution, then the summer resort of aristocratic southern plantation owners, and finally, by midcentury, a quieter, more expensive alternative to Saratoga Springs, New York, after that resort became readily accessible by railroad. At this time, then, when illustrated guides to Newport really began to flourish, the reader's identification with the visible signs of the historical (and recreational) past functioned as a key marker of status. Curtis's alignment of social status with an art form extends beyond a sense of doing things well, without excess, to encompass a certain sense of seeing well. He intimates that the visual elements of mass-market tourism, just beginning to appear in Newport, crowd out a properly refined point of view, which becomes increasingly elusive and thereby exclusive. As the title of his guidebook implies, taken from Alfred Lord Tennyson's 1832 poem "The Lotos-Eaters," this displaced point of view takes the form of a withdrawal from the present and a seeking out of sights that are both fugitive and obsolete.[13] Accordingly, the month of September, the "season" that Curtis recommends for visiting Newport, is when the majority of summer visitors have left and outward appearances have returned, as much as possible, to something like a former state—the cultured past with which he and the reader identify.

Allegiance to the past as a sign of social status is not unusual. This affectation was long an aspect of the picturesque in Europe, but in the context of American scenic tourism and landscape painting, it intersects with visibility in complicated ways. Foremost, as Cole's "Essay on American Scenery" makes clear, what distinguishes the American landscape is the absence of signs pointing to the past.[14] Earlier artists and writers had celebrated a pristine wilderness not far removed from the country's first population centers on the East Coast, frequently by adopting Cole's stance that a landscape without ruins was a landscape with "no ruined tower to tell of outrage—no gorgeous temple to speak of ostentation," as well as a landscape of future possibilities ("Where the wolf roams, the plow shall glisten").[15] By midcentury, however, it was increasingly difficult to ground this forward-looking, future-oriented outlook in the landscape's unspoiled state. Artists either traveled farther afield (especially to the West) or ignored and effaced in their imagery the signs of industrial development in locations revered by a previous generation, so that the image of the northeastern wilderness acquired a distinctly historical aspect. The ongoing transformation of Newport as a tourist destination was a localized version of this process, and it allowed Curtis to position as past not just the actual remains of "southern cottages" but the undeveloped landscape, increasingly restricted to isolated coves, islands, and the sea itself. It is as if the landscape without ruins, once the sign of an absence of history, is now a kind of ruin and an expressive sign of history in its own right. Looking forward to the luminist works of Kensett and Richards, within the context of scenic tourism in Newport and other East Coast resorts, the view devoid of fashion, the view that emphasizes emptiness, stillness, and suspension, sustains the class-specific, past-oriented, and fugitive point of view articulated by Curtis.

The chapters on Newport contain numerous scenes that figure withdrawal from the present in visual terms, often as unusual and insubstantial sights. Wandering the fields above Spouting Horn, the southernmost point of the island, Curtis devotes several pages to a vision of "the Venetian life" that these ramblings inspire, more or less a bittersweet recognition of ruined grandeur.[16] Later he describes a twilight horse-riding excursion, when "gaining the end of the beach we reined up, turned suddenly, and were in another zone, in another world . . . and though it faded every moment and the world resumed its old expression, that glance has bewildered me forever."[17] In perhaps the most extreme nondescription in a book that is nominally a sightseeing guide, Curtis describes the experience of getting lost in the fog on Newport Beach: "I seemed to be upon the hard bottom of the sea, for nothing was visible save occasionally the moon, as the fog thinned over head—the seemingly circular spot of beach upon which I stood—and the long, white seething line of surf that fell exhausted along the shore, . . . I advanced constantly with no sense of progress."[18]

These scenes also stress Curtis's isolation from any onlookers, except the local "bass fishers" and old inhabitants of Newport. The lack of fixity in the visions he describes derives from his penchant for spaces that are delimited in the extreme: "the end of the beach," "another zone, another world," "the hard bottom of the sea," just the "circular spot of beach upon which I stood." Although his search for unusual and fleeting sights eventually reaches an endpoint in blindness ("nothing was visible"), it also dramatically removes him from common scrutiny. In other words, Curtis asserts privileged status through a fugitive view—one outside the present—that situates him in something like the Newport of old, the repository of elite culture. This view consists, moreover, not merely in a visual allegiance to the signs of the past, but in a removal from the degraded viewing activities of the present. Nor does Curtis just report a certain form of spectatorship: he appeals to his readers to project themselves along this socially charged trajectory as well. His readers become the critical, if not the only, members of the exclusive audience he creates by these means.

The Fugitive View of the Past in Kensett's Illustrations for *Lotus-Eating*

John Frederick Kensett was beginning his career as a painter specializing in landscapes when he supplied the drawings on which the illustrations in Curtis's book were based. The two men had been friends for some time and shared a number of acquaintances in the artistic and literary networks of

Boston and New York. Kensett was also a member of New York's Century Association and National Academy of Design, both organizations containing a number of established landscape painters, including Asher B. Durand.[19] Kensett had initially been trained as an engraver, and his friendship with Curtis, whom he met on his first trip to Rome, had facilitated making the social connections that allowed him to pursue painting as a profession.[20] It is possible, then, to interpret Kensett's illustration work for *Lotus-Eating* conservatively, as shoring up a shared set of beliefs about the efficacy of natural scenery, especially since his paintings at this time closely follow the typical subject matter and techniques of the Hudson River school. One of his more popular works from this time was *The White Mountains—From North Conway* (plate 7), painted two years before *Lotus-Eating* was published, which compares closely with Cole's 1843 *River in the Catskills* (plate 3). In both works, there is a slightly elevated viewing position, a winding path into depth (moving from gnarled tree forms to pastureland to the outskirts of a small town), and distant mountains that form a hazy backdrop. Another Kensett painting from the following year, *Camel's Hump from the Western Shore of Lake Champlain,* replicates much of the composition, framing devices, and figures of an illustration of the Hudson River in *Lotus-Eating* (plates 8 and 9). Kensett's membership in the Century Association and the National Academy of Design exposed him to the ideas about nature and the techniques used to convey them that were developed by Cole and adapted by successors such as Durand.[21]

Although Kensett's illustration work in *Lotus-Eating* is conservative in following the dictates of established Hudson River school practice, what I want to show here is that the placement of these images within the text and their appearance in relation to the text more closely conform to Curtis's socially exclusive evocation of the fugitive view. Inasmuch as typical Hudson River school paintings speak to a broader audience (recalling the inclusive tone of Bryant's preface to *American Landscape*), they do so in part by presenting a historical continuum linking past, present, and future through carefully measured spatial transitions. Kensett's illustrations—as they appear in the text in various ways—instead amplify Curtis's privileging of a remote and difficult-to-attain vantage point on the past. Thus, in an earlier chapter, after comparing the Hudson and Rhine Rivers and establishing a basis for landscape beauty in the discovery of historical associations, Curtis then describes an experience of gazing down the Hudson "from [a] garden, at twilight, toward the huge hills . . . that guard the entrance to the Highlands" and alighting on "the white sails of sloops" that "fly, taking my fascinated eyes captive, far and far away, until they glimmer like ghosts and strand my sight upon the distance."[22] This description is placed immediately adjacent to an engraving of the Hudson (plate 9) that captures many of its key elements (gazing figures, the garden, the guardian hills, the tiny sails of distant sailboats). More importantly, the engraving's stationary figures, generalized landscape features, and perspectival pull from dark, crisp forms to faint outlines reenact the text's evocation of a drawn-out movement into distance, one that discourages the continual shifting from foreground to background so common in *American Landscape*. As with the narrator's gaze in the text, the typical picturesque framing devices have the effect here of holding the viewer's "eyes captive," drawn toward the horizon. Finally, this "reverie" is identified as "the seed of such beautiful and characteristic harvests as the Hudson tales of the Sketch Book and Knickerbocker's History"—the fictional past of the Hudson created by Washington Irving—so that the end product of Curtis's vision is linked to the recognition of a kind of history.[23] This coordination of narrative text with landscape engraving to reinforce a point of view that recognizes (or rather emphasizes) the past in a drawn-out contemplation of distance is repeated in the chapters on Newport. The "reverie" of "the Venetian life" induced by Curtis's exploration of the fields around Spouting Horn is immediately followed by an illustration (figure 17) that also shows stationary gazing figures, similar landscape features, and a shift from darker forms to faint outlines. Here, Curtis associates his speculations on the past grandeur of Venice with an elusive vision of aesthetic perfection, "a beautiful mirage" (these words appear right below the print), and then states, "To reach those pleasant places is the aim of all our endeavors."[24] This sense of incorporeality is likewise evoked in the immediate textual framing of the earlier view up the Hudson River, which is positioned to the right of a description of a weightless narrator "float[ing] on the last ray through that mysterious gate [of hills]."[25]

The prints also capture the elusiveness of views, nearly unattainable and hence exclusive, in other ways besides these direct linkages to Curtis's text. Such aspects include their anonymous presentation and lack of a frame, which make the prints seem to crystallize or coalesce from the blank page. In general, the placing of prints as evanescent interruptions in the flow of text, without highlighting any notable location or landscape feature, intensifies in visual form the general sense of an oblique or marginalized point of view, glimpsed now by the reader. Kensett's image of the southernmost cliffs (figure 18) exemplifies several of the presentational strategies involved, beginning with Curtis's framing text: "The southern point of the Island is a rocky bluff, planted now in corn, but from the highest point commanding an unobstructed horizon, including the town removed into picturesque distance."[26] The association of this view with the past occurs later, when it is identified as "the true site of a Newport residence. . . . No one could go beyond you, no one could interfere"; it is "the haunt . . . of the bass fishers," but "in the present rapid settlement of the island, it will not be long before it is occupied."[27] Like the illustrations of the Hudson River or Spouting

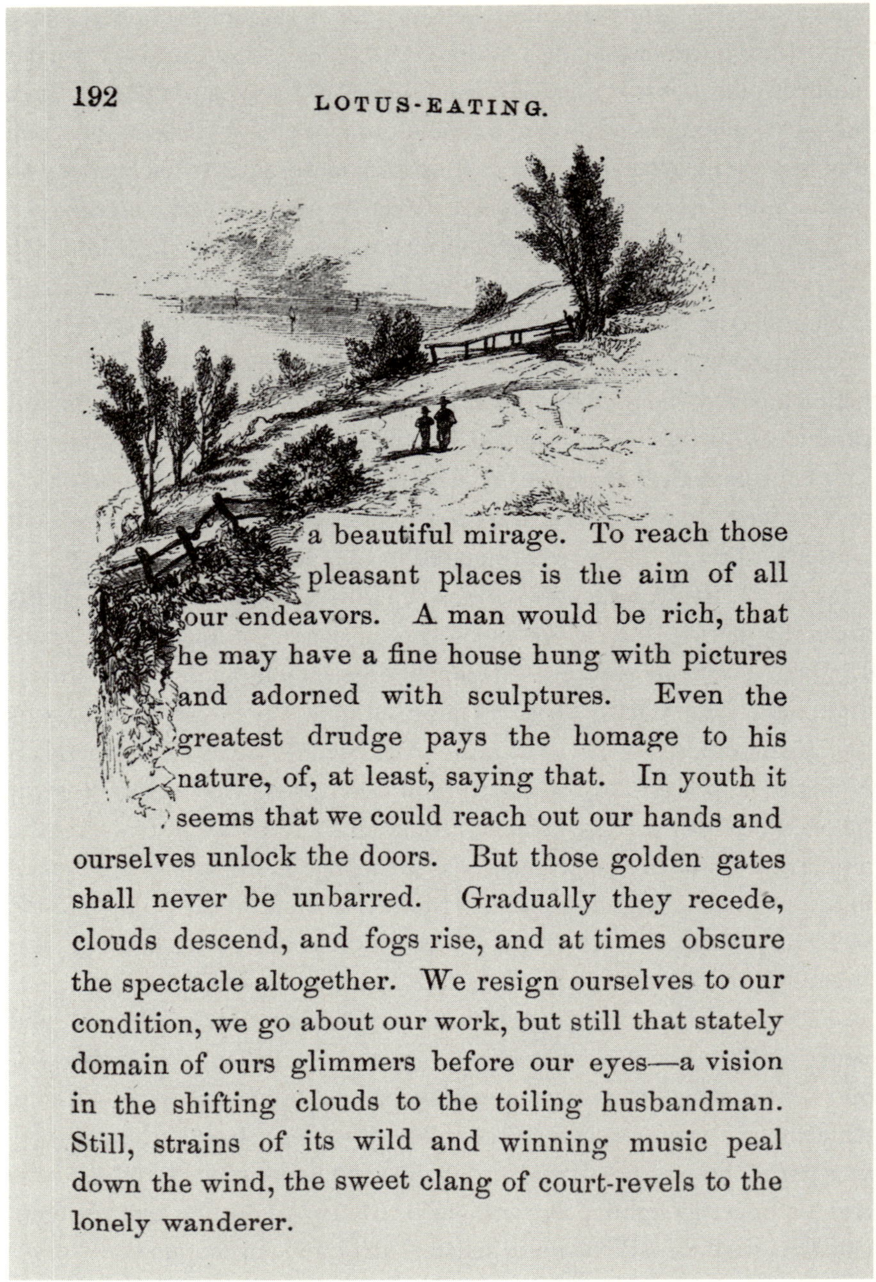

192 LOTUS-EATING.

a beautiful mirage. To reach those pleasant places is the aim of all our endeavors. A man would be rich, that he may have a fine house hung with pictures and adorned with sculptures. Even the greatest drudge pays the homage to his nature, of, at least, saying that. In youth it seems that we could reach out our hands and ourselves unlock the doors. But those golden gates shall never be unbarred. Gradually they recede, clouds descend, and fogs rise, and at times obscure the spectacle altogether. We resign ourselves to our condition, we go about our work, but still that stately domain of ours glimmers before our eyes—a vision in the shifting clouds to the toiling husbandman. Still, strains of its wild and winning music peal down the wind, the sweet clang of court-revels to the lonely wanderer.

FIGURE 17. John F. Kensett, view near the Spouting Horn, Newport. Illustration from George W. Curtis, *Lotus-Eating: A Summer Book* (New York: Harper and Brothers, 1852). Courtesy the University of Chicago Library.

Horn, the print is unframed and seems to float on the page; it additionally takes the shape of an illustrated letter, a "p" for "picturesque distance."[28] The total absence of objects in the image encourages this understanding of it, so that the elusiveness of the view is finally supported by a confusion over its basic signifying status, as picture or text.

It is worth comparing the illustration strategies developed in *Lotus-Eating* with earlier examples of illustrated books that focused on natural scenery. Bryant's *American Landscape* was structured as a series of textual

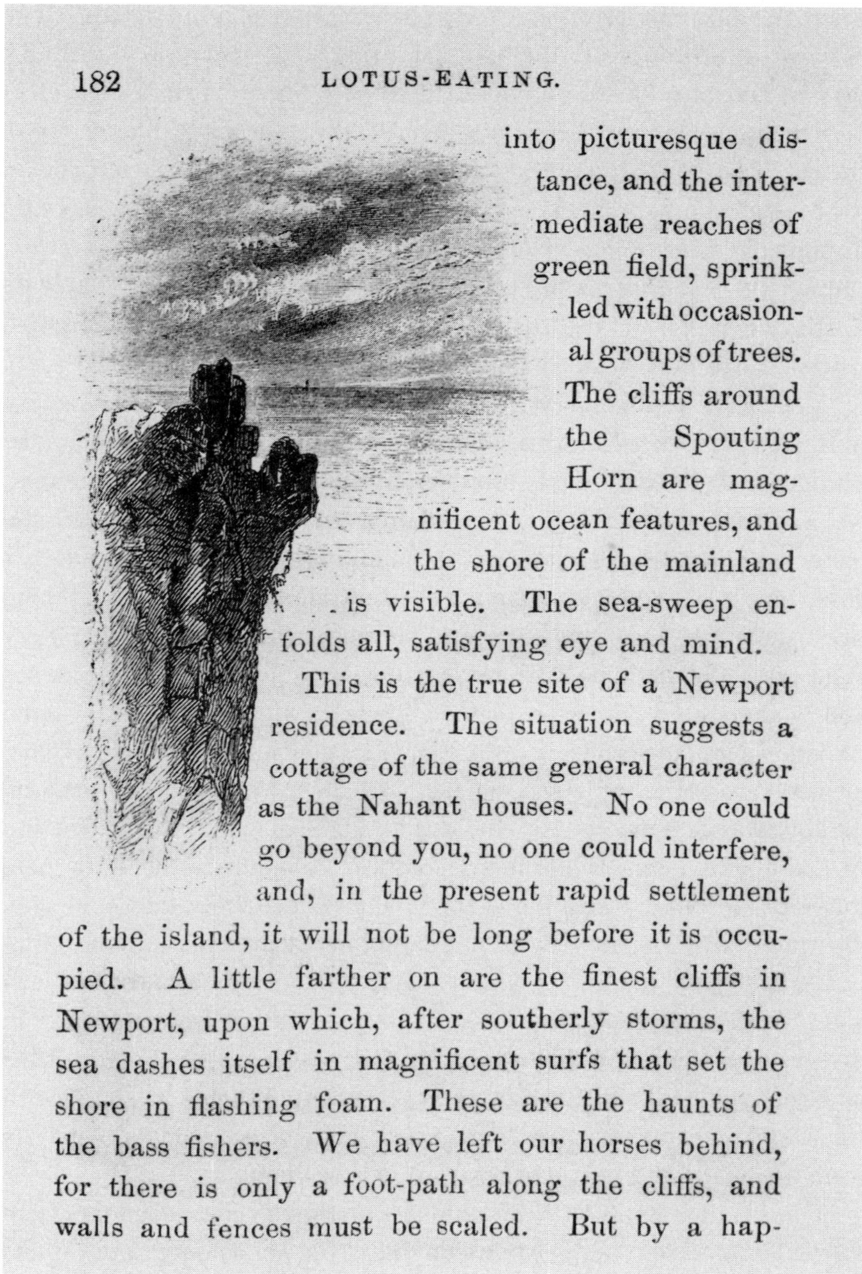

182 LOTUS-EATING.

into picturesque distance, and the intermediate reaches of green field, sprinkled with occasional groups of trees. The cliffs around the Spouting Horn are magnificent ocean features, and the shore of the mainland is visible. The sea-sweep enfolds all, satisfying eye and mind.

This is the true site of a Newport residence. The situation suggests a cottage of the same general character as the Nahant houses. No one could go beyond you, no one could interfere, and, in the present rapid settlement of the island, it will not be long before it is occupied. A little farther on are the finest cliffs in Newport, upon which, after southerly storms, the sea dashes itself in magnificent surfs that set the shore in flashing foam. These are the haunts of the bass fishers. We have left our horses behind, for there is only a foot-path along the cliffs, and walls and fences must be scaled. But by a hap-

FIGURE 18. John F. Kensett, view from the southernmost cliffs, Newport. Illustration from George W. Curtis, *Lotus-Eating: A Summer Book* (New York: Harper and Brothers, 1852). Courtesy the University of Chicago Library.

expositions paired with single-sheet prints. Text and image reflected on each other, cultivating a suspension of readers' attention, an inability to fully immerse themselves into either text or image. This suspended attention in turn increased readers' sensitivity to duration, the passage of time, and hence to the presence of history in the landscape. The basic difference in intention between *American Landscape* and *Lotus-Eating* is reflected in the secure framing, generous size, and isolation of the prints illustrating *American Landscape,* such as *Winnipiseogee Lake* (figure 7), where the reader or viewer is actively encouraged to play out the trajectory of viewing introduced in the text, like using large-size type in a child's primer. Kensett's illustration of the fields near Spouting Horn (figure 17) uses the same picturesque compositional devices (the substitute spectator, the coulisses on the left and right, the winding path into distance, and so forth), while here too the text primes the reader to "look" for history by engaging in a discussion of Venice's past as "a beautiful mirage." Clearly, though, this image of history is not presented as conspicuous, or at least Curtis's narration and the framing of the print have the effect of marginalizing it (the print is, in fact, pushed to the margins of the page by the text).

Most of all, the marginalization of the stable picturesque view of history in the landscape is achieved by the way the familiar effects of distance and duration are noticeably attenuated by their placement in the text. As noted, the kinds of sights described in the text tend to be extreme instances of spatial and temporal marginalization ("we . . . were in another zone, another world," "that glance has bewildered me forever," "taking my fascinated eyes captive, far and far away, until they . . . strand my sight upon the distance"). The size and framing of the prints, however, subtly alter the picturesque pictorial devices within them in the same direction. First, the prints' small size makes it difficult to discern individual elements, so as the eye moves into distance, these elements lose definition and substance more rapidly. Next, their small size and their insertion in small block-outs within the text, without a definite frame, puts them in the background in relation to the text, an effect abetted by such faux illustrated letters as the view of the southernmost cliffs. It is as if the entire image itself were the background of some other image, as if the viewer's sight were "strand[ed] upon the distance"—an effect I return to later in discussing luminist painting. Finally, registering elements within the prints as already distant subtly alters the perception of time associated with them; as distant objects, they "move" slowly, augmenting their remoteness from the hustle and bustle of Newport in the summer.

This is not to imply that the stable picturesque view disappears from scenic guidebooks. A suggestive example of the persistence of the stable picturesque view in genteel scenic literature is Thomas Starr King's *The White Hills* (1860).[29] By the late 1850s, the White Mountains of New Hampshire were, like Newport, a popular destination on the American Grand Tour, a place for the well-to-do to spend the summer admiring pristine natural beauty instead of visiting familiar fashion haunts like Saratoga Springs.[30] Not as bluntly elitist in tone as Curtis, King undertook to actively promote this wholesome form of recreation (giving up-to-date information on travel routes, lodgings, and so forth), but he was also concerned to instruct his readers in the proper aesthetic viewing of landscape. This dual perspective—invitational/didactic—is reflected in the presentation

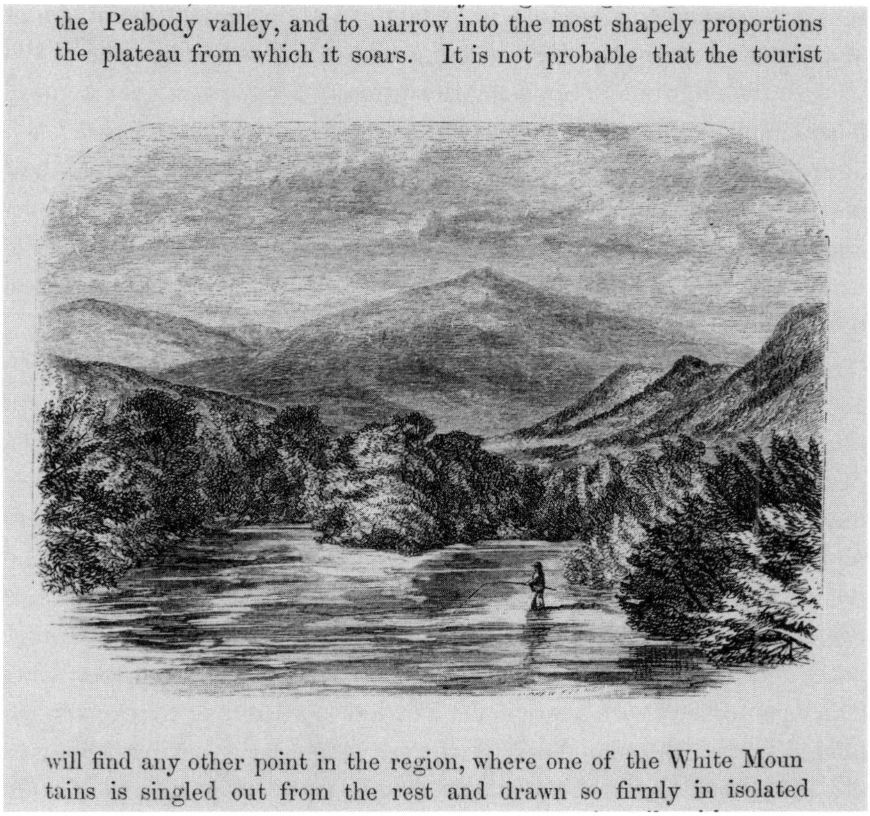
the Peabody valley, and to narrow into the most shapely proportions
the plateau from which it soars. It is not probable that the tourist

will find any other point in the region, where one of the White Moun
tains is singled out from the rest and drawn so firmly in isolated

FIGURE 19. Unknown artist, view of Mount Madison. Illustration from Thomas Starr King, *The White Hills: Their Legends, Landscape, and Poetry* (Boston, MA: Crosby, Nichols, 1860). Courtesy the University of Chicago Library.

of landscape prints in *The White Hills,* in terms of their size, placement, and relation to textual narration, and helps to clarify the class-stratifying emphasis on the fugitive view of the past in Curtis's work.

King's more educational approach becomes explicit in his two basic organizing principles for viewing landscape in a properly aesthetic manner. First, he insists on presenting the scenery of New Hampshire through "poetic passages which illustrate . . . the permanent character of the views."[31] Simultaneously, though, he emphasizes the need to study and become familiar with a map of the region. The poetic extract and the map represent two different approaches for fixing landscape views in memory, and it is fairly easy to align the first approach with the picturesque conventions of earlier albums of landscape views like *American Landscape.* King typically gives a textual description of a specific landscape view, using poetry or a florid prose style to highlight the historical or literary significance of its features, and then follows this description with a print illustration on the facing page. In a print of Mount Madison (figure 19), he is careful to draw attention to how the hills supposedly frame the view, yet it becomes clear that, within his book, the text, the poetic description, primarily frames or structures the image.[32] Although the general arrangement of textual explication followed by a single landscape image recalls *American Landscape,* several features of the illustration of Mount Madison correspond with Kensett's prints for *Lotus-Eating,* such as his view of the environs of Spouting Horn (figure 17). Both scenes contain fairly simplified picturesque elements (compare with *Winnipiseogee Lake,* figure 7). In addition, although the print of Mount Madison is larger and more independent of the text, it notably does not appear on its own page, and it lacks a clear frame. The divided attention of King's book to a certain extent results in illustrations that occupy a representational middle ground between those found in the works of Bryant and Curtis.

King clearly wants his second organizing principle, the map, to function as more than just a traveler's aid. He wants it to serve essentially as an interpretive and mnemonic device in the same way that poetic passages could both give definition to one's view of landscape and activate one's memory of that view. In other words, King conjures an imaginary map to offset a purely practical orientation toward the use of his guidebook. As he puts it, it is important for visitors to have a good "map in their mind's eye of what they have seen" so that "the country which gives them pleasure, may not be distorted and dislocated in their memory."[33] Overall, then, King concerns himself with sequencing as used to structure viewing and to influence how one remembers (or masters) visual experience, in a manner not unlike the ordered sequencing of landscape features in a picturesque view. Certainly the kind of map that King had in mind is not the linear continuous sequence of mile markings and stations that occupies the verso pages of a transportation guidebook like Guild's. Never explicitly defined, King's map comes to function more as a rhetorical device or talisman that wards off the tendency of modern transportation to impose its own networks, its own hours, and its own punctuation of stations and crossings. Moreover, the simplification of landscape features in prints like the view of Mount Madison (and in Kensett's illustrations for Curtis) suggests a deemphasis on specific location in favor of purely picturesque elements that comport well with this specialized, nonpractical sense of the map.

In sum, King advocates an open-ended search for aesthetically satisfying views over and against a kind of touristic activity based on distinct destinations, the kind of protracted visit recommended by Curtis and available only to the tourist of means. In King's words: "By living several weeks in any valley, and driving frequently over the principal roads, a person is able to learn . . . just where the best pictures are to be seen."[34] The class connotations of King's aesthetic advice emerge most famously in his implicit comparison of a finely tuned sight with fine dining: "A large proportion of the summer travellers in New Hampshire bolt the scenery, as a man, driven by work, bolts his dinner at a restaurant. Sometimes, indeed, where railroads will allow, as on the eastern side, they will *gobble* some of the superb views between two trains, with as little consciousness of any flavor or artistic relish, as a turkey has in swallowing corn."[35] Not only is the person in question explicitly identified as working class, but that viewer is also brutified, made into a mere animal. In addition, King specifically figures railroad-mediated tourism as involving a cruder kind of visual satisfaction, based on discrete units and immediate access ("bolt[ing] the scenery," rapidly ingesting those particularly celebrated views that compose "the scenery"). These are the characteristics of narrative viewing adopted in the lower-middle-class scenic guides that I turn to shortly.

It is King's notion of "focus-points" that most clearly connects a socially exclusive form of tourist activity with an especially elusive landscape view reminiscent of Curtis's fugitive view of the past (and Kensett's representation of it in his prints). King introduces his notion of "focus-points" as follows: "A spy-glass is good for nothing, as a help to the sight, unless you get the exact focus. It is quite remarkable how this law of focus-points holds in studying the mountain region. Sometimes the beauty of scenes depends on the hour when you visit them, sometimes on the nicely calculated distance."[36] Like Curtis, King here stresses the fugitive nature of properly aesthetic views, contingent especially on time. King also seems to favor an extension of distance, as his example of the spy-glass and its "nicely calculated distance" call to mind the subtle modification of picturesque conventions in Kensett's prints brought about by their size, framing, and placement. For King no less than for Curtis, establishing a particular view as a picture seemed to depend on a more radical separation of the viewer from the space of the view as well as a focus on the distant background. The historical trajectory attached to landscape features in picturesque compositions frequently located the past in the background, but this location was accompanied by a juxtaposition or comparison with a foreground present. King's "focus-points" modify the traditional Hudson River school adaptation of the picturesque landscape by removing the foreground *repoussoir,* or entry point, for the viewer and focusing instead on the distance, which in Curtis's work became instrumental in demonstrating a privileged point of view.

Narrating Consumer Desire in Popular Guidebooks

Close coordination of narrative text and landscape prints with actual travel typifies the illustration schemes found in Newport guides intended for an emerging group of middle-class tourists. The format compares closely with the characteristics of the railroad narrative (which, after all, was itself a form of scenic guidebook).[37] Whereas Curtis and to some extent King deplore the growth of the tourist industry, these guides actively promote it, adopting a tone of encouragement for the prospective visitor and specifying routes of access correlated with a scale of expense to suit varying levels of financial means. The preface to James H. Bowditch's *"City by the Sea"* (1870) announces: "The aim of this little guide is to supply the requisite information needed by the visitor or traveler . . . *everyday traveling* information, that will enable any stranger, upon arriving at Newport, to move about expeditiously and intelligently from point to point, spending his dimes as freely, or as economically, as fancy or necessity may dictate."[38] An earlier guide, George C. Mason's *Newport Illustrated* (1854), is less specific about its audience and is designed merely "to aid those who would dispense with the services of a guide"; slightly more genteel, it offers "a few historical reminiscences" but is equally invested in describing "the gay scenes witnessed here at the present day, when the season is at its height."[39]

In these more practical guidebooks produced for the mass-market tourist, the primary narrative concern is to communicate a route (this insistent function could be compared with Guild's omnipresent route line as a principle of narrative organization); consequently, whatever illustrations appear within the text mark subdestinations within a larger trajectory of travel. Information relevant to specific sites, including historical events, is given in abbreviated form so as not to halt the flow of the text. These characteristics have the effect of diminishing the capacity of individual illustrations to hold the reader in extended acts of contemplation.[40] The earlier Mason guide seems to include both strategies of coordinating narrative text and landscape prints. In the first chapter, narrator and reader—the present-tense "we" used most often in these books, as opposed to the past tense "I," which Curtis favors—leave Newport and ascend a hill overlooking the harbor. Next follows an extended description of the various islands and landmarks in the bay and a recounting of events in the Revolutionary War that took place in their vicinity. This familiar picturesque exposition is interrupted briefly by an engraving of the harbor, the title of which, *Newport Harbor*, is part of a sentence within the text (figure 20). Although Mason has repeated the familiar ensemble of topographical and historical description followed by a distant view, the treatment of the illustration as a kind of lexical unit propels the forward movement of the reader, instead of encouraging a pause for a more extended perusal of the illustration. What is more, the perspectival pull into depth is not as pronounced in this image as in other, previous guidebooks—the diminution of elements is awkward, and there is a greater incentive to read across the image.[41]

The remaining chapters in Mason's *Newport Illustrated* comprise separate walking tours around Newport and the countryside immediately surrounding it. In contrast to the first chapter's overview of Newport history and a greater amount of exposition between images, in the later chapters,

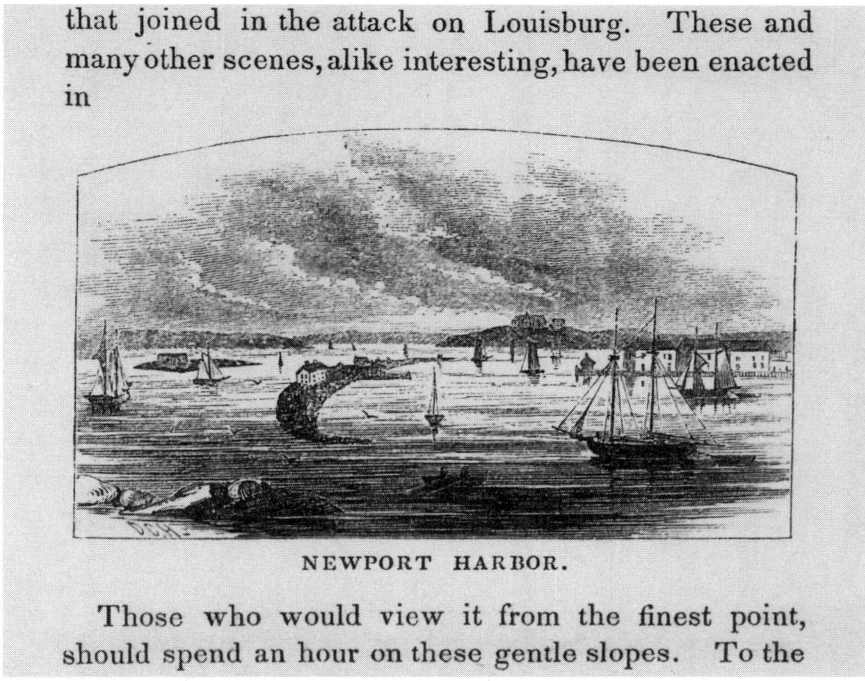
that joined in the attack on Louisburg. These and many other scenes, alike interesting, have been enacted in

NEWPORT HARBOR.

Those who would view it from the finest point, should spend an hour on these gentle slopes. To the

FIGURE 20. Unknown artist, *Newport Harbor.* Illustration from George C. Mason, *Newport Illustrated in a Series of Pen and Pencil Sketches* (Providence, RI: Appleton, 1854). Courtesy Library of Congress.

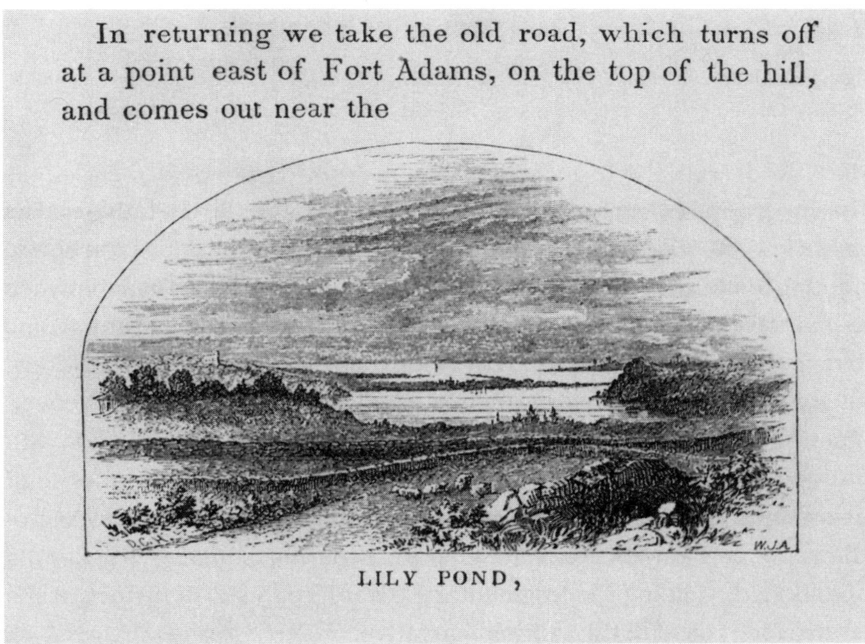
In returning we take the old road, which turns off at a point east of Fort Adams, on the top of the hill, and comes out near the

LILY POND,

FIGURE 21. Unknown artist, *Lily Pond.* Illustration from George C. Mason, *Newport Illustrated in a Series of Pen and Pencil Sketches* (Providence, RI: Appleton, 1854). Courtesy Library of Congress.

text and illustration follow each other in more rapid succession, as the tour narrative proceeds in a more continuous, uninterrupted fashion. Although Newport Harbor received considerable attention in the rehearsal of its component parts and the great historical moments for which they provided a setting, such exposition is subsequently kept to a minimum. The engraving of *Lily Pond* (figure 21) is introduced in the same manner as

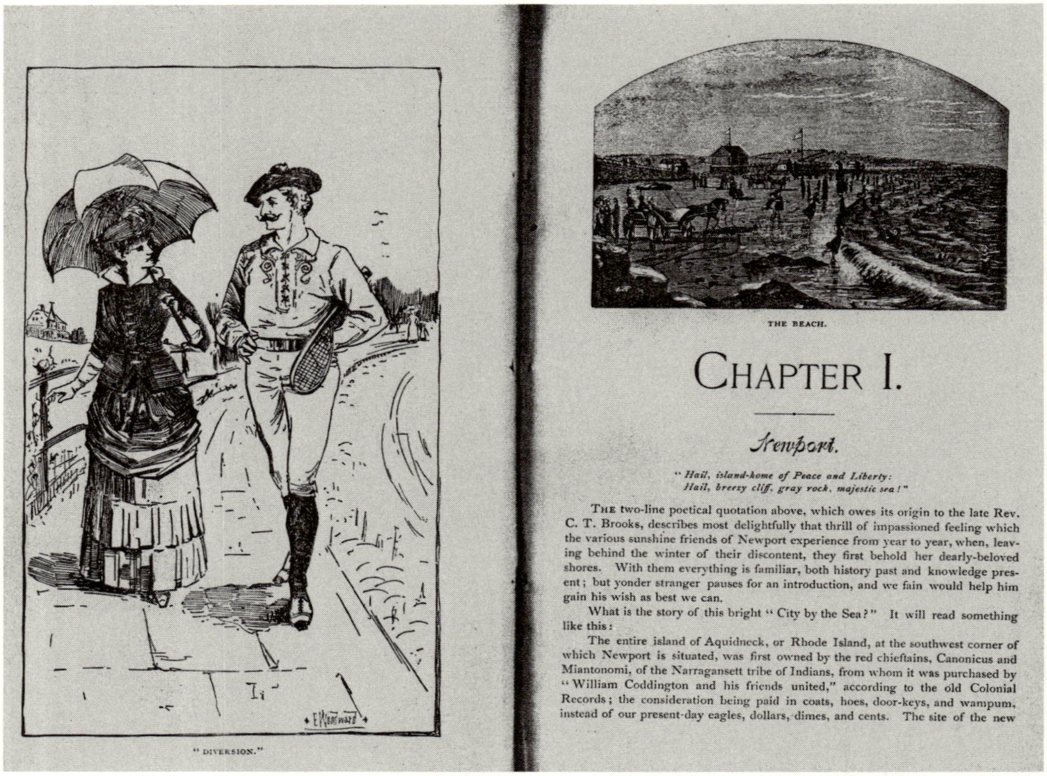

" DIVERSION."

THE BEACH.

CHAPTER I.

Newport.

" Hail, island-home of Peace and Liberty:
Hail, breezy cliff, gray rock, majestic sea!"

THE two-line poetical quotation above, which owes its origin to the late Rev. C. T. Brooks, describes most delightfully that thrill of impassioned feeling which the various sunshine friends of Newport experience from year to year, when, leaving behind the winter of their discontent, they first behold her dearly-beloved shores. With them everything is familiar, both history past and knowledge present; but yonder stranger pauses for an introduction, and we fain would help him gain his wish as best we can.

What is the story of this bright " City by the Sea?" It will read something like this:

The entire island of Aquidneck, or Rhode Island, at the southwest corner of which Newport is situated, was first owned by the red chieftains, Canonicus and Miantonomi, of the Narragansett tribe of Indians, from whom it was purchased by " William Coddington and his friends united," according to the old Colonial Records; the consideration being paid in coats, hoes, door-keys, and wampum, instead of our present-day eagles, dollars, dimes, and cents. The site of the new

FIGURE 22. Unknown artist, *Diversion* and *The Beach*. Illustrations from James H. Bowditch, *"City by the Sea": Newport* (Providence, RI: Reid, 1870). Courtesy Library of Congress.

the illustration of the harbor, as part of the text, but the narrative makes only a few remarks about the pond's popularity as a fishing location before quoting some generic lines of poetry. Overall, the connections between actual travel, textual narration, and landscape imagery mirror the ongoing arrangement found in railroad guidebooks, maximizing access to individual sites and minimizing any prolonged engagement with them. Moreover, Mason's effort to associate the notable features in *Newport Harbor* with a unidirectional narrative of history (the forward-moving sequence of events in the Revolutionary War) is not carried through; in the rest of the guide, this kind of coherent temporal ordering of images is generally abandoned, yielding the fragmentary, disordered view of history in the landscape typical of the railroad narrative.

Bowditch's *"City by the Sea,"* first published almost two decades after *Newport Illustrated,* contains a greater number of images and makes even less of an effort to coordinate them with the flow of a historical narrative. Like *Newport Illustrated, "City by the Sea"* comprises chapters describing distinct walking tours, but here the introductory chapter focuses less on Newport's history than on an outline of various ways to reach the town from New York or Boston, again emphasizing physical access over historical sight. These different routes are novelly presented via a dialogue between the amiable and nondescript everymen Ned and Jack, who prefer to dispense with learned historical disquisitions in favor of practical, self-evident observations.[42] Accordingly, their dialogue, like the narration, identifies sites without exploring their history yet makes room for expressions of needs and desires (relief from the heat, where to mail an urgent letter), as well as immediately locating the means for their satisfaction. Bowditch generates a kind of camaraderie among the narrator, the fictional characters, and the reader, which extends to the satisfaction of material wants.

In King's guidebook, historical and poetical discourse compete with route descriptions; in Bowditch, there is only one kind of trajectory: the physical progression of the tourist. Illustrations depicting locations mentioned in the latter text occur in rough sequential order, but they are not precisely correlated with the pages where they are cited. More importantly, perhaps, the illustrations no longer depict views into depth but feature scenes of fashionable types and crowded beaches (figure 22) or, especially, the houses of the illustrious citizens of Newport (figure 23).

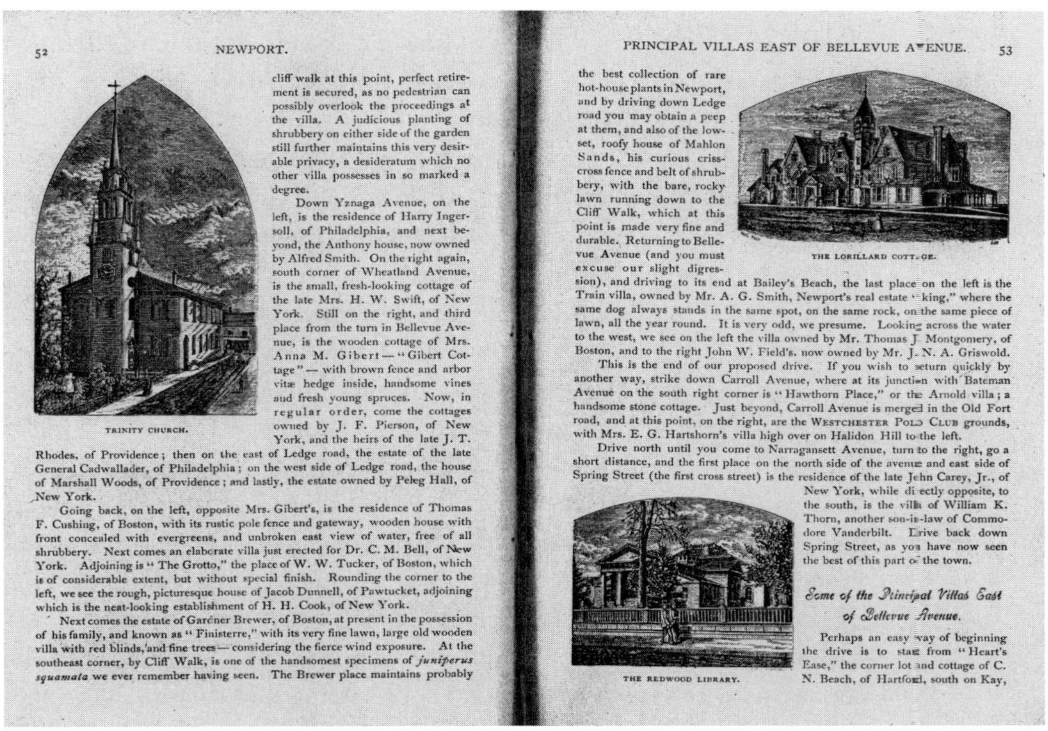

52 NEWPORT.

cliff walk at this point, perfect retirement is secured, as no pedestrian can possibly overlook the proceedings at the villa. A judicious planting of shrubbery on either side of the garden still further maintains this very desirable privacy, a desideratum which no other villa possesses in so marked a degree.

Down Yznaga Avenue, on the left, is the residence of Harry Ingersoll, of Philadelphia, and next beyond, the Anthony house, now owned by Alfred Smith. On the right again, south corner of Wheatland Avenue, is the small, fresh-looking cottage of the late Mrs. H. W. Swift, of New York. Still on the right, and third place from the turn in Bellevue Avenue, is the wooden cottage of Mrs. Anna M. Gibert—"Gibert Cottage"—with brown fence and arbor vitæ hedge inside, handsome vines and fresh young spruces. Now, in regular order, come the cottages owned by J. F. Pierson, of New York, and the heirs of the late J. T. Rhodes, of Providence; then on the east of Ledge road, the estate of the late General Cadwallader, of Philadelphia; on the west side of Ledge road, the house of Marshall Woods, of Providence; and lastly, the estate owned by Peleg Hall, of New York.

TRINITY CHURCH.

Going back, on the left, opposite Mrs. Gibert's, is the residence of Thomas F. Cushing, of Boston, with its rustic pole fence and gateway, wooden house with front concealed with evergreens, and unbroken east view of water, free of all shrubbery. Next comes an elaborate villa just erected for Dr. C. M. Bell, of New York. Adjoining is "The Grotto," the place of W. W. Tucker, of Boston, which is of considerable extent, but without special finish. Rounding the corner to the left, we see the rough, picturesque house of Jacob Dunnell, of Pawtucket, adjoining which is the neat-looking establishment of H. H. Cook, of New York.

Next comes the estate of Gardner Brewer, of Boston, at present in the possession of his family, and known as "Finisterre," with its very fine lawn, large old wooden villa with red blinds, and fine trees—considering the fierce wind exposure. At the southeast corner, by Cliff Walk, is one of the handsomest specimens of *juniperus squamata* we ever remember having seen. The Brewer place maintains probably

PRINCIPAL VILLAS EAST OF BELLEVUE AVENUE. 53

the best collection of rare hot-house plants in Newport, and by driving down Ledge road you may obtain a peep at them, and also of the low-set, roofy house of Mahlon Sands, his curious criss-cross fence and belt of shrubbery, with the bare, rocky lawn running down to the Cliff Walk, which at this point is made very fine and durable. Returning to Bellevue Avenue (and you must excuse our slight digression), and driving to its end at Bailey's Beach, the last place on the left is the Train villa, owned by Mr. A. G. Smith, Newport's real estate "king," where the same dog always stands in the same spot, on the same rock, on the same piece of lawn, all the year round. It is very odd, we presume. Looking across the water to the west, we see on the left the villa owned by Mr. Thomas J. Montgomery, of Boston, and to the right John W. Field's, now owned by Mr. J. N. A. Griswold.

THE LORILLARD COTTAGE.

This is the end of our proposed drive. If you wish to return quickly by another way, strike down Carroll Avenue, where at its junction with Bateman Avenue on the south right corner is "Hawthorn Place," or the Arnold villa; a handsome stone cottage. Just beyond, Carroll Avenue is merged in the Old Fort road, and at this point, on the right, are the WESTCHESTER POLO CLUB grounds, with Mrs. E. G. Hartshorn's villa high over on Halidon Hill to the left.

Drive north until you come to Narragansett Avenue, turn to the right, go a short distance, and the first place on the north side of the avenue and east side of Spring Street (the first cross street) is the residence of the late John Carey, Jr., of New York, while directly opposite, to the south, is the villa of William K. Thorn, another son-in-law of Commodore Vanderbilt. Drive back down Spring Street, as you have now seen the best of this part of the town.

THE REDWOOD LIBRARY.

Some of the Principal Villas East of Bellevue Avenue.

Perhaps an easy way of beginning the drive is to start from "Heart's Ease," the corner lot and cottage of C. N. Beach, of Hartford, south on Kay,

FIGURE 23. Unknown artist, *Trinity Church*, *The Lorillard Cottage*, and *The Redwood Library*. Illustrations from James H. Bowditch, *"City by the Sea": Newport* (Providence, RI: Reid, 1870). Courtesy Library of Congress.

It is as if the readers of Curtis's *Lotus-Eating* have done an about-face to look back at their summer residences, or rather, that these readers (who could be associated with the mansions of Newport) are now fixed and framed as an object of examination and comparison themselves. Bowditch's guide does contain a great amount of historical information, but it is not organized along the path of a picturesque view into distance. In place of this path is a rapid succession of sites associated with moments of the past (histories of the various families who own or owned the depicted houses). Thus, although the progress of narrator and reader is unimpeded by the picturesque view, that view also no longer provides visual support for apprehending a continuous historical trajectory. As a consequence, the experience of history becomes more disjointed, even random in the manner of the constantly shifting perspective of Guild's railroad guidebook. The montage-like character of the illustrations, which appear on almost every page, make the guide into a kind of flipbook charting the surface changes, the minor alterations of cupolas, bay windows, and porticoed verandas, of Newport genteel architecture.

The sequence of illustrations in *"City by the Sea"* might equally well be compared with a commercial or real estate catalog. The series of prints depicting the mansions of Newport's wealthy inhabitants quite closely resembles the pages of advertisements placed at the front of the guide (figure 24). Like the city guides of Rae and Baxter, Bowditch's narration steers the reader from house to house, with clear street directions, while the prints of these houses minimize any sense of a spatial environment, with their shallow proscenium in the foreground and their closing off of views beyond or behind the houses. So, too, the advertisements to *"City by the Sea"* form a succession of street addresses paired with shallow logos or typographical ornamentation. Notices of hotels, such as the Perry House, repeat the depiction of genteel architecture found in the body of the guidebook. Spatial access becomes a thinly veiled metaphor for consumption, as Bowditch's guide offers an efficient mapping of Newport that facilitates a fantasy of instant access to social and material goods.[43] In the process, the viewer is identified with, and brought closer to, those goods.

Before turning to the relation between illustration practices in Newport guidebooks and the landscape paintings of Kensett and Richards, I want to consider how the modifications of picturesque viewing practices within these guidebooks involves the elimination of a key element within earlier picturesque landscape painting, which in turn has class implications connected with viewing behavior. I am referring to the figure of the substitute spectator, which provided a model for viewing in so many Hudson River school paintings, but which is missing from both Curtis's fugitive view and Bowditch's "real estate" view. In a work like Cole's *River in the*

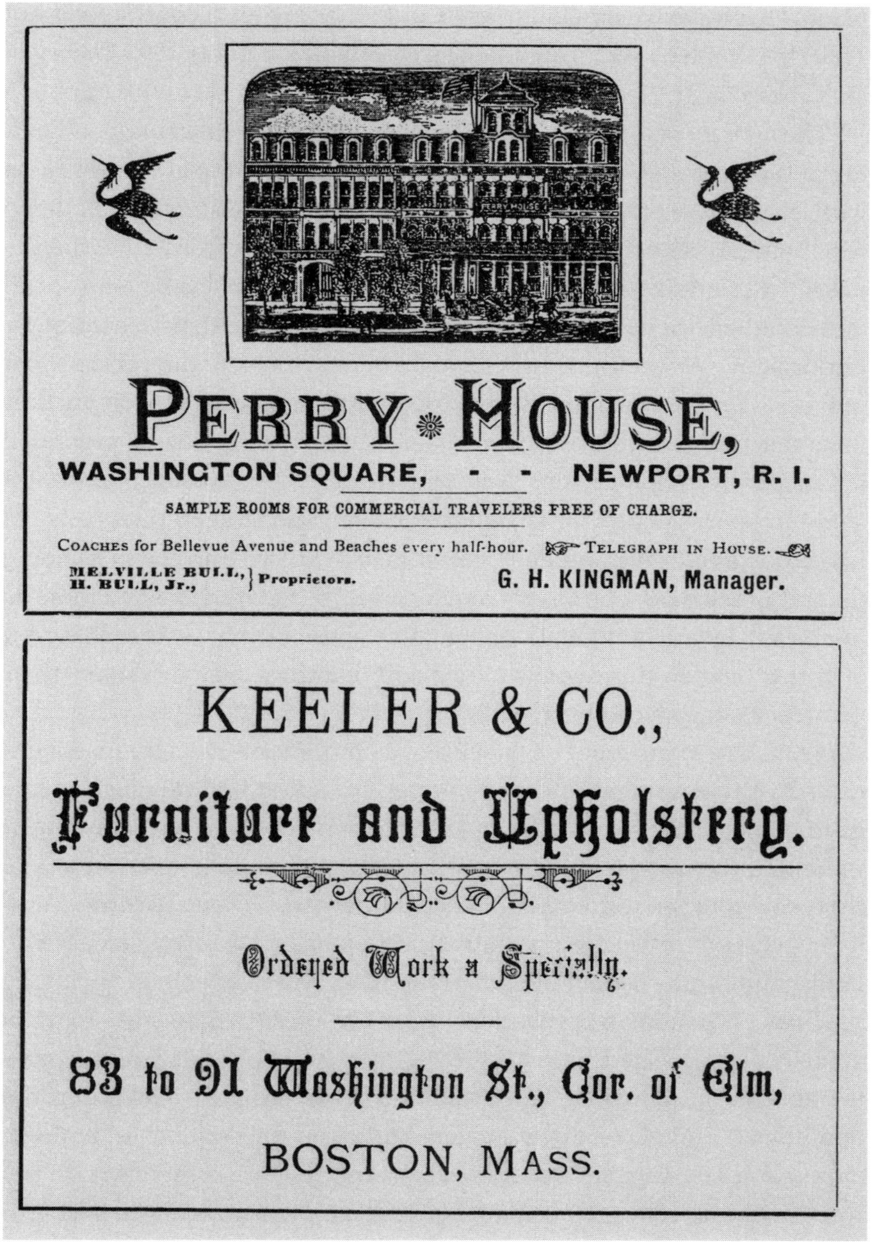

FIGURE 24. Unknown artist, advertisements in James H. Bowditch, *"City by the Sea": Newport* (Providence, RI: Reid, 1870). Courtesy Library of Congress.

Catskills (plate 3), this figure acted as a double for the viewer within the painting, indicating both where and how to look, thus modeling a drawn-out, contemplative perspective on the landscape. The appeal of that figure for viewers lay not only in his elevated social status as indicated by attire and the leisure time to engage in nonutilitarian aesthetic pursuits, but in the viewers' own imaginative sense of self-regard. Put another way, the admiration that viewers (as spectators) have for such a figure is reflected back on the viewers themselves as they imagine themselves in that figure's place. This reflexive dynamic of self and other invites a consideration of Thorstein Veblen's ideas about class identification in his 1899 *Theory of the Leisure Class*.[44]

The activity of tourism was a crucial example for Veblen's understanding of the rituals of class affiliation, because it was almost synonymous with leisure, or what he called the "non-productive consumption of time," which chiefly signified as "the pecuniary ability to afford a life of idleness."[45] Veblen's key concept of "pecuniary emulation" connects social and economic behavior, by redefining "class" as the demonstration or performance of wealth in a society where financial standing is the most universal and pervasive indicator of an individual's worth. He further links this performative behavior to a perception of self that is grounded in imaginative comparison: "And not only does the evidence of wealth serve to impress one's importance on others and to keep their sense of his importance alive and alert, but it is of scarcely less use in building up and preserving one's self-complacency."[46] "Pecuniary emulation" is motivated by an individual's imaginative sense of others' regard, and it is in this fashion that scenic guides and paintings arguably make their greatest persuasive impact.[47]

From the standpoint of "pecuniary emulation," the elimination of the substitute spectator in both upper-class and middle-class scenic guidebooks might seem to figure an affiliation between the classes, but I think that the opposite is at work—namely, a process of differentiation. As scenic tourism is commodified for lower social classes within a system governed by "pecuniary emulation," a pleasurable engagement with landscape scenery itself begins to function more conspicuously along the lines of "pecuniary emulation." Whether lower-middle-class tourists actually posed as landscape aesthetes, the viewing of landscape becomes yet another purchasable item (that is, via the cost of travel and room and board) and accordingly confers status on the purchaser. In these circumstances, Curtis's observer seeks out fugitive sights beyond the reach of appropriation by commercial tourism. For Curtis, the inclusion of a model spectator might reference the increasingly commodified practice of scenic viewing from which he strenuously works to distance his reader/viewer and himself. His practice of cultivating identification with the background and with the past likewise removes Curtis's elite viewer from an increasingly populous foreground.

Landscape views in lower-middle-class guidebooks, such as Bowditch's, initially seem to retain the substitute spectator (see figure 23), but on closer examination, these depicted figures function as models not for seeing but for being seen. Whereas the elegantly dressed gentleman in Cole's *River in the Catskills* encourages the viewer to gaze at length across the depicted expanse of landscape, Bowditch's fashionable couples are mannequin-like figures modeling both clothes and houses, much as if they were giving a preview of the stylish people and places of Newport's upscale neighborhoods. There are certainly illustrations that model touristic behavior (see figure 22), as do engravings of couples strolling in front of elegant housefronts. Nonetheless, their shallow spaces (removing not the foreground but the background of a picturesque view), as well as the transformation of model figures from spectators to display items, reveal the workings of a sense of self-perception that depends crucially on objects. Finally, I want to emphasize once more the active character of this imaginative engagement—one deliberately determines how one wishes to be seen.

The Fugitive View of the Past in the Luminist Works of Kensett and Richards

While a move toward spatial access, or instant access to commercial entities, is prominent in the narrative framing of middle- or lower-middle-class scenic guides to Newport, I argue in this last section that the luminist paintings of John Frederick Kensett and William Trost Richards seem largely to follow the adjustments found in the guidebooks of Curtis and King, so that many of the distinctive traits of luminist painting as traditionally discussed in past scholarship can be connected instead to the class-defining dynamics of evolving print illustration practices in scenic literature. Kensett's and Richards's visualization of the scenic landscape manifests the same tendency to render the picturesque view of history in landscape less accessible, which for Curtis (and arguably King) had been a class-defining response to the increasing phenomenon of middle-class tourist activity. I am not claiming that either painter reacted specifically to the growing prevalence of the railroad narrative in middle-class scenic guidebooks, but, more broadly, their work aligns with the refinement of narrative viewing in upper-class scenic literature that did actively set itself against that model of consumption.

From a biographical standpoint, it is unsurprising that the eastern coastal paintings of Kensett and Richards would reflect the elitist attitude of the more privileged denizens of scenic retreats like Newport and the Beverly Coast in Massachusetts. Both artists began painting these scenes at later stages in their career, when they were well connected to the networks of elite New York and Boston society. Both men were summer guests at mansions like those depicted in *"City by the Sea,"* and many of their patrons were the owners of those houses. During the 1850s and until 1872, the year of Kensett's death, he frequently spent summers at numerous scenic resort locations throughout the Northeast, among them Newport, Massachusetts' North Shore (which included the Beverly Coast and Nahant), New Jersey's Navesink Highlands, and Long Island. Important friends, hosts, and patrons included Curtis (who invited Kensett to the Navesink Highlands, the site of Kensett's first luminist works, in 1853, one year after *Lotus-Eating* was published), Charles Loring (whose prominent Boston family owned a residence in Beverly), Thomas Gold Appleton (son of the Boston textile manufacturer Nathan Appleton, an aspiring artist and a close friend of Kensett's, whose family owned property in Nahant), and Henry G. Marquand (treasurer of the Metropolitan Museum and the owner of the modestly named Marquand Cottage, one of the mansions pictured in *"City by the Sea"*).[48]

Like Kensett, many of Richards's late works (from 1870 on) are devoted to landscape scenes around the fashionable resort locations of the Northeast, but whereas Kensett frequented many of these places, Richards concentrated primarily on Newport itself. This focus coincided with his decision to summer there in 1874 and subsequent years, and then to purchase a permanent residence on nearby Conanicut Island in the early 1880s.[49] In a vein similar to the exclusiveness voiced by Curtis and King, Richards deplored the development of Newport as a tourist destination. Although his Newport house was located at a distance from the town center, and although he stayed there later and later in the summer, from 1881 onward Richards bewailed this development as an unavoidable visual obstruction, writing to his chief patron George Whitney, "They have shut out all my country views of fields and orchards."[50] In a later letter, he complains, "The houses opposite seem to get bigger and bigger and . . . more fashionable and we don't like it at all. All the charm of loneliness has gone out of our place, and it gives me an entirely different feeling from what it did before."[51] In this same letter he lays out his plans for purchasing property on the relatively deserted Conanicut Island, foreshadowing the kind of visionary hermit role that Winslow Homer would cultivate so successfully in connection with Prout's Neck, Maine.[52]

The changes in Kensett's landscape paintings in the last decades of his life, from compositions inspired by Cole and Durand (like *The White Mountains—From North Conway,* plate 7) to the far more austere, even abstract style of his luminist work (like the 1872 *Eaton's Neck, Long Island,* plate 10), have traditionally been explained in terms of the specific topographical features of the East Coast, the influence of his early background as an engraver, and an increase in introspection. Thus, in *John Frederick Kensett: An American Master,* John Paul Driscoll writes, "Kensett's new stylistic concerns were intimately tied to his decided preference for a new subject: American coastal scenery," and Oswaldo Rodriguez Roque notes, "The chief features of that style . . . cannot be separated from the work he did in that particular locale and seems as much a response to its

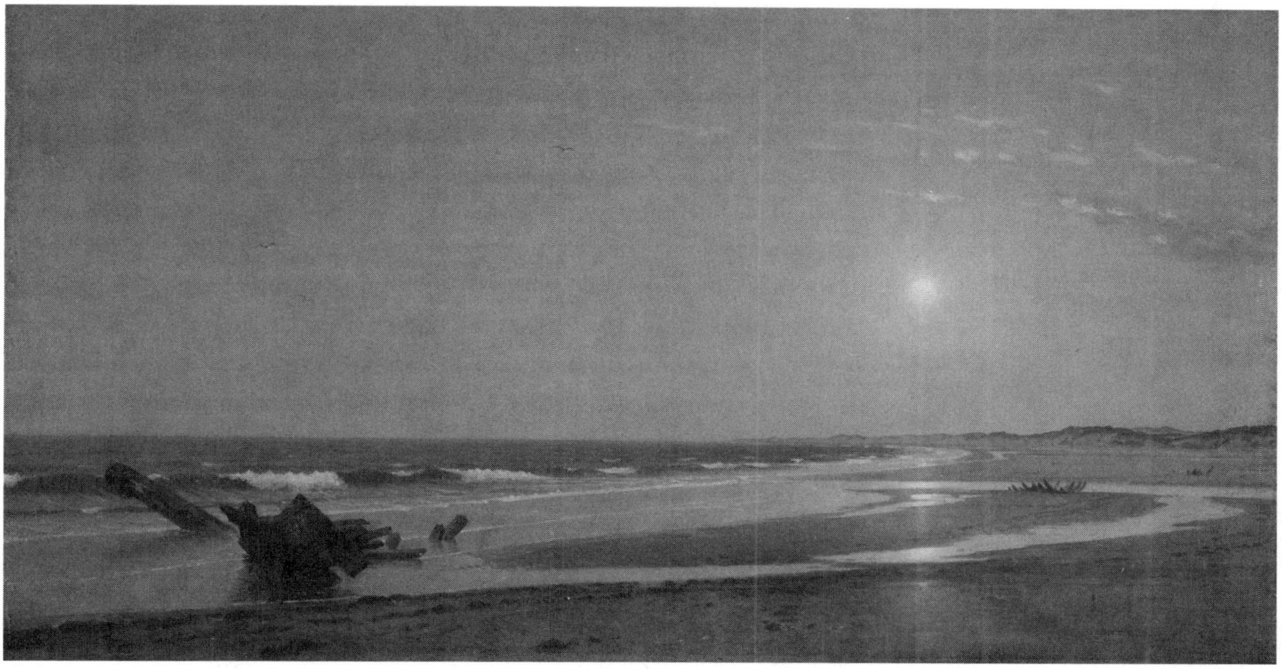

FIGURE 25. William Trost Richards, *Newport Beach*, 1873. Oil on canvas; 24 × 44 in. Private collection.

physical qualities as to any abstract ideas of style."[53] In *American Light: The Luminist Movement, 1850–1875,* a number of scholarly contributors identify a growing mood of privacy and intimacy in Kensett's luminist works, while Lisa Fellows Andrus and Linda S. Ferber relate this mood to approaches to pictorial design that characterized nineteenth-century American practices of draftsmanship and engraving.[54]

Richards's move to Newport has been interpreted as a similar turn toward a private engagement with nature—in his case, departing from detail-oriented work involving dense forest scenes that were heavily influenced by John Ruskin's writings and Pre-Raphaelite artwork in the United States.[55] The influence of the Pre-Raphaelites and Ruskin on Richards's work, as on the work of many of his American contemporaries, has often been explored as a pictorial problem involving an interest in quasi-scientific accuracy and an abiding, intrinsically American, concern with landscape as a genre. The evolution of Richards's Pre-Raphaelite style is seen as a process of reconciling carefully observed foreground scenes with the spatial depth found in landscape painting, a process that echoes criticisms of early Pre-Raphaelite stylistic development.[56] Around the time that Richards moved to Newport to concentrate on marine paintings, attentiveness to space gave way to an increasing abstraction, an interest in "radical" horizontality without interrupting foreground detail. A dramatic example is the 1873 *Newport Beach* (figure 25), which, as in Kensett's work, evokes a "lonely mood" and an "intimate" engagement with nature.[57]

Comprehensive characterizations of luminism as an artistic movement similarly emphasize the increasing intimacy associated with the late careers of Kensett and Richards. In *American Light,* David C. Huntington situated luminist practice in relation to evolving American religious attitudes, taking Kensett's work to exemplify the connections between luminist style and transcendental conceptions of the Deity: "The implied space and time of [his paintings] are, seemingly, no longer limited by the parochial scale of man's recorded history. Unobtrusively this painting brings the spectator in touch with a universe that is superhuman. Barbara Novak's invocation of Emerson's words comes automatically to mind: 'I become a transparent eyeball: I am nothing; I see all; the currents of the Universal Being circulate through me; I am part or parcel of God.'"[58] In *The Empire of the Eye,* Angela Miller addressed an "atmospheric luminism" that "expressed—and in turn shaped—a growing midcentury appreciation for nature as a complex organic realm surrounding the human world. . . . The aesthetic of atmospheric luminism was grounded . . . in an identification with nature rather than an insistence on one's physical separateness from it."[59] Both Huntington and Miller characterized luminist paintings as putting the viewer into unmediated contact with a deified or expanded nature. More recent studies of luminist artists have downplayed such a religious or moralistic dimension, but they continue to stress the works' evocation of private engagement.[60] I do not contest any of these interpretations, but it seems to me that underlying them is an intrinsic impulse to read luminist work (however this grouping is defined in terms of specific artists) in markedly inclusive terms, with the viewer as a seeker of connections with a larger social or natural order, or with shared religious, spiritual, or aesthetic beliefs. There is also a tacit assumption in such interpretations that luminism addresses a national audience; as if luminism, a successor to the nationalist aspirations of the Hudson River school, in some sense answers for the failures of that earlier vision.[61] Luminism figures as the endpoint, after all, of a rise and fall, the development and subsequent decline of a certain "image" of landscape painting that arguably remains current.[62]

I want to argue instead that the tendency toward "privacy" in the late work of Kensett and Richards is socially exclusive, as in the sense of a posted "private property" sign, and that they modify the picturesque conventions of the Hudson River school in the service of such exclusion. Not only were the two men steeped in the privileged cultural life of East Coast scenic tourism, but their paintings display the same elusive and exclusive strategies for framing the experience of landscape scenery that are found in the work of Curtis and King. Luminist paintings like Kensett's *Eaton's Neck, Long Island* and Richards's *Newport Beach* (plate 10 and figure 25)

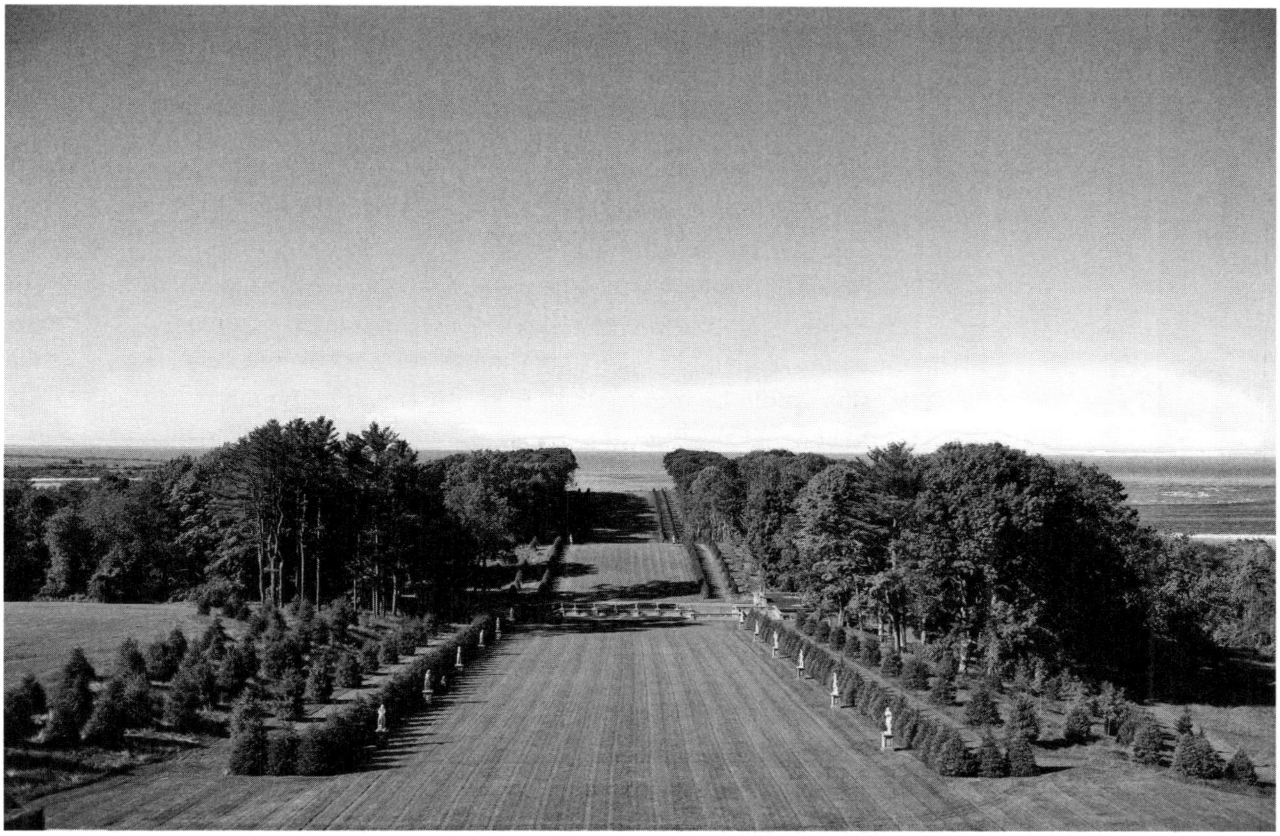

FIGURE 26. Photograph of the ocean and *grande allée*. Crane Estate, Ipswich, Massachusetts. Photograph courtesy of Sarah Bastille.

manifest the same absence of a foreground, as though the painter were giving us the background of a larger scene or we were looking through King's "spy-glass." Such a perspective corresponds closely, in its distancing effect, with the *grand allées* of the most lavish Massachusetts retreats, such as the Crane Estate near Ipswich, built in the early twentieth century by the Chicago plumbing fixture magnate Richard T. Crane (figure 26).[63] The emptiness of space between the mansion and the ocean along the avenue of the grand allée directs attention specifically toward the distant view.

The works of Kensett and Richards are also smaller in scale compared with earlier landscape scenes—especially the supersized canvases of Frederic Edwin Church and Albert Bierstadt of the 1860s—so that, despite their crispness, individual elements cannot be registered as easily as might be expected when the eye moves back into the depicted space. Whereas paintings by Cole or Durand represented depth through a measured, rationalized series of transitions—a viewing path along which objects steadily decreased in size, lending itself to analogy with progressing historical stages—works by Kensett and Richards stretch depth or distance beyond the capacity of observable measurement. Perhaps the most important effect of these spatial modifications is on the viewer's sense of time. "Strand[ed] upon the distance," time is perceived as moving slowly or not at all, like distant boats creeping across the horizon. Such effects of extended or exaggerated distance and duration, of infinity and eternity, are among the most common attributes ascribed to luminist works.[64] The perception of time gained from the view of extremely distant objects is also crucially associated with the past, with history, like light from distant stars that gives the astronomer a view of cosmic entities millions of years old. Without ascribing any scientific sophistication to either Kensett or Richards, one could say that the slow and almost imperceptible movements of distant objects are themselves past events, relative to the time that would be required to physically traverse the intervening distance, to connect the time of the observer with the time of the distant object.

Moreover, as with Curtis, both Kensett and Richards seem to ignore the touristic present. Although Richards's earlier intense observation of natural detail seems to suggest a modern scientific concern with accuracy, his work throughout his career addresses subjects redolent of the past or of removal from the present, as in his own version of Tennyson's poem, *The Land of the Lotos* (1860). Likewise, Kensett's images of resort landscapes obscure the signs of recent tourist development, as in his 1869 depiction of Lake George, one of the destinations described by Curtis in *Lotus-Eating.* On the apparently deserted lake, the figure of an Indian in a birch-bark canoe is barely discernible just beneath and in front of the middle-ground island, second from the left (plate 11).[65] It is difficult to juxtapose the crowded scenes of fashion depicted in contemporary scenic guides (figure 22, right side) with the deserted, depopulated shorelines of Kensett's and Richards's paintings and not sense a kind of misanthropy. Especially in Kensett's works (like *Lake George* or *Forty Steps, Newport, Rhode Island*, 1871; figure 27), it seems that the past viewpoint, the old, "quiet" Newport, can be achieved only by eclipsing figures in distance.

Earlier scholars have discerned connections between the stylistic traits of luminism and these artists' background in the graphic arts. The heightened precision and clean contours that prevail in their works, the precise and prolonged perspectival recession, the quadrangular compositions, and even the absence of movement have been traced to the training in draftsmanship, watercolor, or engraving that began many of their careers.[66] The small scale of luminist paintings can also be related to graphic practices. Perhaps most telling in terms of the relationship between Richards's paintings and contemporary scenic literature are the postcard-size watercolors Richards executed in his later career. These were a series of small watercolor sketches, known as "coupons," which he produced in and around Newport between 1875 and 1884, and which he regularly enclosed in his letters to his primary patron, George Whitney. These sketches were records of his travels around the Newport area

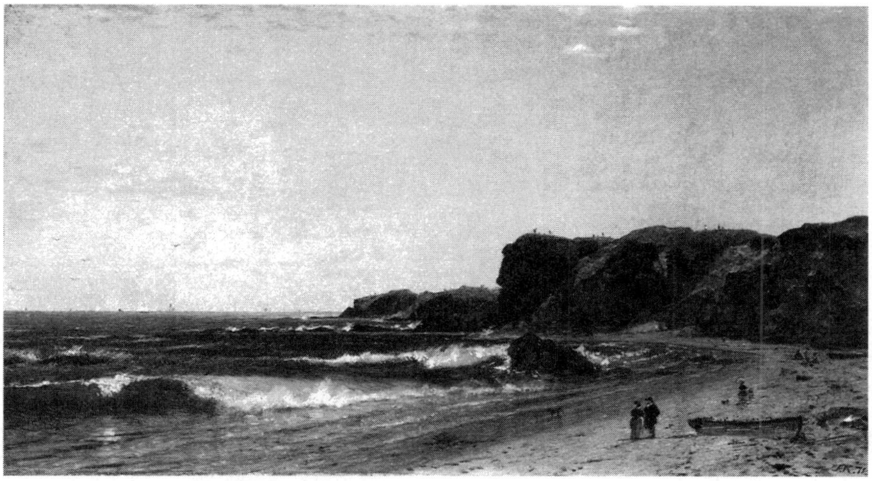

FIGURE 27. John F. Kensett, *Forty Steps, Newport, Rhode Island*, 1871. Oil on canvas; 10½ x 18½ in. Private collection.

and elsewhere as well as previews of forthcoming finished paintings. Whitney collected them in an album that likewise performed a dual role, as a collection of personal mementos of his artist friend and as a public catalog of prospective works that interested buyers could consult when visiting Whitney's gallery in Philadelphia.[67] Such collections of drawings were not unusual in this period, but Whitney's collection is distinguished by its multiple different images of Newport and the way it acts as a pointed alternative to the presentation of views in the lower-middle-class scenic guides, especially in terms of the album's status as an object.[68]

As drawings, watercolors, and small-scale works, these coupons were an arena where Richards worked out his ideas, giving insight into his original intentions and thought processes. As postcards, however, they had a finished quality, especially since they were shown in Whitney's gallery. They feature the same barren scenes of rocks, meadows, sea, and sky found in Richards's paintings: depopulated, vast, and without incident (plate 12). Like his paintings, moreover, many of the coupons depict sites associated with Newport's past, such as views of ruined Revolutionary War fortifications (plate 13; Fort Dumpling is the small stone structure on the slip of land in the background). Richards's interest in rock formations appears almost architectural, as if these were manmade structures eroded beyond the point of recognition (figures 28 and 29; the former is actually another view of Fort Dumpling). In the decade in which Richards produced his coupons, he also traveled to England and spent almost two years making landscape studies; scholarship on his coupons has noted their possible relation to collections of J. M. W. Turner prints, such as the *Liber Studiorum* and the *Southern Coast,* which also include many ruined castles and fortresslike cliffs.[69] Just the size of Richards's coupons indicates an affinity with prints of landscape scenery more than finished paintings.

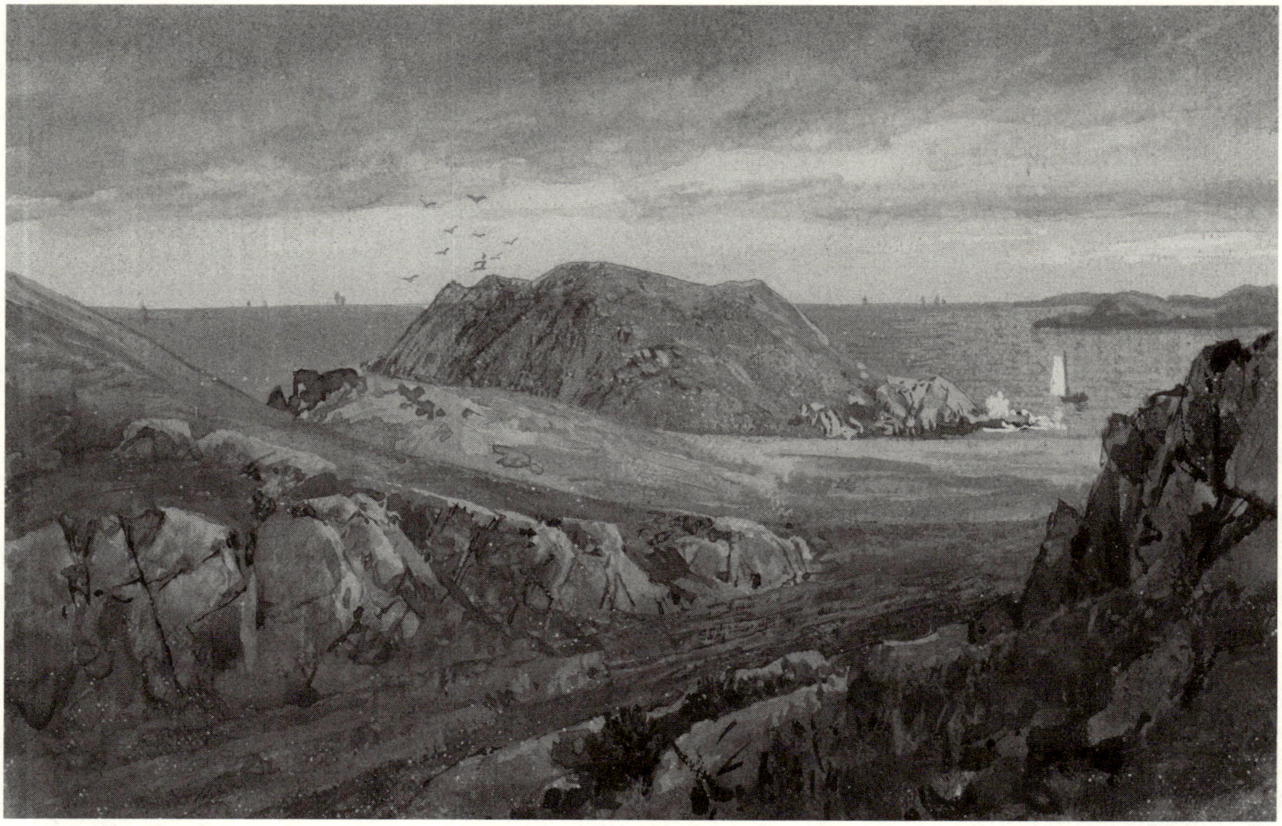

FIGURE 28. William Trost Richards, *High Hill, Conanicut Island*, 1877. Watercolor and Chinese white on paper; 3⁵⁄₁₆ × 4¹⁵⁄₁₆ in. 17.5.2008. Courtesy of the Pennsylvania Academy of Fine Arts, Philadelphia. Promised gift of Dorrance H. Hamilton in memory of Samuel M. V. Hamilton.

Collected in an album, though, Richards's coupons seem to almost tantalizingly assume aspects of landscape presentation found in the middle-class guidebooks, as if flirting with a more mass-market commercial logic. The most obvious point of comparison is that both have a plenitude of imagery that can seem disconnected in terms of any larger narrative organization of them. The guides produced for the emerging middle class, however, organize their illustrations as a unidirectional succession, suppressing an extended engagement with them of the kind provided by the textual framing in more genteel guides. In contrast, the album format restores agency to the viewer in the construction of a narrative explanation for their arrangement, almost as a kind of hypertext—the viewer can order them as he or she sees fit. Then again, just as the engravings of mansions in *"City by the Sea"* titillated the reader with fantasies of the good life, Richards's coupons point toward some other object to be possessed—the finished painting—and yet they curiously stand for those objects themselves: they are almost the same size as Richards's large-scale watercolors, and they possess an unusual degree of finish for mere studies. What is more, these coupons, as their monetary title suggests, are objects meaningful within a commercial context; that is, they connote monetary value as much as they do a landscape view.[70] Readers or viewers of scenic guides and paintings ascribed distinct kinds of value to landscape images, based on the interpretations shaped by conventions in either form of representation but also on the object's relation to other objects, or goods, available for a price. Scenic tourism was a business, and the publishers of guidebooks, to a certain degree, increasingly translated the value system undergirding the aesthetic experience of picturesque viewing to a more commercial and consumer-friendly universe of purchasable goods. This process is apparent in the Bowditch guidebook's enumeration of costs for various aspects of visiting Newport. The fragmentation, or atomization, of the railroad narrative abets this process in its insistence on discrete and measurable units of experience as opposed to the open-endedness encouraged by picturesque viewing. The modifications that Richards and Kensett made to picturesque compositional devices and viewing practices can be understood in part as an effort to redefine paintings as objects in the face of tourism's marketing of aesthetic experience.

Viewed in this light, the high resolution and dense colors of the coupons could be said to give them a jewel-like appearance that replaces the proprietary, elevated view of earlier Hudson River school painting with another visual analog for proprietary desire—a precious stone. This impression activates a contrast of scale—the vast luminist space versus the actual size of the coupon or of its jewel-like associations—that

FIGURE 29. William Trost Richards, *The Road to the House of W. T. Richards on Conanicut Island*, 1882. Watercolor on paper; 3⅛ × 4^{15}⁄16 in. 73.5.2008. Courtesy of the Pennsylvania Academy of Fine Arts, Philadelphia. Promised gift of Dorrance H. Hamilton in memory of Samuel M. V. Hamilton.

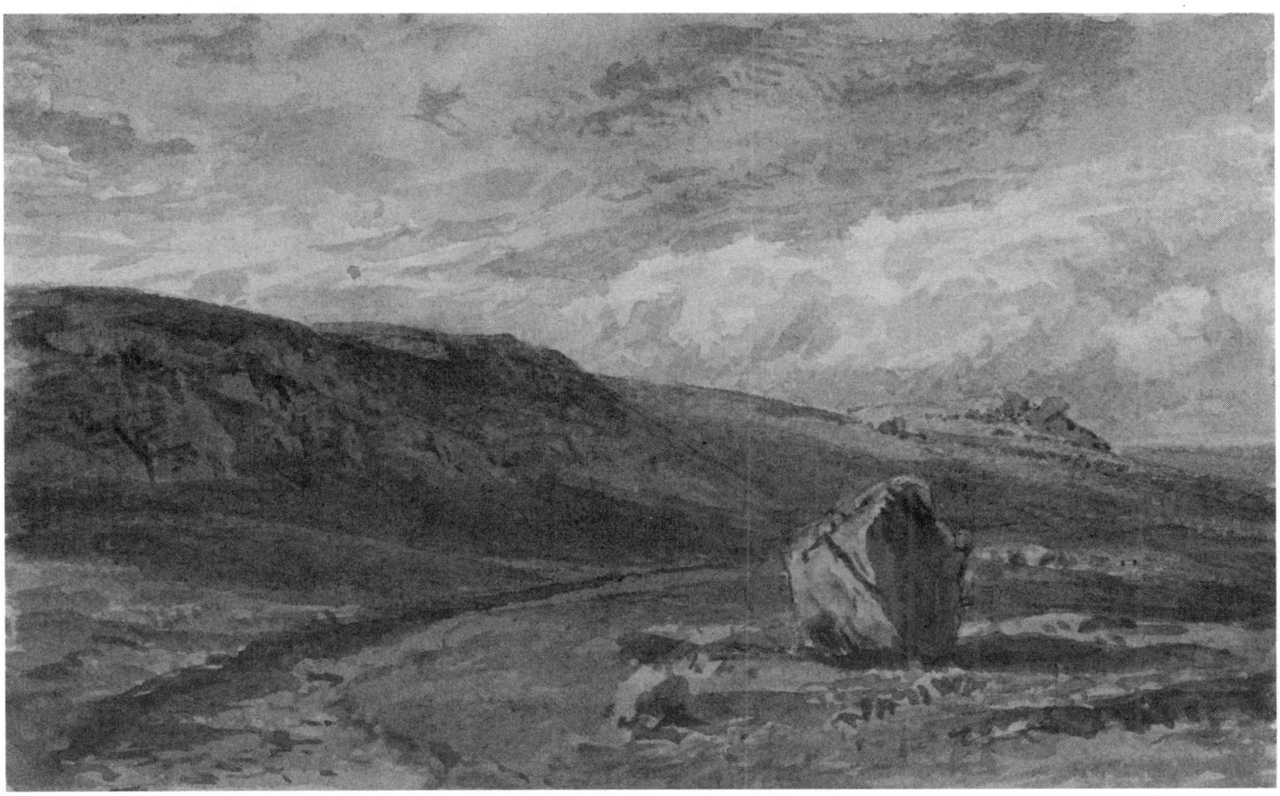

heightens the sensation of poignant loss cultivated by Curtis. The intention seems to be to remove the distant view (of the past) from the background of a picturesque view, what had been a painting, and place it in a gemstone-like setting, for the viewer to possess. This operation is similar to the framing of ocean views in grande allées in the realm of landscape architecture. These object connotations contrast with the dilemma of value arising from mass-produced goods, easy to access but valueless in the scheme of pecuniary distinction.[71] If the scenic view is cheapened through its representation in inexpensive scenic literature and through the increased affordability of travel, Richards's coupons gesture toward some less easily depreciable object of value. These object valuations can also carry behavioral associations, as if there were a sense of agreement between the activities of the readers or viewers who engage scenic guides and paintings and the sense in which these objects themselves "behave," and with similar class-defining implications. Richards's coupons, like his paintings, insist on stasis—they restrain the viewer's rush to access their spaces imaginatively (both through the exaggeration of distance, with its corollary denial of proximity, and through the sense of timelessness that pervades them). Alternatively, in these compositions conspicuously lacking in objects and features, there is also nothing for the viewer to possess, nothing with which to gratify a gross material passion. Either way, the coupons seem to insist on decorum and good behavior.

In their own separate ways, then, both Kensett and Richards produced work in reaction to the development of East Coast locales as popular tourist destinations. This reaction extended beyond subject matter to participation in print-related projects that competed with the format of scenic guidebooks aimed at lower-middle-class audiences, projects that in turn shaped the distinctive appearance of the artists' luminist paintings. Opposition to a growing mass-market tourist industry is reflected in their work by their increasing emphasis on isolation as a narrative strategy. As the railroad narrative begins to appear across a range of print materials, facilitating a fantasy of access to commodities as opposed to mastery over an unfolding of history, the already small size of Richards's luminist paintings becomes even more diminished, the depicted landscapes even more remote, just as Richards himself moves further away from the "Fashion" and "cottage heaven" of Newport. As I show in the second half of this book, chapters 3 and 4, a similar dismantling of picturesque viewing models takes place in the evolution of professional science in the United States, a testimony both to the early dominance of that picturesque tradition and to the increasing capacity of print materials to mold visual culture on their own terms.

3

"Walking Statues"

Narrative and Landscape in Early American Ethnology

AS CHAPTERS 1 AND 2 SHOW, the narrative structuring of spectatorship was an important means by which landscape images conveyed concepts of history, consumption, and identity in the nineteenth century, not only in painting but in a diverse body of print publications as well. Correlations between movements in time, movements in space, and movements of the eye (whether looking or reading) underwrote a rich set of strategies for juxtaposing text sections with illustrations in printed books, allowing them to imitate and to surpass older picturesque conventions for encoding narrative meaning in landscape imagery. Besides transportation aids, scenic guides, and aesthetic treatises, such strategies were used in other types of publications, where they worked to frame other kinds of time besides written history and patterns of consumption. In this and the following chapter I examine how early scientific works developed notions of past time extending before and beyond recorded history and communicated those concepts largely through the narrative presentation of landscape imagery, focusing on the emergence of professionalized ethnology and geology.

My choice of publications is not arbitrary. Just as various kinds of touristic literature contributed to shaping patterns of land use and development over the course of the nineteenth century, early scientific expeditions and reports, especially those devoted to ethnology and geology, played key roles in facilitating settlement in the new territories and states.[1] Such scientific works likewise initially relied on picturesque conventions of landscape representation, and professional artists were often centrally involved in their production. Here, too, they incorporated new ways of engaging with landscape imagery that departed from the compositional and viewing precedents of earlier paintings and prints. Whatever categorical differences exist today between tourism and science—for example, the distinction between cultivating consumer interest (advertising) and supporting a particular scientific theory (evidence)—in the nineteenth century such differences were not as sharp, especially in terms of relating images to narrative text.[2] My central aim in chapters 3 and 4 is to trace how the kinds of knowledge produced in these sciences became established as being different from the concerns of touristic literature, specifically through practices of relating narrative texts and landscape images.

In both tourism and science, new kinds of illustrated books were produced in tandem with the evolution of these discourses, beginning at midcentury. While tourism began to cultivate a lower-middle-class audience, the disciplines of ethnology and geology moved toward a higher level of professionalization. The development of distinctly upper-class and lower-middle-class tourist cultures (which I have traced through the evolution of scenic guidebooks) reveals itself, though, as a process of specialization analogous to the trend of increasing professionalization in science. Moreover, in both cases, such developments required establishing discrete temporal frameworks (uses of time and spans of time), which in ethnology and geology meant a radically expanded time range that could encompass ancient civilizations and the history of the earth. Finally, the new methods for narratively organizing landscape perception, developed to convey such expanded ranges of time, share some of the characteristics of the railroad narrative found in lower-middle-class tourist publications. There is a key difference, however, in the effects of the railroad narrative within these scientific publications, namely that fragmentation and superficiality supply the preconditions for knowledge, for reassembling data into new, more ostensibly rigorous, scientific narratives. Put differently, the legitimation of ethnological and geological time involves the decomposition of other kinds of time suggested by observable phenomena, creating isolated data sets unattached to any other competing narrative order or organization of time. In turn, by virtue of their isolation, these data sets become amenable to enlistment in the construction of specifically scientific knowledge.

In touristic and scientific publications, land and landscape are simultaneously a central subject matter and a critical tool of persuasion—a state of affairs that might seem anomalous in the field of ethnology, the study of people, not places. The figure of the Indian, however, frequently anchored nationalistic conceptions of a teleological progression from wilderness to civilization, imagined as spatial domains, in many nineteenth-century American landscape paintings and in a host of related fine art and popular representations. Many scholars have explored how such representations endorsed the displacement or outright eradication of American Indian societies in the course of western expansion by casting these events as inevitable by-products of Manifest Destiny.[3] In images of this kind, the Indian is typically associated with primeval nature, and

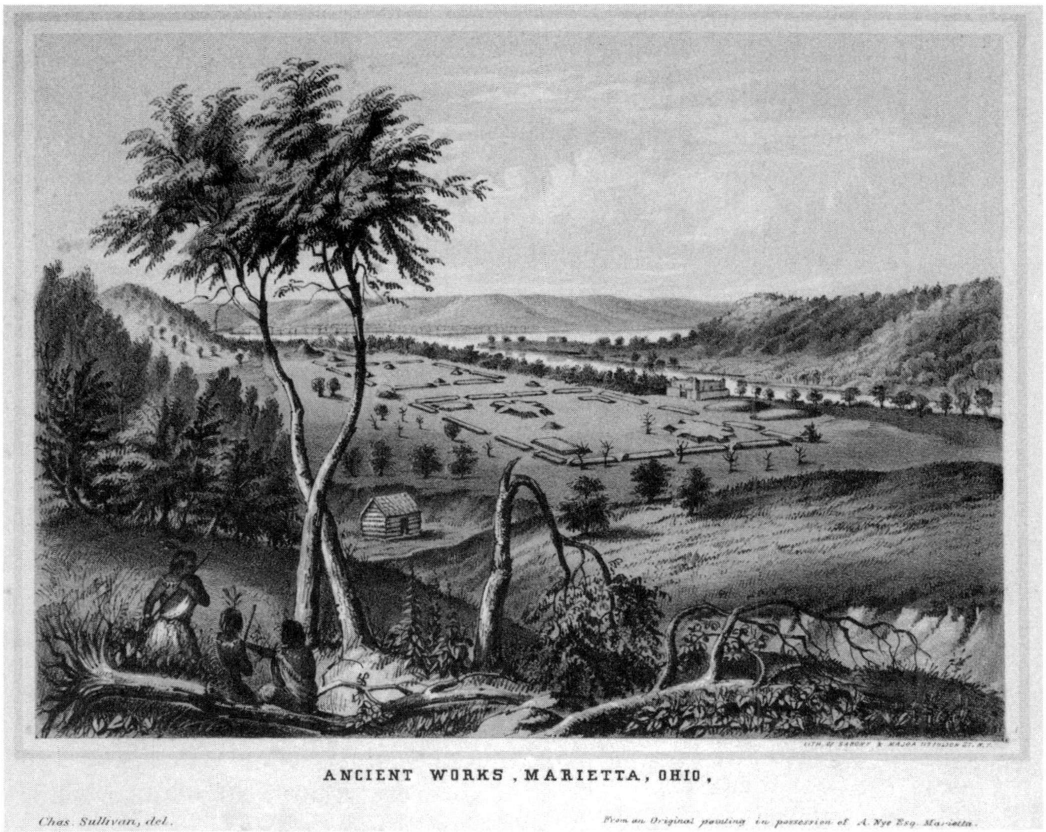

FIGURE 30. Unknown artist, *Ancient Works, Marietta, Ohio.* Illustration from Ephraim G. Squier and Edwin H. Davis, *Ancient Monuments of the Mississippi Valley* (New York: Bartlett and Welford, 1848).

in fact becomes an emblem for the undeveloped wilderness landscape, existing in an ahistorical zone that sets off and thereby implicitly justifies the serial advance of improvements displayed for the white American viewer. The persuasive force of such images is produced by combining racial identification with the narrative organization of the spectator's eye movement. In Durand's *Progress* (plate 2), for example, the story of the march of civilization on the right side of the painting is promoted as much by appealing to a viewer's disinclination to identify with the group of Indians hidden in the lefthand foliage as by contrasts of light and dark (moving from a left foreground shrouded in darkness to a right background bathed in light) and directional cues (the road leading to a canal leading to a railroad leading to a shipping lane).[4]

Such representations of Natives existed in early anthropological studies as well, as in the frontispiece (figure 30) to the Smithsonian Institution's first scholarly publication, Ephraim Squier's and Edwin Davis's *Ancient Monuments of the Mississippi Valley* (1848).[5] As in Durand's *Progress*, an elevated foreground group of Indians, ensconced in a wilderness zone of shrubs and trees, contrasts with a historical sequence of built environments laid out on the river terrace below. Here, however, the Indian is excluded not just from the history of white American settlement, but also from a prior history of land development carried out by the so-called Mound Builders, the subject of Squier's and Davis's catalog.[6] The Mound Builders' ziggurat-like platforms stand on a floodplain between a log cabin and the "Old Stockade" (located right next to the river), which signify the beginnings of the town of Marietta, Ohio. In this frontispiece, the historical sequence, projected as spatial depth in *Progress,* is represented in truncated form as only the starting point of that historical vector (the first signs of settlement) and confined to a single site (the floodplain adjacent to the river), while also strangely coexisting with an antecedent historical sequence (that of the Mound Builders) as a kind of palimpsest. In a subsequent detailed plan of the mounds at Marietta, the later stages of white American settlement are depicted, with the grid pattern of the modern town's streets serving as a convenient lattice to fix the location of Mound Builder remains and to suggest their size.

This peculiar opposition between the Indian's supposed lack of history, suggested by association with the untouched wilderness landscape, and two separate sequences of civilization conformed to the authors' outlook on the Mound Builders and current American Indians. Squier in particular was a proponent of polygenism, the theory that living American Indians were an inferior race distinct from both European stock and that of the ancient Mound Builders; and Indians' perceived lack of enduring monuments was seen as negative evidence of that inferiority. Squier regarded *Ancient Monuments* as an adjunct to the craniological work of Samuel Morton, the theory's most respected advocate, and he later lent his research in support of Josiah Nott's *Types of Mankind,* the most prominent polygenist defense of slavery, published in the decade before the Civil War.[7] The Smithsonian Institution avoided further potentially inflammatory polygenist anthropological work, but the denial of American Indian historicity, the claim that the Indian was somehow equivalent to nature in lacking a history of tangible human achievement, was not confined to adherents of polygenism; it permeated studies with other orientations.[8] The widespread and persistent idea of the "vanishing American"—the assumption of American Indians' doomed status in the face of advancing civilization—increasingly positioned the Indian emphatically *in* history, as a past or left-behind entity.[9] The latter notion clearly subsumed the Indian within the nation's history, but even so, as monogenist anthropology regained ascendancy in the 1860s, the question of the relationship between earlier indigenous civilizations and contemporary Native cultures became both more difficult and more urgent to clarify. Given such contrary

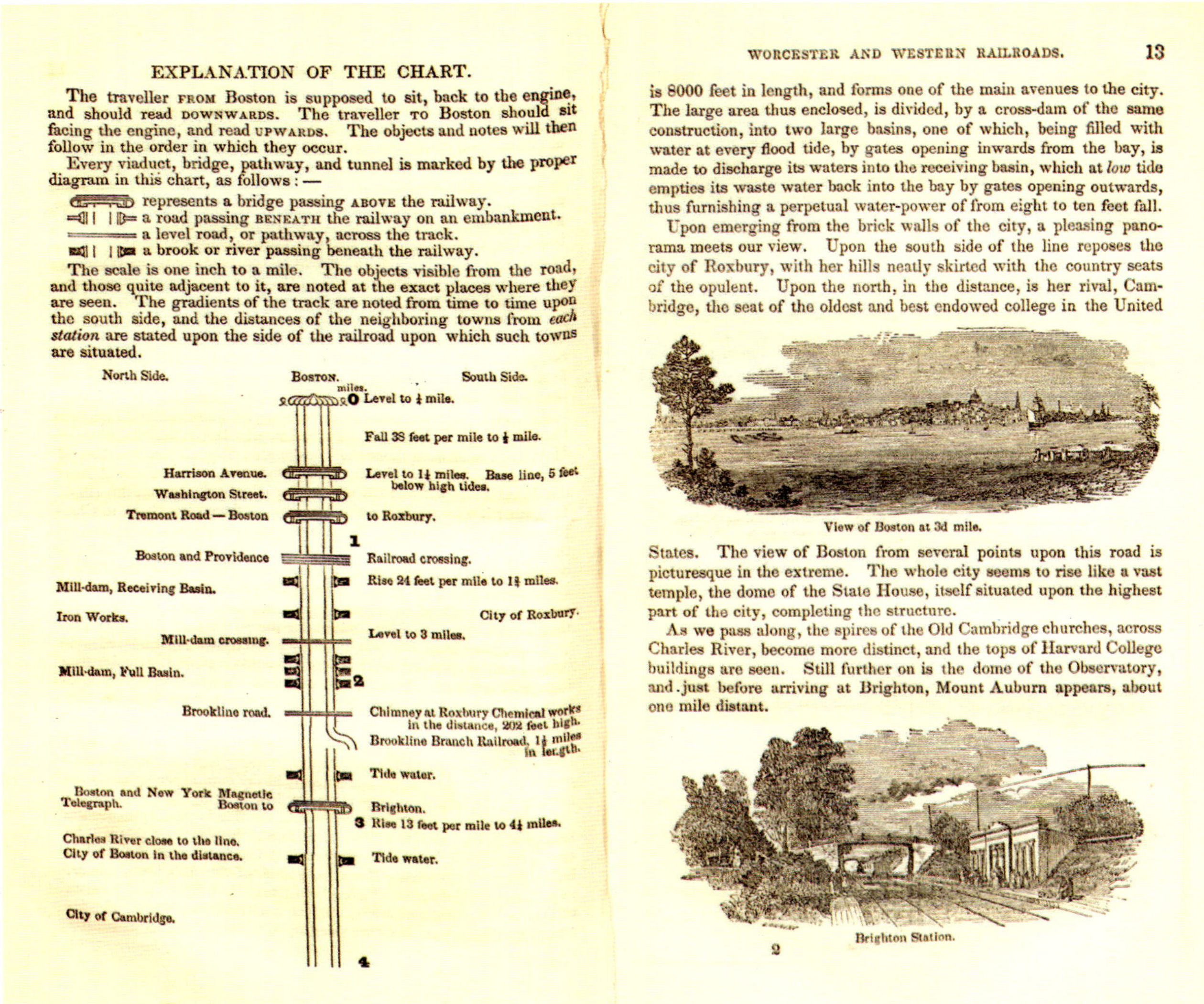

EXPLANATION OF THE CHART.

The traveller FROM Boston is supposed to sit, back to the engine, and should read DOWNWARDS. The traveller TO Boston should sit facing the engine, and read UPWARDS. The objects and notes will then follow in the order in which they occur.

Every viaduct, bridge, pathway, and tunnel is marked by the proper diagram in this chart, as follows: —

[bridge symbol] represents a bridge passing ABOVE the railway.
[symbol] a road passing BENEATH the railway on an embankment.
[symbol] a level road, or pathway, across the track.
[symbol] a brook or river passing beneath the railway.

The scale is one inch to a mile. The objects visible from the road, and those quite adjacent to it, are noted at the exact places where they are seen. The gradients of the track are noted from time to time upon the south side, and the distances of the neighboring towns from *each station* are stated upon the side of the railroad upon which such towns are situated.

WORCESTER AND WESTERN RAILROADS. 13

is 8000 feet in length, and forms one of the main avenues to the city. The large area thus enclosed, is divided, by a cross-dam of the same construction, into two large basins, one of which, being filled with water at every flood tide, by gates opening inwards from the bay, is made to discharge its waters into the receiving basin, which at *low* tide empties its waste water back into the bay by gates opening outwards, thus furnishing a perpetual water-power of from eight to ten feet fall.

Upon emerging from the brick walls of the city, a pleasing panorama meets our view. Upon the south side of the line reposes the city of Roxbury, with her hills neatly skirted with the country seats of the opulent. Upon the north, in the distance, is her rival, Cambridge, the seat of the oldest and best endowed college in the United

View of Boston at 3d mile.

States. The view of Boston from several points upon this road is picturesque in the extreme. The whole city seems to rise like a vast temple, the dome of the State House, itself situated upon the highest part of the city, completing the structure.

As we pass along, the spires of the Old Cambridge churches, across Charles River, become more distinct, and the tops of Harvard College buildings are seen. Still further on is the dome of the Observatory, and just before arriving at Brighton, Mount Auburn appears, about one mile distant.

Brighton Station.

2

PLATE 1. Unknown artist, *View of Boston at 3d Mile* and "Explanation of the Chart." Illustrations from William Guild, *A Chart and Description of the Boston and Worcester and Western Railroads* (Boston, MA: Bradbury and Guild, 1847). Courtesy the University of Chicago Library.

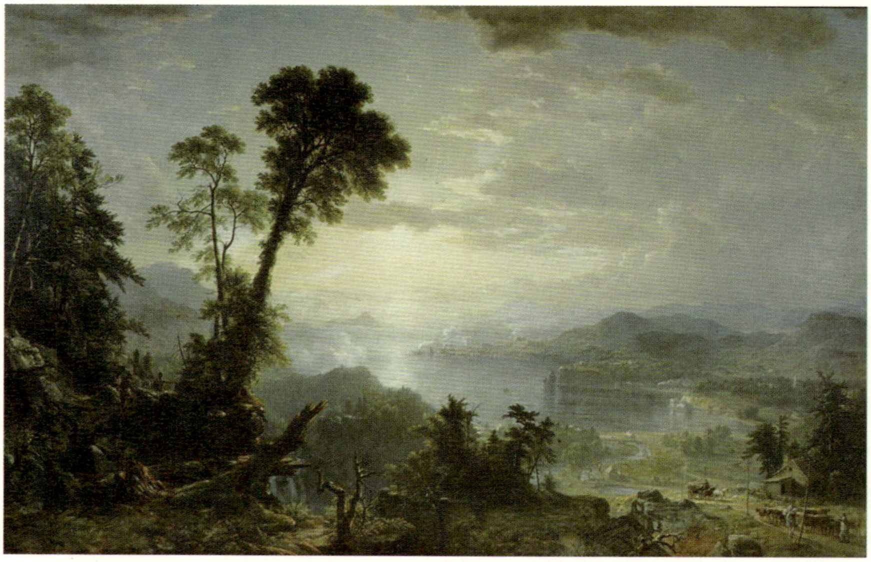

Plate 2. Asher B. Durand, *Progress*, 1853. Oil on canvas; 48 × 72 in. Private collection.

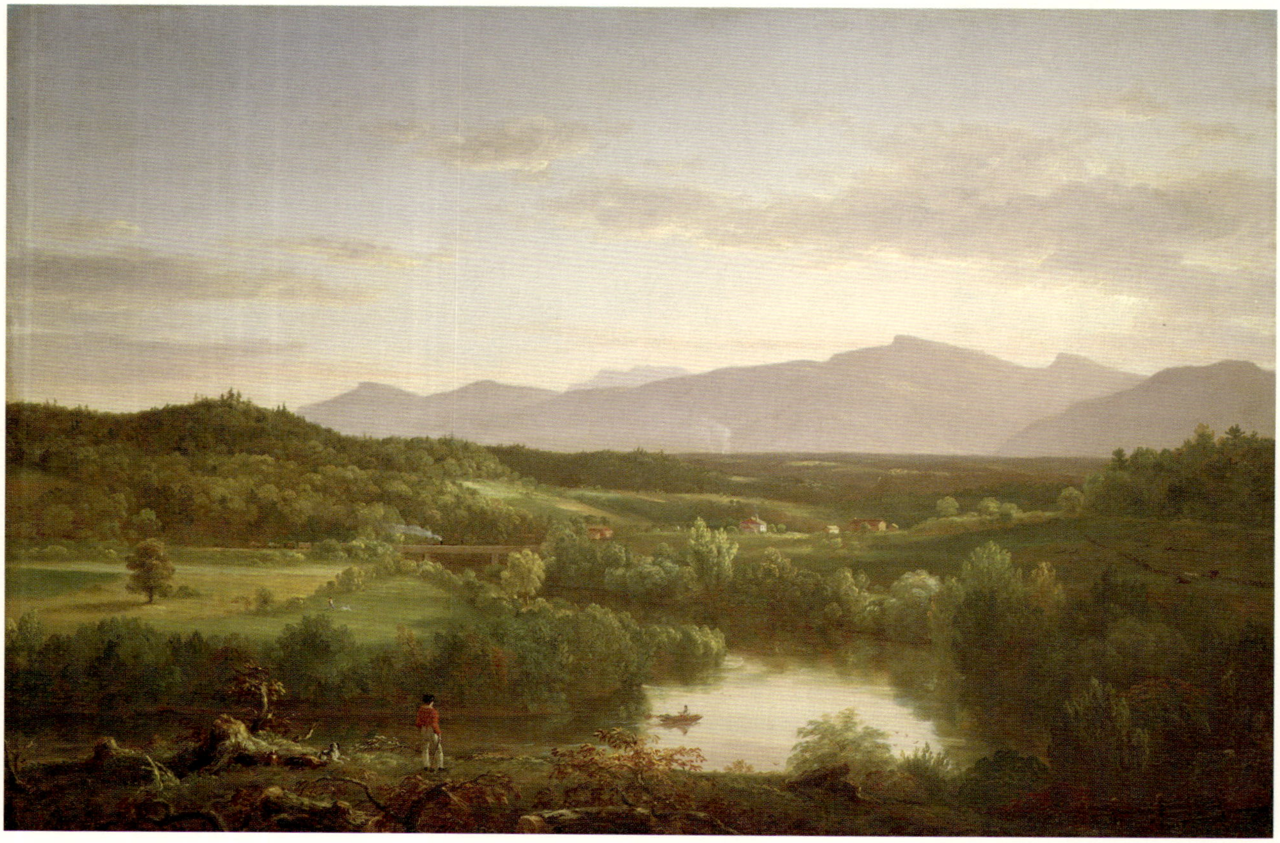

Plate 3. Thomas Cole, *River in the Catskills*, 1843. Oil on canvas; 27½ × 40⅜ in. Museum of Fine Arts, Boston, Massachusetts. Gift of Martha M. Karolik for the M. and M. Karolik Collection of American Paintings, 1815–1865, 47.1201. Photograph © 2015 Museum of Fine Arts, Boston.

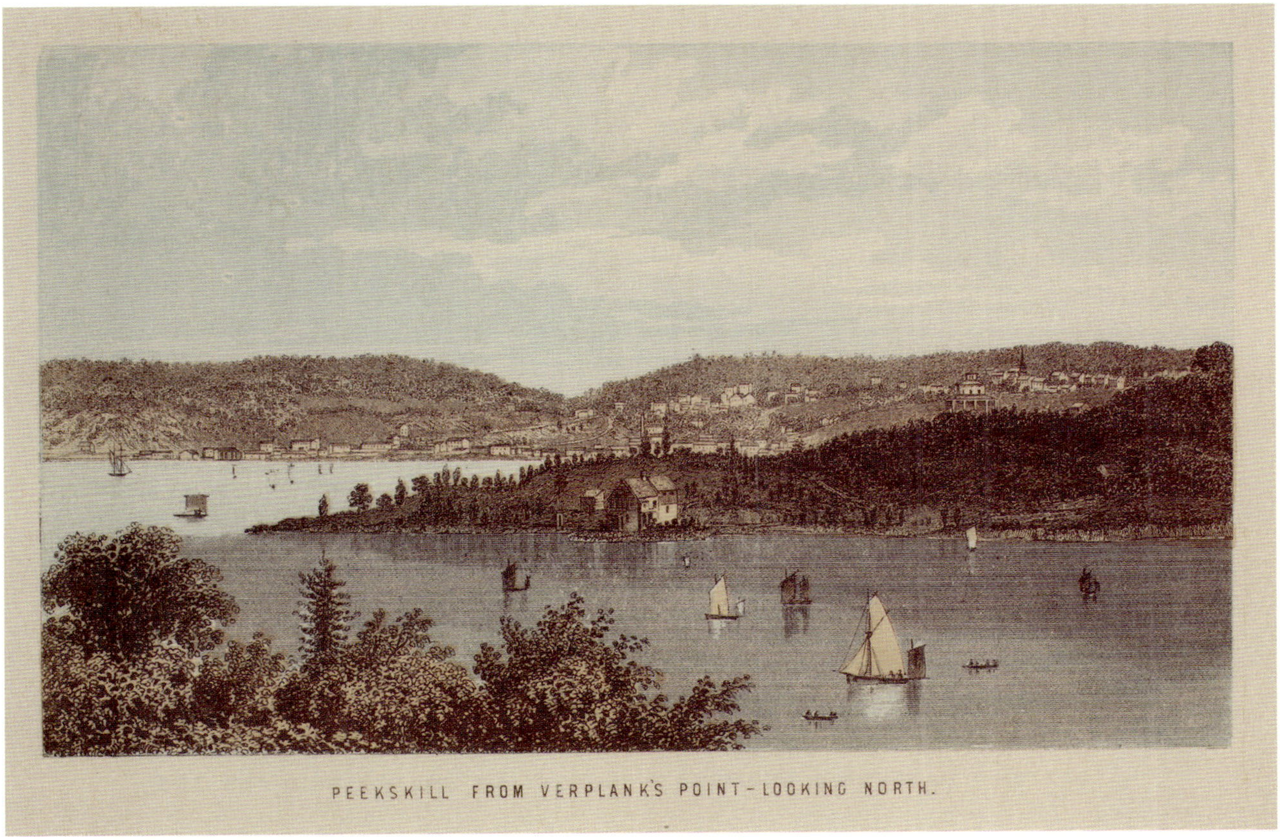

PLATE 4. Unknown artist, *Peekskill from Verplanck's Point.* Illustration from Thomas Nelson, *Nelson's Illustrated Guide to the Hudson and Its Tributaries* (New York: Nelson and Sons, 1860). Courtesy the University of Chicago Library.

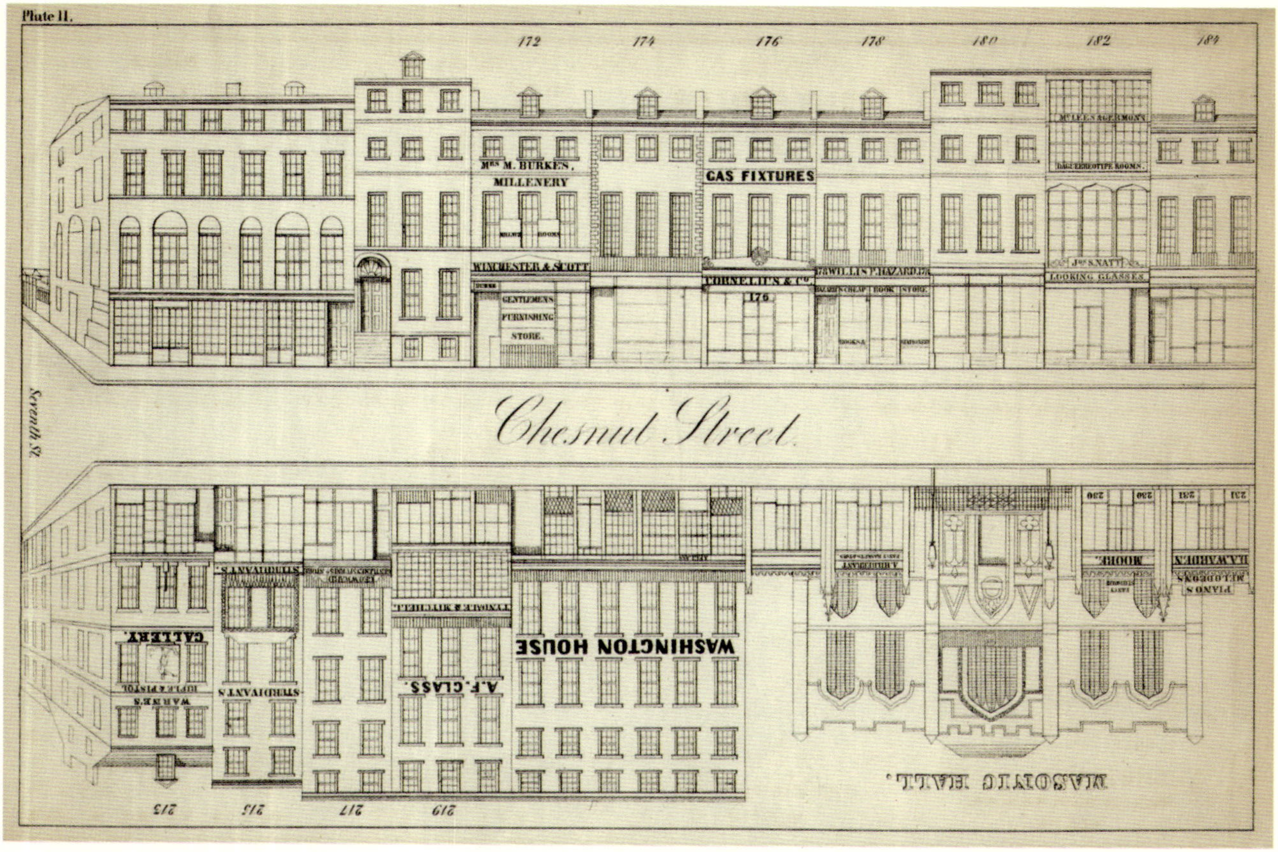

PLATE 5. Unknown artist, profile views of Chestnut Street from Seventh Street to Eighth Street (upper row pictures the south side; lower row, the north side). Illustrations from Julio H. Rae, *Rae's Philadelphia Pictorial Directory and Panoramic Advertiser* (Philadelphia, PA: Rae, 1851). Courtesy the Library Company of Philadelphia.

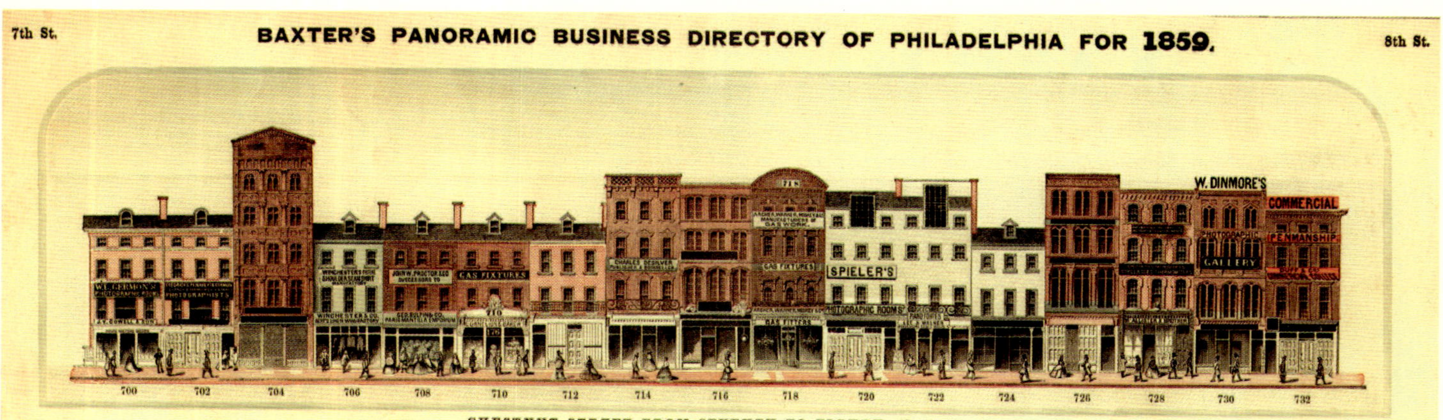

PLATE 6. Unknown artist, profile views of Chestnut Street from Seventh Street to Eighth Street (*above*, south side; *opposite*, north side). Illustrations from DeWitt Clinton Baxter, *The Baxter Panoramic Business Directory* (Philadelphia, PA: Baxter, 1859). Courtesy Athenaeum of Philadelphia.

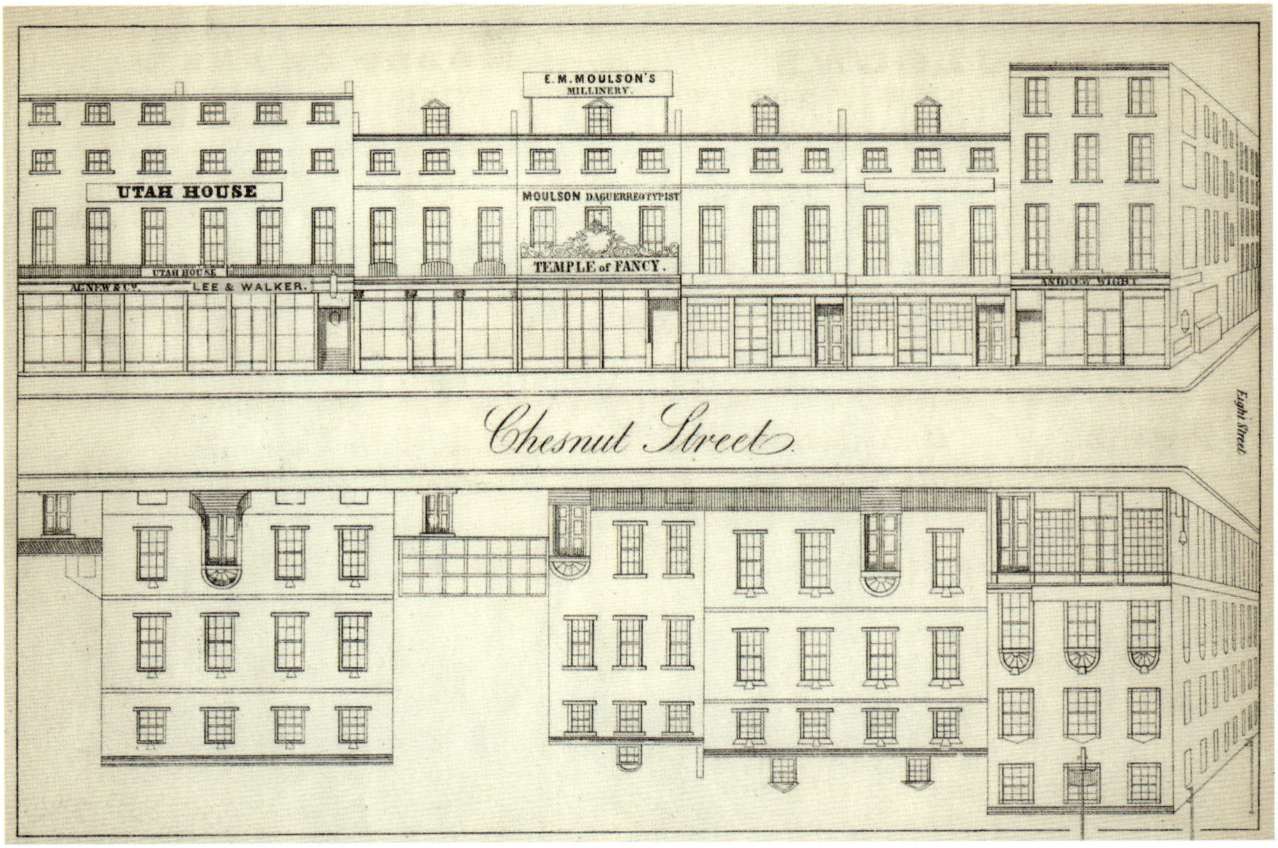
E. M. MOULSON'S MILLINERY.
UTAH HOUSE
MOULSON DAGUERREOTYPIST
TEMPLE of FANCY.
LEE & WALKER.
Chesnut Street
Eight Street

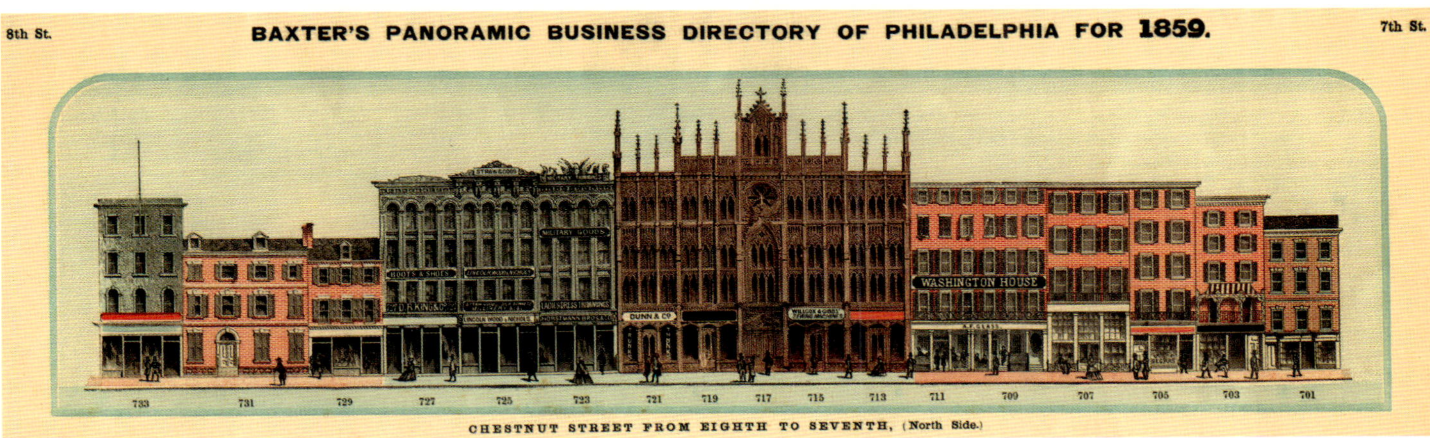
8th St.
BAXTER'S PANORAMIC BUSINESS DIRECTORY OF PHILADELPHIA FOR 1859.
7th St.
WASHINGTON HOUSE
DUNN & CO.
733
731
729
727
725
723
721
719
717
715
713
711
709
707
705
703
701
CHESTNUT STREET FROM EIGHTH TO SEVENTH, (North Side.)

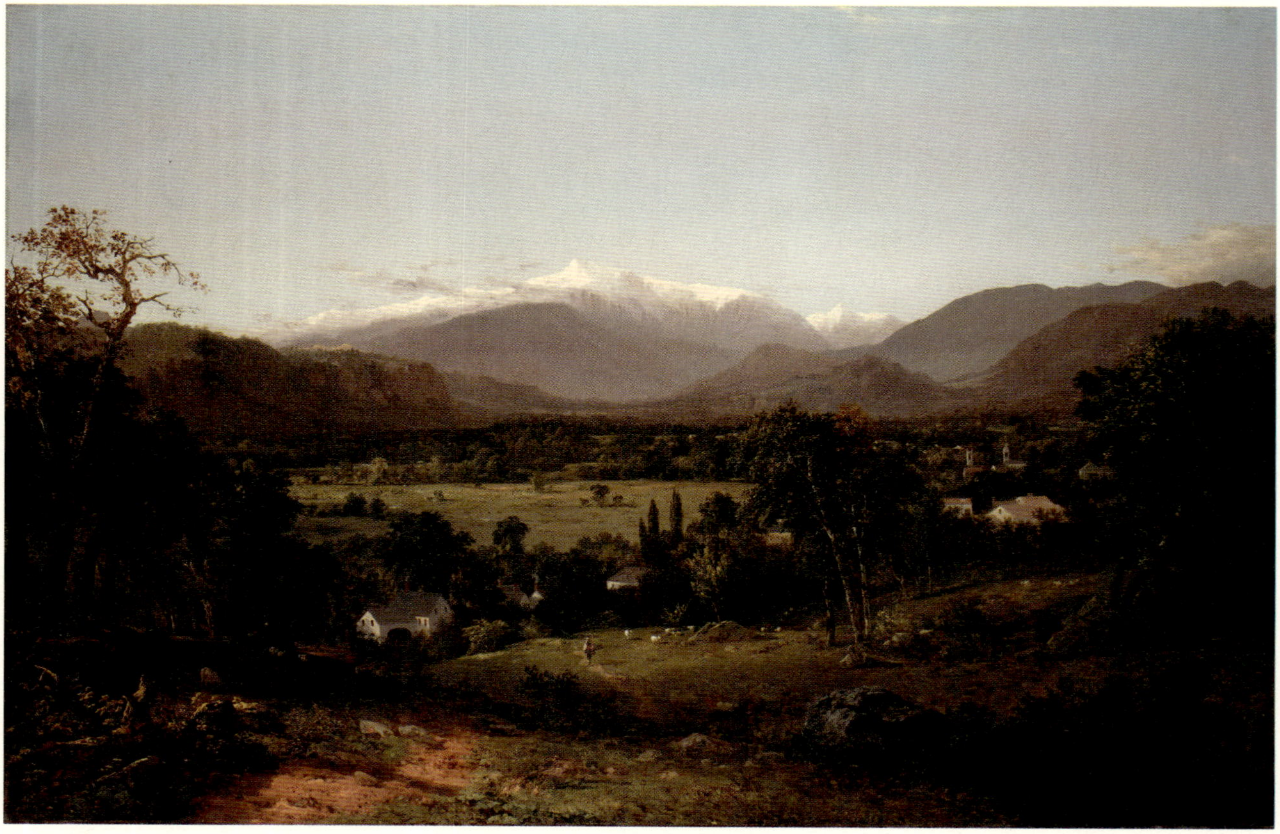

Plate 7. John F. Kensett, *The White Mountains—From North Conway*, 1851. Oil on canvas; 40⅜ × 60⅜ in. Courtesy Davis Museum at Wellesley College, Wellesley, MA. Gift of Mr. and Mrs. James B. Munn (Ruth C. Hanford, Class of 1909) in the name of the Class of 1909, 1977.37.

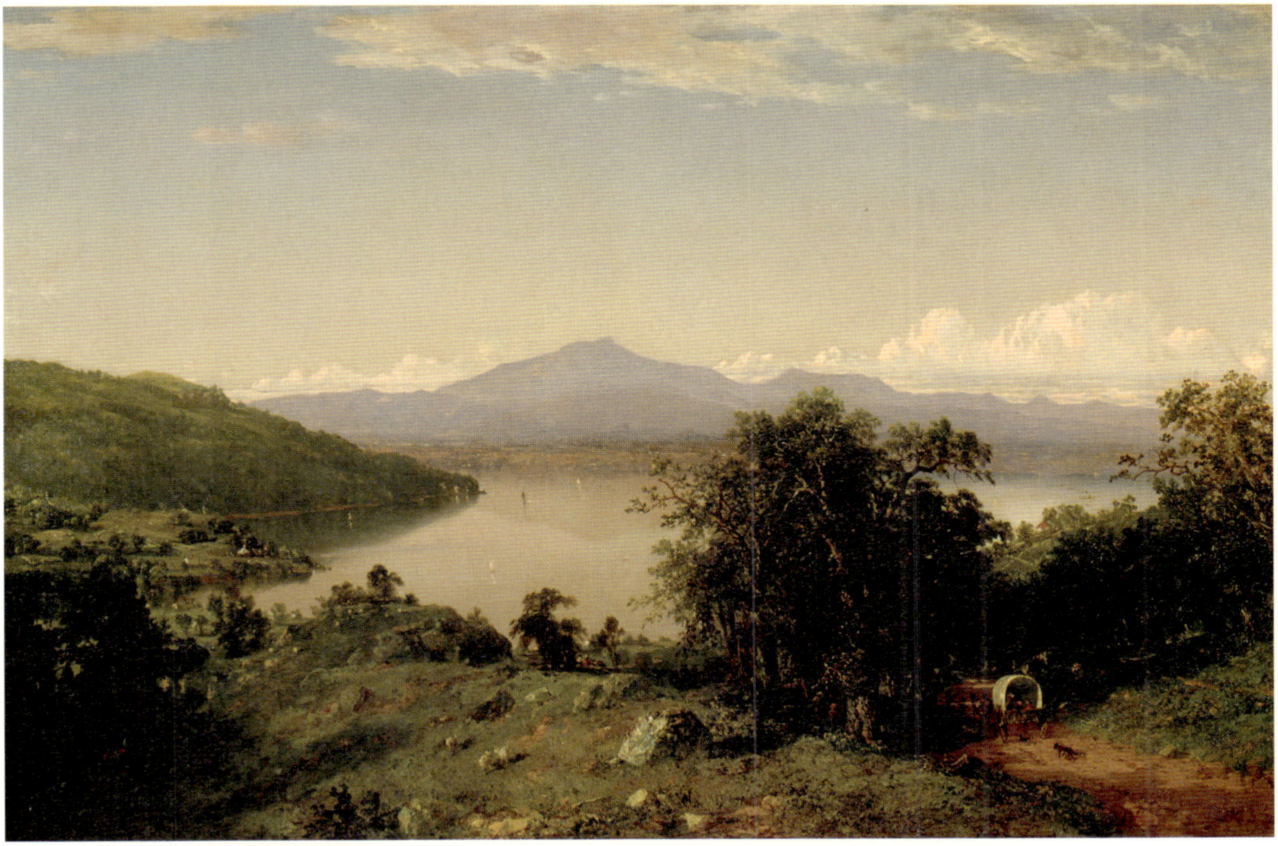

PLATE 8. John F. Kensett, *Camel's Hump from the Western Shore of Lake Champlain*, 1852. Oil on canvas; 31 × 42 in. Courtesy High Museum of Art, Atlanta, Georgia.

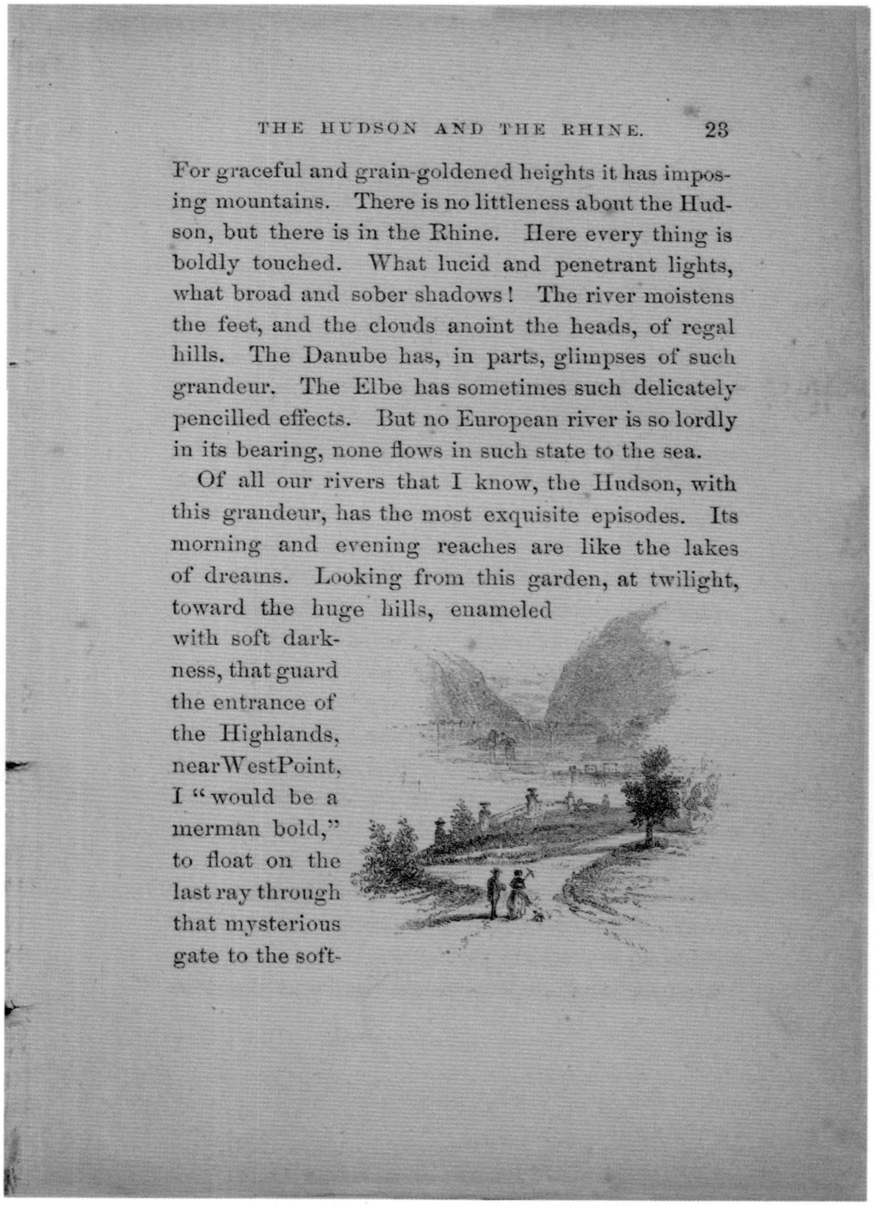

THE HUDSON AND THE RHINE. 23

For graceful and grain-goldened heights it has imposing mountains. There is no littleness about the Hudson, but there is in the Rhine. Here every thing is boldly touched. What lucid and penetrant lights, what broad and sober shadows! The river moistens the feet, and the clouds anoint the heads, of regal hills. The Danube has, in parts, glimpses of such grandeur. The Elbe has sometimes such delicately pencilled effects. But no European river is so lordly in its bearing, none flows in such state to the sea.

Of all our rivers that I know, the Hudson, with this grandeur, has the most exquisite episodes. Its morning and evening reaches are like the lakes of dreams. Looking from this garden, at twilight, toward the huge hills, enameled with soft darkness, that guard the entrance of the Highlands, near West Point, I "would be a merman bold," to float on the last ray through that mysterious gate to the soft-

PLATE 9. John F. Kensett, view up the Hudson River. Illustration from George W. Curtis, *Lotus-Eating: A Summer Book* (New York: Harper and Brothers, 1852).
Courtesy the University of Chicago Library.

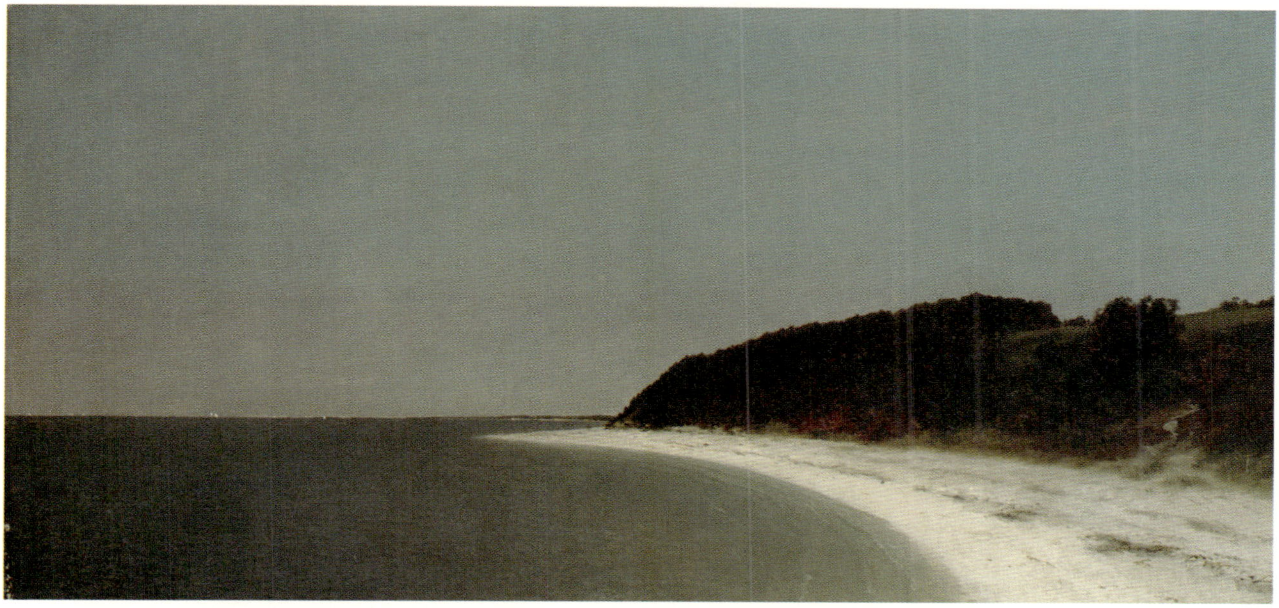

PLATE 10. John F. Kensett, *Eaton's Neck, Long Island*, 1872. Oil on canvas; 16 × 36 in.
Courtesy the Metropolitan Museum of Art. Gift of Thomas Kensett, 1874.

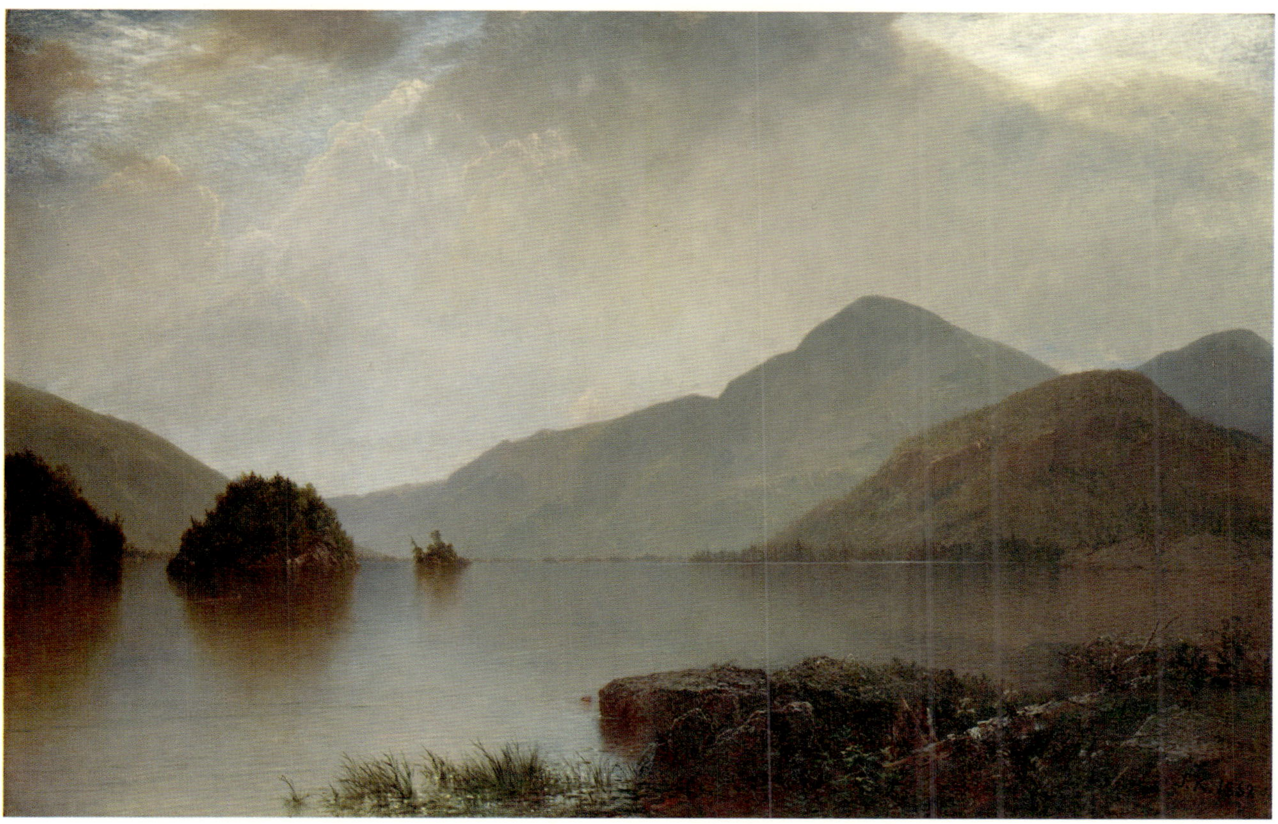

PLATE 11. John F. Kensett, *Lake George*, 1869. Oil on canvas; 44⅛ × 66⅝ in.
Courtesy the Metropolitan Museum of Art. Bequest of Maria DeWitt Jesup, from the collection of her husband, Morris K. Jesup, 1914.

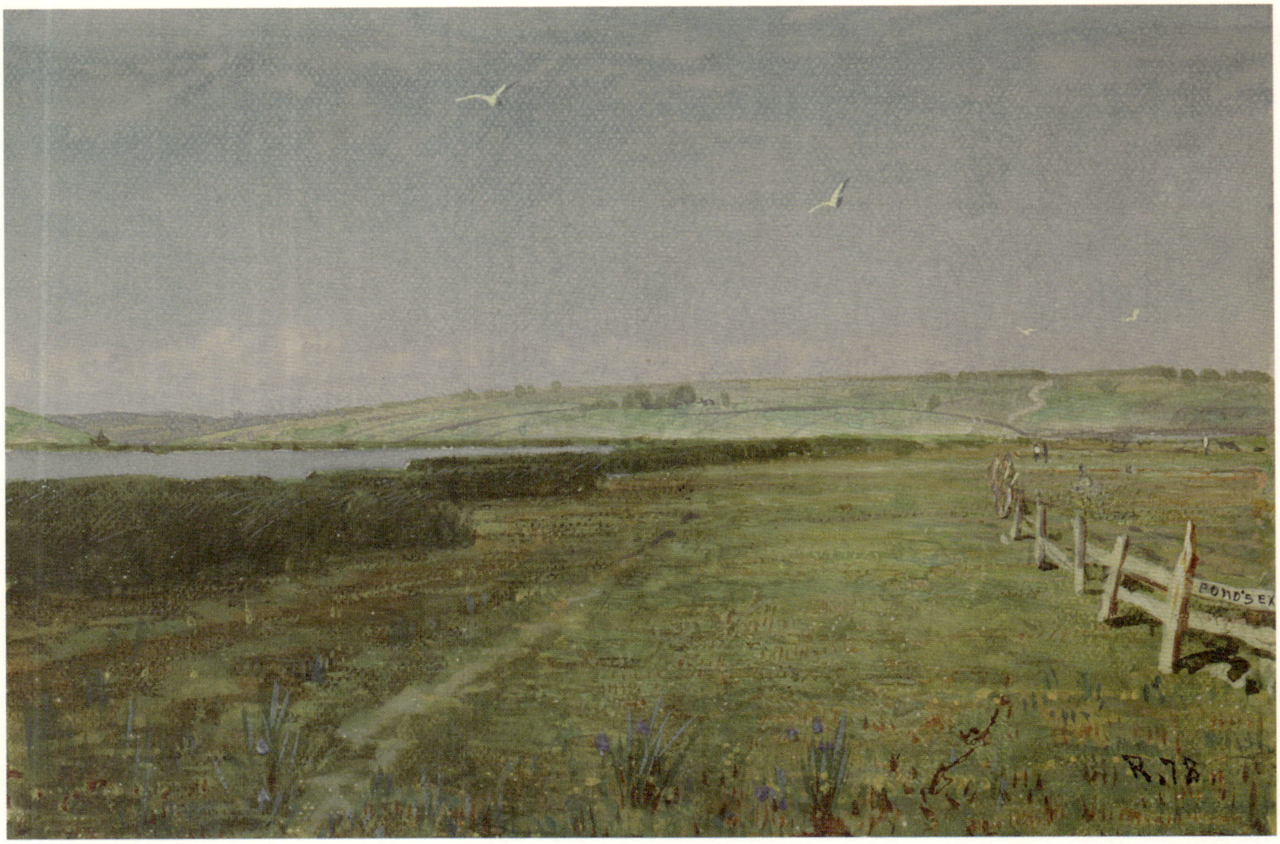
BOND'S EX
R.78

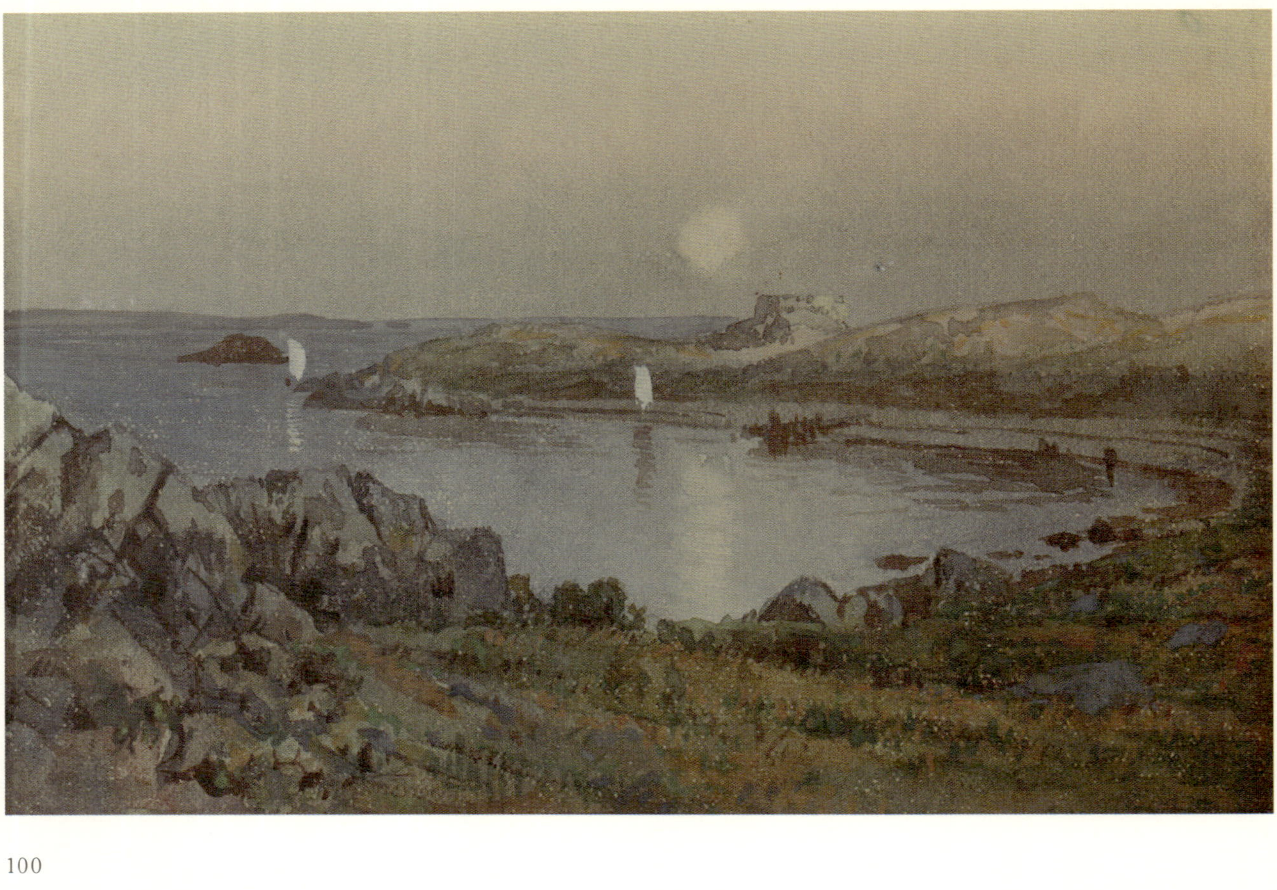

PLATE 12. *(opposite top)* William Trost Richards, *The South Side of the Pond, Newport*, 1878. Watercolor on paper; 3½ × 5¹⁄₁₆ in. 28.5.2008. Courtesy of the Pennsylvania Academy of Fine Arts, Philadelphia. Promised gift of Dorrance H. Hamilton in memory of Samuel M. V. Hamilton.

PLATE 13. *(opposite bottom)* William Trost Richards, *Salt Works Beach, Conanicut Island*, 1877. Watercolor and Chinese white on paper; 3¼ × 5 in. 18.5.2008. Courtesy of the Pennsylvania Academy of Fine Arts, Philadelphia. Promised gift of Dorrance H. Hamilton in memory of Samuel M. V. Hamilton.

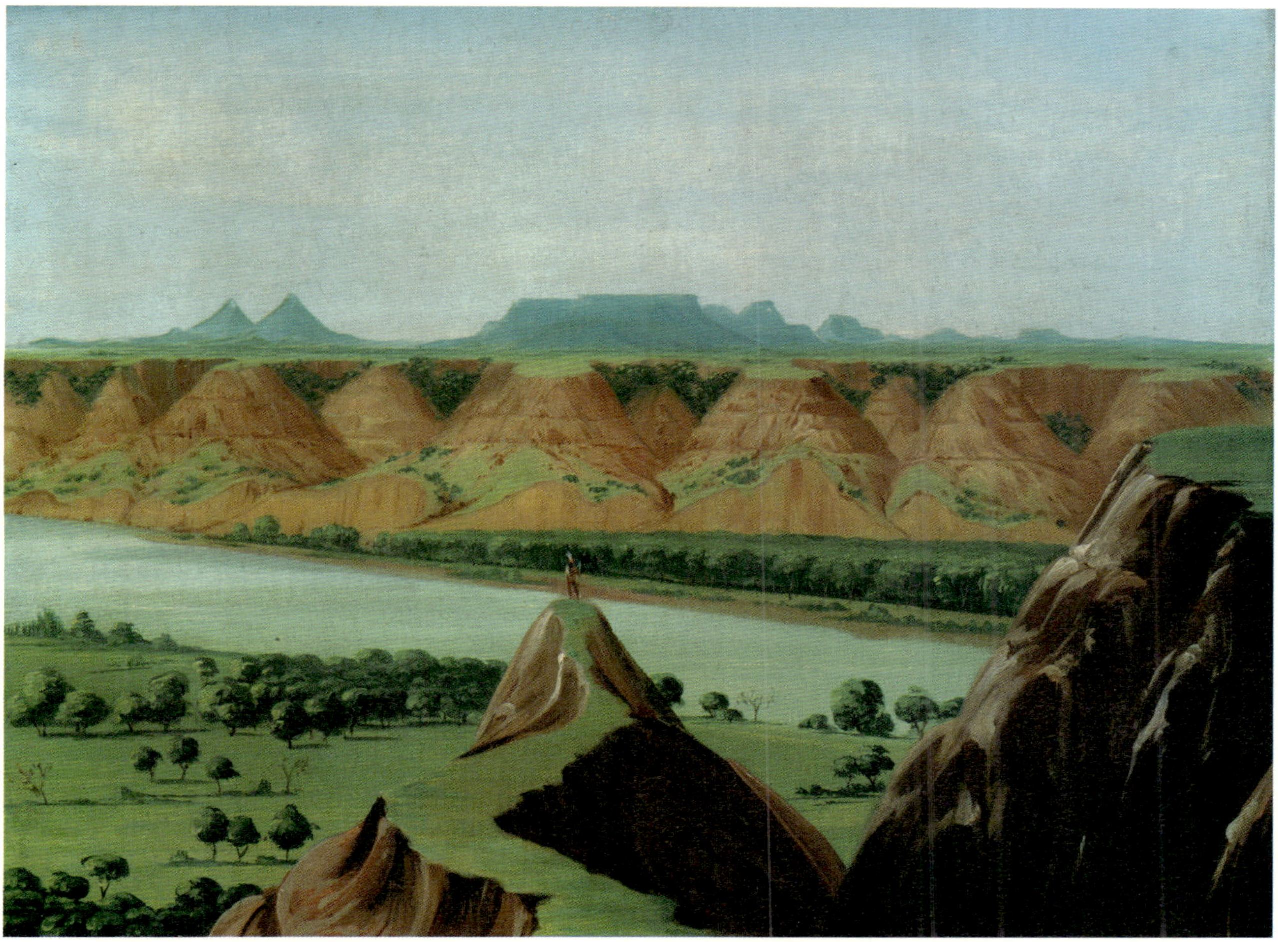

PLATE 14. George Catlin, *Big Bend on the Upper Missouri, 1900 Miles above St. Louis*, 1832. Photo credit: Smithsonian American Art Museum, Washington, DC / Art Resource, New York.

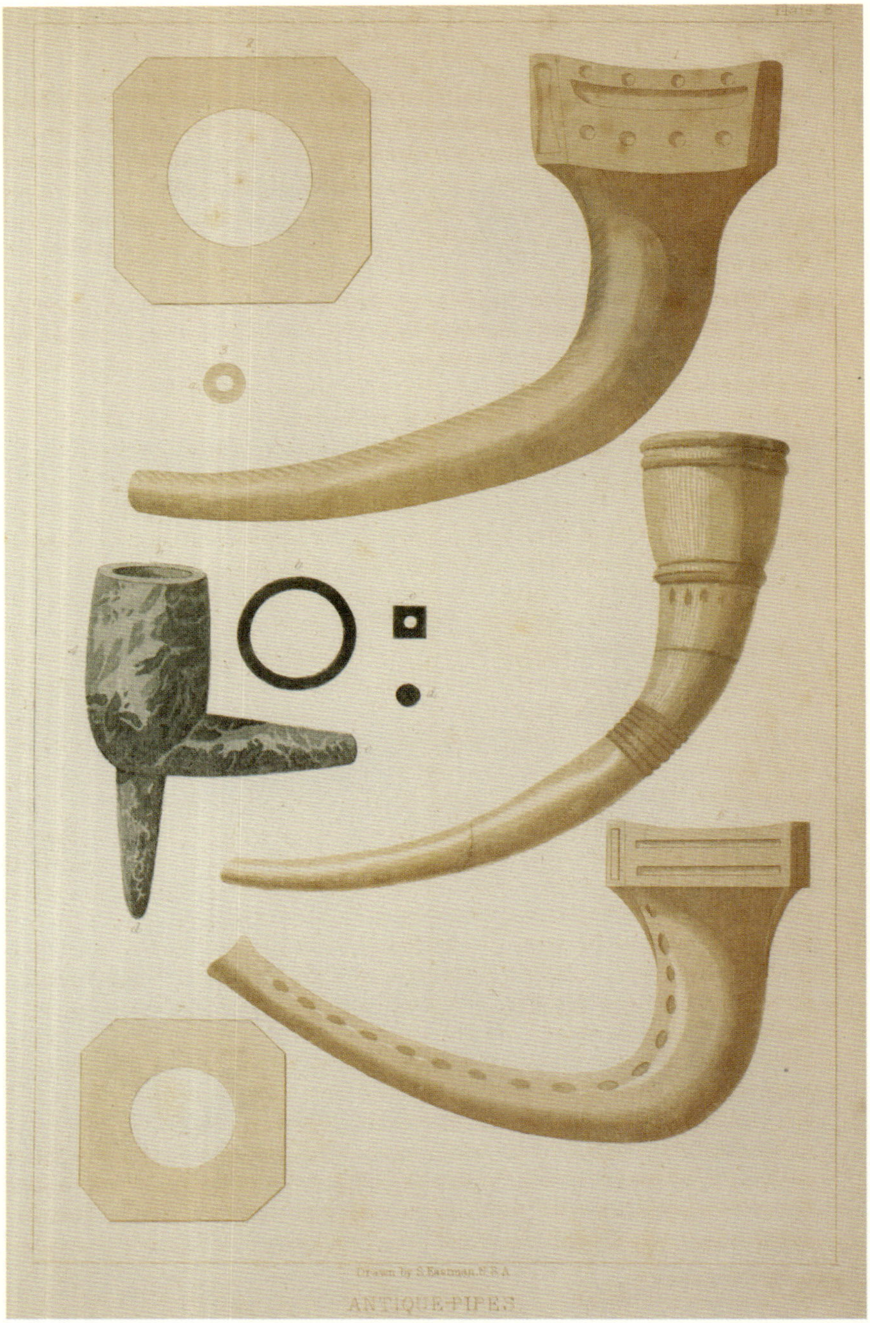

Plate 15. Seth Eastman, *Antique Pipes*. Illustration from Henry Rowe Schoolcraft, *Historical and Statistical Information Respecting the History, Condition, and Prospects of the Indian Tribes of the United States*, vol. 1 (Philadelphia, PA: Lippincott, Grambo, 1851–1857). Courtesy the University of Chicago Library.

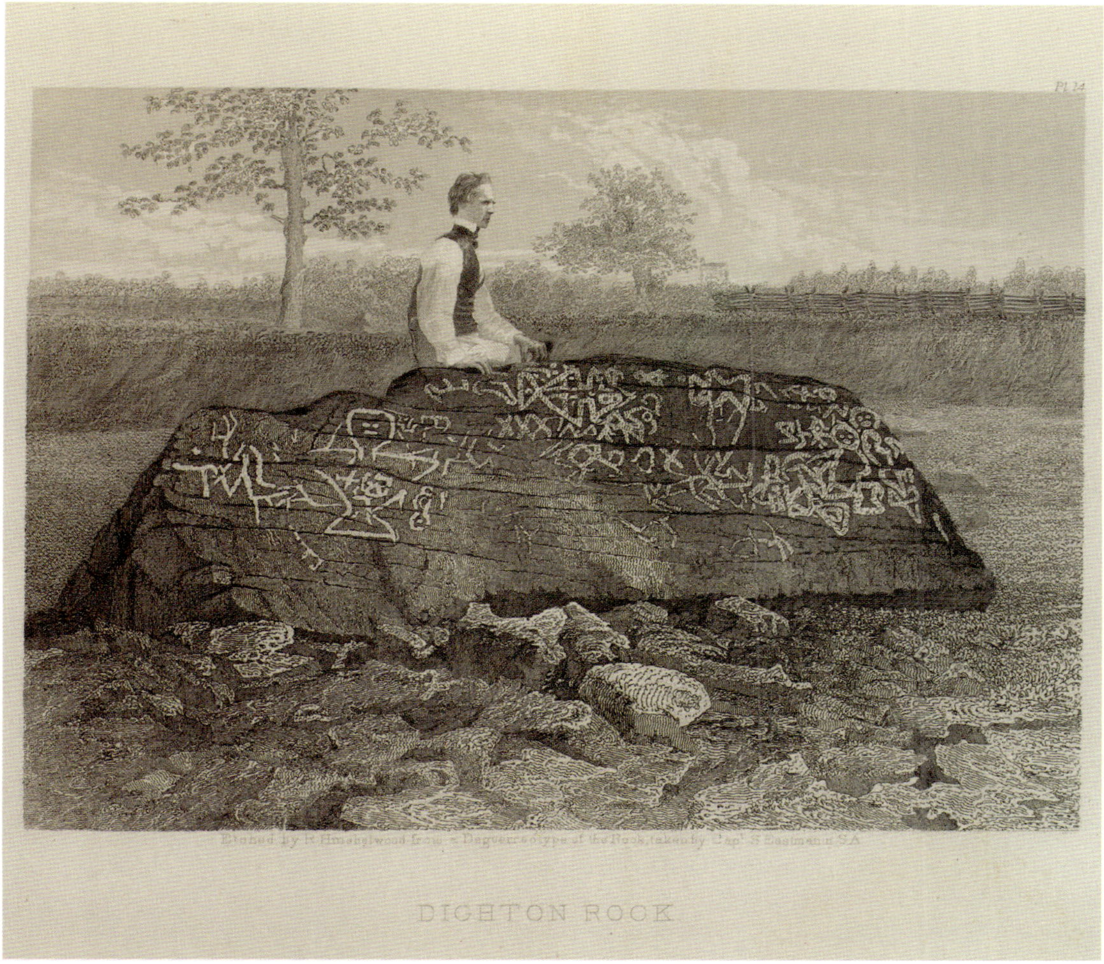

Plate 16. Seth Eastman, *Dighton Rock*. Illustration from Henry Rowe Schoolcraft, *Historical and Statistical Information Respecting the History, Condition, and Prospects of the Indian Tribes of the United States*, vol. 4 (Philadelphia, PA: Lippincott, Grambo, 1851–1857). Courtesy the University of Chicago Library.

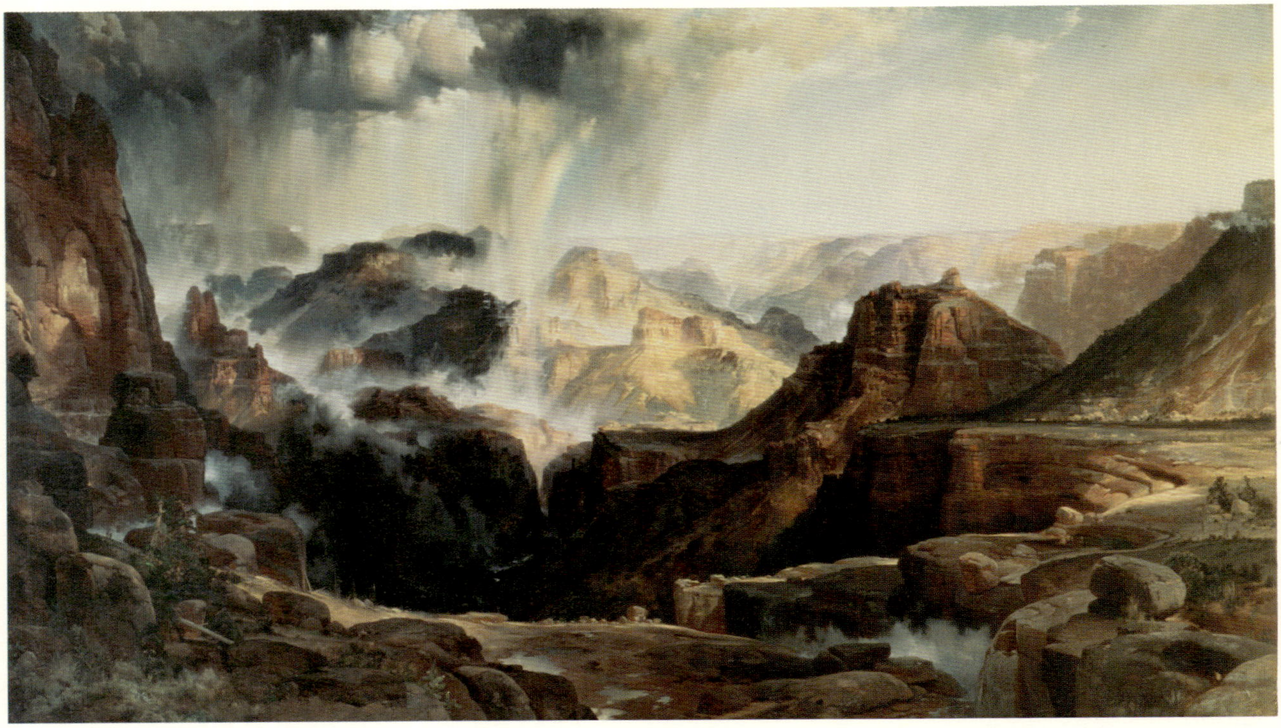

Plate 17. Thomas Moran, *The Chasm of the Colorado,* 1873–1874. Oil on canvas; 84⅜ x 144¾ in. Lent by the U.S. Department of the Interior, Office of the Secretary. Photo credit: Smithsonian American Art Museum, Washington, DC / Art Resource, New York.

Plate 18. *(opposite top)* Timothy O'Sullivan, *Tufa Domes, Pyramid Lake, Nevada,* 1867. Courtesy Davis Museum at Wellesley College, Wellesley, Massachusetts. 1984.6.2.

Plate 19. *(opposite bottom)* Timothy O'Sullivan, *Pyramid and Tufa Domes, Pyramid Lake, Nevada.* Illustration from Clarence King, *Systematic Geology,* vol. 1 of *Report of the Geological Exploration of the Fortieth Parallel* (Washington, DC: Government Printing Office, 1878). Courtesy Sandel Library, Northeast Louisiana University.

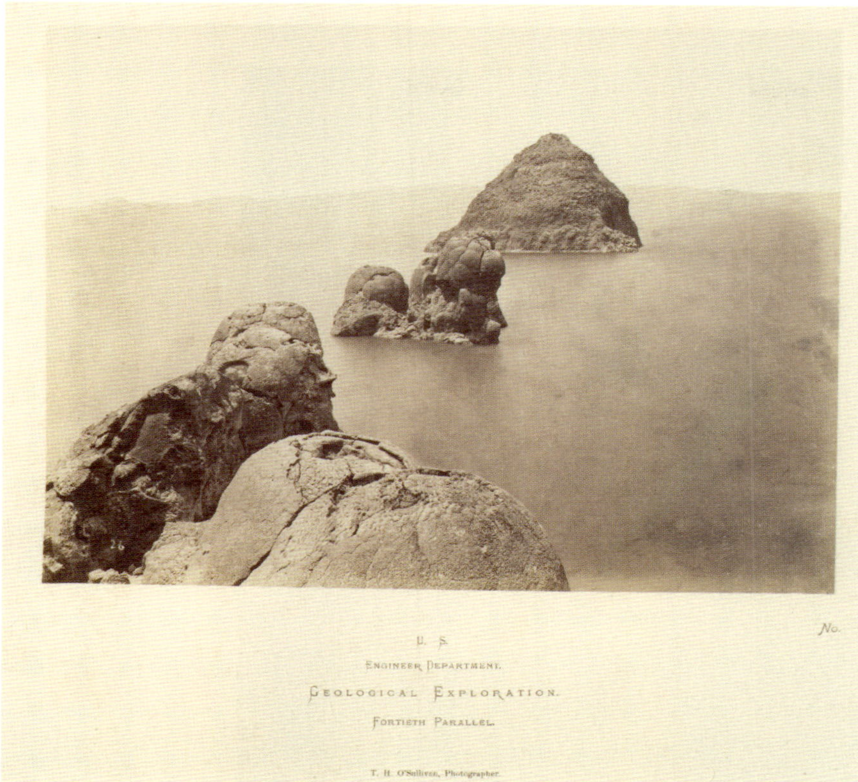
No.
U. S.
Engineer Department.
Geological Exploration.
Fortieth Parallel.
T. H. O'Sullivan, Photographer.

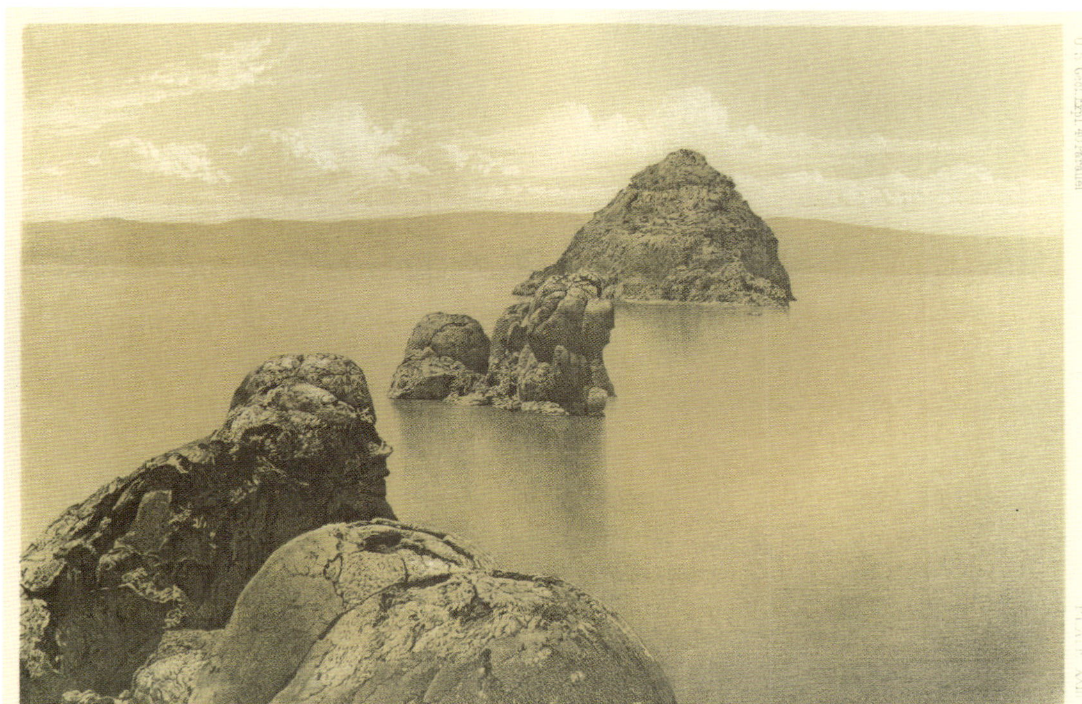
U.S. Geol. Expl. 40 Parallel
PLATE XXII
PYRAMID AND TUFA DOMES, PYRAMID LAKE, NEVADA.

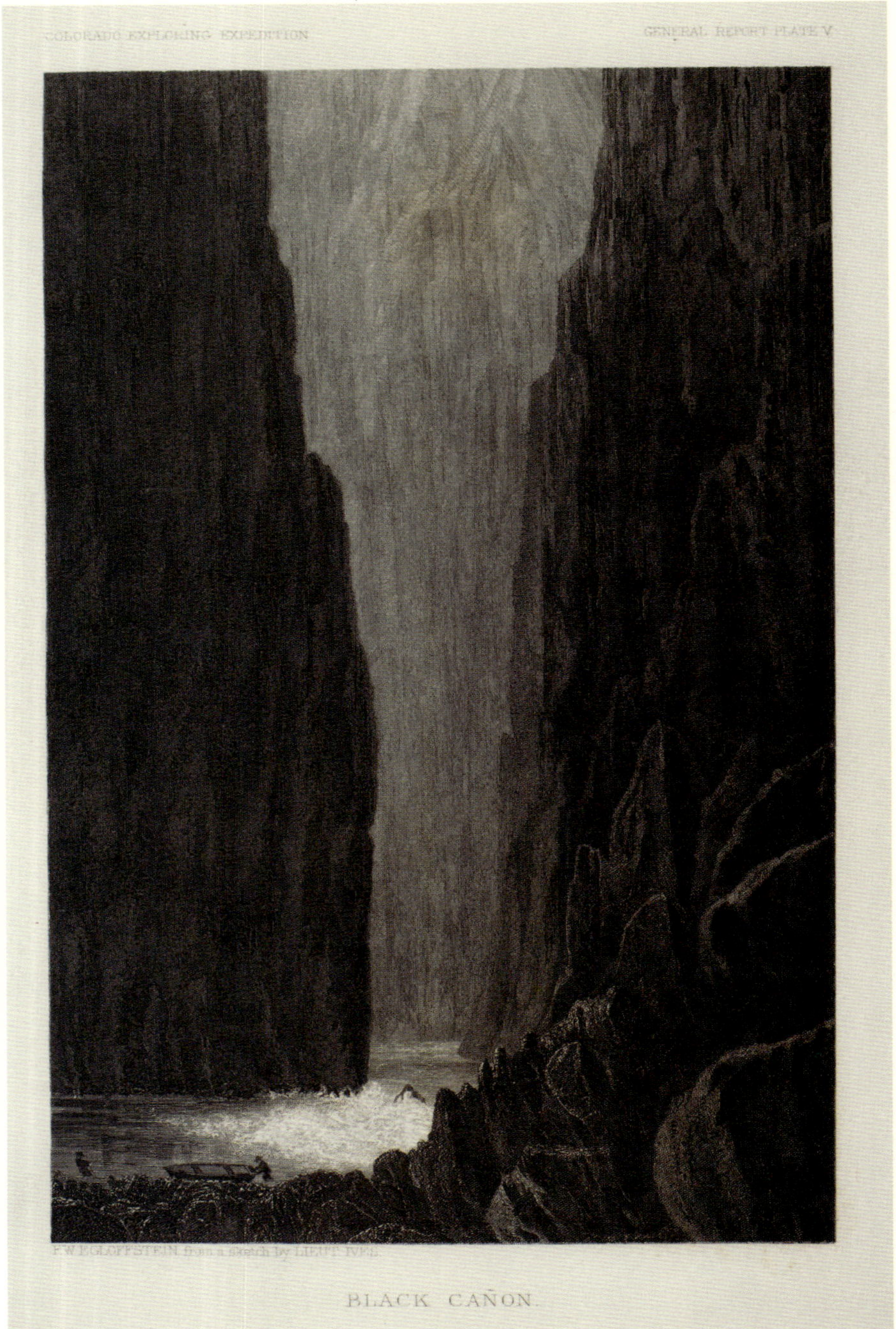

PLATE 20. F. W. von Egloffstein, *Black Cañon*. Illustration from Joseph C. Ives, *Report upon the Colorado River of the West, Explored in 1857 and 1858* (Washington, DC: Government Printing Office, 1861). RB 2676. Courtesy the Huntington Library, San Marino, California.

perceptions, then, what kind of historical understanding or conception of the past was brought to bear in the early development of scientific studies of American Indian cultures?

One influential approach can be associated with Henry Rowe Schoolcraft, a principal figure in midcentury ethnology and the author of the first comprehensive, federally funded survey of Natives in the United States. Addressing a recently formed New York antiquarian society (the "New Confederacy of the Iroquois") in 1846, Schoolcraft characterized the nation-building potential of ethnology by shifting away from one temporally significant location for the Indian (ahistoric nature) to another (the ruin), emphasizing the specifically archaeological character of the ethnological object:

> No people can bear a true nationality, which does not exfoliate, as it were, from its bosom, something that expresses the peculiarities of its own soil and climate . . . [drawn] from the broad and deep quarries of its own mountains, foundation stones, and columns and capitals, which bear the impress of an indigenous mental geognosy. . . .
>
> The tomb that holds a man derives all its moral interest *from* the man, and would be destitute of it, without him. America is the tomb of the Red man.[10]

Schoolcraft's exhortation remains immersed in natural metaphor, but his geological language urges a transition to ancient monuments, from "mountains" to "columns and capitals"—and indeed, he later likens contemporary Natives to "walking statues" of their ancestors.[11] The odd phrase "indigenous mental geognosy" condenses a sense of vast stretches of past time and natural and manmade formations—is the intention to assert that an "indigenous mental[ity]" has marked the American soil or to equate knowledge about Native culture and history to "geognosy," knowledge about the earth? The phrase also suggests a bridge between Native and white American civilizations, based on an archaizing view of the Indian, which transforms ethnology's object into its building blocks, as Roman masonry was reused in the construction of Renaissance churches. For Schoolcraft, saying that "America is the tomb of the Red man" is not so much forecasting the extinction of a people as it is predicating the nation, or at least American ethnology, on the archaeological framing of indigenous cultures, appropriating those cultures as a past that would otherwise be absent. In other words, the living "Red man" does not precisely "vanish" but is imagined as a presence, a monument, signifying "vanished" time.

In the present chapter, I examine the transition in temporal framing imposed by studies of American Indians in the mid-nineteenth century, from ahistoric nature to past monument. I focus on the works that were arguably most representative of either approach: George Catlin's *Letters and Notes on the Manners, Customs, and Conditions of the North American Indians*

(1841) and Schoolcraft's *Historical and Statistical Information Respecting the History, Condition, and Prospects of the Indian Tribes of the United States* (1851–1857).[12] For both authors, locating American Indian civilization in a history that was not continuous with the historical present was motivated in part by aspirations for government patronage in an era before the dominance of university science.[13] Catlin's numerous trips in the upper Missouri and Mississippi drainage, the basis for his *Letters and Notes,* its subsequent editions, and his Indian Gallery, were undertaken between 1830 and 1836, during the presidency of Andrew Jackson and immediately after the Indian Removal Act, a period that saw the most massive relocations of eastern Native tribes.[14] Although Catlin emphasized that settlement west of the Mississippi was a fast-approaching actuality, stressing a close connection between Indian and unimproved nature was still consonant with a federal Indian policy, which treated such settlement as a distant prospect. Similarly, Schoolcraft's six-volume work was published just before the opening of the transcontinental railroad, the instrument that effectively ended the policy of Indian removal and ushered in the reservation system. In such circumstances, the treatment of Native cultures as phenomena of the past would have appealed to a government confronted with diminishing open lands for relocation and eager to disavow its own role in bringing about the extinction of those cultures.[15]

In light of the factor of available land (what is "unimproved" or "wilderness") as an influence on federal Indian policy, it makes a certain sense that Catlin would privilege its existence, and thereby its plenitude, in forming a description of Native societies, while Schoolcraft would transform that landscape into an agent of obsolescence, a locality attesting to absence. More than merely agreeing with prevailing Indian policy, however, both authors conceived of their work as memorials of Native civilization, essentially as substitutes for that civilization, which they could present to the national government as a public service—in a sense, then, creating a memorial of the nation's past. At an early point in a subsequent edition of *Letters and Notes,* Catlin explained his motivation in studying "an interesting race of people, who are rapidly passing away from the face of the earth," as "snatching from a hasty oblivion what could be saved for the benefit of posterity, and perpetuating it, as a fair and just monument, to the memory of a truly lofty and noble race . . . to perpetuate them in a *Gallery unique,* for the use and instruction of future ages."[16] And again, slightly later, Catlin infamously declared:

> At last sunk into the earth, and the ploughshare turning the sod over their graves . . . I have flown to their rescue—not of their lives or of their race (for they are "*doomed*" and must perish), but to the rescue of their looks and their modes . . . phoenix-like, they may rise

> from the "stain on a painter's palette," and live again upon canvass, and stand forth for centuries yet to come, the living monuments of a noble race.[17]

Letters and Notes was intended in part to spur government interest in acquiring Catlin's Indian Gallery, the collection of portraits, genre scenes, and various artifacts that he had amassed during his travels; over the remainder of his life, he repeatedly but unsuccessfully lobbied Congress to purchase it as a vital component of the nation's heritage.[18] In the same vein, Schoolcraft's work was intended as a definitive record of American Indian civilization, to be used in the shaping of federal Indian policy. Schoolcraft conceived of that civilization as closed off in the past, however, accessible only through a kind of archaeological investigation, so that his record, like Catlin's, takes on the aspect of a memorial.

Both of these examples of early American ethnology exhibit a reifying impulse that has been the target of numerous critiques of past anthropological practice. As Mary Louise Pratt writes of Alexander von Humboldt's treatment of South American antiquities in his *Ansichten der Kordilleran und Monumente der eingeboren Völker Amerikas* (1810; *Views of the Cordilleras and Monuments of the Indigenous Peoples of America*): "The European imagination produces archaeological subjects by splitting contemporary non-European peoples off from their precolonial, and even their colonial past. To revive indigenous history and culture as archaeology is to revive them *as dead.* The gesture simultaneously rescues them from European forgetfulness and reassigns them to a departed age."[19] The central concern of the present chapter is to examine the crucial role played by the narrative deployment of landscape imagery in bringing about this kind of erasure.[20] Reification, making something abstract into something concrete, was another objective in coordinating text sections and printed illustrations in scenic guides, which provided their readers with a vivid experience of various models of the nation's history or different experiences of ownership and consumption. But a key difference is that Catlin and Schoolcraft endeavor to bring their readers close to a Native civilization that they also locate far away from their readers' temporal context. In the process, history, or rather the nullity of past time, is grasped to the extent that it figures as absent or lost—in Pratt's words, history is "revive[d] *as dead.*"[21]

In *The Predicament of Culture,* James Clifford describes how modern museum collections "create the illusion of adequate representation of a world by first cutting objects out of specific contexts (whether cultural, historical, or intersubjective) and making them 'stand for' abstract wholes—a 'Bambara mask,' for example, becoming an ethnographic metonym for Bambara culture. Next a scheme of classification is elaborated for storing or displaying the object so that the reality of the collection itself, its coherent order, overrides specific histories of the object's production and appropriation."[22] The works I examine are also in a sense collections, deliberately created assemblages of text and illustrations. Narrative itself is an ordering, "a scheme of classification for storing or displaying," and what I want to isolate in these ethnographic and ethnological works is how landscape (as text or illustration) facilitates modes of engagement with these texts that in turn influence the reader's impression of the temporal frame in which Native cultures are placed. Landscape is an especially effective form of mediation because its perception slips easily between an imaginative traversal, where one projects oneself into represented space, and an apprehension of something like an apparent totality. In general terms, as I articulate further in what follows, Catlin emphasizes the former in order to keep the reader in an ahistoric "now." Schoolcraft stresses the latter in order to present a subject whose time has already passed and who is thus rendered suitable for archaeological investigation.

George Catlin: The Artist as Ethnographer

The scholarly literature of today views George Catlin as a decidedly split personality: he is consistently credited with providing an important and vivid record of Plains Indian life on the edge of the nation's frontier during the Jacksonian era as well as consistently criticized for devising some of the most enduring and misleading tropes to figure those same people.[23] He is depicted both as a consummate showman and as a case study for artistic and entrepreneurial failure.[24] Catlin poses a severe challenge to modern historians who ponder the value of his work, seeking to determine to what degree his project can be taken seriously and whether to treat it as ethnography, art, or even a work of literature. A further complication in assessing Catlin's work is that the composite character of his published accounts and his Indian Gallery reflects the eclectic nature of ethnographic collecting, research, and writing at this time. The first secretary of the Smithsonian Institution, Joseph Henry, regarded this eclecticism as a strength, an opportunity for fruitful synthesis in a still relatively new and unconstrained field, but Henry's optimism could just as well be viewed as a generous outlook on a pervasive lack of rigor or system.[25]

The structure of *Letters and Notes,* and the effects of that structure in imposing a temporal frame on Catlin's subject, derive less from the eclectic nature of early ethnography than from his resolve to use *Letters and Notes* as an instrument of promotion for his Indian Gallery. Catlin's biographers generally portray his career as a series of frustrated attempts to turn his western travels in the 1830s into financial and cultural profit. Although he was able to exhibit his Indian Gallery quite successfully as a traveling show in East Coast cities and abroad, he additionally wanted to make his findings permanently public in the manner he thought most appropriate, as a national collection, or "*Gallery unique,*" containing his paintings and artifacts.[26] Various permutations of *Letters and Notes* were sources of stop-gap financing and crucial publicizing to elicit the interest of prospective government patrons for his gallery.[27] In other words, Catlin's marshaling of various established artistic, scientific, and literary perspectives in his descriptions of Plains Indian life can be understood as much for their value in legitimating his larger project, the Indian Gallery, for an audience of nonprofessional patrons with a diverse set of interests and agendas, as for their value in bringing out specific characteristics of those societies. What I examine here is how Catlin's promotional aims drive his articulation of his interests in recording Native cultures—especially in terms of art and history—toward a kind of immediacy and urgency that in turn conditions the temporal framing of his description of those cultures in *Letters and Notes*. If Catlin presents his work as a last chance to rescue some vestige of those cultures, soon to be eradicated or bastardized, this sense of mission is in part a transposition of his urgency to secure patronage onto his subject.

The promotional aspect of *Letters and Notes* translates into a perceptible ambiguity about how complete a representation he makes of his subject in this book, or more specifically about whether the book or the gallery is the fullest representation. The book itself comprises a series of "letters" that record Catlin's travels in the upper Missouri and Mississippi regions, accompanied by engravings based on the paintings he produced there. The first letter is actually a preface written just before publication, in which Catlin constantly shifts between introducing the book, subsequent books, and his gallery as the proper object of his reader's attention. He begins by apologizing "for making a book at all," then swiftly assumes the vantage point of a later work, from which he can look back at *Letters and Notes* and "take some considerable credit for not having trespassed too long upon [the reader's] time and patience."[28] As a result, *Letters and Notes* is already cast as a preliminary effort intended to gauge interest in what he later alludes to vaguely as "a subsequent and much more elaborate work, for which I have procured the materials, and which I may eventually publish."[29] Then, having explained that some parts of the book were originally published in the New York press, Catlin enumerates the collection of paintings made during his travels and then proceeds to reassure the reader that *Letters and Notes* faithfully reproduces them, while also remarking that the reader who visits his gallery will find that it, in turn, faithfully reproduces his narrative.[30] A kind of circularity is therefore generated that keeps the question of representational accuracy in motion among the various textual and pictorial forms of Catlin's travels.[31] Finally, the numerous endorsements reproduced at the end of the first letter uniformly attest to the accuracy of the gallery, variously titled "Indian Gallery" or "Collection," in a way that implies it is a truer record than the book itself.

Moreover, as Catlin's biographers consistently point out (with some frustration), *Letters and Notes* is actually a condensed version of several trips he made in the 1830s, now presented as a single travel account, "hastily compiled, at the urgent request of a number of my friends."[32] As a consequence, there is a conspicuous absence of dates, some confusion as to his route, and a tendency to reduce the "plot" of the narrative to the gathering of materials for his project, especially in those letters where he is actually describing different tribes, as opposed to traveling. Connections between letters are most often presented as returns to the scene of painting portraits: Catlin begins the seventh letter by noting a break in "the 'thread of my discourse' . . . leav[ing] my painting-room . . . to be taken up and discussed; which I will now endeavour to do," while he starts the eighth letter with "Since my last Letter, nothing of great moment has transpired at this place; but I have been continually employed in painting my portraits."[33] *Letters and Notes* ultimately reads as an account of how Catlin put his materials into a final form that may or may not be the book itself. This ambiguity becomes most apparent in Catlin's characteristic shifts in identifying his recording activity with writing or painting, with the book or the gallery. Thus, in the preface, he refers to his "literal and graphic delineation" and later states that he will "speak and paint" about the "primitive wildness" of the upper Missouri tribes, that he "will paint with my brush and scribble with my pen."[34]

By condensing his trips into one travel account, Catlin endeavors to attain two all but contradictory goals: one, to emphasize the authenticity and accuracy of his observations, made on the spot and presented without mediation; and two, to organize them into a polished form, one that will also bring out their value both as art and as history. Catlin seems to want to operate on the level of ethnography by preserving the freshness of his paintings (his "fieldwork"), while translating them into book form to meet demands for a more fully formed and adequate expression that will merit national attention—not an ethnology per se but a creation aspiring to that level of completeness. In the final analysis, Catlin wants the paintings to stand on their own, and this desire manifests itself even as he *writes*. A revealing instance occurs in his preface, where he states:

> It would be impossible at the same time, in a book of these dimensions, to explain *all* the manners and customs of these people; but as far as they are narrated, they have been described by my pen, upon the spot, as I have seen them transacted; and if some few of my

> narrations should seem a *little too highly colored,* I trust the world will be ready to extend to me that pardon which it is customary to yield to all artists whose main faults exist in the vividness of their colouring, rather than in the drawing of their pictures.[35]

Here Catlin proposes that the reader regard his writing as a work of art, one subject to a certain critical latitude, or, more accurately, indicates that he does not want to abandon that form of expression. Catlin thought of himself, after all, as an artist, and a work of art presumably requires no further accompanying exposition.

This split perspective on the book (one could say "raw" versus "finished") is especially evident when he situates *Letters and Notes* in relation to other texts. Thus, Catlin disdains the learned, specifically antiquarian, exposition of Native languages, origins, and relationships between tribes, undertaken by scholars who had never actually traveled west.[36] Simultaneously, though, he alternately emphasizes the error or the validity of viewing his record of direct observation according to prevailing literary genres: that is, as a written work whose completeness is determined by familiar literary conventions. Error is uppermost in the strikingly literal correspondence he often assumes between observation and writing; in his eyes, a given amount of writing takes a somehow equivalent amount of time away from experience.[37] Validity is uppermost in Catlin's likening of his experiences to the novels of James Fenimore Cooper and Washington Irving; in his eyes, his travels enabled him to actualize the fictional worlds of these authors in an experience that he terms "literally true."[38]

To maintain the impression of unmediated observation, while validating the adequacy of his work as art or history, Catlin effectively empties both his art and his history of any sense of depth or requirements of specialized knowledge. The world he describes is entirely self-enclosed, lacking any previous—and, as he forecasts, future—record resembling his own. There are no models of Indian portraiture (the "true" Indian, captured on the spot) and no models of Indian history (taken directly from the source) by which to judge his account. An even more important point for Catlin is that the Indian is accessible and knowable through immediate contact alone; there is no need for a more nuanced approach that would, for example, seek to understand Native codes of visual signification or traditions regarding the past. Catlin's emphasis on immediacy is transformed, finally, into urgency in his dramatic enlistment of the notion of the vanishing American, a theme to which he returns throughout his account. Thus, in his preface, he portrays the Indian as eminently accessible through contact, but in an assertion that both attacks current expansionist attitudes and establishes the value of his account, he simultaneously denies the possibility of such access.[39]

To justify the artistic value of his work, Catlin employs the association of Indian and nature in comparing his portraits to ancient Greek sculpture, particularly as it exemplified artistic beauty according to notions of purity and absence of artifice, as articulated in Johann Joachim Winckelmann's 1755 *Reflections on the Painting and Sculpture of the Greeks* and 1764 *History of Ancient Art*.[40] Catlin explains that his travels in the West furnished him with "those conditions, on which alone I was induced to pursue the art as a profession. . . . I mean the free use of nature's undisguised models."[41] As Winckelmann had rejected rococo excess and artifice, Catlin shuns "the specious refinements of the accomplished world" and "the ridiculous fashions of civilized society."[42] Similarly, he echoes the terms by which Winckelmann promoted his version of the Greek ideal of beauty as a sensuous evocation of a society solely concerned with the fullest realization of the body's athletic (and aesthetic) potential. For Winckelmann, the beauty of Greek art ultimately derived from the beauty of the Greek body. For Catlin, the same is true of the beauty of the Indian body: "I have for a long time been of opinion, that the wilderness of our country afforded models equal to those from which the Grecian sculptors transferred to the marble such inimitable grace and beauty. . . . [The Indians are] knights of the forest; whose whole lives are lives of chivalry, and whose daily feats, with their naked limbs, might vie with those of the Grecian youths in the beautiful rivalry of the Olympian games."[43] For Winckelmann and Catlin, then, artistic beauty is actually dependent on the absence of a more developed culture.

As Catlin scholars have noted, his paintings appear to be sensitive likenesses, capturing idiosyncratic details and suggesting definite personalities that are frequently elaborated by the commentary in *Letters and Notes,* but most often the individuals are identified by name only, and the general focus of textual explication is on peculiarities of costume, face painting, and weaponry.[44] Thus, the text accompanying one of the most frequently reproduced portraits, that of *Stu-mick-o-sucks (Buffalo's Back Fat)*, tells us only that he is a Blackfoot chief, "good-looking and dignified . . . and superbly dressed" (figure 31).[45] Certainly the fact that Catlin rarely resided for extended periods with a particular tribe put limits on the amount of information he could gather about specific individuals, and exceptions to his usually brief descriptions of individuals predominate among the Mandans, with whom he was able to stay for several months. His longest character sketch, for Mah-to-toh-pa (Four Bears), second chief of the Mandans, begins with an exhaustive inventory of his costume and ornaments, followed by numerous pages recounting his battles with the Sioux, Cheyenne, and Riccaree, which Catlin learned about by asking Mah-to-toh-pa to decode the pictographs on his robe. If Catlin largely avoids these kinds of detailed histories of interactions between tribes, he also characteristically condemns instances

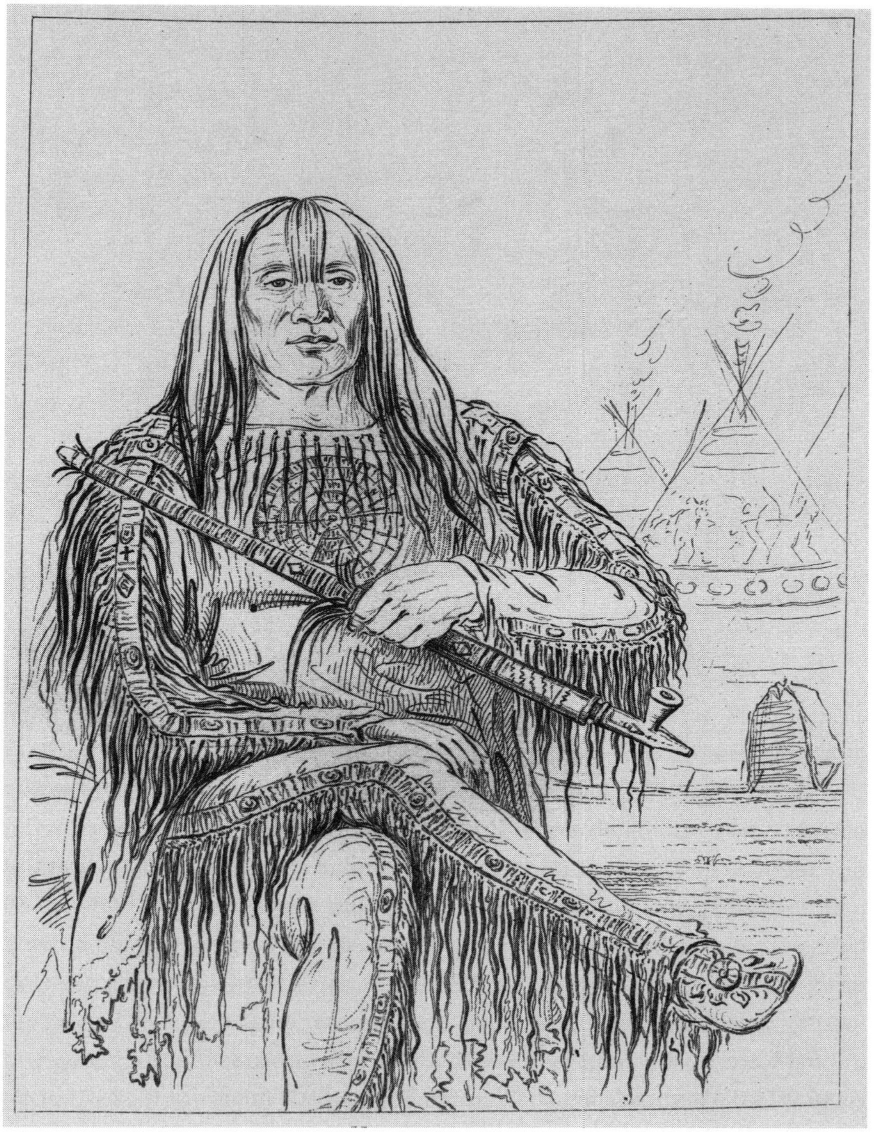

FIGURE 31. George Catlin, *Stu-mick-o-sucks (Buffalo's Back Fat).* Illustration from George Catlin, *Illustrations of the Manners, Customs, and Condition of the North American Indians* (1841; London: Bohn, 1851). Courtesy the University of Chicago Library.

when they adopt white American habits.[46] Contrarily, though, he also stresses the accessibility of Native customs to his readers, as pleasurable sport or theatrical spectacle, encouraging a visceral engagement with his text and the people he describes.[47]

This focus on the body and surface aspects such as clothing and ornamentation reinforces Catlin's comparison of the natural Indian to Winckelmann's Greek athlete; besides Winckelmann's interest in the Greek body, he devoted several chapters of the *History of Ancient Art* to the rendering of drapery in sculpture. Moreover, it might not be unjustified to see in the engraving style of *Letters and Notes* an effort to imitate the strong, almost geometric linearity of British neoclassical book illustration, exemplified by John Flaxman, as

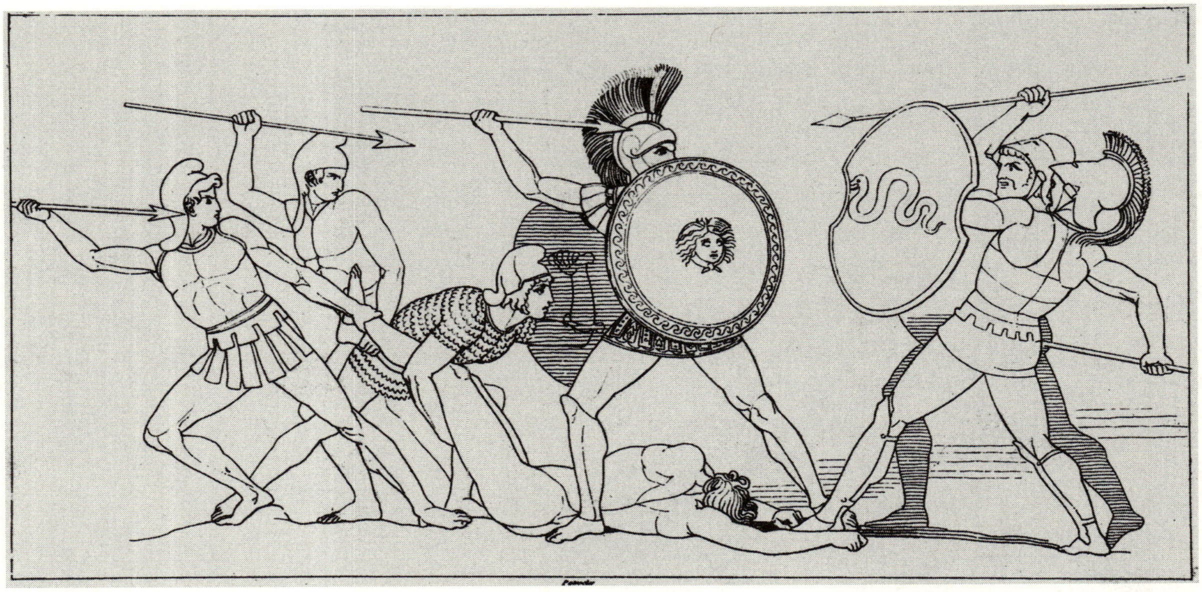

FIGURE 32. John Flaxman, *The Fight for the Body of Patroclus*. Illustration from *The Iliad of Homer Engraved from the Compositions of John Flaxman R. A.* (London: Parker, 1805).

in his illustrations for Homer's *Iliad* (figure 32). Flaxman's figures were in part based on the outline illustrations found in many archaeological works of the period, and illustrated editions of the *History of Ancient Art* from the nineteenth century continued to use a similar style.[48] In transposing the paintings into printed form, a similar vocabulary of bold contour outlines and faint, sometimes stippled interior lines for facial features and musculature is used; the absence of modeling and the necessary regularization of expression further results in figures that seem both generic and perfected. Especially in his pictures of groups of individuals, Catlin approaches the geometric regularity of Flaxman's figures (figures 32 and 33). This is not to say that he transforms his subjects into stone. The activities and postures depicted and certain small-scale differences in the use of the engraved line (the faint line running along the inside of women's faces, suggesting a sheen or glow to the skin) indicate animation. Perhaps not coincidentally, though, one of Catlin's English publishers, Henry George Bohn, was well known for his classical editions, and he acquired Flaxman's *Odyssey* plates and used them in an edition of Homer's epic that he published in 1841, the same year that *Letters and Notes* appeared.

I want to emphasize, though, how Catlin's equation of the natural Indian with Winckelmann's models for ancient Greek sculpture relocates the aesthetic value of his Indian portraits away from comparisons with other (contemporary) artists' work (as he remarks, "I have not here the benefit of that feeling of emulation, which is the life and spur to the arts, where

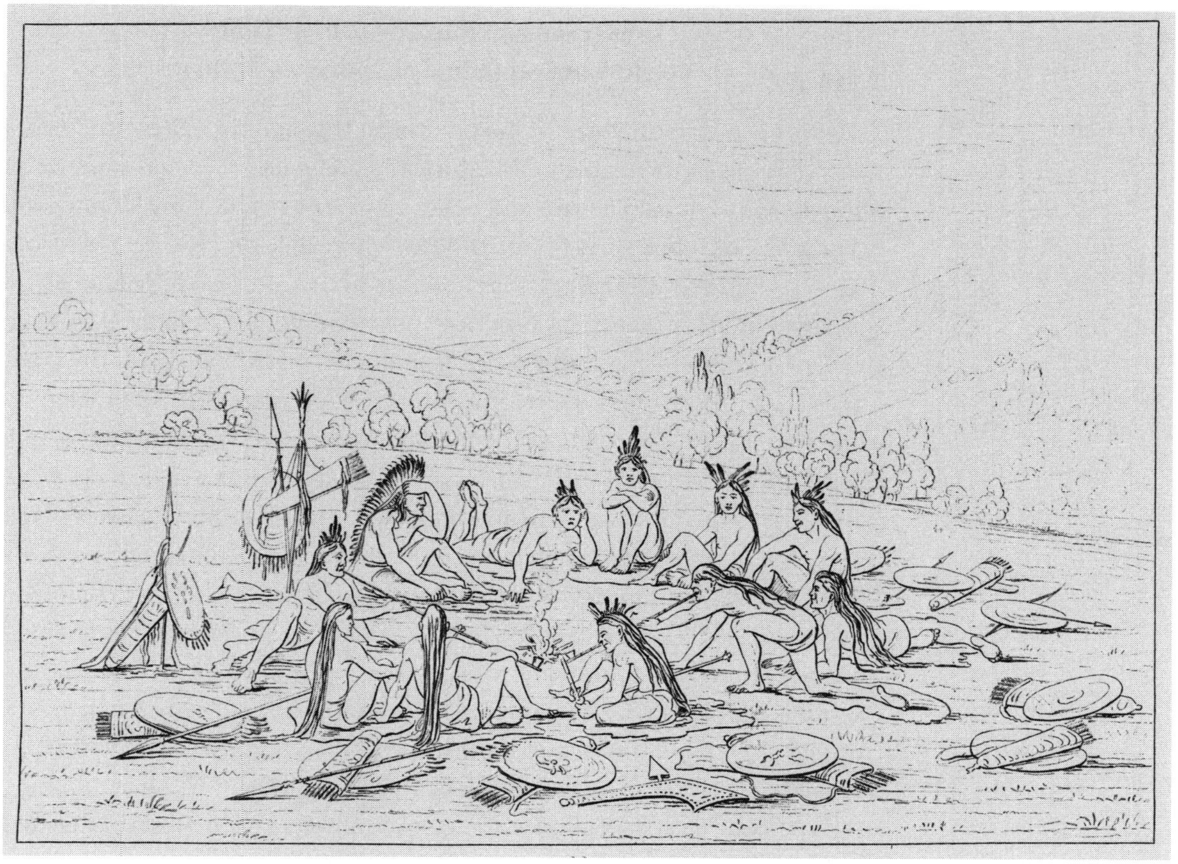

FIGURE 33. George Catlin, *Mandan War-Party.* Illustration from George Catlin, *Illustrations of the Manners, Customs, and Condition of the North American Indians* (1841; London: Bohn, 1851). Courtesy the University of Chicago Library.

artists are associates together"). Instead, their value as art rests on the reader's appreciation of Catlin's portrayal of the Indian as a purely physical, uncivilized being, a view he cultivated through his surface-oriented approach to portraiture. In addition, objections to Catlin's paintings' lack of finish, or the prints' summary descriptive quality, become recognitions of his lack of artifice and his more transparent recording of the beautiful Indian body. Finally, as I will address in the next section on his use of landscape, Catlin suppresses the relevance of history as a meaningful category by which to define Native culture. Buffalo hunts and rain dances are thrilling because they are experienced for the first time, as opposed to being habitual practices, connected to a history of migrations, conflicts, and other events. Immediacy legitimates the value of Catlin's work as art or history, and the experience of landscape offered by his narrative text and its relation to his prints is a primary device by which he reinforces that sense of immediacy for the reader/viewer.

Landscape and Narrative out of Time: The Ahistorical Indian of *Letters and Notes*

Besides the artistic value of his paintings, throughout *Letters and Notes* Catlin stresses their eventual historical significance: "In addition to the knowledge of human nature and of my art . . . the result of my labours will doubtless be interesting to future ages; who will have little else left from which to judge of the original inhabitants of this simple race of beings."[49] In affirming this historical function, however, he not only assumes the lack of a future for the Indian, but also denies the relevance of the past. This is not to say that questions of origin and alterations over time do not arise in the observations he made of the Native societies he visited. Especially with regard to the manufacture of weapons, articles of clothing, and other aspects of outward appearance, Catlin carefully gleans as much information as he can, often pointing to the past.[50] Generally, though, he emphasizes that his Native informants regard past events as "involved in mystery" or, to use the Native neologism that he favors, "medicine." Catlin is no doubt faithfully reporting his informants' attitudes, but the continual repetition of "medicine" in his book, "habitually applied to every thing," has the effect of solidifying a sense of the past as irrelevant or nonexistent. If the past is medicine, and the medicine bag is a common ritual object, a sack "stuffed with grass, or moss, or something of the kind . . . [and] religiously closed and sealed, and seldom, if ever, to be opened," the implication is that Indian history is significant only as an unknown, that investigation would find nothing there.[51]

Instead, Catlin depicts the Indian as fully realized and contained in the present, and nowhere is this portrayal more evident than in his letters on the Mandans. The principal village of this tribe was located about a week's journey by boat from the American Fur Company's outpost at the mouth of the Yellowstone River—the starting point of his narrative. Catlin was able to reside in this village for much of the summer in 1833, painting portraits; recording the Mandan hunting habits, kinds of games, and other distinctive activities; and finishing with his sensationalistic account of the "Mandan religious ceremony" (or *okipa* ritual). Catlin's biographers have noted how he uses the Mandans to emphasize a contrast between natural and civilized modes of living, reviving the tradition of the Noble Savage to energize his critique of an increasingly complicated and materialistic modern society:

> No one can look into the wigwams of these people . . . without being at once struck by the conviction that small-talk, gossip, garrulity, and story-telling, are the leading passions with them, who have little else to do in the world, but to while away their lives in the innocent and endless amusement of the exercise of those talents with which Nature has liberally endowed them . . . they are free

> from, and independent of, a thousand cares and jealousies, which arise from mercenary motives in the civilized world; and are yet far a-head of us . . . in the real and uninterrupted enjoyment of their simple natural faculties.[52]

This natural, pleasurable, and virtuous mode of living is directly related to the absence of concerns for past and future, a predisposition that is in turn fostered by the Mandans' environment. As he puts it: "They live in a country and in communities, where . . . their inclinations and faculties are solely directed to the enjoyment of the present day, without the sober reflections on the past or apprehensions of the future."[53] Although Catlin is at times hopeful about acculturation, subsequent critics have long noted that his preferred solution for encroachments on Native land is the creation of a natural park that would enable his Indians to continue living in their wholly natural manner.[54] His own enthusiasm for what he sees as the pristine, at times explicitly edenic, landscape of the Great Plains is conspicuous, and he offers a model for viewing this landscape that recreates his description of the Mandans' idyllic society. In turn, the many prints of scenic views in his book give the reader an opportunity to experience it vicariously as well; the reader's visual engagement with the landscape can viscerally reinforce what he claims it is like to live as a Mandan.

Nevertheless, Catlin's prints notably fail to reproduce the richness and saturation of his original paintings, even though some limited editions included hand coloring. The saturated hues of a painted view of the Missouri River, at Big Bend—just upstream from the Mandan village—is matched by the text's attention to color—repetitions of "rich," "deep," "verdant," and so on—but this intensification is absent in the accompanying illustrations (figure 34 and plate 14). While the text's focus on color acts as an expedient measure to offset the necessity of printing in black and white, it is also possible to interpret the lack of color in the illustrations as emphasizing a temporal aspect similar to how the portraits' graphic reproduction references a classicizing figure style. Instead of the lush environment described by Catlin, the book's prints show a landscape that seems arid, blanched, altogether emptied or drained, creating the impression that whatever richness it possessed is no longer there (figure 35). The prints' sterility may be a means of further drawing attention to Catlin's paintings, produced on the spot and therefore closer to the moment of edenic experience, just as his painted portraits more fully capture the expression and personality of his sitters than their print versions.

More specifically, this difference between painting and print is one of many aspects of Catlin's representation of landscape in *Letters and Notes* that work to convey his dual perspective on the temporal frame enclosing the Plains Indians: being fully realized in the present and yet doomed to a swift and inevitable extinction. This dual perspective squeezes the Indian's

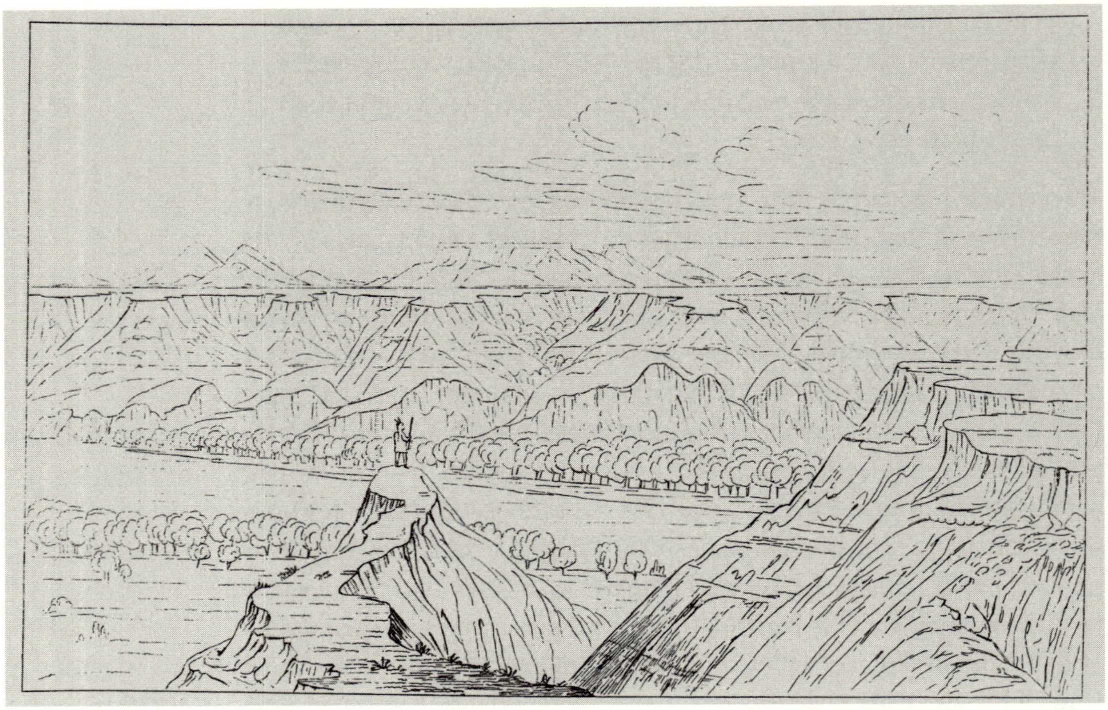

Figure 34. George Catlin, *View of the Missouri River from the Big Bend.* Illustration from George Catlin, *Illustrations of the Manners, Customs, and Condition of the North American Indians* (1841; London: Bohn, 1851). Courtesy the University of Chicago Library.

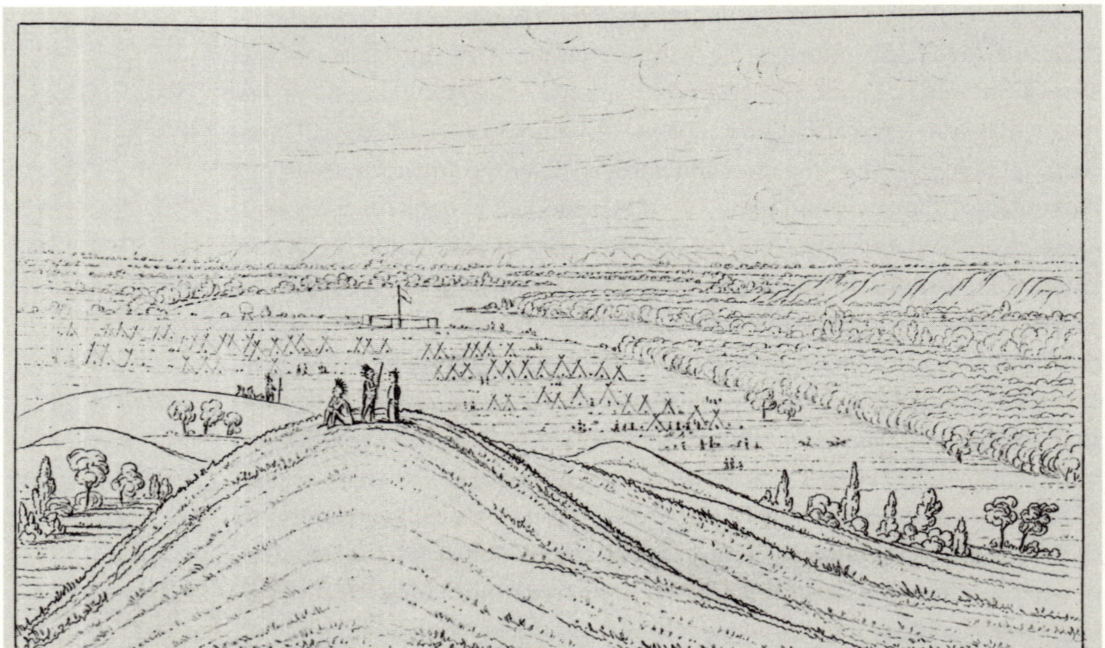

Figure 35. George Catlin, *View of the American Fur Company Fort.* Illustration from George Catlin, *Illustrations of the Manners, Customs, and Condition of the North American Indians* (1841; London: Bohn, 1851). Courtesy the University of Chicago Library.

place in time into a present that rapidly vanishes, a vanishing instant, which Catlin, like many of his contemporaries, localizes in the notion of the frontier.[55] Such a collapsing of time registers the impoverishment of the expansive eighteenth-century notion of the natural and timeless Noble Savage by the nineteenth-century version, now fast approaching the status of history (which is in part accepted and promulgated in Schoolcraft's work). In his book, Catlin offers an experience of the frontier by coordinating narrative text and landscape prints to promote a form of spectatorship in sympathy with the characteristics of historical time associated with the frontier. The early scenic guidebooks discussed in chapter 1 stressed prolongation, the eye moving from point to point and recognizing the signs of the past or lingering in distance, but here the perception of landscape is reformulated as a passing glance that slips over points in space too quickly to register any enduring element or presence.[56]

This association of the passing glance with the frontier emerges most clearly in Catlin's ninth letter. Having arrived at the American Fur Company fort at the mouth of the Yellowstone, he reflects on the moving location of "the *classic* West" that is home to the Plains Indians:

> the bane of this *blasting frontier* has regularly crowded upon them . . . and, like the fire in a prairie, which destroys everything where it passes, it has blasted and sunk them, and all but their names, into oblivion. . . .
>
> Few people even know the true definition of the term "West"; and where is its location?—phantom-like it flies before us as we travel, and on our way is continually gilded, before us, as we approach the setting sun.[57]

Catlin then recounts how the "West" has moved west over time, from Niagara Falls to Buffalo to Cincinnati to St. Louis, concluding by reporting a comical conversation he had with his landlady in this last city about the elusive "West." In other words, the textual dynamic propels the reader from historical exposition into the immediacy of dialogue just as Catlin arrives at the frontier. The whole excursus, however, is preceded by a description of the country around the fort: "A traveller on his tour through such a country as this, has no time to write. . . . Impressions, however, of the most vivid kind, are rapidly and indelibly made by the fleeting incidents of savage life. . . . The mind susceptible of such impressions catches volumes of incidents which are easy to write."[58] He is baldly explaining here his own role in recording "savage life," taking down "Impressions . . . of the most vivid kind," like his paintings, another shift from writing to painting that becomes explicit as Catlin goes on to describe "this *shorn* country": "it is but to paint the splendid panorama of a world . . . with its thousands of miles . . . where nought but silence reigns." This evocation of an empty, vast, silent landscape, redoubling the bleached appearance of the book's prints, is then followed by his remarks on the frontier.

Catlin reverts to the passing glance again and again as he travels over the Great Plains: he "indulg[es his] eyes in the boundless and tireless pleasure of roaming over the thousand hills." "The summit level of the great prairies stretch[es] off to . . . an almost boundless extent," and "the prairies . . . sweep off from the brink of the precipice [adjoining the Missouri], almost level, to an unknown distance."[59] His descriptions of animals and people moving swiftly across the landscape, especially in his accounts of the buffalo hunt, function similarly to evoke smaller-scale versions of the correlation of vision, movement, and time represented by the frontier. In addition, objects on the prairie are most frequently seen at a distance, with the eye passing quickly over the intervening and undifferentiated landscape to identify specks on the horizon as game or potential enemy. Despite the prints' small scale, they replicate this impression of rapidly traversed vastness, as in a view from his trip to the American Fur Company fort (figure 35). These spaces contain a minimum of arresting points along the viewing path, while objects relatively near at hand are already diminished in size, mimicking the distance-seeking gaze of the traveler on the prairie.[60] Catlin's simplified outline forms further reduce the capacity of the viewer to distinguish objects as figures, trees, and tents, which become so faint that the horizon almost disappears and the eye moves back into the whiteness of the page. Finally, elevated views follow the course of the riverbed in a direct progression into depth, stretching out the serpentine compositional elements of the picturesque view that retarded the eye's progress, as in Cole's *River in the Catskills* (plate 3).

Although these prints are related to spatial constructions found in contemporary landscape painting, they contain nothing to hold the viewer's attention, in terms of either visual or historical interest. Whereas the features in Cole's painting (the foreground stumps, the farms, the town's buildings, the distant railroad) evoke a history of development, any such narrative is generally absent in Catlin or presented in a much more abbreviated form, as in a compressed transition from a foreground group of Indians to tents to fort, the first sign of the frontier's inevitable disappearance (figure 35). Catlin does frequently compare landscape features with picturesque ruins, a familiar staple of the picturesque travel account, but the prints of such (generally geological) forms seem more strange than suggestive of crumbling edifices. Conversely, human habitations are often compared with natural formations. Just before reaching the Mandan village, Catlin encounters "an extensive village of prairie dogs": "I have subjoined a sketch of one of these *sub-terra* communities . . . their houses or burrows are all alike, and as their location is uniformly on a level and desolate prairie, without timber, there is little room for variety or dissimilarity."[61] Arrived at the Mandan village, he describes it in similar terms; it is located on "an extensive plain" and is "semi-subterraneous," "built entirely of dirt," and comprising lodges that "all have a circular form."[62] The accompanying print shows the Mandans socializing on their rooftops, perched on mounds like the chatty prairie dogs. Both the geological formations and the human or animal earthworks are represented as largely transient, surface phenomena, reinforcing the surface orientation of Catlin's portraits. The variegated, artificial shelves and towers abutting the river are composed of loose dirt and gravel, easily eroded by the action of rain, ice, and flooding, while the Mandan lodges are quickly erected—a necessity for a seminomadic people—and they have neither basement nor upper story, thus barely modifying the level expanse of the prairie.

Besides this agreement in the textual and pictorial treatment of landscape, the notion of time localized in the frontier and experienced as a passing glance structures the organization of narrated events, but not the exposition of the customs of the Plains Indians that validates the documentary status of Catlin's book. *Letters and Notes* is, after all, a travel account, dedicated to giving the reader the pleasure of vicariously participating in Catlin's journeys, and the impression made by his observations relies in part on the reader's immersion in this story of movement through the Great Plains. At the same time, however, Catlin's determination to capture and preserve American Indian culture gravitates away from too closely tying or reducing his description of that culture to the story of movement. Instead, the book divides into two distinct kinds of letters, ones recounting his travels, and ones containing observations on various tribes. Each of these two kinds of accounts is controlled by a different narrative time. On the river, there is a clear sequence of events leading to a definite end, a destination, and these sections are also often dated. At the American Fur Company fort, the Mandan village, and the other Native habitations that Catlin visits, letters more often develop as accounts of various aspects of social life without any real sense of a story line and without chronology. This distinction might be merely a convenient characterization of two different kinds of writing except for two key considerations. In the first place, the repeated pronouncements of the Indians' doomed fate lead the reader to expect the descriptions of customs and social life to serve a more ambitious historical purpose than being mere sketches of an existing and locatable people. In the second place, access to the Indian in Catlin is insistently framed in terms of travel.[63] It might be said that Catlin equates geographic and temporal distance, in the manner faulted by anthropological criticism. It is more accurate to see him as foregrounding a negative comparison between the sequence and permanence of the record of his travels and the kind of present-tense narrative that would capture the life of the natural, ahistoric Plains Indians. If there can be no history of a people who are totally immersed in the present, they are equally denied a position in a record of movement through space, and this dual eclipsing is how the frontier passes over its victims. Catlin often employs the present tense in making his observations in the Mandan village ("There is really a newness and rudeness in every thing that is to be seen. There are several hundred houses or dwellings about me"), but his "now" attaches itself, in the sense of a narrative order, to nothing; like the objects of the passing glance, it too is passed over.[64]

The fact that Catlin places illustrations of landscape primarily in these sections that recount his travels enacts this eclipsing of Indian time in several ways. Occurring in groups, these landscapes form a chain that reinforces the sequence of events recorded in the text, while their relative suppression of duration and other picturesque compositional devices prompt viewers to project themselves into the depicted space in an imagined form of travel that associates them more closely with the narrator's movement. In contrast, landscape prints appear infrequently in the sections describing the Plains Indians, and when they do, they usually contain little in the way of identifying landmarks. They neither form a chain within the book, nor are their features connectable to a larger recognizable environment, as if the Mandan village rises up out of nowhere. Finally, sequential time seems to happen on the river in a way that excludes the Indian. Not only is the ordered and dated travel account associated with the river (as the route and as the repeated focus of the landscape prints), but the progressive incursions of explorers and trappers are recorded there as well. Even Catlin's tentative geological speculations tend to focus on the river as the main agent of erosion, producing the supposedly picturesque bluffs on either bank. Thus, when Catlin leaves the river to immerse himself in the world of the Crows, Blackfeet, Sioux, and Mandans, he also leaves behind the chain of time, a departure embodied in the tiny Indians routinely depicted on the hilltops, helplessly gazing down at but detached and distanced from the flowing Missouri River below them (figures 34 and 35).[65]

Henry Rowe Schoolcraft: The Problem of the Indian's Past for American Ethnology

Whereas Catlin employs textual and pictorial representations of landscape to convey and reinforce the absence of past and future for the Indian, Schoolcraft's *History, Condition, and Prospects of the Indian Tribes* deploys the image of landscape more variably to qualify the perception of history, reflecting a complex set of motivations and representational tactics that tug at the relationship he draws between the past and American Indian civilization. Schoolcraft's multivolume report was intended to aid the formulation of a general federal Indian policy by providing more precise data on the location, population, languages, and basic customs of all American Indian tribes currently inhabiting the nation's territory. The focus of the report was thus ostensibly on the present and the future; as he writes in his preface to the first volume:

> Occupying the peculiar relation of a mixed foreign and domestic character, the intercourse [between the United States and the Natives living within its borders] has called for the exercise of a paternal as well as an official policy. . . . What line of policy is best suited to advance their prosperity? The present plan of collecting information respecting their actual condition, character, and prospects, is based on an appeal to the entire official organization of the Department on the frontiers . . . and may serve as the record from which the tribes are to be judged.[66]

Schoolcraft's appeal to "the entire official organization of the Department on the frontiers" refers to the transfer of the Office of Indian Affairs from the Department of War to the recently created Department of the Interior (in 1849), marking a new era in the government's relationship with Native tribes. Instead of concluding treaties with different tribes as "foreign" powers to accommodate the pressures of westward expansion, a policy based on the availability of land, henceforward the Native population would be more intensely managed within areas explicitly conceived as lying within the nation's territorial limits, a change that would later culminate in the reservation system.[67] Indeed, one of the primary goals of Schoolcraft's report was to clarify, belatedly, the distribution of the Native population after the serial relocations of tribes following the Indian Removal Act of 1830 and subsequent treaties concluded to facilitate white settlement of lands west of the Appalachian Mountains.

Despite this practical and immediate purpose, however, Schoolcraft's opus is striking in the way it keeps returning to the subject of the past. Although its title suggests a forward movement in time, it keeps reverting to historical topics in its larger organization. Much of the report comprises accounts, surveys, papers, and completed questionnaires written by explorers, army officers, specialists, and Indian agents. The sections actually authored by Schoolcraft are not only typically historical, but they also often evince a higher level of interest, a more involved thought process, and a greater amount of effort than the sections that address contemporary customs, practices, and beliefs. In a fundamental fashion that determines how the report conceives and presents ethnological knowledge, the Indian is perceived as a phenomenon of the past—an artifact. Schoolcraft articulates this perspective again and again:

> the Indian tribes . . . remain unchanged to this day; a monument . . . far more inscrutable, than the pyramids of Egypt, if for no other purpose, it would seem, yet to operate as a stimulus to our humanities, national virtues, and sense of justice. . . .
>
> The most antique things in [the United States], appear to be the people themselves. . . .
>
> The extreme antiquity of Indian society appears to be attested by their adherence to the patriarchal state.[68]

I want to trace how Schoolcraft promotes this "archaeological" view through the orchestration of various kinds of narratives, which has the ultimate effect of collapsing contemporary Native civilization into the past. The past is presented as the implied totality of that civilization, the contours of which are progressively delineated in the course of his reports. In *Letters and Notes,* the historical frame surrounding the Indian was reinforced by immersing readers in the travel account and the landscape illustrations, a recurring emphasis on the "now" or this-is-happening. In Schoolcraft's reports, even accounts of present conditions seem to be directed toward shedding light on preexisting ones. The overall sense is that of reconstruction or, better put, decipherment—the implication that anthropological knowledge is characteristically produced in relation to a preexisting whole not subject to change in the present.[69] In turn, images of landscape strengthen this orientation by appearing to be self-contained in various ways, suggesting or at least allowing the impression to form of an already completed passage of time. More importantly, a certain kind of landscape, the ruin, critically empowers Schoolcraft to give substance to this impression. Schoolcraft's principal means of accessing Native civilization is through language. Both contemporary and earlier Native texts are translated or otherwise represented (as phonetic transcriptions) within the reports as anthropological knowledge. Although he juxtaposes these texts in a way that suggests the "pastness" of that civilization, only in his putative deciphering of pictographs—rock inscriptions—does he succeed in establishing a concrete location for that civilization (which is elsewhere more generically described) and a method of producing knowledge that is correspondingly "concrete." Place and method in Schoolcraft are symbiotic: they reinforce their respective concreteness as well as the sense of pastness they impart to Native civilization. Place and method together yield effects of crystallization that forcefully impose a pastness on Native civilization that is only implied elsewhere in the reports.

History, Condition, and Prospects of the Indian Tribes was written during a period of renewed interest in Native American archaeological remains, prompted by the discoveries of ancient (as well as recently deserted) villages in survey expeditions of the Southwest after the conclusion of the U.S.-Mexican War of 1846–1847.[70] These explorations were documented and usually published for a restricted governmental readership—that is to say, a congressional one—although Schoolcraft would certainly have had access to them. The accounts of these discoveries included a number of efforts to locate a viable route for a transcontinental railroad, as well as the results of the official U.S.-Mexican Boundary Survey.[71] The significance of Native monuments and artifacts is a recurring subject in the early history of the United States because these monuments and artifacts belie the perception of the Indian as a purely natural being amenable to the teleology of advancing civilization underwriting western expansion.[72] Polygenists such as Squier sharply distinguished between ancient and modern Natives, but Schoolcraft sought to conflate living American Indians with their ancient ancestors, to view them as "walking statues." His report gave him the opportunity to establish this perspective as inherent in the discipline of ethnology.

Yet I want to emphasize that this archaizing impulse does not merely or even primarily arise from a common set of ideas about the Indian as barbaric, primitive, or backward. Nor do the effects of the archaizing impulse manifest themselves only in an unbalanced form of synthetic reasoning and a methodology that diverts information about contemporary Natives to the project of illuminating the archaic Indian. For Schoolcraft, the past itself seems to be *the* issue, because a precise understanding or articulation of the past could condone or condemn current relations between white and Native Americans. In his various prefaces and dedicatory letters, Schoolcraft appears preoccupied with justifying federal Indian policy by the standard of its past fairness. He gives the impression that he is aware of past *un*fairness but also of being unable to shake the force of a connection between developments in current policy and prior courses of action.[73] Similar ambivalence shows in Schoolcraft's vacillating attitudes toward the possibility of acculturation and the question of the unity of mankind.[74] In the same vein, his ongoing interest in the distribution of Native tribes at the moment of initial contact with Europeans, under the rubric "General History" in volumes two and three, appears to be motivated by a tacit recognition of the consequences of that contact over the subsequent centuries. Schoolcraft distills excerpts from explorers' and early colonists' accounts as well as speculations about the migration of *Zea mays* (maize) into an *Ethnographical Map of the Indian Tribes of the United States* A.D. *1600* (figure 36). The rationale underlying this map is

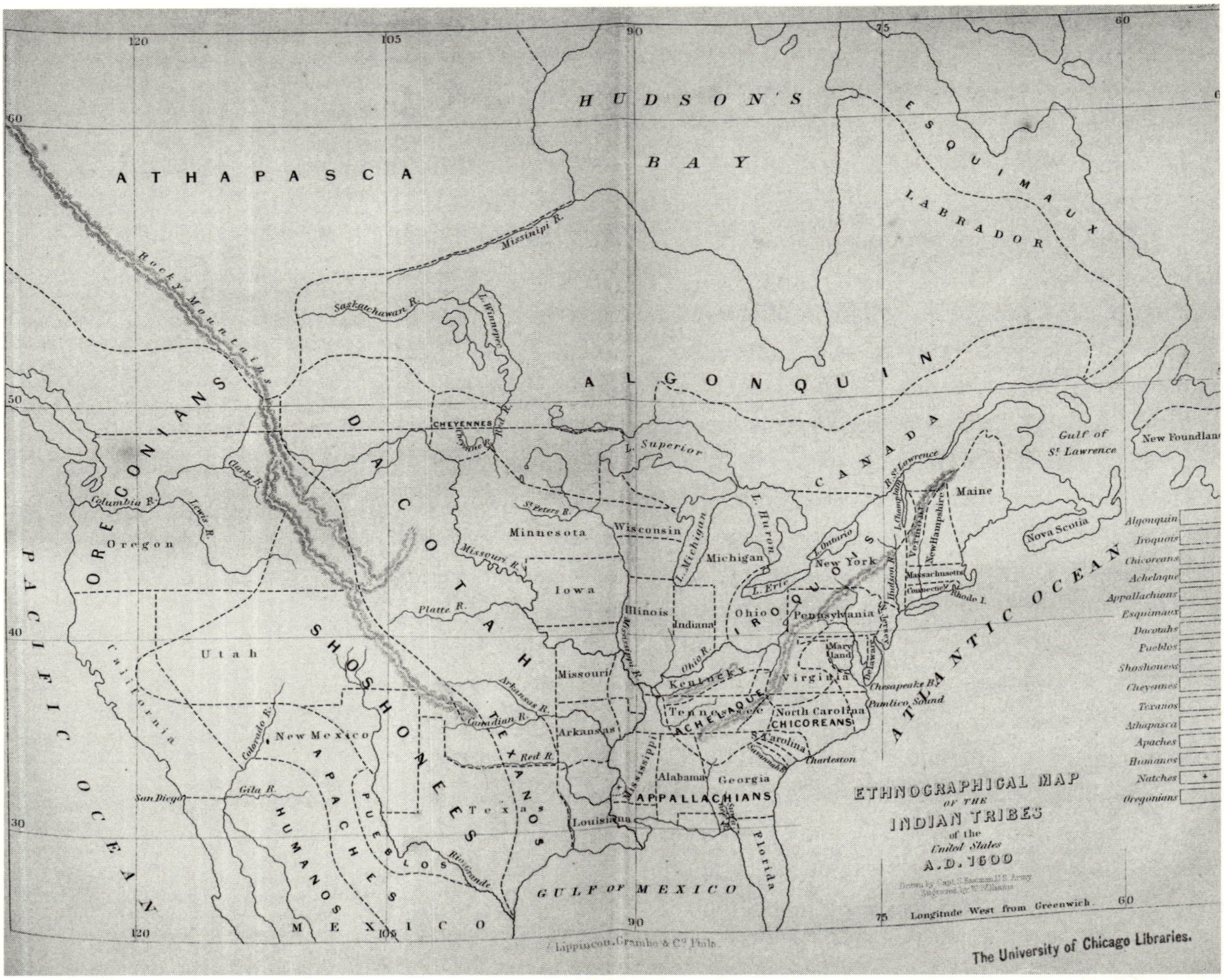

FIGURE 36. *Ethnographical Map of the Indian Tribes of the United States, A.D. 1600.* Illustration from Henry Rowe Schoolcraft, *Historical and Statistical Information Respecting the History, Condition, and Prospects of the Indian Tribes of the United States*, vol. 2 (Philadelphia, PA: Lippincott, Grambo, 1851–1857). Courtesy the University of Chicago Library.

left conspicuously unexplained; however, by using those accounts retroactively to reconstitute a past reality, Schoolcraft also avoids assessing the consequences of contact.[75] This avoidance takes on graphic form in the map: the different ancestral tribal zones are juxtaposed with the country's current state boundaries. There is no intermediate sequence of stages, no history, delineated to figure the transition between the past distribution of tribes and the political boundaries of the present; instead, there is a distinct past (the Indian) and a distinct present (the United States). This dichotomy informs his presentation of Native civilization throughout the report.

Schoolcraft's work was not well received in the relevant scholarly journals, the most important of which was the Boston-based *North American Review,* to which he had personally contributed reviews of ethnological works over the past decade.[76] The author of the *North American Review* article on his report is identified as Francis Bowen, then the editor of the journal, leaving open the possibility that an anonymous reviewer could have done the actual writing. Schoolcraft was convinced—as later scholars have been—that the review's negative assessment pointed to Squier, his current nemesis in the small world of American ethnology, but other reviews did find similar faults with Schoolcraft's report.[77] Squier or Bowen first dwells on the report's great expense (it eventually cost more than twelve times the initial investment of ten thousand dollars), then proceeds to identify "the want of system" as the report's key defect as a work of ethnological science, concluding, "The whole work forms only a huge repertory, in which are jumbled together all the materials that the editor can lay his hands on."[78] Schoolcraft envisioned his report as a cumulative project, with subsequent papers, vocabularies, and statistical tables appearing in later volumes and arranged according to a fixed sequence of sections, or "divisions." Within each section, however, successive writings do not sustain a line of inquiry or set of interests contained in prior volumes, except in certain cases (especially "Manners and Customs" and "Language"), where the aim is clearly to treat one tribe after another. Even here, though, there does not seem to be a rationale to the order in which tribes are treated, nor is there a sense that a particular volume is primarily devoted to a single family of tribes. The reasoning behind the sequence of sections is never explained, and Schoolcraft seemed to be aware of its counterintuitiveness, stressing in a dedicatory letter in the fourth volume that "the subject has been systematically divided, by sectional and diacritical marks (vide formula herewith,) in each volume, thus connecting kindred with kindred matter."[79] But in that volume's "Division of the Subject," the titles of sections are followed by "letters" or "numbers" (the "formula") indicating their proper groupings, and this proves quite different from the actual order of sections, as if Schoolcraft was revising, as he went along, whatever rationale lay behind his original schema.

As one examines this original schema and reads individual volumes, the overriding impression is one of moving backward and forward in time. "General History," an account of classic moments from the early history of European contact, is followed by "Manners and Customs," a survey of contemporary, and generally material, cultural practices: hunting and foraging techniques, different kinds of wigwams and tents, and so on. Next in the schema is "Antiquities," then "Geography of the Indian Country" (frequently comprising accounts of recent survey expeditions), then "Intellectual Capacity" (oral traditions and pictography), then "Topical

History" (accounts of famous European explorers from the sixteenth to the eighteenth century), and so forth. This disjointed sequencing resembles the disordered quality of the railroad narrative, while the constant returns to the past establish it as the proper temporal frame in which to locate Native civilization. Moreover, this perspective is repeated within the sections themselves: those that address modern topics typically assert either the changelessness of that aspect of Native culture or its potential to yield insight into the past. In volume one, "Manners and Customs" culminates in the claim that the Indian race exhibits an "indestructibility of type . . . [The Indian] mind appears to have no intellectual propulsion, no analytic tendencies. It reproduces the same ideas in 1850 as in 1492," and the later section on "Intellectual Capacity" analyzes pictography and mythology, concluding that they support this thesis. In volume two, the section on "Language" begins by affirming that it, "more than any other [topic], appears suited to throw light on the obscure origin and history of the tribes."[80]

Very few of the report's sections contain anything like archaeological investigation per se—a partial consequence of Schoolcraft's animosity toward practitioners like Squier.[81] More basically, Schoolcraft's education and past scholarship focused on the study of Native languages and oral traditions, although he lacked sufficient training to carry out a truly comparative philological investigation.[82] The back-and-forth sequencing of sections and the prose within them can be viewed as part of an effort to continue to use language "to throw light on the obscure origin and history of the tribes." Myths, rituals, phonetic transcriptions—various Indian "texts"—are all shuffled between one or another temporal framework, some connected to the present, others exclusively historical. In the process, the Indian "text" becomes a kind of artifact, pointing toward the past and treated as an object that can be transported from one section to another. These sections in turn function like the armature of Clifford's museum collection, as described earlier, for which "a scheme of classification is elaborated for storing or displaying the object ['vide formula herewith'] so that the reality of the collection itself, its coherent order, overrides specific histories of the object's production and appropriation."[83] By fragmenting chronological order, Schoolcraft endeavors to establish an ethnological order, which for him is an archaeological approach to the Indian. Nonetheless, despite the applicability of Clifford's allusion to the "reality of the collection itself," and despite Schoolcraft's claims that his text is "systematically divided" like a well-ordered collection, that collection remains virtual because the "object" (the various myths, rituals, and so on) does not achieve concreteness except as text within the report. Instead, Schoolcraft achieves this kind of concreteness only in his deciphering of pictographs, texts that are also, critically, physical objects located in physical spaces.

The shuffling between different registers of time also violates one of the most basic principles of archaeological investigation, that of superposition, and its accompanying inference, that objects found in the lower layers of an excavation antedate those found in upper layers. In his actual treatment of objects, Schoolcraft shows himself particularly sensitive to the ongoing modification of traditional materials, techniques, and practices through exposure to white American civilization. His primary concern is to isolate the characteristics of an authentic and antique material culture, with the result that contemporary objects are either relegated to a more distant time or eliminated as a component of American Indian life. Before proceeding to examine how images of landscape relate to his orchestration of narrative texts, especially Indian "texts," I want to look briefly at Schoolcraft's flouting of superposition in his presentation of Native material culture as a partial template for his archaizing approach to language. More specifically, as in the sequencing of sections, Schoolcraft collapses Native material culture into the past, except that he further tries to substantiate that collapse by heightening a sense of the described and pictured object as a tangible, physical artifact.

Although there are two separate sections treating "Antiquities" and "The State of Indian Art," Schoolcraft's interest clearly lies with the former. Not only is the section on "Antiquities" located closer to the work's beginning in the "Division of the Subject," but it is larger (in fact there is no section on modern manufactures in the first volume), and it contains a much greater amount of analysis, which Schoolcraft sometimes, and uncharacteristically, carried over from one volume to the next (as in his discussion of Dighton Rock and the inscription on Cunningham's Island). By contrast, like other modern sections, "The State of Indian Art" is frequently preoccupied with ancient remains. In volume four, the discussion of antiquities in this section is explained as a necessary step in differentiating ancient from modern, to arrive at "a just view of the state of the Indian arts at the respective periods of the discovery and settlement of the country, to judge accurately of their antiquity."[84] Schoolcraft is alluding specifically to the wealth of objects found in recent surveys of the Southwest, where deserted villages could date from the distant Anasazi or Ancestral Pueblo period up to more contemporary occupation by Pueblos, Zunis, and Moqui. Schoolcraft tries to ameliorate this indeterminacy by looking for Spanish and Mexican stylistic and technological influences and concluding that their absence indicates a "lingering taste for the gross imitative forms of the true Indian period."[85] For example, the recognizable shapes of a puma and a man on horseback in "Earthen Vessels from the Pueblos of New

Mexico" are taken as evidence of this stylistic inertia. Schoolcraft's comparative approach clearly equates authenticity with age, with the result that the antiquity of "the true Indian period" stretches out and absorbs the present. In another instance, the depiction of the Pueblo method of spinning thread is taken as an illustration of an ancient Aztec practice. Schoolcraft's general preference, in fact, is to show only those examples of "Indian Art" that resemble artifacts unearthed from graves and produced in a similar fashion. As he states in volume four, "We must admit that the ancient Indian was a better artist than the modern."[86] Schoolcraft's conflation of past and present is further advanced by the similarity in his representations of ancient and modern objects. In volume one, the lithograph *Antique Pipes* (plate 15) depicts pipe bowls that were unearthed from graves in western New York in the 1840s, while the engraving *Dacota Pipes* (figure 37; from volume two) shows such items as they "have been observed among the Dacotas." The parallel format—same-size objects grouped together within an otherwise blank rectangle and organized to fit within that rectangle—obtains throughout the report. This uniform approach is reinforced by Schoolcraft's opening paragraphs on "Modern" pipe sculpture immediately preceding *Dacota Pipes*, in which he discusses the recent discovery of "ancient smoking pipes" in graves in the Scioto Valley of Ohio—here too, then, chronological order is disjointed in such a way that the past can function as the authentic temporal frame enclosing American Indian civilization.

Whereas genre scenes of existing customs receive a more cursory and generalized mention in Schoolcraft's text, the majority of the pictured pipes, arrowheads, and pottery fragments—the examples of the antique "true Indian art"—stand in a much more direct and specific supplemental relation to it. These various artifacts are paired by number with textual descriptions, and they are accompanied by additional information in the form of measurements and cross-section views. This greater specificity of textual connection and elaboration anchors these objects more securely in the here and now of the reader's engagement. Their visual presentation is calculated to induce the reader to take them for the things themselves, and as artifacts within an antiquarian setting. They are shown more often than not as actual size, and they are grouped as they would appear in an antiquarian collection, the shadows cast by the objects redefining the blank page as the antiquarian's display table. The use of color here, relatively scarce in the reports' other illustrations, likewise points to a greater effort to capture the specificity of the object. The beige color of the engraving *Dahcota Written Music* is explained by a note penciled on the back of the artist's preliminary sketch to "print the entire ground of this plate in Nankin color to resemble [the] birch bark" of its original.[87]

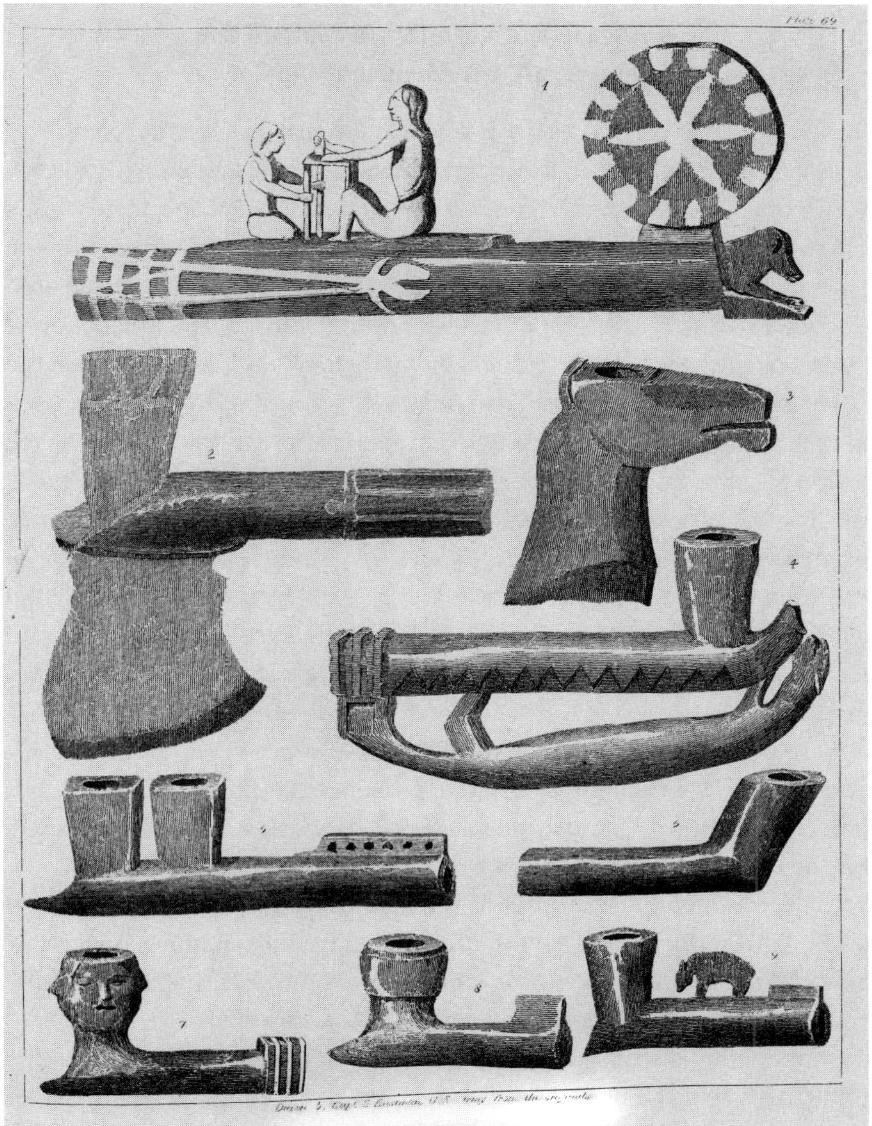

FIGURE 37. Seth Eastman, *Dacota Pipes*. Illustration from Henry Rowe Schoolcraft, *Historical and Statistical Information Respecting the History, Condition, and Prospects of the Indian Tribes of the United States*, vol. 2 (Philadelphia, PA: Lippincott, Grambo, 1851–1857). Courtesy the University of Chicago Library.

In this way, it is the past and not the present that is realized within the report—up to a point. On the one hand, the depiction of artifacts within an antiquarian setting suggests pastness but necessarily obscures their original location. On the other hand, although these objects are closely tied to the text in terms of references to them, these notices are generally confined to physical attributes alone: their dimensions, weight, and color. In a basic sense they do not speak; they remain alien to the order of textual explication. Schoolcraft attempts to overcome these limitations in his analysis of pictographs, an analysis in which landscape plays an instrumental role.

Landscape and Narrative Buried in Time: Schoolcraft's Archaeological Indian

Illustrations that contain landscape imagery in *History, Condition, and Prospects of the Indian Tribes* fall into three basic categories: historical scenes, views of contemporary Native customs and practices, and pictographs (or ruins), corresponding to the first three sections of the report—the sections most likely to be actually read. Just as ancient objects dominated Schoolcraft's presentation of modern manufactures, the adjacency of "Manners and Customs" to both "General History" and "Antiquities" in the "Division of the Subject" works to position "Manners and Customs" back in time. The spatial settings depicted in each of the three sections provide a kind of common thread that reinforces this association, particularly as the illustrated scenes all give an appearance of containment, whether as dramatic moment, generic activity, or isolated ruin. This impression of containment, or completeness, is also suggested by how they correspond with the familiar subject categories of academic art: history, genre, and landscape proper. Moreover, these scenes suggest an interlocking progression: from recreated history (fixed back in time, but pointing forward), a more or less ahistorical, "natural" cultural practice (unfixed in time), and the modern remains of a Native presence (fixed in the present, but pointing backward). Landscape imagery furnishes a vehicle of expression for the reifying impulse evident in the illustration of objects, but it is the pictograph that gives full play to the aspiration to treat language itself as an artifact. Instead of actual-size objects casting shadows on a page, Schoolcraft deciphers the past into letters and words, installing it fully within the space of his writing as ethnological knowledge.

A recurring dilemma for nineteenth-century readers of Schoolcraft's report was that the illustrations that could be categorized as history or genre scenes were perceived as being so inadequately and variably related to the main text that it was difficult to "see" what information they were supposed to convey in supplement to the text. The author of the *North American Review* article criticizes illustrations such as *Defeat of Vasques d'Ayllon by the Chicoreans* (figure 38) for appearing to have "no historic or antiquarian significance," further asserting, "It will not be contended . . . that the costumes either of the Indian or European actors . . . are here depicted with historic accuracy."[88] Schoolcraft's declared intention in "General History" was not "to narrate scenes of conquest," but "to notice events as they brought to light new tribes . . . from which a coup d'oeil of the Indian history may be seen."[89] In using the history of early European contacts to sketch the outlines of Native civilization at that time, he identifies key moments from that history, and although he does not concentrate on

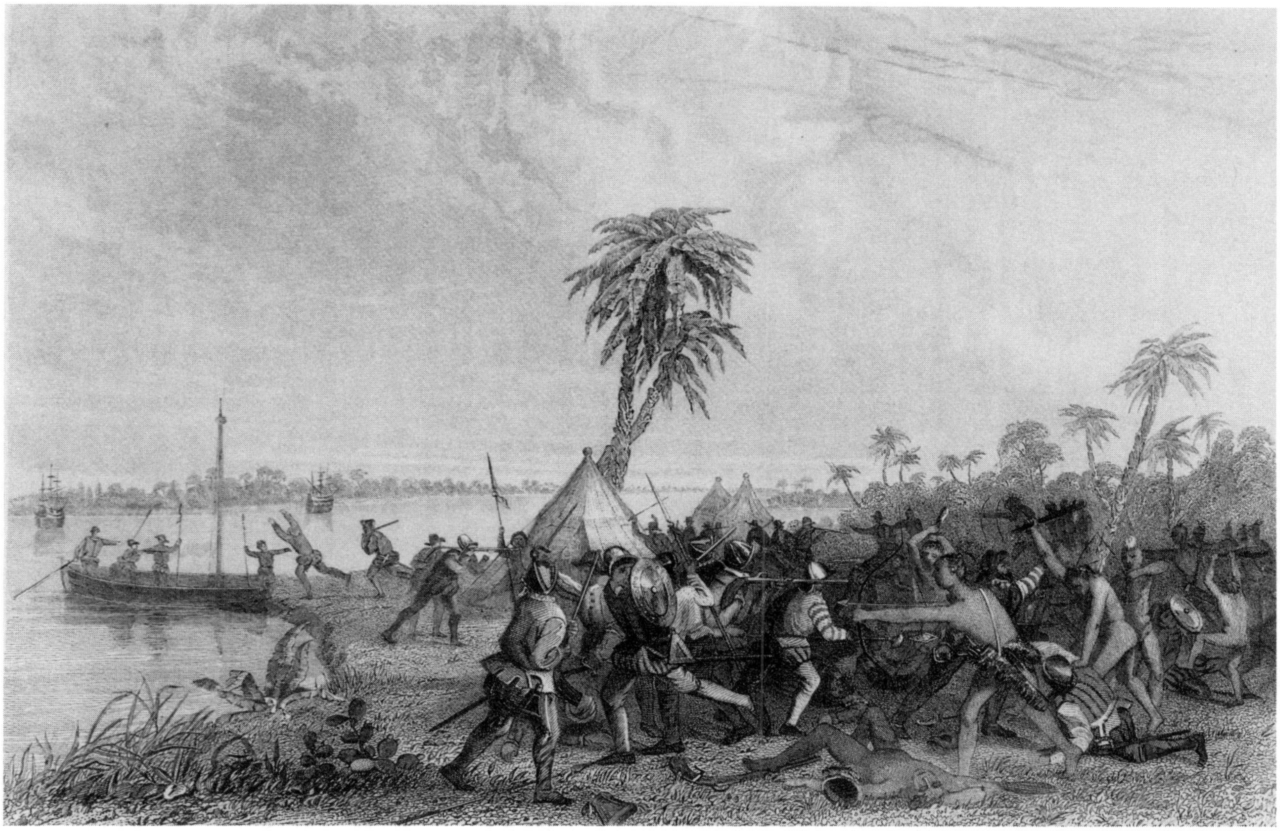

FIGURE 38. Seth Eastman, *Defeat of Vasques d'Ayllon by the Chicoreans.* Illustration from Henry Rowe Schoolcraft, *Historical and Statistical Information Respecting the History, Condition, and Prospects of the Indian Tribes of the United States,* vol. 3 (Philadelphia, PA: Lippincott, Grambo, 1851–1857). Courtesy the University of Chicago Library.

the events of contact but on the distribution of tribes, the illustrations preserve the format of extant history paintings of the colonial era and are comparable to works by John Vanderlyn, Emanuel Leutze, and others. As a result, the illustrations portray events through a familiar set of dramatic poses and configurations that had been established over the course of the genre's evolution. Schoolcraft does not explicate them in the text because they are iconic, or emblematic, and surely Squier or Bowen was aware of this aspect. But in the context of Schoolcraft's report, this illustration is doubly sealed off from the reader's perspective because it represents major colonial episodes from a supposedly alien vantage point: we look from the shore at the approaching European longboat; we see a battle won by Natives.

Most of the illustrations in "Manners and Customs" were based on drawings of Dakotas made by the report's chief artist, Seth Eastman, while he was stationed as an army officer at Fort Snelling, Minnesota, in the 1840s—that is, before he was assigned to Schoolcraft. Even though they predate his work for the report, such images as *Indian Sugar Camp* (figure 39) have the potential to serve a documentary function and link customs and practices described in the text to a specific time and place.

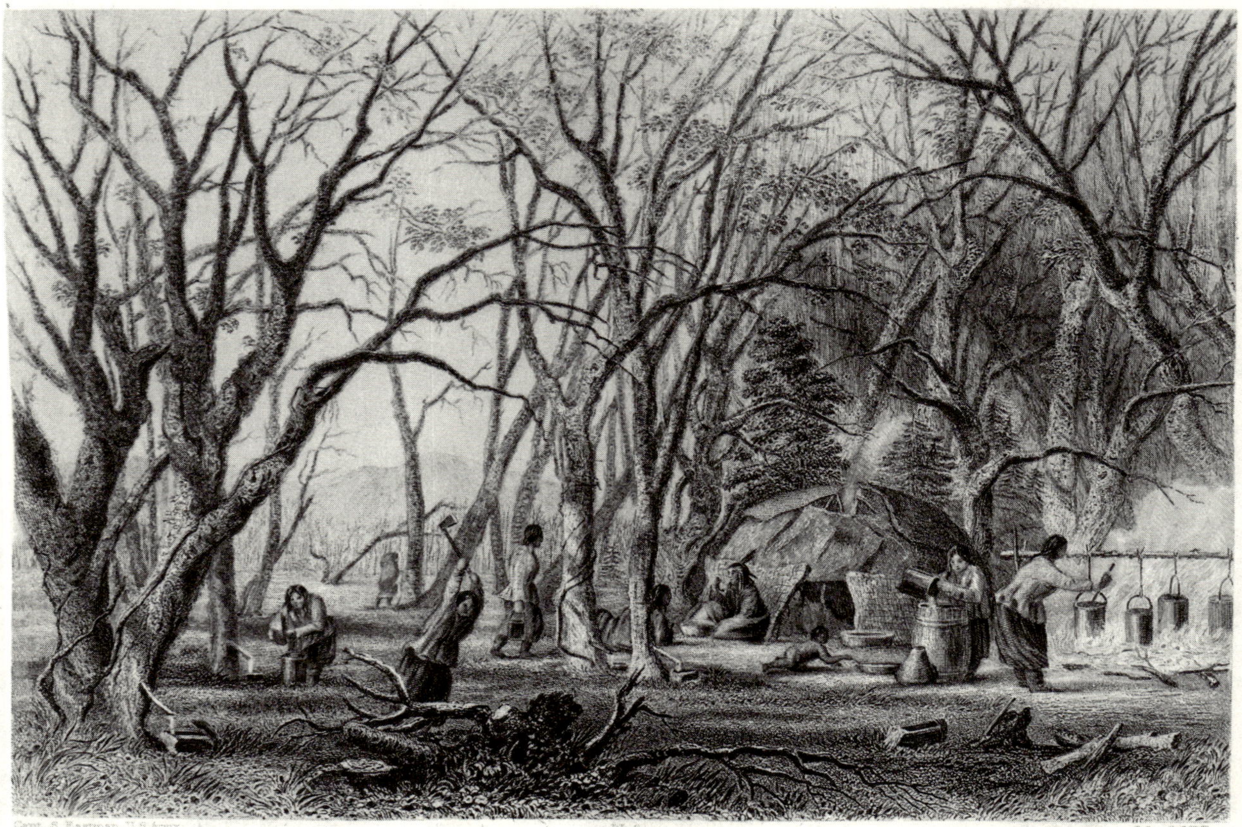

FIGURE 39. Seth Eastman, *Indian Sugar Camp*. Illustration from Henry Rowe Schoolcraft, *Historical and Statistical Information Respecting the History, Condition, and Prospects of the Indian Tribes of the United States*, vol. 2 (Philadelphia, PA: Lippincott, Grambo, 1851–1857). Courtesy the University of Chicago Library.

Yet here again, the figures and activities are only summarily indicated, as the text fails to engage them in any point-by-point explication. Moreover, the historical prints refer to dated and locatable events, supported by a written record, the explorer's account, but the images in "Manners and Customs" are typically presented as illustrations of "universal" Native activities—for example: "As the spring season approaches, and the sap begins to ascend the still leafless trunks . . . the Indian families, throughout all the northern and middle latitudes, repair to their sugar-camps."[90] In some cases, these generic characterizations are applied to tribal groups that would necessarily exclude the Dakotas. Again, the prints' relation to established categories of painting, in this case genre painting, predisposes them against any close connection to the text. If anything, their emphasis on timeless—and, to the reader, unfamiliar—activities in the round of life, their nondescript wilderness settings, and most of all, their occurrence right after the section on "General History" makes possible their application to any time before the present. No historical account fills the gap between "General History" and the recent discoveries related in "Antiquities"; moreover, the fact that the point of "General History" is to give an outline of tribal distributions at the outset of European contact makes it very possible to associate Eastman's scenes with Native life before recorded history. In volume two, "Manners and Customs" actually begins by attempting to date the immigration of the Indians' ancestors to North America by reference to Archbishop James Ussher's biblical account of history.

As spatial settings, the illustrations in Schoolcraft's first two sections share several characteristics. They demarcate a stage for human activity through the placement of rocks, trees, or bodies of water, while preventing the eye from moving back into the space beyond that stage by screening off or obscuring the transition to the background, not unlike the museum diorama with its two or three rows of figural space and a flat backdrop of landscape. Often there are central trees or tents that act as magnets for the figures' activities, as well as other devices that have the same effect: the line of impact between Spanish and Chicoreans in *Defeat of Vasques d'Ayllon,* the curving tree branches in *Indian Sugar Camp* that repeat the curves of the wigwam. As spaces, the illustrations are compositionally self-contained, an effect analogous to their independence from the text in which they are inserted. Again, their evocation of distinct genres of painting—images independent of text—is confirmed and amplified by their brief mention in the text. This self-containment reinforces the perception of an alien Indian subject both closed off from the reader and completely realized in that separate space.[91] The kind of space the illustrations depict, coupled with their minimal relationship to the text, closely parallels the features of the temporal frame surrounding American Indian civilization that Schoolcraft develops and imposes throughout his report.

Nevertheless, this sealed-off archaic Indian has still not been fully rendered as an object of ethnological or archaeological knowledge. The first two sections of Schoolcraft's report, and the kind of illustration practices used within them, distinguish themselves from previous histories and descriptions of Native civilization primarily through the claim of comprehensiveness.[92] For both Catlin and Schoolcraft, much of the value of their work was based on its status as an original and definitive contribution ("the record from which the tribes are to be judged"), and Schoolcraft's section on "Antiquities" provides him with his most focused and localized opportunity to demonstrate the effectiveness of his language-based approach to illuminating the archaic Indian; it is the culmination of his first three sections. "Antiquities" enables him to engage in conflating past and present aspects of Native civilization found in other sections. But "Antiquities" also allows him to go beyond what is more or less an "environmental" effect (with the "environment" being the report's overall organization and the relationship between narrative text and landscape prints), to give the treated material a more concrete presence as, first, an

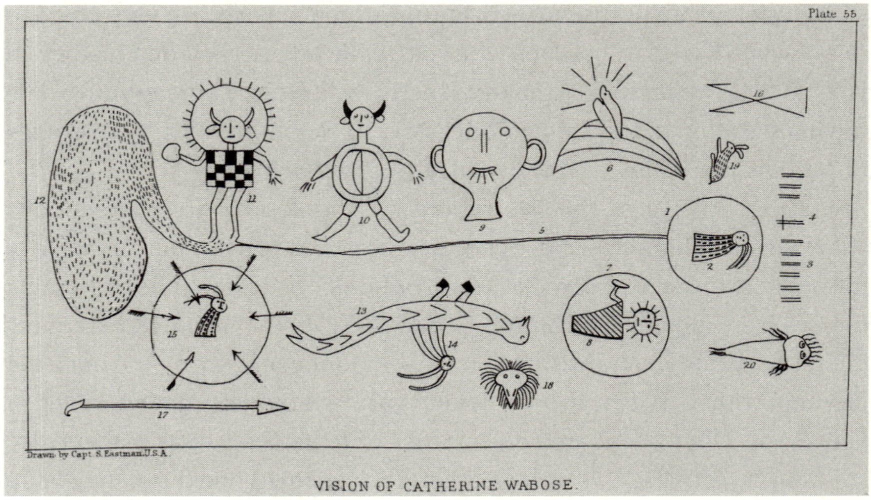

FIGURE 40. Seth Eastman, *Vision of Catherine Wabose.* Illustration from Henry Rowe Schoolcraft, *Historical and Statistical Information Respecting the History, Condition, and Prospects of the Indian Tribes of the United States,* vol. 1 (Philadelphia, PA: Lippincott, Grambo, 1851–1857). Courtesy the University of Chicago Library.

artifact (by virtue of its location in a specific place), and second, an object of ethnological and archaeological knowledge (via its decipherment).

Schoolcraft's investigations into pictography had two foci: a well-known inscription on Dighton Rock (which he dates before 1680), located on the Assonet River in Massachusetts, and a pictograph drawn by an Ottawa named Catherine Wabose during Schoolcraft's residence in Michilimackinac (plate 16 and figure 40). Even though the Dighton Rock inscription was apparently almost two centuries old and located far from Ottawa territory, in both cases Schoolcraft provided a tentative translation by asking Ottawas whom he knew around Michilimackinac to read the pictographs for him. An Ottawa named Chigwauk interpreted an engraving of the Dighton Rock inscription, while Wabose simply told him what she meant to communicate by her drawings. Although Schoolcraft resorts to contemporaries for translations, to systematize pictographs he compares them with apparent equivalents from European antiquity. The practice of pictography, whether past or present, is acknowledged by Schoolcraft in his discussion of Dighton Rock as being of the same importance for American antiquarians as Egyptian hieroglyphics are said to be for French antiquarians, such as Jean François Champollion. Striking notes of nationalistic appropriation, Schoolcraft writes of Dighton Rock:

> It is but the other day, as it were, that we began to look around the northern parts of the continent for objects of antiquarian interest. Every thing in our own history and institutions is so new and so well known . . . it appears refreshing to light on any class of facts which promises to lend a ray of antiquity to our history. The Indian race is, indeed, the oldest thing in American antiquity, and they bid fair to take the place of the inscribed shaft and undeciphered medal of the old world.[93]

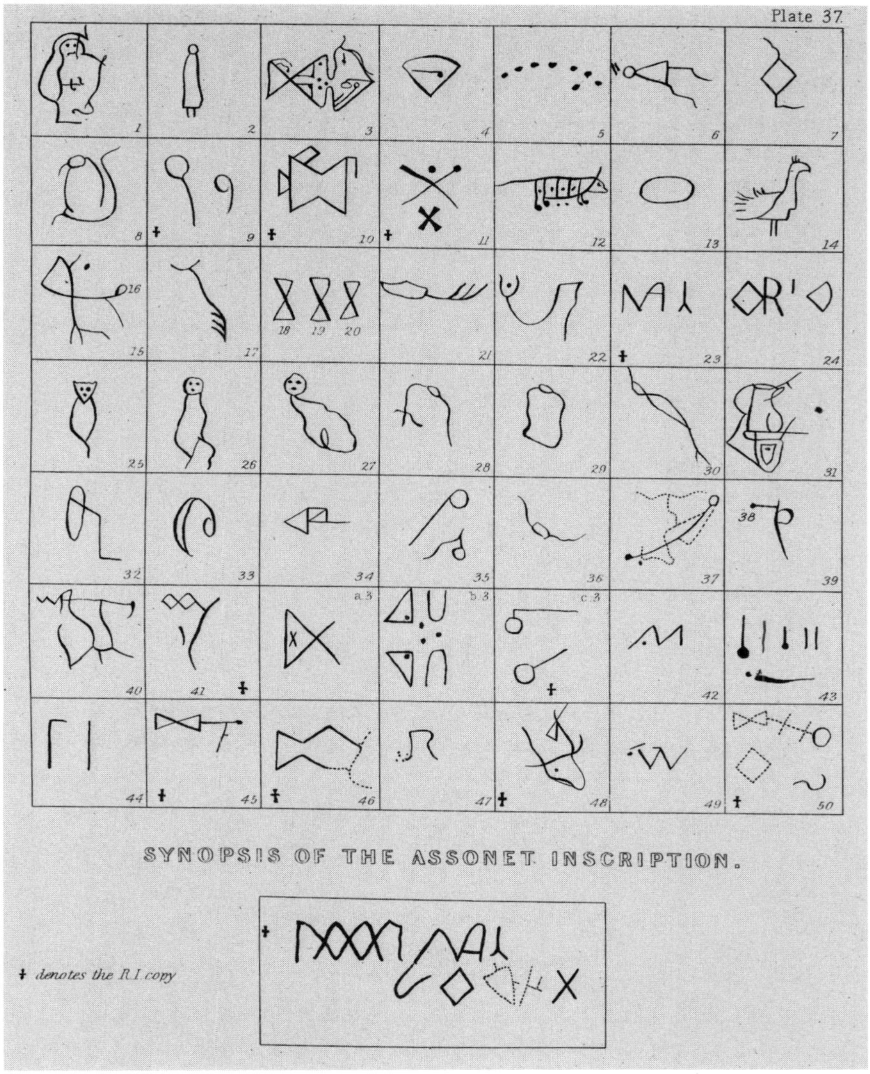

FIGURE 41. Henry Rowe Schoolcraft, "Synopsis of the Assonet Inscriptions." Illustration from Henry Rowe Schoolcraft, *Historical and Statistical Information Respecting the History, Condition, and Prospects of the Indian Tribes of the United States*, vol. 1 (Philadelphia, PA: Lippincott, Grambo, 1851–1857). Courtesy the University of Chicago Library.

Pictography is conceived of as "the thread which ties up the scroll of the Red Man's views of life and death," but its analysis takes the form of antiquarian investigation.[94]

Fortified with Chigwauk's translation of Dighton Rock, a kind of American Rosetta stone, Schoolcraft constructs a grid of symbols as a first step toward a more regular linguistic schematization (figure 41). This grid recalls the ethnological order, or "scheme of classification," that Schoolcraft aims to impose on his subject, and here as well it involves a prior process of chronological fragmentation (seventeenth-century inscription and modern translation). This process of transformation from the pictograph to a table of the pictograph's operative signs imitates the process by which European antiquarians, in particular Champollion, systematized Egyptian hieroglyphics as phonetic signs. In the famous

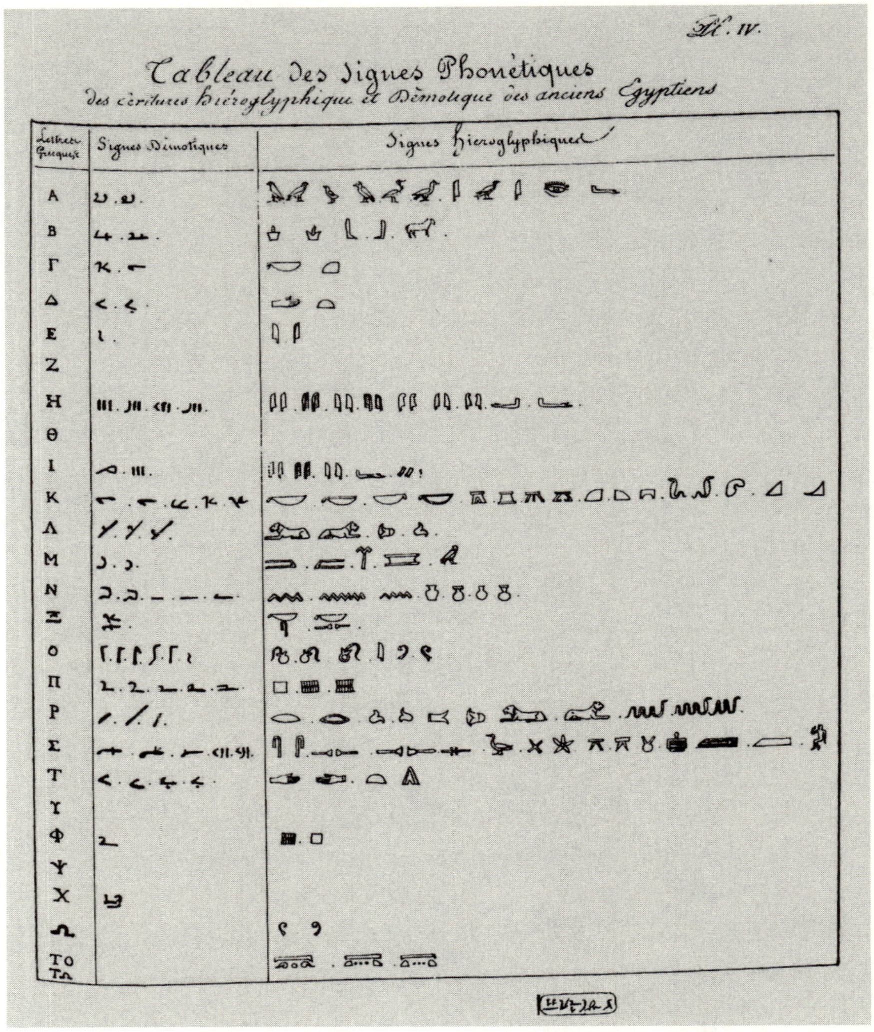

FIGURE 42. Jean François Champollion, "Tableau des Signes Phonétiques." Illustration from Jean François Champollion, *Lettre à M. Dacier, relatif à l'alphabet des hiéroglyphes phonétiques* (Paris: F. Didot père, 1822). Courtesy the University of Chicago Library.

Lettre à M. Dacier, Champollion separated out proper names (located within cartouches) from the stream of symbols on the Rosetta stone and eventually paired specific symbols with phonetic values (figure 42).[95] Schoolcraft's table of symbols was distilled in the course of investigating more recently produced pictographs, including those by Wabose. This synthetic approach to visual evidence—contemporary translations, antiquarian decipherment—crucially results in a product. Schoolcraft engages in the same conflation of ancient and modern found in his work's other sections, collapsing the present time of Wabose and Chigwauk with the presumed antiquity of pictography. But the conflation has the force and effect of a transposition, carrying something over from the sealed-off archaic Indian (the pictograph) and resituating it as ethnological and archaeological knowledge within his report (the translation).

Schoolcraft's enlistment of Ottawas to decipher Native pictographs, and his subsequent repositioning of these translations within an established European antiquarian investigative tradition, resembles his handling of American Indian songs and chants, some of which provided the basis for Henry Wadsworth Longfellow's "Hiawatha." In "Schoolcraft as Textmaker," William M. Clements analyzes the process by which Schoolcraft produced English text versions of Indian narratives, first making word-for-word, or "literal," translations with the assistance of his mother-in-law, a daughter of the Ojibwa chief Waubojeeg, and then reworking them in accordance with his sense of nineteenth-century American poetic standards.[96] In Clements's view, Schoolcraft's refashionings of Indian tales and songs reflected his desire to transmit—by making palatable or familiar to his audience—their literary qualities. This interpretation, however, curiously rests on the presumption of an original but now irretrievable Indian art form. Clements stresses the relative incapacity of Schoolcraft's translations to enable the reconstruction of their originals, even as he concedes that "we can learn something about the content of Ojibwa oral literary performance . . . from Schoolcraft's texts," despite their nineteenth-century American stylistic trappings.[97] But Schoolcraft's translations are a matter of not just adjusting Indian tales and songs, but of substituting other creations for them, specifically in the form of fragments or remnants. There is an ironic concurrence between Clements's view of these translations—as a residue, however mistakenly "beautified" or adjusted, of some past and largely irretrievable cultural event—and the antebellum ethnologist's own statement of purpose, to rescue Indian "oral tales and fictitious legends" from an impending extinction of the race.[98] Schoolcraft's collection of Indian songs and chants is the launching point of a trajectory in which the Indian is already closed off in the past, just as his translations of pictographs establish them as American versions of ancient hieroglyphics.

The conception of American Indian pictography as analogous to the antique monuments of Europe is dramatically set forth in the illustrations depicting rock inscriptions in situ (plate 16 and figure 43). Like the illustrations in "General History" and "Manners and Customs," these prints are based on a familiar model, that of vedute, views of ancient Roman remains. This subject was a primary theme for American artists who toured Europe, often funding their travels by executing commissions to paint specific ruins, as was the case with Cole's 1832 *Aqueduct near Rome* (figure 44).[99] Like vedute, Schoolcraft's prints of Native pictographs present the ruin as a landscape feature, just another rock to be negotiated for the shepherds and fishermen who are generally ignorant of its significance, emphasizing the lostness of the civilization that originally built these structures.[100] If anything, the prints stress this lostness more, in how

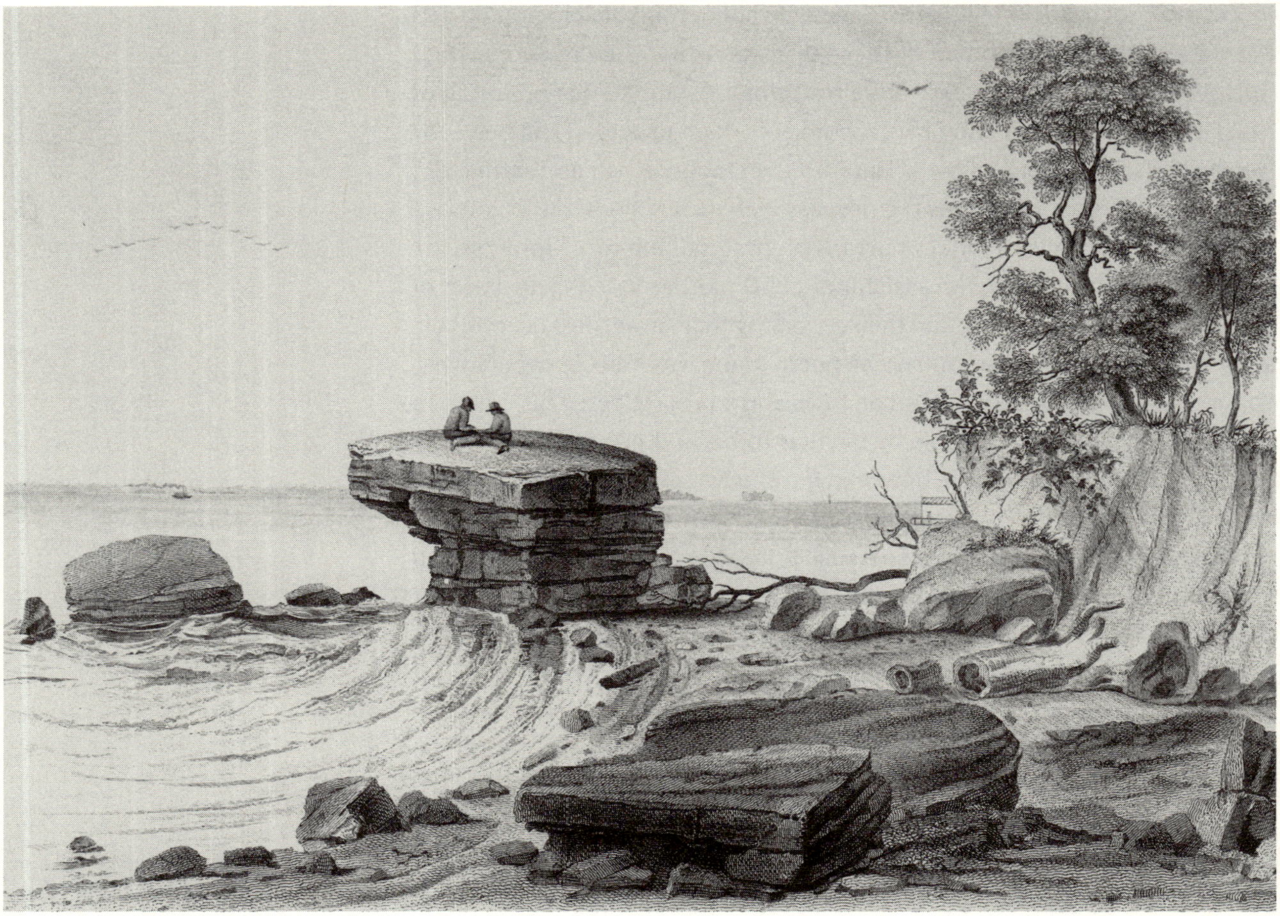

FIGURE 43. Seth Eastman, *View of Inscription Rock on South Side of Cunningham's Island, Lake Erie.* Illustration from Henry Rowe Schoolcraft, *Historical and Statistical Information Respecting the History, Condition, and Prospects of the Indian Tribes of the United States,* vol. 2 (Philadelphia, PA: Lippincott, Grambo, 1851–1857). Courtesy the University of Chicago Library.

they show figures sitting or standing on the ruin, in positions that may be alluding to principles of stratigraphy in archaeology and geology. For, in both of the Schoolcraft illustrations, the rocks appear to have been unearthed by water erosion, and by standing on them, the figures are raised to a higher, more recent stratigraphic level.

Although these landscape images are tied to the illustrations in the previous two sections—as spatial settings, and as familiar painting genres—they are also more explicitly discussed as distinct places visited on specific dates by Schoolcraft or one of his sources. They are fixed in time and space, aspects highlighted by the contemporary figures shown standing on the ruins, who are often scientists or at least figures engaged in examining the inscriptions (plate 16 and figure 43). The view of Dighton Rock is based on a daguerreotype, one of the few times in which this relatively new technology was employed in the report, and it shows Schoolcraft himself perched on the rock, touching the inscriptions. As was the case in the presentation of artifacts, these images of places and settings are more closely tied to the

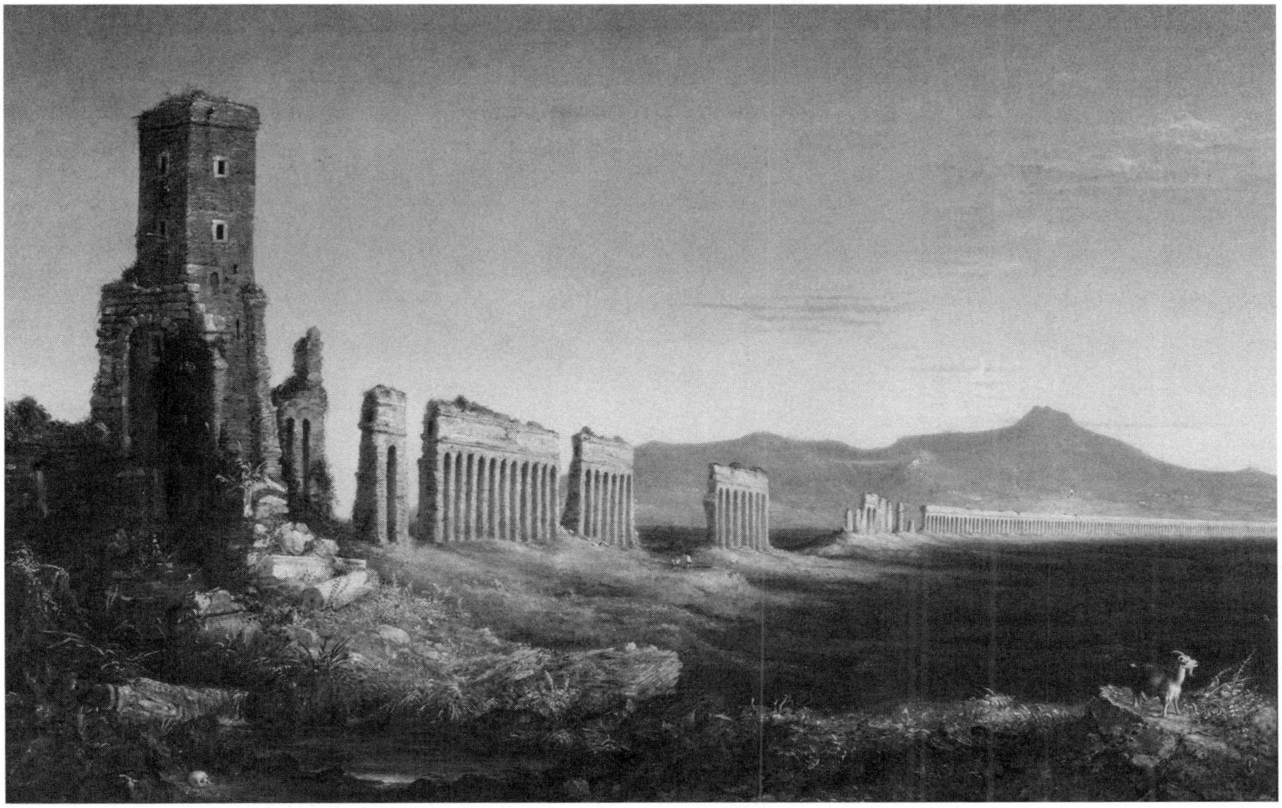

FIGURE 44. Thomas Cole, *Aqueduct near Rome,* 1832. Oil on canvas; 44½ × 67⁵⁄₁₆ in. Courtesy Mildred Lane Kemper Art Museum, Washington University in St. Louis. University purchase, Bixby Fund, by exchange, 1987.

text by specific references to them than are the illustrations in "General History" and "Manners and Customs." This greater specificity indicates the much greater material importance accorded to pictography as an ethnologically investigated feature of an archaic Indian civilization. Finally, these picturesque views of pictographs undergo successive redepiction, dismantlement, and reassembly—as a modeled rock face with incisions, in which scratches on the rock are undifferentiated from incised symbols or those symbols are actually invisible (plate 16 and figure 43); then as a simplified rock face parallel to the picture plane, the outlines of which begin to function as the edges of a sheet of paper, in which only the incised lines deemed to be symbols are shown (figures 45 and 46); and last as an ordered grid in which the symbols appear as lexical units (figure 42).

The multiply transmuted pictograph takes as its final form one not far removed from that of the actual printed letters of the text, thus reifying their opacity as mysterious signs almost within the body of the text itself.[101] While his other landscape images are detached from the text, Schoolcraft's American versions of vedute are not only identified as specific places, they are also decomposed into ethnologically significant elements and

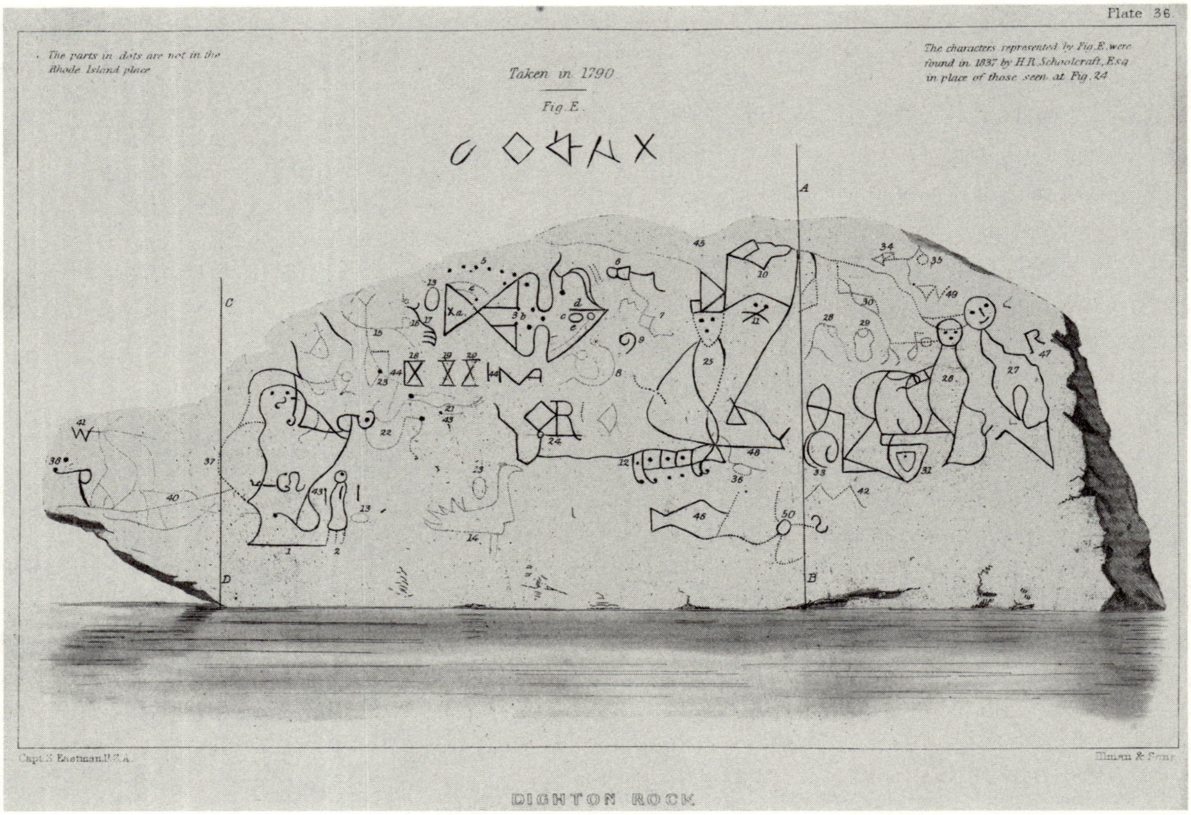

FIGURE 45. Seth Eastman, *Dighton Rock*. Illustration from Henry Rowe Schoolcraft, *Historical and Statistical Information Respecting the History, Condition, and Prospects of the Indian Tribes of the United States*, vol. 1 (Philadelphia, PA: Lippincott, Grambo, 1851–1857). Courtesy, the University of Chicago Library.

progressively incorporated into the text as stages in a process of decipherment. While their identity as vedute suggests the antiquity of the pictographs (whatever their actual dates of creation), the application of decipherment retroactively solidifies that impression. The "reality" of ethnological knowledge as knowledge of the past is likewise established by reaching into a familiar landscape image strongly associated with antiquity (the veduta) and then reconstituting the retrieved Indian sign within its own textual space. The paralleling of place and method in Schoolcraft's report is thus a procedure that both assumes and confers antiquity.

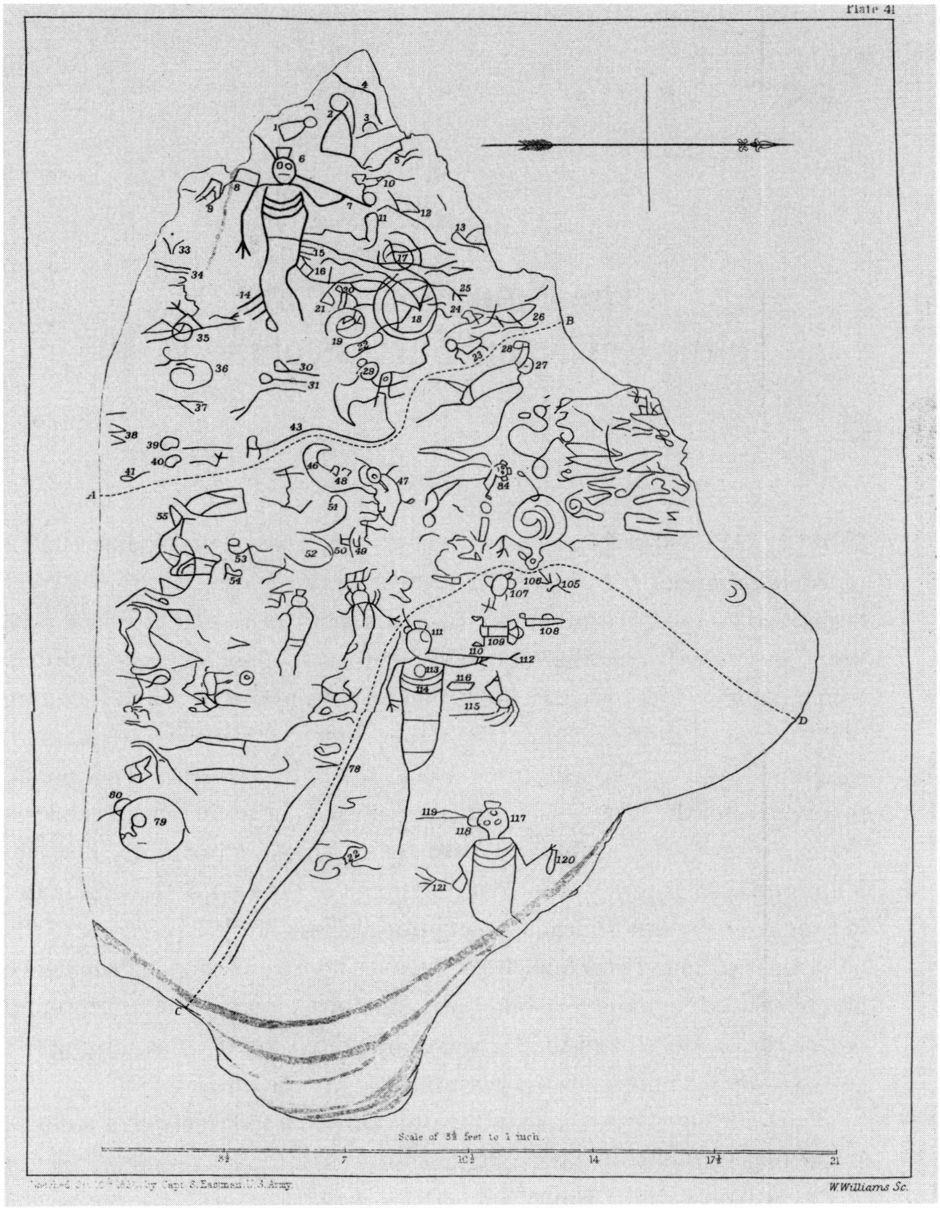

FIGURE 46. Seth Eastman, *Sculptured Inscription on a Rock, South Side of Cunningham's Island, Lake Erie.* Illustration from Henry Rowe Schoolcraft, *Historical and Statistical Information Respecting the History, Condition, and Prospects of the Indian Tribes of the United States,* vol. 2 (Philadelphia, PA: Lippincott, Grambo, 1851–1857). Courtesy the University of Chicago Library.

4

The Figuration of Time in the Geological Surveys of the West

SCHOOLCRAFT'S REPORT was part of an increasingly systematic assessment of the inhabitants, terrain, and resources of the Trans-Mississippi West organized by the government in the years just before and after the Civil War. The Union Pacific Railroad, completed in 1869 to form a continuous transportation link between the urban centers of the East and the state of California, was the culminating achievement in this process of exploration and was viewed as a pivotal instrument of the nation's economic recovery after the war.[1] On its own, the railroad certainly helped refill the Treasury's coffers as a sharp investment, but most importantly, it at last afforded rapid access to the vast resources of the rest of the continent. In President Ulysses S. Grant's inaugural address of 1868, referring to the challenges of Reconstruction, he observed: "It looks as though Providence has bestowed upon us a strong box in the precious metals locked up in the sterile mountains of the far west and which we are now forging the key to unlock, to meet the very contingency that is upon us."[2]

The building of the transcontinental railroad was largely enabled by a series of geographical and geological surveys, initially conducted by the U.S. Army through the Topographical Corps of Engineers.[3] The corps was eventually succeeded by civilian agencies in the 1860s and 1870s; during this time, however, the army continued important survey operations, and the corps provided an influential model for later geographical and geological work. The end of this period was reached with the completion of four major expeditions, under varying degrees of military control: Clarence King covered a swath of territory approximately one hundred miles wide along the route of the transcontinental railroad (1867–1879); Ferdinand Vandiveer Hayden mapped much of what is now Nebraska, Colorado, and Wyoming, including the Yellowstone region (1867–1879); John Wesley Powell explored the Colorado River, from the Green and Grand

Rivers south to the Grand Canyon (1869–1879); and Lieutenant George Montague Wheeler charted major portions of the Southwest lying south of the railroad, in present-day California, Nevada, New Mexico, Arizona, Utah, and Colorado (1871–1879).

The military and the later civilian surveys were primarily directed toward mapping and assaying unknown terrain and locating viable stage, water, and railroad routes, but they served a range of other functions as well.[4] They assisted in the government's intensified management of American Indian populations, which went hand in hand with opening areas for settlement, principally by noting the location of tribes and gathering census information (excerpts of survey reports touching on Native subjects found their way into Schoolcraft's report). These surveys also assembled extensive collections of specimens and raw data relating to the region's flora and fauna, as well as soil, minerals, and fossil remains. Officers of the corps were trained in the applied earth sciences at West Point, while their nonmilitary counterparts were educated in the emerging geology departments at the Sheffield School at Yale and the Lawrence School at Harvard, and both groups tried to incorporate the latest European geological theories in describing the topography of the West.[5] The western surveys as a whole were conducted shortly after the revolution in geological science marked by the publications of Georges Cuvier, Charles Lyell, Louis Agassiz, and others.[6] These writers introduced or won credence for several notions that overturned the traditional biblical account of the earth's history, including a vast timescale for that history, the extinction of species, the existence of past ice ages, and the formation of the continents through prolonged processes of sedimentation, compaction, and uplift, as well as abrupt volcanic action and earthquakes. Many of these theories were still being debated at midcentury, especially the primacy of gradual (or uniformitarian) versus sudden (or catastrophic) change in the shaping of the continents, and the unique rock formations of the West supplied dramatic proving grounds in which modern geological science could be tested and confirmed. Since the four major surveys following the Civil War were less restricted than earlier corps expeditions to the task of mapping terrain and locating transportation routes, their reports attempted to synthesize their findings into master narratives charting the earth's development, embracing wide expanses of terrain and vast stretches of geological time.

The maps, descriptions, collections, and statistical records of the terrain produced by these surveys were also accompanied by an extensive body of images—sketches, watercolors, and photographs, depicting landscape, people, plants, and animals—that multiplied in turn via the manifold avenues through which information obtained on expeditions reached various different audiences.[7] The official annual and summary reports of the surveys, distributed to a restricted governmental and scientific audience, were usually accompanied by prints based on sketches and often by actual photographs assembled in portfolios or tipped in to the publications themselves. Photographs and drawings were the basis for prints that appeared in newspapers, journals, and railroad promotional material, under a variety of working arrangements among survey leaders, artists, and publishers. Certain photographers and artists, officially or informally connected with different expeditions, retained considerable control over negatives and sketches, making them available as stereoscopic views or individual prints, or working them up as finished landscape paintings exhibited in annual shows, galleries, or by themselves as blockbuster events.

This multiplicity of medium and venue has complicated efforts to assess the meaning and impact of these images, a condition no less exacerbated by the highly charged intersections between scientific, nationalistic, economic, and aesthetic interests represented by the surveys themselves.[8] Indeed, to a certain extent many of these images, especially the photographs and prints, seem to directly contradict fundamental assumptions about originality, authorship, intention, and audience associated with traditional art historical investigation, explaining their belated and frequently vexed arrival as serious objects of study. The visual material associated with the Powell and King surveys, whose official reports featured prints based on the work of the painter Thomas Moran and the photographer Timothy O'Sullivan, has been a recurring touchstone in efforts to make sense of the multiplicity of forms and contexts of survey imagery. Although scholars have taken a variety of approaches, what unifies them is a basic concern with the precise manner in which these images illustrate the geological theories of Powell and King. Their ideas about geological history and development are frequently seen to anchor the work of Moran and O'Sullivan, to explain its specific appearance, as distinct from or in spite of prevailing, specifically artistic, conventions governing the composition and interpretation of paintings and photographs. But it remains unclear how the articulation of scientific theory itself—which occurs in the survey reports on a number of levels, as various kinds of texts, diagrams, illustrations, and so forth—affects the pictorial decisions made by these artists. I argue that an important thread connecting the expression of scientific theory with the landscape images of the surveys, particularly governing their use as illustration, is the search for a narrative form capable of communicating that theory. "Reading" the geological landscape, tracing a certain kind of order in topography, strata, and fault lines, posed a dilemma that was simultaneously visual and literary. The present chapter examines how images of landscape organize and substantiate narratives of geological history in the major publications produced in connection with these two surveys, Powell's *Exploration of the Colorado River of the West* (1875) and King's *Systematic Geology* (1878).[9]

Recent scholarship on Moran and O'Sullivan has pointed toward a closer affiliation between the survey enterprise and the work of these artists. But such an approach has been hampered by the striking character of their work outside the immediate context of the survey report, as well as by an art historical bias toward the primacy of particular media (painting and photography over print), the uniqueness of the art object, and the isolated nature of artistic effort. Although Moran produced hundreds of engravings based on his sketches, for survey reports and for several newspapers and journals, scholars have tended to focus on his painted masterpieces, such as *The Chasm of the Colorado* (1873–1874), which are viewed as culminating expressions in painted form of his experiences on the Hayden and Powell expeditions, paralleling their written summary reports (plate 17). Thus, Joni Louise Kinsey's definitive study of Moran devotes several chapters to each of these surveys, beginning with a visual analysis of the paintings themselves. This analysis is then followed by a careful reconstruction of his involvement with the expeditions, a summary of the geological theories of Hayden and Powell, and an explanation of how the paintings represent them, so that the appearance of the paintings organizes what follows in the remainder of the book. Kinsey's later chapters then discuss his printed work, but they focus on prints in newspapers and journals as opposed to his illustration work for the survey reports.[10] As a result, any appreciable instrumentality exercised by Moran's prints (or those of other artists involved in the survey) in reinforcing or participating in Powell's presentation of the story of erosion and uplift in the Colorado River Basin is obscured, as is any close relationship between the articulation of that story and the formal organization of print images.

Elizabeth Childs's more recent article on Moran and Powell departs from this concentration on painting as a definitive and essentially individual expression, paying equal attention to the prints, drawings, photographs, and maps created in connection with the survey and fostering a closer proximity between these images and the total enterprise of producing scientific knowledge.[11] Childs further ventures to speculate on "what impact the artist had on the geologist," even if her answer restricts itself to identifying a similar flair in Moran's art and Powell's writing.[12] Just as Kinsey elucidates the geological significance of Moran's master paintings, Childs identifies what "the geologically minded viewer"—perhaps even the surveyors themselves—would find in the various visual materials of the expedition, but these materials also begin to function more actively as tools that enable a story of geological development to be articulated.[13]

Childs finally characterizes Powell's understanding of his surveying activity as a kind of reading, even if she treats her characterization as essentially a "metaphor": "The Grand Canyon is an open book, the stone layers are pages, and the viewer is a privileged reader."[14] My sense of it is that this kind of reading is not simply metaphorical, but that the activity of surveying required a distinct kind of viewing, registered in the survey images themselves—including those by the less illustrious draftsman involved, H. H. Nichols—that delimited as well as enabled narrative form.

A similar inertia restricting inquiry to the unique, personal, and self-contained image persists in studies of O'Sullivan's photographic work for the King and Wheeler surveys. When O'Sullivan's pictures, such as *Tufa Domes, Pyramid Lake, Nevada* (1867), were first "rediscovered" by artists and curators in the twentieth century, their striking features were evaluated according to noticeably modernist aesthetic values (plate 18). Here, the pyramidal and spherical shapes of the islands—reinforced by the point of view—coupled with their separation by an expanse of water without ripples—so that recessional depth is negated—calls to mind modernist traits of "stark geometric relations, radical value contrasts, [and] instances of insistent planarity."[15] Although later generations of scholars pointed out the mistakenness of assimilating such pictures to an anachronistic modernist narrative of photography's development, efforts to resituate them within the discourse of the survey have shied away from attributing any formative role to these pictures in constructing and communicating geological theory. Instead, the relationship between photograph and theory is generally construed as being sympathetic at best, with the notable exception of Robin Kelsey's more recent work on O'Sullivan and the Wheeler survey.[16] Kelsey persuasively associates the visual characteristics of the Wheeler photographs with the graphic values and conventions found in the diagrams, maps, and topographical notations used in preparing and illustrating the survey reports.[17] I want to push this approach further, or rather elsewhere, and consider how O'Sullivan's pictures—meaning specifically their lithographed form within the King report—structure a new kind of geological narrative.

Within the Powell and King reports, illustrations, especially landscape illustrations, critically act as a kind of master key, directing the reader between familiar and unfamiliar kinds of narrative. Both Powell and King endeavor to present a new kind of story, one that departs from the linear travel account characteristic of earlier corps reports, in order to chronicle the geological changes that resulted in the unique topography of the West. The typical linear travel account was anchored by landscape imagery that more or less conformed to prevailing picturesque conventions, which, significantly, offered particular ways of experiencing and accessing duration and history. In other words, previous narrative form and landscape viewing composed an interdependent ensemble of narrative viewing that structured the scope and direction of inquiry—specifically the kind of "time" that both textual account and printed illustration could describe. In turn, the radicalness of Powell's and King's inquiries required corresponding changes to that ensemble.[18] Cognizance of the history of geological change demanded a new approach to viewing landscape, of ascertaining the record of time in a perusal of its features. Although to some degree the compositional and iconographical significance of the picturesque view could be bent toward describing a geological frame of time—as, for example, in Moran's paintings—Powell's and King's reports move away from the linear travel account toward a new kind of narrative viewing that more effectively captures that time frame. Just as the picturesque view found in the travel account—or in publications like Bryant's *American Landscape* or *Nelson's Illustrated Guide to the Hudson*—allowed the reader to experience history palpably as duration, the prints of Moran and O'Sullivan, and their placement within the text, provided their own distinct visceral analogs of time in relation to the task of reconstructing and persuasively describing geological history.

"Wandering Astray Somewhere in the Labyrinth": Narrative and Landscape Illustration in the Early Corps Reports

The corps surveys of the West that immediately preceded the expeditions of Powell and King, extending back to Lewis and Clark, were for the most part conceived of and carried out as reconnoiters proceeding along a single line of travel, following waterways or other amenable features of the terrain to trace convenient water routes and trails between a starting point and objective destinations, like water seeking its level.[19] Before the state geological surveys or land surveys that marked out plots for settlement had been produced, the imperative within newly acquired territories was rarely to engage in a systematic survey of an entire area. In the 1850s, in preparation for the transcontinental railroad, the corps did conduct a coordinated series of expeditions along different parallels proceeding west from the Mississippi River; however, even then the objective was to locate a line of travel, one possessing the easiest grades and plentiful supplies of timber. Individuals and institutions in the emerging scientific community in the East were given the opportunity of assimilating the specimens, data, descriptions, and images collected during these western surveys into something like a complete picture, but within the survey reports themselves, the orientation was one of linear progress.[20] This orientation was reflected in the narrative presentation used in these reports, as well as in the kind of time being registered in describing, analyzing, and picturing the landscape. To clarify the special character of the narratives that Powell and King develop, I begin with practices of writing and illustration found in these earlier reports, concentrating on Lieutenant Joseph Christmas Ives's *Report upon the Colorado River of the West* (1861).[21]

Ives's expedition was intended to chart the lower Colorado River and, in the process, to establish relations with Native tribes in the region and assess the terrain for its agricultural potential and its amenability to the construction of stage and railroad lines. Specifically, Ives was to assess the navigability of the Colorado River by steamboat, proceeding north from the Gulf of California to Fort Yuma, at the confluence of the Gila River, then moving on through largely unexplored territory until further progress became impossible.[22] There was also the intention of exploring the Grand Canyon, which had been encountered and described by Spanish missionaries and fur trappers, but not cartographically fixed or systematically surveyed. As it turned out, the expedition only reached the Black Canyon by steamboat, just above what is now the Hoover Dam, but by moving overland, it was able to catch glimpses of the Grand Canyon from its southern side.[23] Finally, mineral assays and data collection relating to the geology of the Colorado River were conducted by the geologist John Strong Newberry, while sketches of the terrain were made by two artists, F. W. von Egloffstein (who had accompanied John Charles Frémont on an 1853 expedition) and Heinrich Baldwin Möllhausen (who had participated in Lieutenant Amiel Weeks Whipple's railroad survey of 1853, and who was sent by famed naturalist Alexander von Humboldt).[24]

Ives's report is divided into three sections: the first, taking up the most space, recounts the expedition's progress day by day; the remaining two sections, considerably shorter, make summary statements on the geology and zoology of the areas covered by the survey. Each chapter in the first section corresponds to some convenient division of the journey, usually geographical (such as the route through a particular valley or network of canyons), and is preceded by a foldout outline panorama of the terrain traversed in that section. For example, chapter 4 opens with

FIGURE 47. F. W. von Egloffstein, *Colorado River, Chemehuevis Valley*. Illustration from Joseph C. Ives, *Report upon the Colorado River of the West, Explored in 1857 and 1858* (Washington, DC: Government Printing Office, 1861). RB 2676. Courtesy the Huntington Library, San Marino, California.

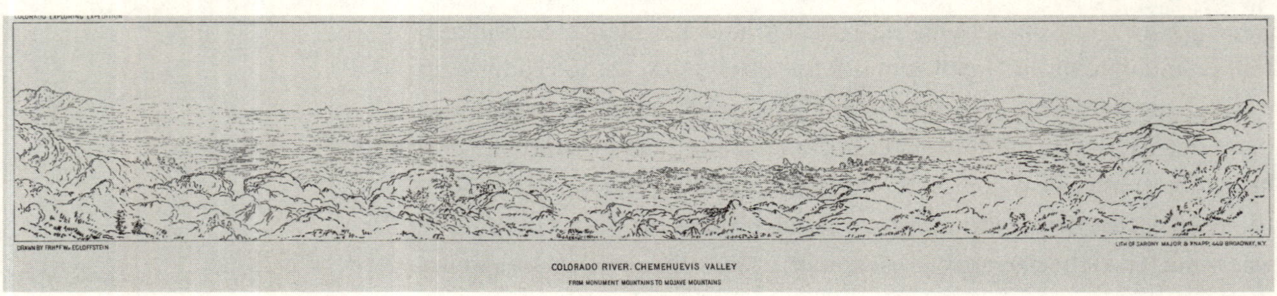

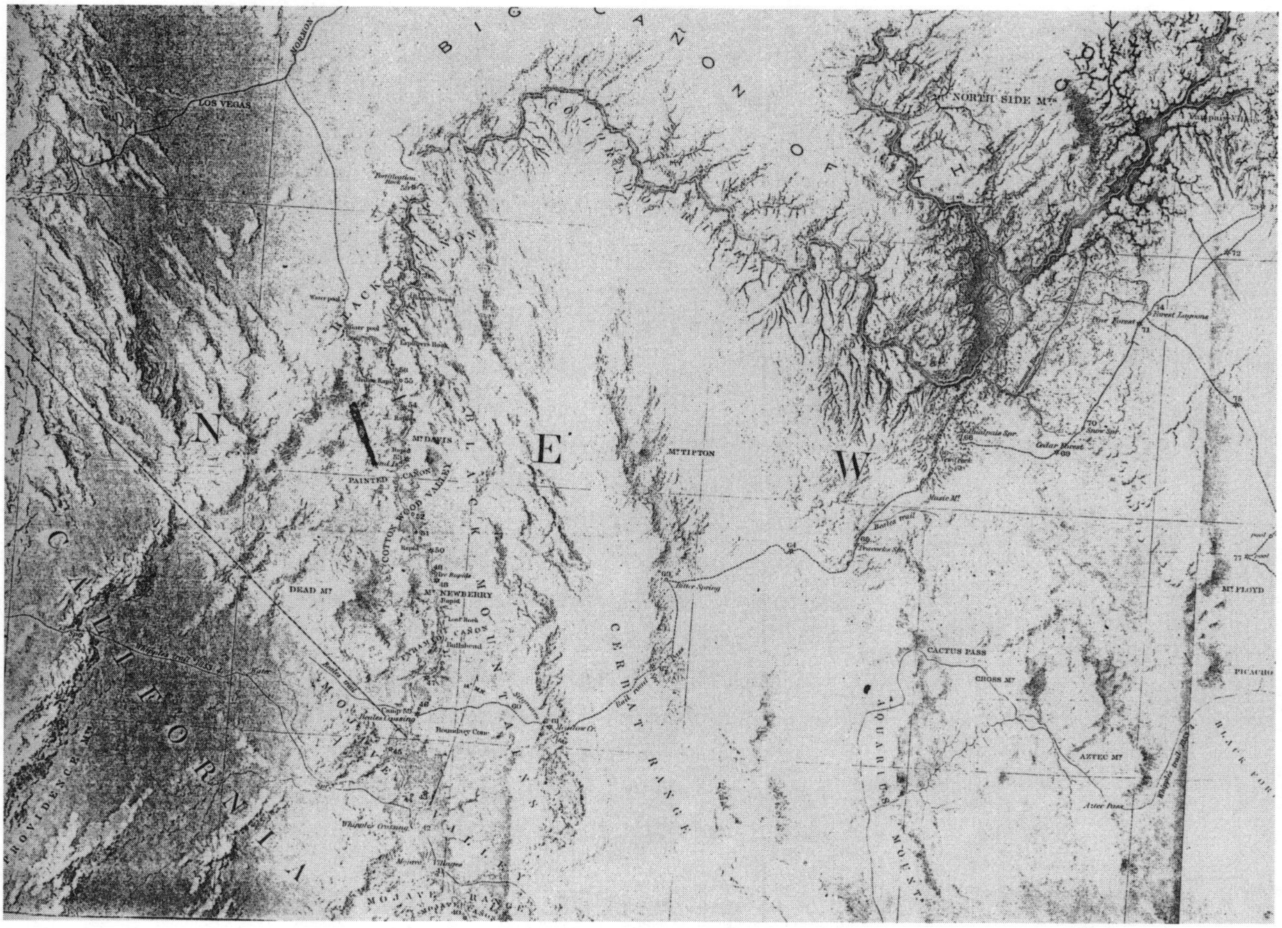

FIGURE 48. F. W. von Egloffstein, *Map No. 2, Rio Colorado of the West* (detail). Illustration from Joseph C. Ives, *Report upon the Colorado River of the West, Explored in 1857 and 1858* (Washington, DC: Government Printing Office, 1861). RB 2676. Courtesy the Huntington Library, San Marino, California.

the panorama *Colorado River, Chemehuevis Valley*, allowing readers to preview what the corps would encounter in that chapter, firmly giving the subsequent narrative the task of taking them from one point—or stopping place, where the expedition would establish a camp—to another (figure 47).[25] The expectation of a linear narrative is intensified by the outline appearance of the print, which the subsequent text would presumably fill in. This kind of organization associates the account of the corps' progress with a particular kind of landscape view, essentially a topographical view, establishing a template for the kind of narrative, and the kind of time, that such a view makes possible.[26] The foldout maps at the beginning of the report, which depict the progress of the expedition as a dotted line marked by numbers representing stopping places, repeats this arrangement on a larger scale, which is further suggested by the lack of definition or even blankness in the rendering of terrain outside that line of travel (figure 48).

This expectation about how landscape views can support a certain kind of narrative explication is borne out by the vignette wood engravings (based on Möllhausen's sketches) and full-page lithographs (based on Egloffstein's work) of passing views found within each chapter. Here the frequent delays caused by the grounding of the steamboat in shallow water, as well as the great number of unusual topographical features and the presence of two prolific draftsmen, resulted in a welter of illustrations, interspersed in the text every two or three pages. Their frequency and the text's focus on movement—for example, ignoring successive days that are spent in camp—has the effect of rendering what was a slow and tedious journey into a much more rapid and fluid experience of travel for the reader, despite the reports of delays and even embarrassment caused by the presence of Native onlookers who were evidently amused by the expedition's troubles. Ives's report, in effect, is the corps version of the illustrated steamboat guidebook, comparable with such productions as *Nelson's Illustrated Guide to the Hudson.* The temporal significance of landscape, its capacity to offer historical meaning for the apprehension of the astute viewer, is likewise understood within the conventions of picturesque illustration; however, the absence of historical content attached to landscape features foregrounds the fact that traversal, physical progress, is the primary temporal experience those features can offer.

Like other authors of corps reports, Ives is highly sensitive to the idea that landscape elicits aesthetic appreciation. Along with dry repetitions of mineral composition, the repeated use of mineralogical terms like "ferruginous" (rust colored) and "argillaceous" (resembling clay), he describes the passing terrain in specifically pictorial terms. Time and time again, moreover, the narrative of the steamboat's progress presents scenic views as sudden disclosures produced by changes in course, rounding obstructing canyon walls, and so forth. The terrain is encountered as a sequence of purely visual phenomena, an experience conveyed to the reader through the strategic placement of vignette illustrations. Thus, the view of Chimney Rock in the Purple Hills (figure 49) is immediately preceded by the words "a sudden turn brought Chimney Rock full in view. Its turreted pinnacles towered directly in front, and almost seemed to block up the head of the cañon. The vista was beautiful, and the channel looked promising."[27] The employment of typical picturesque literary devices that described landscape views in pictorial and architectural terms is matched by the print's serpentine path into depth; the measured intrusions of points of land into the river; the elevated repoussoir, or foreground viewing station; and the focus on and regularization of Chimney Rock as an architectural form. These moments of encountering landscape beauty are also typically accompanied by Egloffstein's full-page lithographs (in this case, *Cane Brake Canyon*), where the narrative text disappears altogether and only the pictorial realm remains. Concurrently, aesthetic

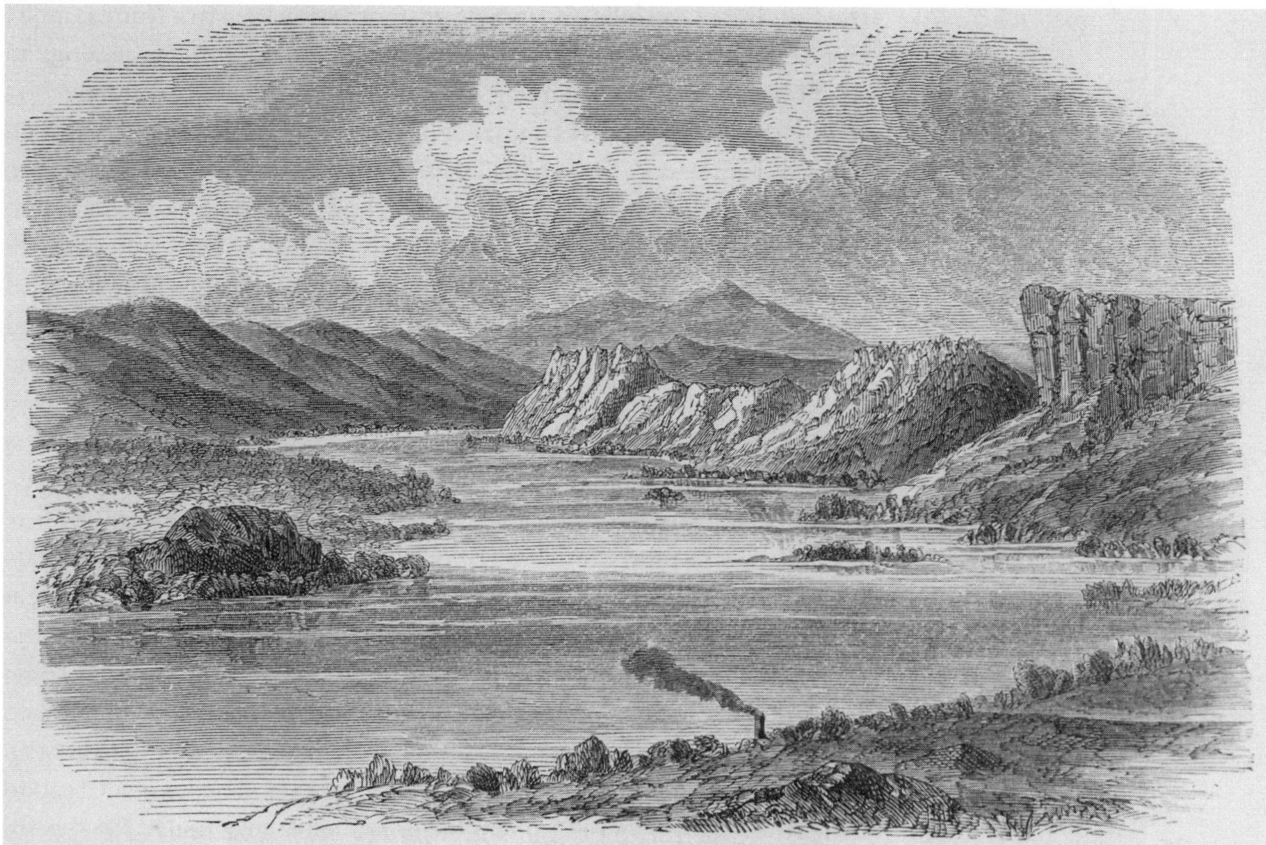

Fig. 3.—Purple Hills.

FIGURE 49. Heinrich Baldwin Möllhausen, *Purple Hills*. Illustration from Joseph C. Ives, *Report upon the Colorado River of the West, Explored in 1857 and 1858* (Washington, DC: Government Printing Office, 1861). RB 2676. Courtesy the Huntington Library, San Marino, California.

beauty is paired with physical progress ("The vista was beautiful, and the channel looked promising"), its significance connected to a certain kind of duration understood in topographical terms—that is, in terms of the ease of traversal. Beyond the predominant orientation of printed views with the winding course of the river (faithfully matching the orientation of the text), the prints often include the steamboat itself (here Möllhausen shows us its smokestack, while Egloffstein presents the entire boat with a winding wake pointing to its path), or they present schematized movement back into depth by way of waterfowl depicted in successive stages of flight, as in a view of the Riverside Mountains.

These pictorial devices were also characteristic of illustrations in steamboat and other scenic guidebooks in the East. What is lacking here is the historical exposition that would prepare the passenger to identify, within a view, specific features relatable to some narrative of colonial or Revolutionary War history. This is not to say that Ives ignores this aspect of picturesque description; like other authors of corps reports, he insistently looks for resemblances to architecture—specifically to ruins—in the features of the hills and mountains bordering the river (for example, the "turreted pinnacles" of Chimney Rock). This search for analogs to human presence in the terrain also involves the anthropomorphizing of landscape features, recognizing likeness to the human body—such as "Sleeper's Bend," "a little hill" that bears "a ludicrous resemblance to a sleeping figure."[28] These formulations, however, are purely aesthetic; they derive from insistence on a picturesque mode of perceiving history in the landscape. Although Ives encounters numerous signs of past Native habitation—abandoned dwellings, old path markings, and the like—and although he reports incidents from Native history, he does not associate such physical traces and past events within a view. Despite being peopled by Yumas, Mojaves, Chemehuevis, Hualpais, and Yampais, the landscape is apparently unaltered by their presence; its essential availability for settlement is thus tied to its exclusively topographical temporal significance.

Other than periodic usage of mineralogical terms and references to Newberry's activities, Ives's report is generally devoid of geological observations and conclusions. As the expedition draws closer to the Grand Canyon, though, an implicit awareness builds: processes shaping the landscape have operated here on much vaster scales than immediate experience or (largely unremarked) human history. References to geological change earlier in the report, if they can be said to occur at all, tend to be restricted to observable phenomena—chiefly the action of the river in shaping banks, sandbars, and channels via agents like drifting logs and loose stones (often depicted in the engravings). Just before encountering Chimney Rock, still at some distance from the Grand Canyon, Ives notes that "the banks of the stream for the first time exhibit no appearance of having been recently formed or washed away," and within the next few chapters, the expedition increasingly encounters series of canyons with walls rising directly from the river, with no soil or vegetation forming a transition between the rocky cliffs and the water.[29] As the domesticated landscape components of the picturesque view begin disappearing from the terrain, the presence of geological time looms greater and greater behind the textual descriptions and printed views, even if it is never explicitly named or identified. More precisely, the practice of picturesque description paired with printed illustration proves increasingly inadequate to register the kind of history that views of the terrain imply. Geological time asserts itself as a mounting apprehension of the terrain's sublime—that is, terrifying—character that overpowers picturesque conventions. This overpowering of the report's default mode of landscape presentation occurs most notably because the expedition's progress stops, and with it the association of aesthetic beauty with ease of traversal.

As the expedition enters the first real systems of canyons with heights equivalent to the walls of the Grand Canyon, the chapters are no longer illustrated, because the artists have been left behind in the face of frequent portages and towing episodes. The text, though cognizant of the striking appearance of the landscape, dwells more on the difficulties of continued movement up the river. Eventually the expedition is compelled to turn around, having reached Black Canyon, at the point where the river turns east, just before the Grand Canyon itself. The chapter ends with the only illustration found in this part of the report, a lithograph, *Black Cañon*, in which topographical, traversable (and hence knowable) space has disappeared altogether (plate 20). The pictorial characteristics of the sublime in such an image have been recognized, but I want to focus on the way it forcefully overturns or negates the kind of landscape illustrations encountered earlier in the report.[30] The print is oriented vertically, there is no path into depth, and the ability to register forms—the shape of hills and the course of the river, with their picturesque broken lines—ends as their outlines either stretch to sheer verticality (the cliff walls) or compress to a mere point (the river entering the canyon). In a sense there is a spectrum between the blank, or white, spaces of the report's opening map (in which landscape features are yet to be represented because the terrain has not been explored), the gray appearance of the domesticated picturesque view found in the earlier chapters (achieved through either close parallel engraved lines or softly applied lithographic crayon), and the blackness of the anti-image exhibited here (what is unrepresentable).

Forced to turn back, the expedition now attempts to reach the Grand Canyon by an overland route, leaving the domain of the steamboat excursion altogether and entering the barren landscape of the plateaus topping the canyons of the Colorado River and its tributaries. Although illustrations of the landscape reappear in this part of the report (Möllhausen and Egloffstein have rejoined the survey team), glimpses of the Grand Canyon itself and its subsidiary branches are depicted in a manner that, like the *Black Cañon* lithograph, compromises the components of the picturesque view, while the text dwells on the difficulties of traversing this space: climbing canyon walls, getting lost, locating potable water. The *Cataract Cañon* vignette shows almost no horizon; the principal lines of landscape features are more or less vertical; and the path into space has dropped out of sight (figure 50). This vignette appears, like many of the illustrations in this sequence of chapters, at a point where progression stops, as opposed to the appearance of picturesque views discovered over the course of the steamboat's steady forward movement. The outline panoramas inserted at the beginnings of these later chapters likewise depict a landscape of cliffs and walls that overwhelms the frame and gestures toward the incapacity of the succeeding text to narrate progress from point to point (figure 51).

Concurrently, the text characterizes these views no longer as pictures but as vertiginous visual experiences ("dizzying," "crazy looking,"

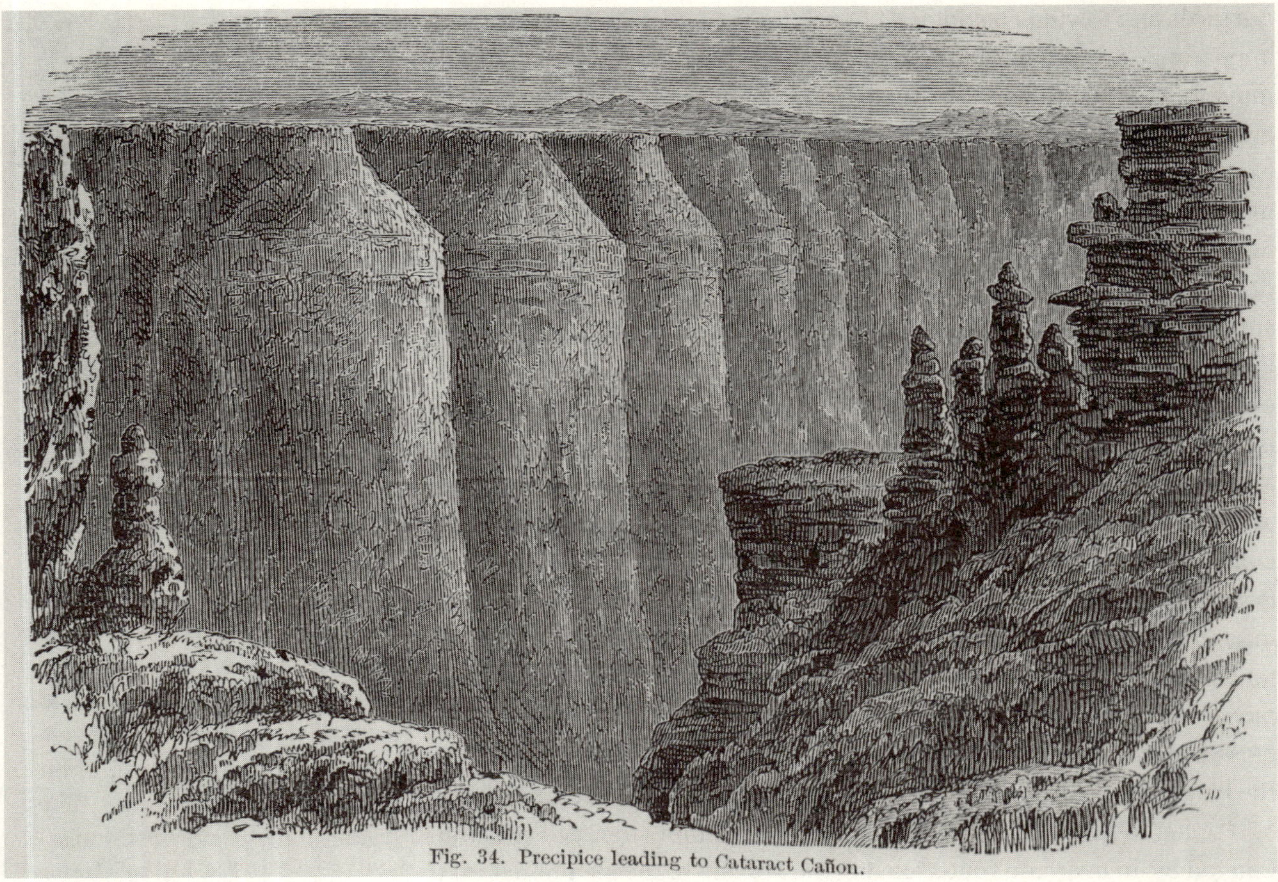

FIGURE 50. Heinrich Baldwin Möllhausen, *Precipice Leading to Cataract Cañon.* Illustration from Joseph C. Ives, *Report upon the Colorado River of the West, Explored in 1857 and 1858* (Washington, DC: Government Printing Office, 1861). RB 2676. Courtesy the Huntington Library, San Marino, California.

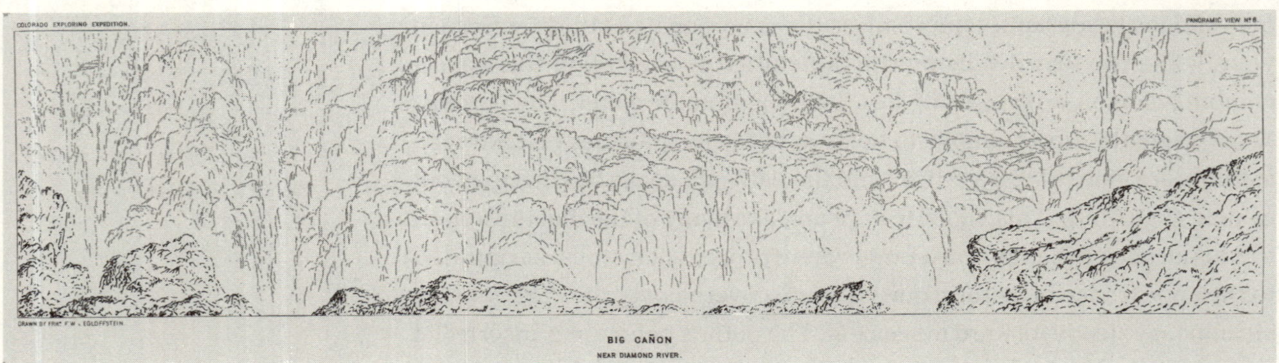

FIGURE 51. F. W. von Egloffstein, *Big Cañon.* Illustration from Joseph C. Ives, *Report upon the Colorado River of the West, Explored in 1857 and 1858* (Washington, DC: Government Printing Office, 1861). RB 2676. Courtesy the Huntington Library, San Marino, California.

"frightful," "giddy"). Within this strange space, a "labyrinth" or "maze" resembling a "vast ruin," time measured by physical progress winds down.[31] Lacking the means to describe or narrate the action of geological processes evidently shaping the landscape, Ives finally registers time as a nullity of "solitude and silence":

> Our reconnoitering parties have now been out in all directions, and everywhere have been headed off by impassable obstacles. . . . It seems intended by nature that the Colorado river, along the greater portion of its lonely and majestic way, shall be forever unvisited and undisturbed. . . . Excepting when the melting snows send their annual torrents through the avenues to the Colorado, conveying with them sound and motion, these dismal abysses, and the arid table-lands that enclose them, are left, as they have been for ages, in unbroken solitude and silence.[32]

Ives is generally aware of the agent responsible for creating the shape of the canyons: the erosion caused by rain and the sediment transported by water. But he is unable to describe its action within a measurable frame of time or narrate its effects as different stages resulting in the distinctive appearance—likewise scarcely representable—of the canyons themselves.

Following Ives's account of the expedition is a short section written by Newberry on the geology of the Colorado River and the adjacent terrain. Its brevity and lack of illustrations or diagrams—except for a geological section, a cross-section displaying the range of sedimentary layers visible in the portions of the Grand Canyon they visited—testifies to a geological history yet to be constructed.[33] Like other geologists on corps surveys, besides looking for signs of valuable mineral deposits, Newberry was engaged in identifying strata as belonging to particular geological epochs, with the long-term objective of constructing a geological section embracing the entire visible stratigraphy of the continent. The history of upheavals, erosion, subsidence, and volcanic action, the alternation of gradual and sudden changes in the transformation of the continent over time, would be compiled and assembled by comparing geological sections from various points throughout the West. At this stage, however, Newberry can offer only general speculations about the location and extent of a western continent during the Paleozoic era, after which erosion caused by the Colorado River carved out the canyons. In 1859 Newberry participated in a survey led by Captain John Macomb that followed the San Juan River to the Colorado, at a point above the Grand Canyon, but he was unable to expeditiously publish a more nuanced geological report. In fact, he seems to have been disappointed with the incompleteness of his "geological narrative" and at a later time worked up his findings into a more comprehensive and detailed history of the Colorado River Basin.[34]

"A Whole Land of Naked Rock": Struggling to Read and Represent Geological Time in the Powell Report

Powell's surveys of the Colorado River were conducted ten years after Ives's ascent from the south, during a seven-year period from 1867 to 1873.[35] Initially Powell's efforts proceeded without government support, financed largely by Illinois educational institutions, until, having descended the Grand Canyon in 1869, he finally secured substantial congressional appropriations for later expeditions.[36] Surveys conducted in 1871–1872 and 1873 involved photographic documentation (chiefly by E. O. Beaman and Jack Hillers), with Moran taking part only in a portion of the last survey. Whereas the first expeditions followed the course of different parts of the river, these later reconnoiters frequently went inland, with the purpose of filling in the cartography and correlating the geological sections of the region. Thus, the process of visual documentation in Powell's report coincides not with the exigencies of physical progress, in locating and following a line of travel between points, but with a more thorough and systematic assessment of the topography and geology of an entire area.

The report does, nonetheless, essentially conform to the structure and use of illustrations found in Ives's account and other earlier corps publications. A larger initial section in Powell recounts a descent of the Colorado River from the point at which the Pacific Railroad crosses the Green River (one of the Colorado's tributaries), through the Uinta Mountains and past junctions with the Grand and San Juan Rivers, into and out of the Grand Canyon, and ending with its confluence with the Virgin River (just up from the farthest point reached by Ives's steamboat). This narration is accompanied by engravings of Moran's work, some based on his sketches made in 1873, but most based on drawings after the photographs of Beaman and Hillers. The last section is again a summary of the geological composition and history of change in the Colorado River region, and it includes numerous diagrams and schematic illustrations by H. H. Nichols. If this last section is a summation, however, the earlier narration of travel also condenses multiple expeditions (not unlike Catlin's *Letters and Notes*), including apparently the first two trips (which covered the extent of the river described in the narration and generally stayed close to the river's course) and, in some way, the later trips as well (during which the photographs and sketches were made). Although this travel narration presents itself as a straightforward account of physical progress, I suggest that it actually comes close to the correlating, synthesizing process underlying the articulation of geological history found in the last section, and that this proximity becomes most evident in the value ascribed to views of the Colorado River landscape.

Scholars have generally regarded the first section as "a flowery adventure narrative" or "tense adventure story," in which Powell dramatizes the difficulties of descending the Colorado River—capsized boats, lost supplies, desertion, and so forth. This narrative, reinforced by Moran's striking illustrations, avoids any substantive scientific exposition.[37] The accounts of the expedition and the images by Moran that appeared in contemporary newspapers certainly stressed this character, as was the case with Powell's updates for *Scribner's Monthly,* illustrated by prints such as *The Grand Cañon of the Colorado*, which would later figure in the report.[38] In this regard, both the narrative and the illustrations in this first section correspond with the first section of Ives's report, especially the portions describing the failure to navigate the river and the strenuous effort involved in traversing the plateaus above it. Images like *Pa-ru'-nu-weap' Cañon* and *Noon-Day Rest in Marble Cañon* reprise the exaggerated scale and perspective, relative to picturesque proportions, that are found in the later prints of the Ives report, as well as their emphasis on darkness and the eclipsing of the horizon (figures 52 and 53). Here again a stable viewing platform is compromised—loose rocks and timber that would be swept away by rushing torrents, a tiny shingle of beach bordering cliffs that rise directly from the water—while the path into depth is variously obstructed, compressed, or too rapid. Childs has noted how Moran's versions of the survey photographs tended to heighten pictorial drama; in *Noon-Day Rest in Marble Cañon,* this is achieved by "accentuat[ing] the height of the cliffs and straighten[ing] their profiles to increase their verticality. . . . The result is both a sense of claustrophobia and of human diminution."[39] She further describes how Moran's prints consistently return attention to the plight of the expedition's members, dwarfed by canyons, tossed by rapids, struggling to ascend sheer walls of granite.

This pictorial dramatization of physical progress is further augmented by the kind of space depicted in the prints and their relationship to the travel account given in the text. As in the Ives report, there are places—usually calm stretches of the river—where the textual description employs a picturesque vocabulary of architectural form, and the printed views feature something like serpentine recession and regularized quasi-architectural shapes. The view of *Glen Cañon*, with its easy sweeping river; modest, uniformly smooth cliff walls; and stable, elevated vantage point, is preceded by the observation that "We have a cool, pleasant ride today, through this part of the cañon . . . the curves are gentle, and often the river sweeps by an arc of vertical wall, smooth and unbroken" (figure 54).[40] Whereas Ives was unable to extend the apparatus of travel narrative paired with printed landscape views into the largest canyons, in particular Black Canyon, here there is an alternating rhythm linking text sections and

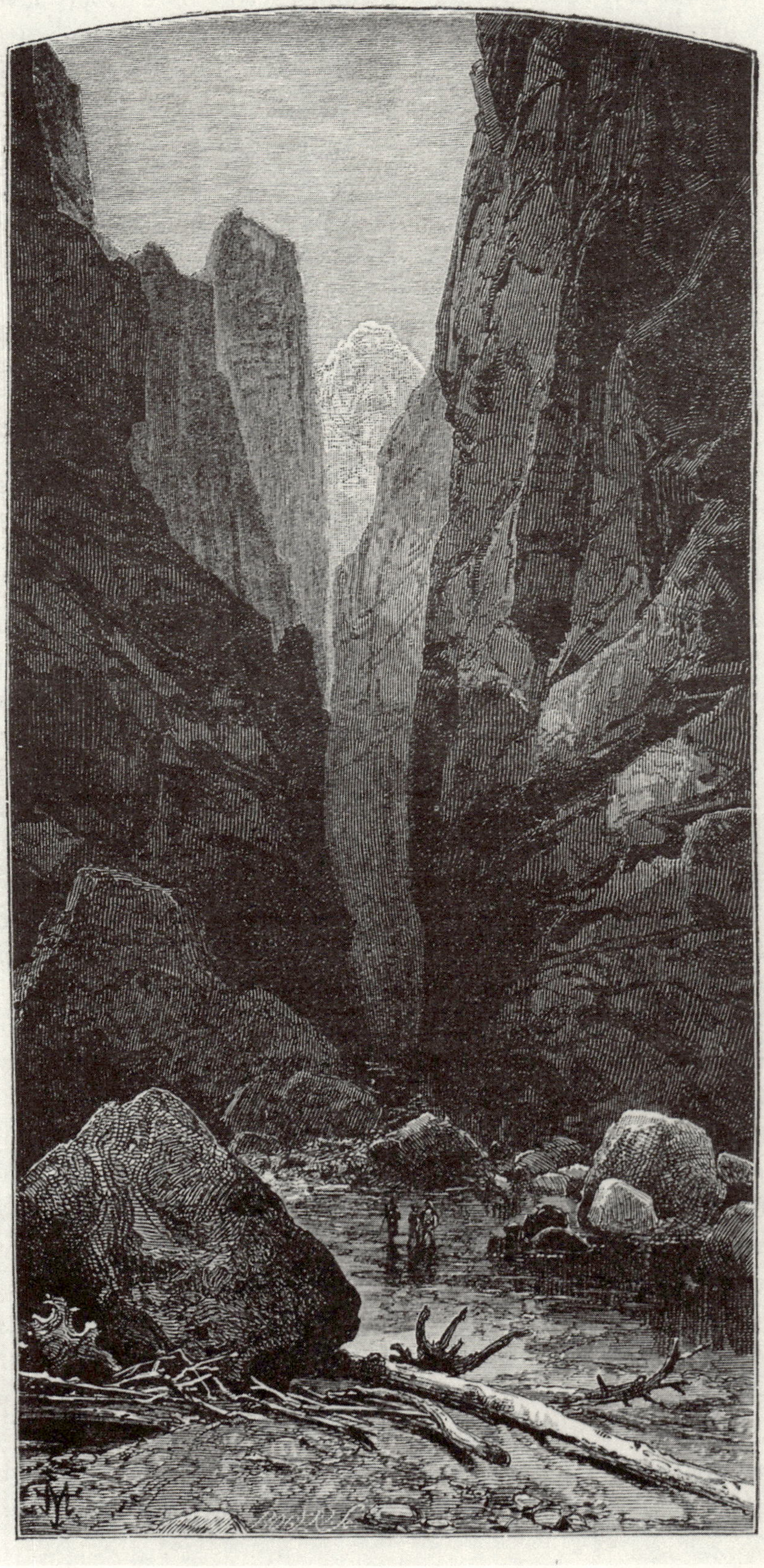

FIGURE 52. Thomas Moran, *Pa-ru'-nu-weap' Cañon*. Illustration from John Wesley Powell, *Exploration of the Colorado River of the West and Its Tributaries* (Washington, DC: Government Printing Office, 1875). RB 751274. Courtesy the Huntington Library, San Marino, California.

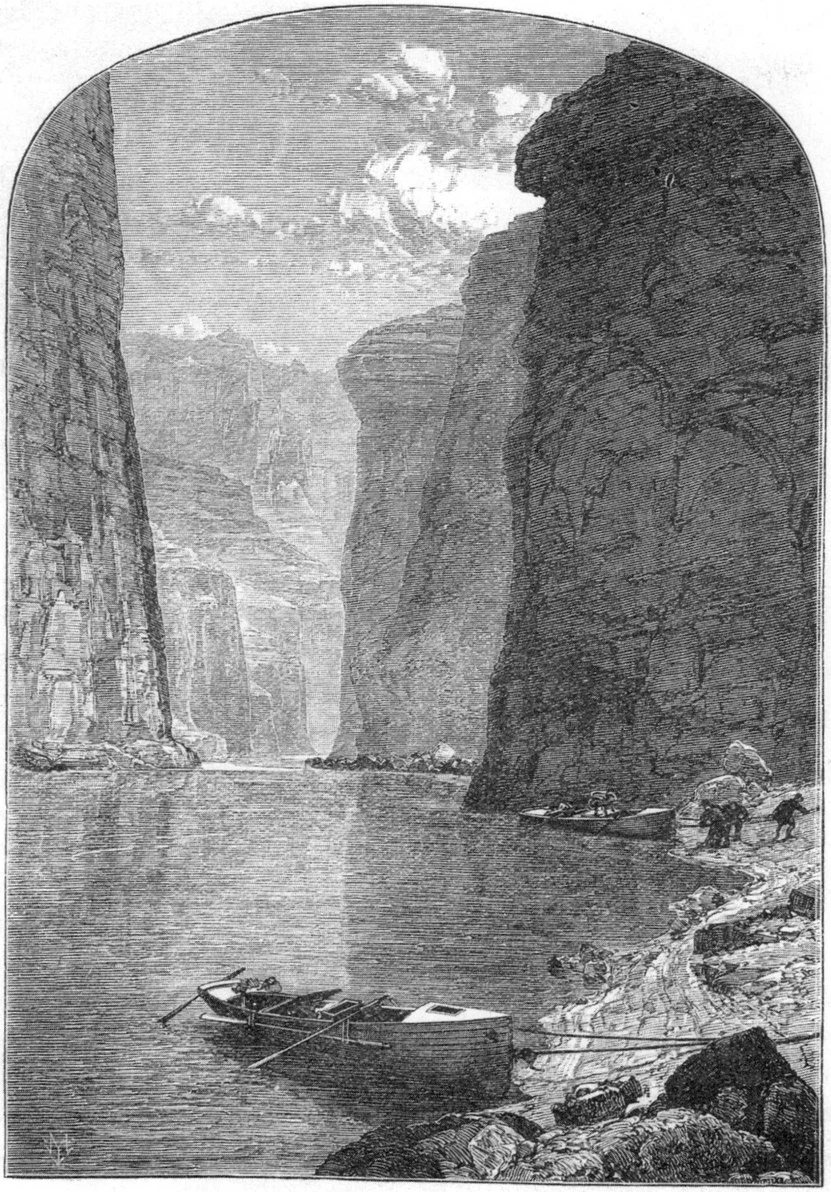

Figure 53. Thomas Moran, *Noon-Day Rest in Marble Cañon*. Illustration from John Wesley Powell, *Exploration of the Colorado River of the West and Its Tributaries* (Washington, DC: Government Printing Office, 1875). RB 751274. Courtesy the Huntington Library, San Marino, California.

printed views, which effectually simulates the oscillation between dead stops and unchecked velocity that characterizes the physical progress described by Powell in descending the Colorado River. Where the text emphasizes speed, confining walls, and the movement of massive volumes of water, multiple engravings tend to follow in rapid succession, featuring views with an almost tunnel-like perspective. *Noon-Day Rest in Marble Cañon* is almost immediately followed by *Marble Cañon*, another view with a rapid, almost geometrically precise path into depth, as the straight lines of the sandbar converge toward the river's exit through the canyon

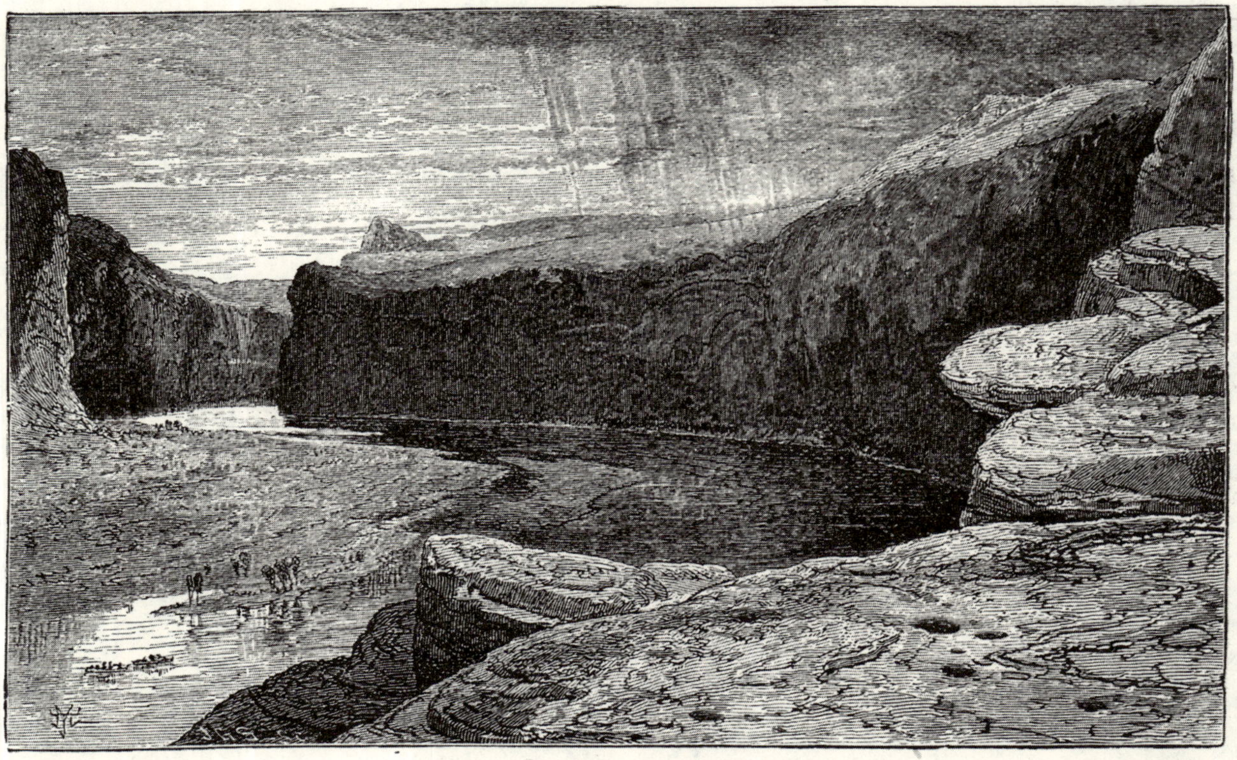

FIGURE 54. Thomas Moran, *Glen Cañon*. Illustration from John Wesley Powell, *Exploration of the Colorado River of the West and Its Tributaries* (Washington, DC: Government Printing Office, 1875). RB 751274. Courtesy the Huntington Library, San Marino, California.

(figure 55). The text in these pages describes "a long, rocky, mad rapid," "walls still higher; water, swift again"; the water is moving too quickly, the shoreline is barely existent, and the members of the expedition struggle to prevent their boats from being swept away, engaging in a series of risky shots down sections of rapids ("tossed enough by the waves to appreciate the rate at which we are traveling") or attempting to lower their boats downriver with lines.[41]

These episodes of scarcely checked progress alternate with stretches when the expedition grinds to a halt, usually for the purpose of scaling the canyon walls to calculate elevation and obtain geodetic observations to correct for the curvature of the earth's surface. Illustrations of such stopping points tend to be relatively scarce, while the text rehearses the difficulties of locating side canyons leading away from the river and up toward the plateaus, or the dangers of scaling the cliffs themselves. Where prints occur, they depict tiers of cliffs and rocky shelves without paths of access between them and reduce the horizon to a distant sliver. *Water Basin in Gypsum Cañon* is accompanied by a lengthy account of the expedition's ascent, filled with repeated expressions of frustration: "our way seems cut off," "we can go no further," "we turn back," "it will be impossible to climb" (figure 56).[42] If the text describing the running of

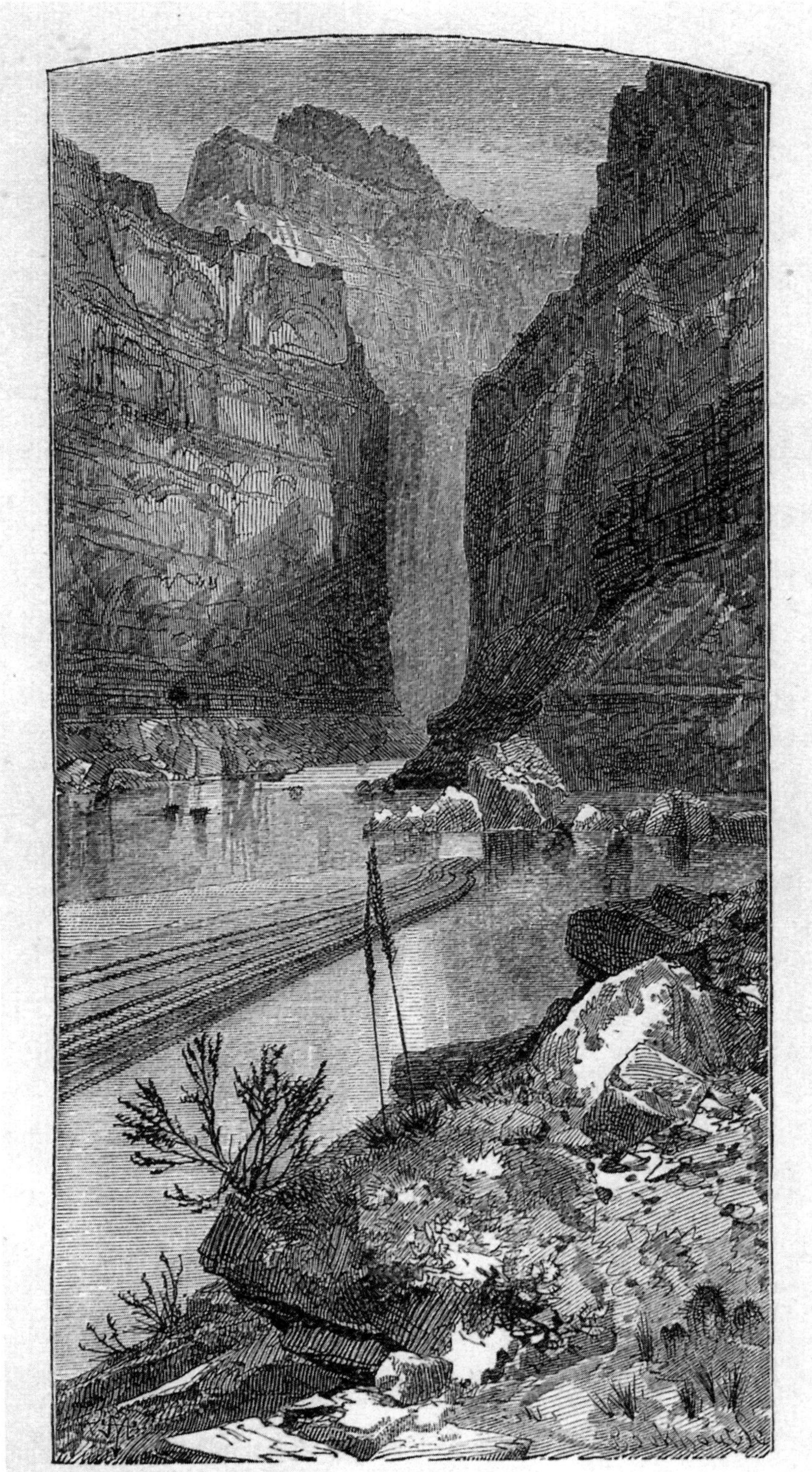

FIGURE 55. Thomas Moran, *Marble Cañon*. Illustration from John Wesley Powell, *Exploration of the Colorado River of the West and Its Tributaries* (Washington, DC: Government Printing Office, 1875). RB 751274. Courtesy the Huntington Library, San Marino, California.

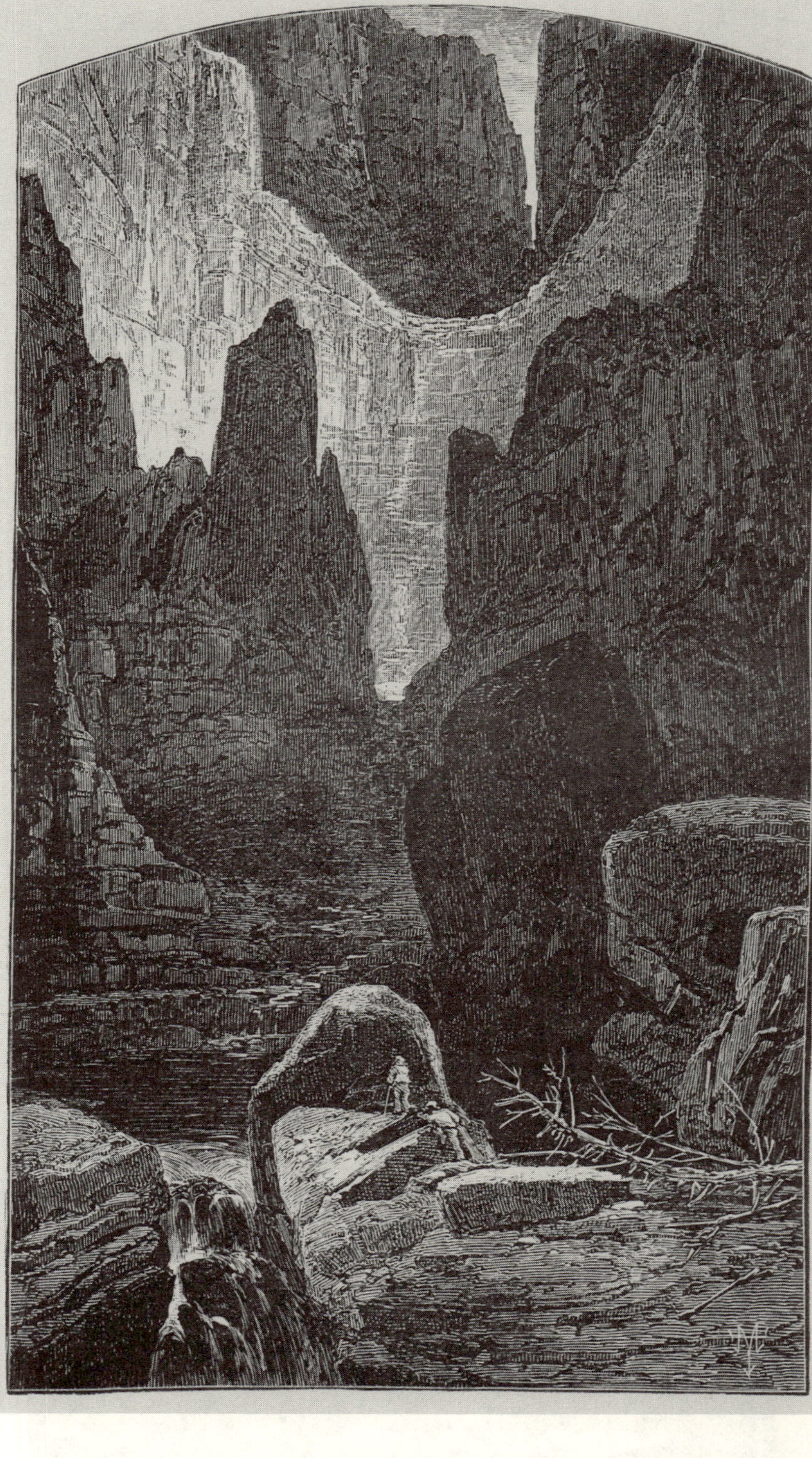

FIGURE 56. Thomas Moran, *Water Basin in Gypsum Cañon*. Illustration from John Wesley Powell, *Exploration of the Colorado River of the West and Its Tributaries* (Washington, DC: Government Printing Office, 1875). RB 751274. Courtesy the Huntington Library, San Marino, California.

rapids stresses the sense of the Colorado River as an unstoppable force, an agent of uncontrolled speed, accounts of these excursions up the canyon walls emphasize the impossibility of traversing a space that so greatly exceeds the units of measurement involved in human locomotion: the span of a stride or step compared with the calculation of horizontal or vertical distance.[43] Although the kind of space depicted in the illustrations (tunnel versus wall) and the grouping of illustrations (on every other page or in isolation) do not always precisely correlate with the mode of travel described in the text, to the extent that they evoke alternations of rushing and halting movements, they evoke an environment antagonistic to human navigation in the form of the reader's own navigation of Powell's report.

In many key aspects, the textual and pictorial representation of progress through landscape in this report resembles the alterations to familiar modes of traversing space imposed by railroad travel and represented in railroad guidebooks. The river cuts through mountain chains (as do railroad tunnels and embankments), and the members of the expedition struggle to maintain their own rate of travel against the rushing water (just as the train sweeps along at uniform speeds exceeding previous forms of travel). Above all, Powell and his companions are restricted, confined to the river (as passengers in a train car are sealed off from the outside). The railroad guidebook labored to assign a coherent historical narrative to the passing sights visible from the train car window, and this perceptible effort fostered a sense of history as fragmented, uncontrollable, and superficial. Powell's report certainly registers the inadequacy of picturesque conventions of description and illustration as means for representing a navigation of the Colorado River. But the report can also be read as representing the difficulties of conjoining a series of views that in this case purport to relate geological time. Powell surveyed the Colorado River and its adjacent territory with the intention of reconstructing the history of geological change that had produced that landscape. Although the first section of his narrative focuses on the drama of descending the river, it nevertheless recounts a process of taking measurements and making observations. The vast environment, more or less devoid of plant and animal life, through which Powell and his associates travel is a species of pure geometric space whose coordinates are a lattice of equally vast stretches of time, and Powell's efforts to traverse that space are equally efforts to apprehend that lattice in its proper relations: "All the scenic features of this cañon land are on a giant scale, strange and weird."[44] In this context, the experience of rushing and halting movements evoked by Moran's prints simultaneously gesture toward the difficult process of apprehending geological time.[45]

At certain junctures, Powell equates traversal of space with traversal of geological time, most often when scaling cliff walls to measure the thickness of their strata, formed by deposition and compaction over millennia:

> Howland and myself determine to climb out, and start up a lateral cañon, taking a barometer with us, for the purpose of measuring the thickness of the strata over which we pass. The readings of the barometer below are recorded every half hour, and our observations must be simultaneous. Where the beds, which we desire to measure, are very thick, we must climb with the utmost speed, to reach their summits in time. Again, where there are thinner beds, we wait for the moment to arrive.[46]

The imposition of an artificial sequence of time by means of the barometric readings mediates between the movement of the two men up the wall and the measurement of the strata's widths, which correspond to particular geological epochs. The seemingly arcane instrumentation of nineteenth-century geological science—the theodolites, barometers, and sextants—provide a precise recording of position and distance, but the apprehension and correlation of geologically significant features occur as a sort of specialized reading, a new way of coordinating discrete views.[47] In summing up the history of geological change in the Colorado River Basin, Powell contrasts the limited perspective obtainable on the river with the increasing legibility of landscape as one ascends to the higher plateaus:

> The varying depths of [the Grand Canyon], due to the varying altitudes of the plateaus through which it runs, can only be seen from above. . . . One might imagine that this [the strata and their erosion into side canyons] was intended for the library of the gods; and it was. The shelves are not for books, but form the stony leaves of one great book. He who would read the language of the universe may dig out letters here and there, and with them spell the words, and read, in a slow and imperfect way, but still so as to understand a little, the story of creation.[48]

The process that Powell describes here consists of the identification and correlation of geological sections, a kind of reading constituted by recognition, vantage point, and arrangement in a sequence.

Wrestling with the inadequacy of the picturesque mode of description and pictorial representation, the first section of Powell's report is littered with odd sights, points of view, and optical illusions. Looking up at the night sky in one of the earlier camps of the expedition, Powell reflects, "I see a bright star, that appears to rest on the very verge of the cliff overhead to the east . . . as it moves out from the rock, I almost wonder that it does not fall. In fact, it does seem to descend in a gentle curve. . . . The stars appear to be in the cañon."[49] Later, he again notes the distortion of vertical distance within the canyon: "The light above, made more brilliant by the bright-tinted rocks, and the shadows below more gloomy by the somber hues of the brown walls, increase the apparent depths of the cañons, and it seems a long way up to the world of sunshine and open sky."[50] While the canyon stymies the optical equipment of the human observer, Powell nevertheless simultaneously records a process of adjusting that equipment and overcoming such distortion, judging heights through a kind of stereoscopic perspective or comparing cliffs to city buildings to establish a more accurate succession of vertical heights.[51] These adjustments are components of geologically sensitive vision; Powell is not a neutral observer but looks about him for visual data pertinent to his surveyor's mission. Similarly, the printed illustrations do not just present a range of picturesque, vertiginous, or obstructing views, they also advance the process of familiarization with the optical environment of the canyon. Moran's prints are notably striking for their odd frames, apparent waste of page space, and unusual vantage points.

Above all, I want to stress the dual nature of the first section of the report as a record both of physical progress and of efforts to identify and integrate place-specific observations in the articulation of geological history. This process turns on developing a geologically sensitive eye, one that can surmount the visual shock that accompanies the sensory distortions of an unfamiliar environment and move toward a mode of vision that finds meaning. Powell's summation following this section endeavors to integrate the observations and measurements obtained on his surveys into a properly geological narrative. This summation contains illustrations that exemplify the capabilities of this more astute spectator, but some of the prints in the first section already anticipate this kind of viewing in their function as a record of its development. The section of the report titled "On the Physical Features of the Valley of the Colorado" divides the terrain encountered on the expeditions into several groupings and then offers localized explanations for the shapes found in these areas—specific instances of Powell's general understanding of the activity of erosion occurring all along the Colorado River. These explanations are generally uniformitarian, stipulating that the river antedates the network of plateaus and mountains through which it runs and has maintained its level while cutting through them as they rose over the course of millennia.[52] As Kinsey notes, a wood engraving of Moran's painting *The Chasm of the Colorado* appears at the end of this section as a final pictorial restatement of this geological history (figure 57).[53] Evidence of uplift and folding is largely

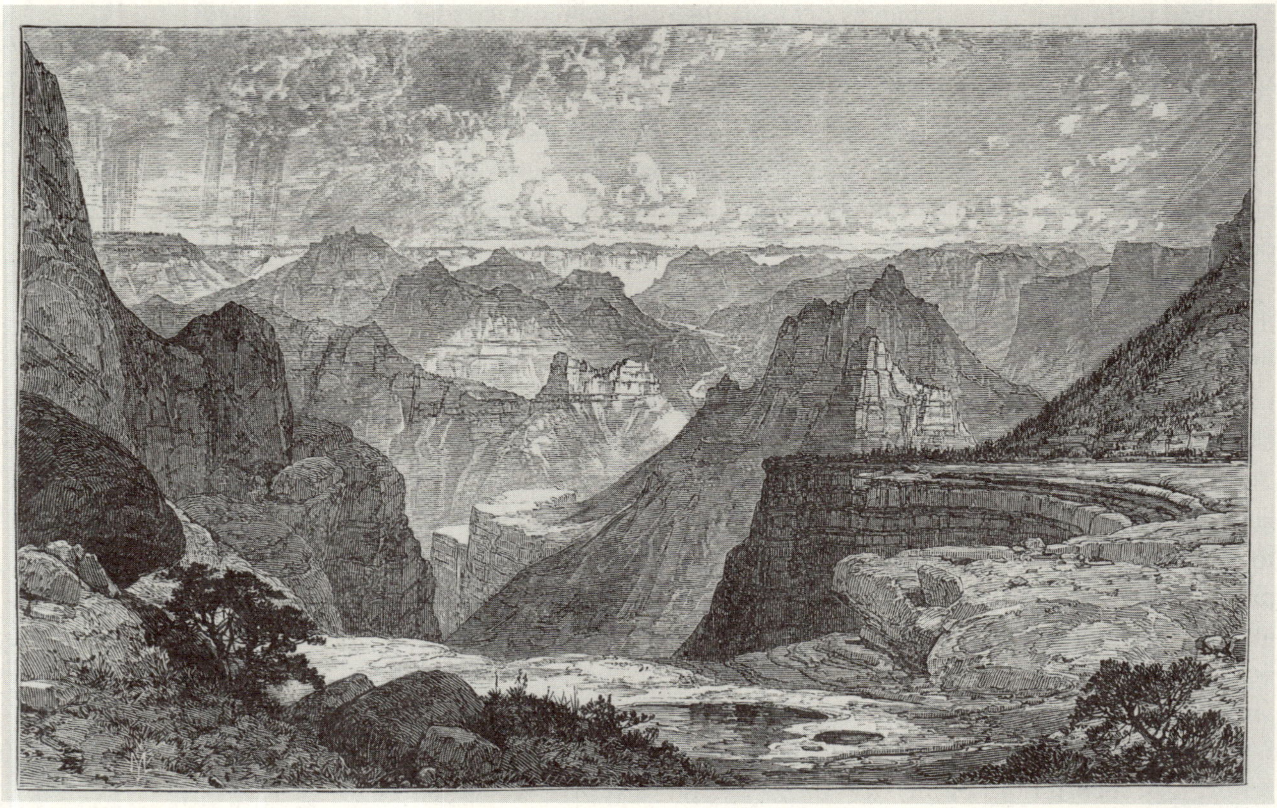

Figure 57. Thomas Moran, *The Grand Cañon of the Colorado.* Illustration from John Wesley Powell, *Exploration of the Colorado River of the West and Its Tributaries* (Washington, DC: Government Printing Office, 1875). RB 751274. Courtesy the Huntington Library, San Marino, California.

missing, although we do see bands of strata, and the upward-pointing forms of hills and our elevated viewpoint suggest uplift. This image still records an epic process of erosion, however, with the tiny ribbon of the river itself, just visible in the middle background, stretching the time frame necessary for that process to carve the vast system of canyons through which the river winds.

If Moran's print supplies a kind of pictorial conclusion, its inclusion in this final section is also exceptional. The other illustrations are predominantly diagrams and schematic renderings of landscapes, based on drawings by Nichols, that clarify their particular geological forms and their place within the master story of uplift and erosion. In discussing the folding of the Uinta Mountains and the carving of canyons, Powell describes a series of valley types classified by their relation to the axis of uplift, each of which is illustrated by Nichols in a simplified, bird's-eye view. Thus, a diaclinal valley passes directly through a fold, and an anticlinal valley runs across its apex (figures 58 and 59). While simplified and diagrammatic, these prints also represent a geologically illuminating view: a vantage point, a frame, and a focus on specific features of rock, corresponding with the cliff-top observations that were particularly instrumental for Powell in

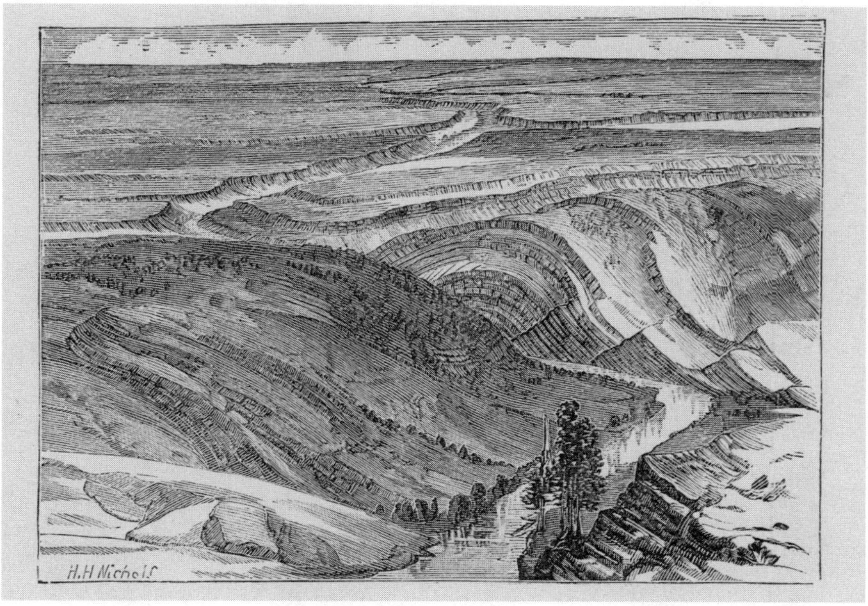

Figure 58. H. H. Nichols, *A Diaclinal Valley.* Illustration from John Wesley Powell, *Exploration of the Colorado River of the West and Its Tributaries* (Washington, DC: Government Printing Office, 1875). RB 751274. Courtesy the Huntington Library, San Marino, California.

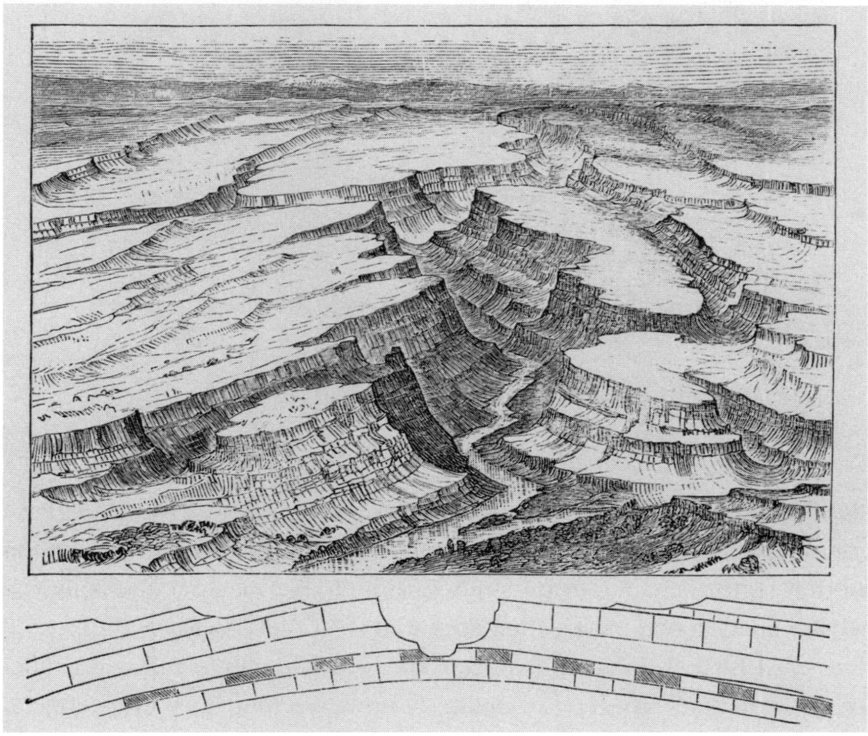

Figure 59. H. H. Nichols, *An Anticlinal Valley.* Illustration from John Wesley Powell, *Exploration of the Colorado River of the West and Its Tributaries* (Washington, DC: Government Printing Office, 1875). RB 751274. Courtesy the Huntington Library, San Marino, California.

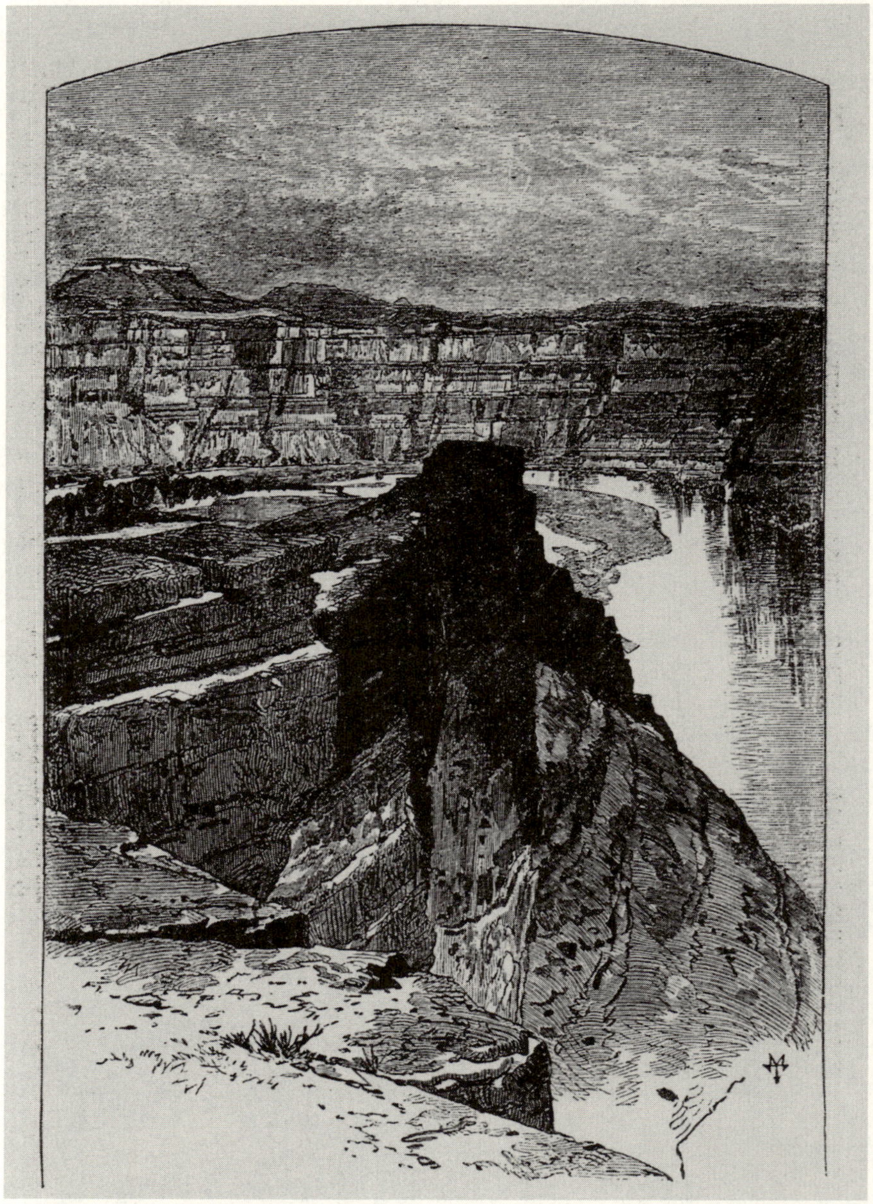

FIGURE 60. Thomas Moran, *Sumner's Amphitheater.* Illustration from John Wesley Powell, *Exploration of the Colorado River of the West and Its Tributaries* (Washington, DC: Government Printing Office, 1875). RB 751274. Courtesy the Huntington Library, San Marino, California.

developing his understanding of geological history. These elevated views function both as illustrations and as constitutive parts of the articulation of that history. Such elevated views, though, likewise occur within the earlier section recounting the descent of the Colorado River (figures 60 and 61). The text does not explicate the depicted cliff forms as diaclinal or anticlinal, nor are they correlated in relation to a story of geological development. Such views do, however, register the increasing sophistication of geologically directed vision in competition with the picturesque, the dramatic, and the distorted view. *The Grand Cañon* represents a vast space that can be read aesthetically as sublime. But it also gives us the view available to the surveyors, shown gazing into the canyon, perhaps equally impressed by the scene's majesty but also engaged in detecting those perspicacious views of diaclinal and anticlinal valleys.

This function of the view in constituting a history of geological development is further suggested by the readiness with which these earlier prints of elevated views lend themselves to larger composite pictures. Following *The Grand Cañon* is a second print of the canyons of the Colorado River depicting a wider extent of hills and channels and thus embracing a larger

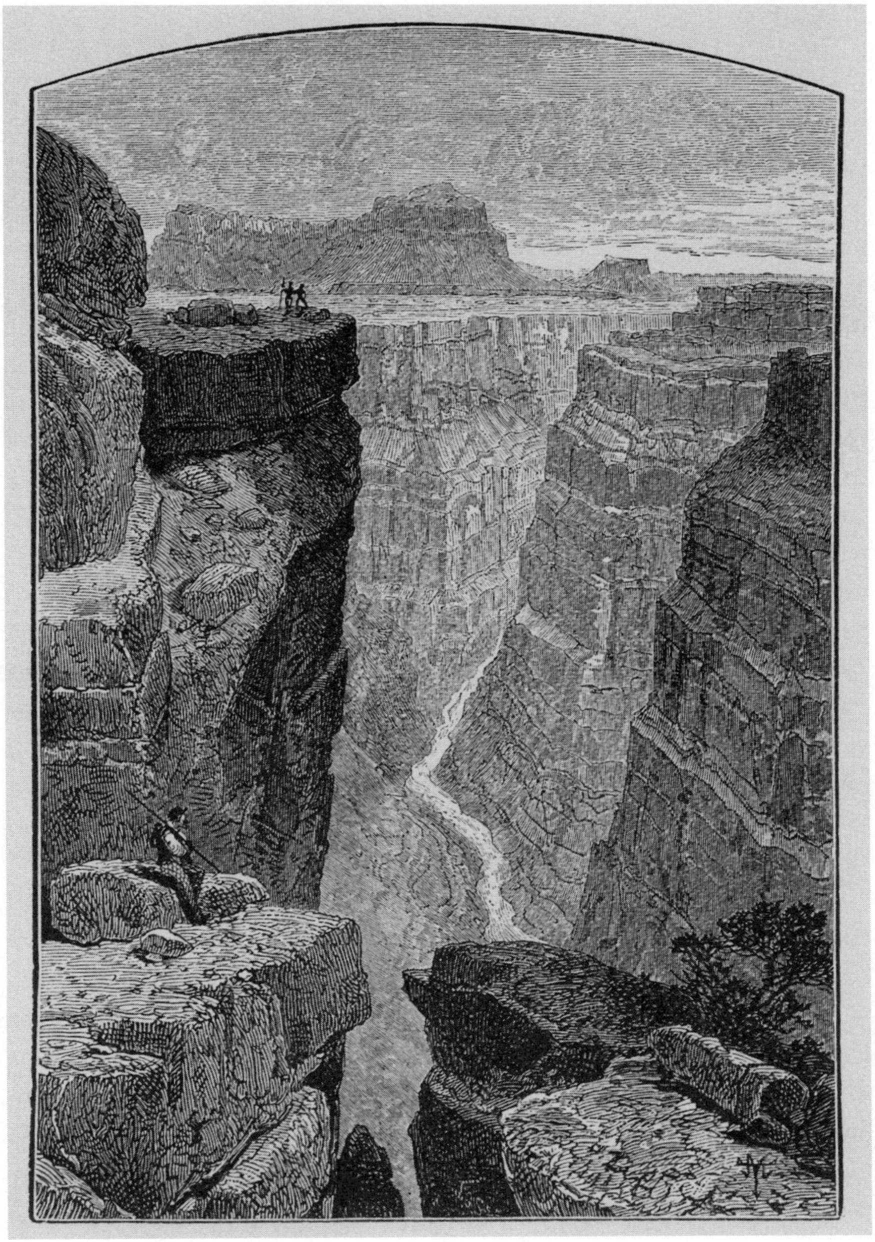

FIGURE 61. Thomas Moran, *The Grand Cañon, Looking East from To-ro-weap.* Illustration from John Wesley Powell, *Exploration of the Colorado River of the West and Its Tributaries* (Washington, DC: Government Printing Office, 1875). RB 751274. Courtesy the Huntington Library, San Marino, California.

segment of the overall geological story. The salient point is that, while Moran's prints have been associated with an understanding of Powell's report as a sensationalistic account of travel, they equally relate to Powell's attempt to construct a true "geological narrative" (to use Newberry's phrase). The parallels between the reports of Ives and Powell, including the use of illustration, extend as well as to the incompleteness of that attempt on the part of either author. Powell's competitor, King, would proceed even further in modifying the narrative of physical progress characteristic of corps reports to fashion such a "geological narrative," an initiative that, crucially, also involved adjusting the role of landscape illustration.

Narrating the Geological Column in the King Report

Both King's survey and his report were more ambitious in scope than his predecessors'. Appointed the civilian head of a military-sponsored and funded enterprise, he enlisted a full complement of scientists to systematically describe the geological, mineralogical, hydrographical, meteorological, paleontological, botanical, and zoological profiles of the territory they covered from 1867 to 1873—a band one hundred miles wide that followed the route of the Pacific Railroad from the Sierra Nevada to the Rocky Mountains.[54] King's own principal interest was the geology of the region, and this focus came to determine the geographical limits of survey activities. By compiling geological sections one hundred miles wide across the east-west extent of the Cordilleras (the total system of mountain chains on the western part of the continent), King hoped to gain a clear understanding of its structure and history. As he remarked, "One well observed section traced across a single range or a complex chain, or even through the whole broad system, would in most cases simply mislead the student. A parallel section five miles either side of it might result in a totally different reading."[55] King also authored the first volume of the survey's many published reports, a synthetic account of the geological composition and history of this area.[56]

King's report replicates many structural and narrative aspects of the corps publications. Its first chapters generally follow a route from east to west—actually the opposite of the expedition's course of travel, which started from the Sierra Nevada—and they restrict themselves to describing terrain, while the final chapter brings these observations together in a comprehensive "geological narrative." The sense of movement along a linear path, however, is diffused across the width, north to south, of the surveyed area ("A parallel section five miles either side of [a line of geological observations] might result in a totally different reading").

Critically, also, the account of movement from east to west is repeated; each chapter goes over the entire area surveyed. Instead of recounting a linear path of physical progress, chapters are organized to enumerate the instances of rock from particular geological eras where they occur as one moves across this hundred-mile band from east to west. The result is a fragmented sense of progress as the survey moves west, with notices of various rock types unattached to any clear directive or narrative development. What King is attempting to do, however, is reorient the corps narrative of physical progress across terrain, a horizontal perspective, to movement up the strata representing different geological periods, a vertical perspective that corresponds to geological history. As he explains in the introductory chapter: "In these chapters the method of treatment adopted is, to begin at the bottom of the geological column, and present all the important facts we have accumulated on each successive formation [each instance of rock from a particular geological era encountered from east to west], always attempting to correlate the wide-spread data and construct a continuous piece of geological history."[57]

Like the outline panoramas in the Ives report, each chapter in King is accompanied by an overview of the terrain surveyed, here appearing at the end rather than the beginning of chapters and taking the form of an elevation map—a map of vertical distances above sea level—in which rocks from the geological era described in that chapter are displayed as colored areas. The first three maps depicting the instances of Archean, Paleozoic, and Mesozoic strata are cumulative, so that in an approximate way, as one moves from map to map (in the manner of a flipbook), the western continent emerges from the primarily white space of the map like a series of islands emerging from the sea (figures 62 and 63).[58] Whereas the outline panoramas in the Ives report project a linear path of travel that the text then recounts, these maps set an orientation that moves up the "geological column," tracking the overall temporal dynamic of geological history.

What is more, while Ives and Powell dramatically narrate the difficulties attending their expedition's movement through terrain, King effaces his presence in describing strata across the area of the survey. The activities of surveying, of human agents moving, observing, collecting specimens, taking measurements, are entirely implicit, inferable only through specified locations and the results of those activities. This effacement of human presence has the effect of further reorienting the reader's perspective away from the traditional corps account of physical progress, particularly its encouragement of the reader's vicarious participation in the expedition. In King's account, rocks from different strata are encountered according to no explicit division of time into days of travel or series of camps, and are

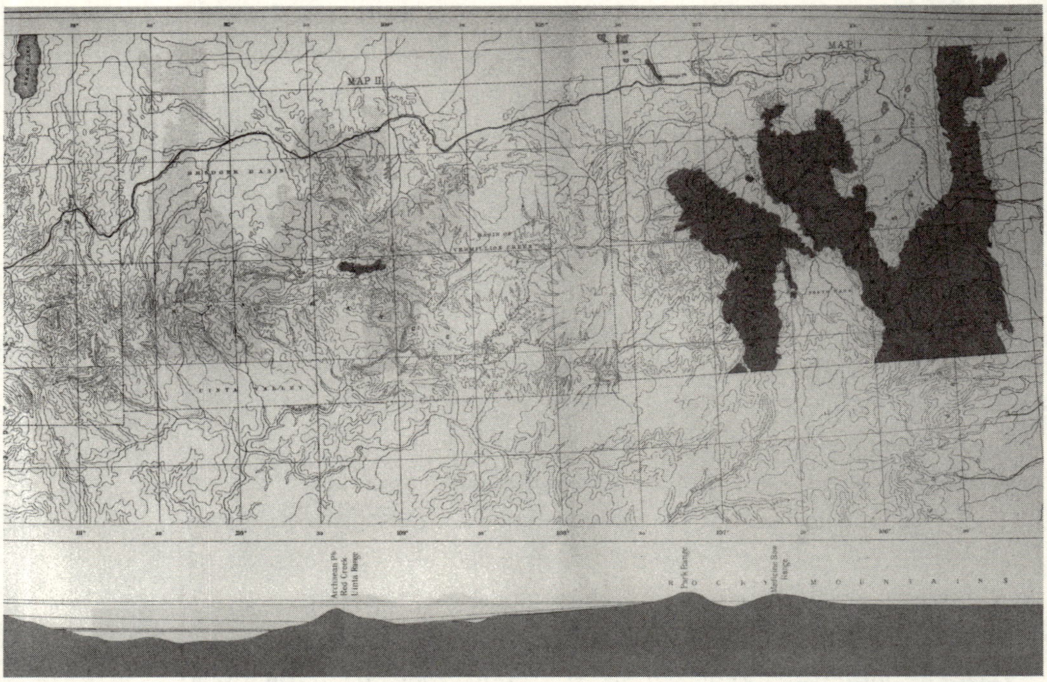

FIGURE 62. Unknown artist, *Archaean and Granitic Exposures.* Illustration from Clarence King, *Systematic Geology,* vol. 1 of *Report of the Geological Exploration of the Fortieth Parallel* (Washington, DC: Government Printing Office, 1878). Courtesy Sandel Library, Northeast Louisiana University.

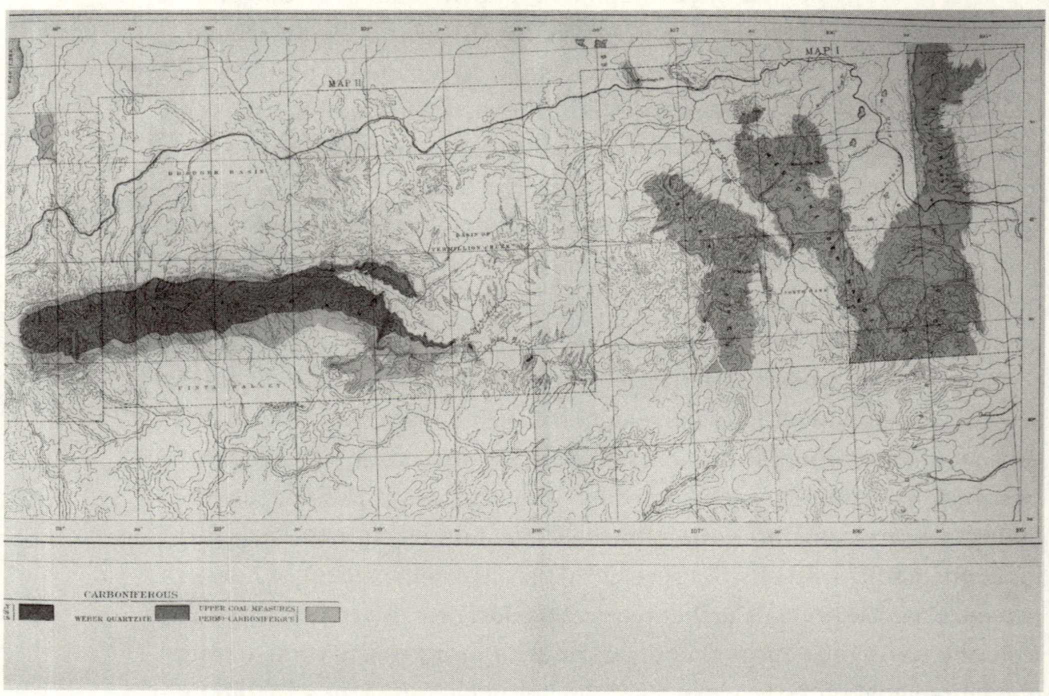

FIGURE 63. Unknown artist, *Archaean, Granitic, and Palaeozoic Exposures.* Illustration from Clarence King, *Systematic Geology,* vol. 1 of *Report of the Geological Exploration of the Fortieth Parallel* (Washington, DC: Government Printing Office, 1878). Courtesy Sandel Library, Northeast Louisiana University.

consequently referable to other, vaster periodizations of time. Describing geological characteristics is thus closer to a retelling of geological history, as the listings of sedimentary rock layers rehearse periods of erosion, accumulation, and compaction. Even the conditions of viewing strata evoke this vaster scale of time: "The [Wasatch] range itself is really a great mountain wall, the result of a profound break in the earth's crust; the western half of the range has been carried down beneath the level of the present plains, leaving a lofty face presented to the west."[59] The range of strata composing the western faces of the Wasatch Range reveal themselves as the result of a specific geological episode; to see them is almost to witness that episode.

After the series of chapters identifying the locations of strata (or exposures), King undertakes to narrate the history of their deposition and later transformations in a final chapter on "Orography." Covering a wider range of territory and geological time than Ives and Powell do, King proposes nothing less than a reconstruction of the western continent's mutations of shape and topography, through periods of both rapid and gradual change, since before the appearance of life on the planet. He is leery of identifying principal causes and instead restricts himself primarily to determining when which parts of the land mass existed above and below the levels of seas or lakes, as well as the likely starting and stopping times of folding and faulting.[60] King's history divides into five parts, or stages, that roughly correspond with the first chapters: Archean, Paleozoic, Mesozoic, and Cenozoic, divided into the Tertiary and Quaternary periods. Thus, the division of space into various zones corresponding to eras, periods, and epochs is finally transmuted into a division of time according to various configurations of the shape and topography of the western landmasses.[61] At least, this is King's method of proceeding; nowhere does he consider his reconstruction satisfactory in terms of precision, and in many cases he admits the incompleteness of both his data and his theory in respect to such a reconstruction.[62]

King's report is illustrated with some thirty toned lithographs based on photographs by O'Sullivan and drawings by Gilbert Munger (who often based his drawings on other photographs by O'Sullivan). The toned lithographs of O'Sullivan's work reflect the black-and-white palette of photography; although not photomechanical reproductions, they translate his pictures with surprising fidelity.[63] The marks of the lithographic crayon can be too exclusively directed toward clarifying conditions of light and dark or emphasizing the tonality of areas of colored rock, while the view can be cropped or tilted. Other, more dramatic alterations include the insertion of human figures and the depiction of cloud forms and waves on bodies of water (see plates 18 and 19).[64] For studies of O'Sullivan's work, however, these differences are crucial because they reduce the specificity of the photographic image to some version compromised by the conventions of landscape illustration, taking an image that was unfamiliar and strange and normalizing it through a received pictorial language that holds no surprises.[65]

This perspective on the reproduction of O'Sullivan's pictures then drives a wedge between the photographs and King's report. Seemingly, nothing is more conventional or further from unique, individual expression, and thus less deserving of analysis, than illustration, reinforcing an approach that, like readings of Moran's paintings, tends to find the influence of King's ideas on the photographs solely in their parallel evocation of an environment hostile to human presence (reflecting the catastrophic forces King favored as the leading agents of geological change).[66] The illustrations may belong to a different "discursive space" than the photographs, but they are still based on the photographs; more importantly, that "discursive space"—the kinds of utterances permissible in the articulation of scientific theory (including both narrative and illustration practice)—is not fixed but in a state of flux.[67] Möllhausen's prints in the Ives report intensified the narrative presentation of landscape as having only one kind of temporal dimension, that of traversal. King's report modifies that narrative form to present the geological history of landscape, and the prints of O'Sullivan's photographs correspondingly intensify this altered narrative form.

On a basic level, these prints reorient the inclination to move back into representational space, which was characteristic of the picturesque view, to upward movement instead. Numerous prints depict sheer cliff walls, with no possibility of moving around them, as in *Eocene Bluffs, Green River, Wyoming* (figure 64).[68] Kelsey relates this two-dimensional vertical orientation to other graphic practices used in the surveys, but to clearly see the width, torsion, and vertical relations of strata is also to reconstitute the history of accumulation and upheaval in its correct order.[69] The specific episodes of geological history are revealed as widths, fluctuations, and alterations occurring on a vertical axis, however much the reader may expect to move back into depicted space (just as the reader may expect to move along the route of the expedition's traversal of terrain within King's narrative). In a related fashion, several prints depict a vertiginous path into depth, such as *Archaean Quartzite, Humboldt Range, Nevada*, in which a bluff thrusts sharply and tangentially into space, and middle-ground debris falls away equally abruptly in a vector pointing downward and backward (figure 65). This kind of swooping, dizzy perspective is characteristic of many other O'Sullivan photographs, an effect often heightened by tilting the horizon line, as in *Ridge of Columnar Trachyte, Nevada* (figure 66). Such a perspective has been read as a pictorial analog of the thrusting, violent action of upheaval, but its vertigo additionally stems from a conflict

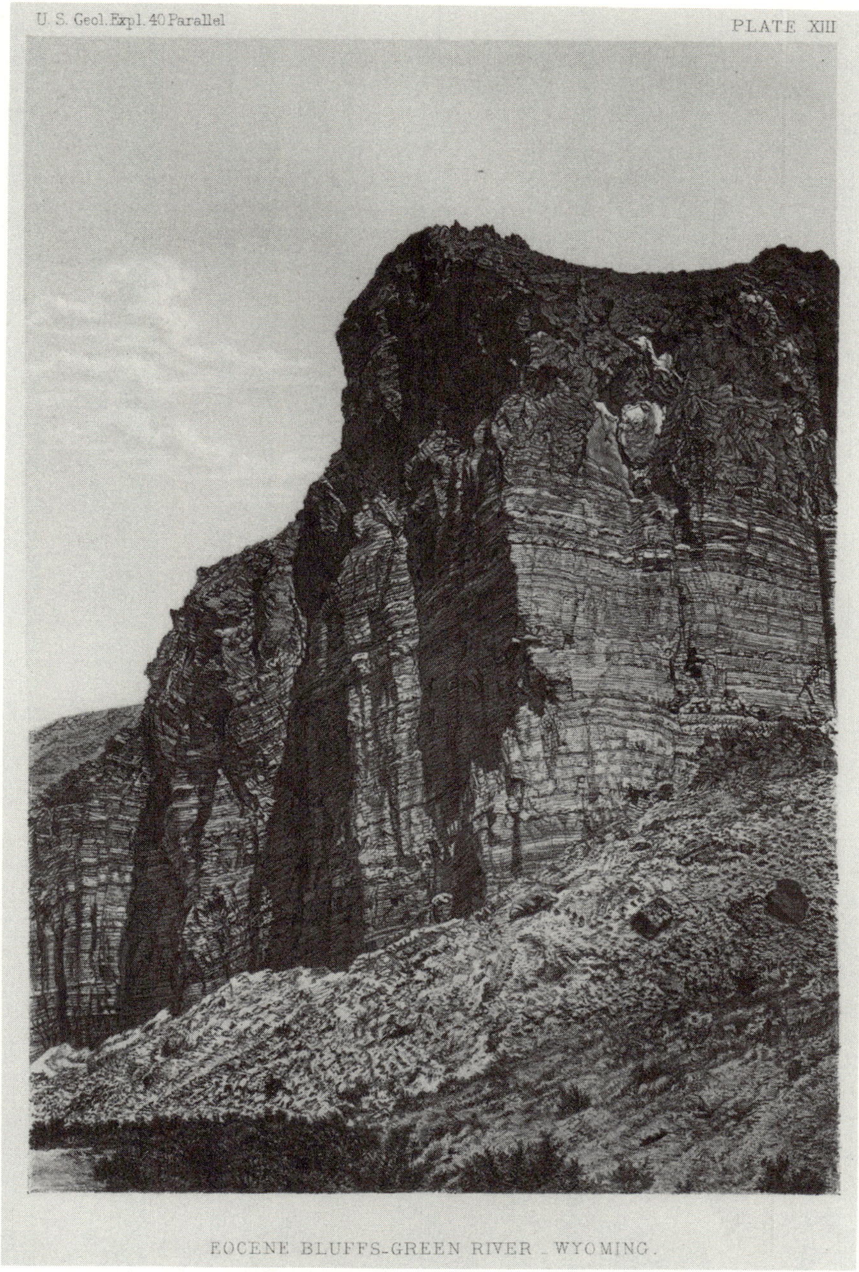

FIGURE 64. Timothy O'Sullivan, *Eocene Bluffs, Green River, Wyoming.* Illustration from Clarence King, *Systematic Geology,* vol. 1 of *Report of the Geological Exploration of the Fortieth Parallel* (Washington, DC: Government Printing Office, 1878). Courtesy Sandel Library, Northeast Louisiana University.

between this implied vertical movement and the viewer's expectation to move back into space.[70]

O'Sullivan's photographs and the lithographed versions found in the report record a hostile landscape, inimical to human habitation and traversable and knowable only to scientific specialists; but, like Moran's prints in the Powell report, they also record the formation of a viewer or reader who is able to perceive historical order in that landscape.[71] The emergence of a specifically scientific viewpoint in the observation of

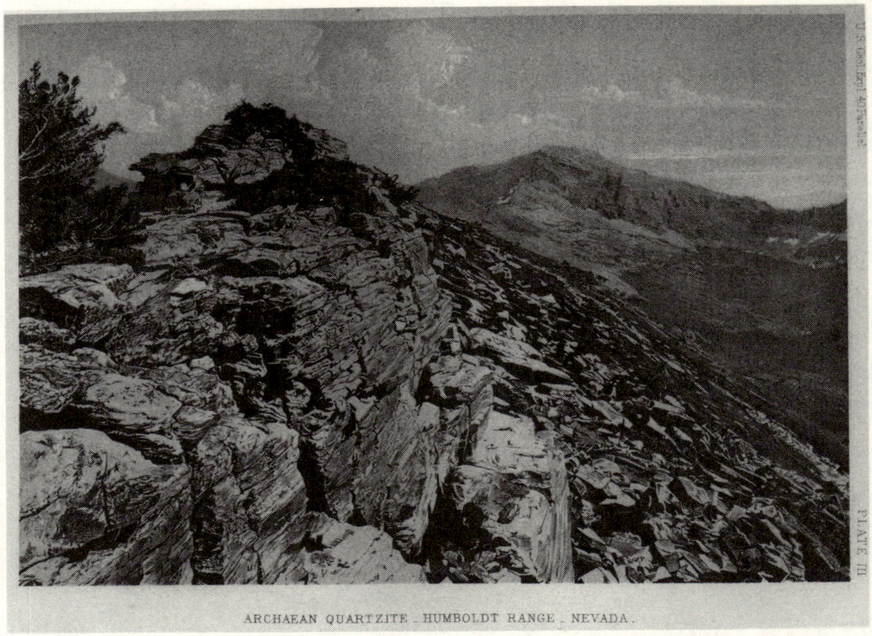

FIGURE 65. Timothy O'Sullivan, *Archaean Quartzite, Humboldt Range, Nevada*. Illustration from Clarence King, *Systematic Geology,* vol. 1 of *Report of the Geological Exploration of the Fortieth Parallel* (Washington, DC: Government Printing Office, 1878). Courtesy Sandel Library, Northeast Louisiana University.

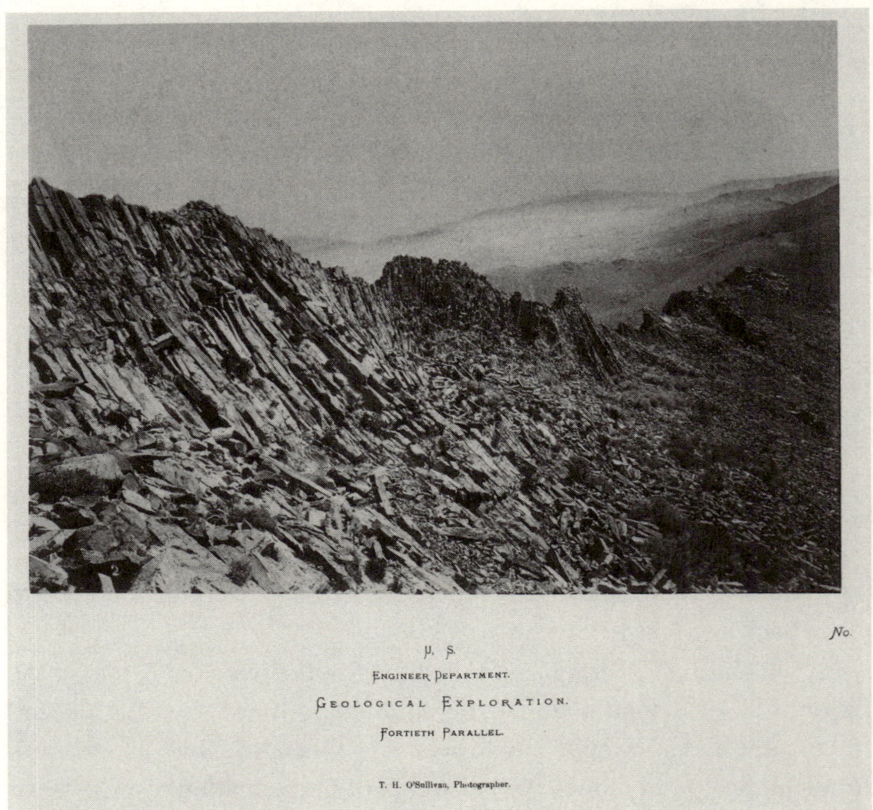

FIGURE 66. Timothy O'Sullivan, *Ridge of Columnar Trachyte, Nevada,* 1867. Courtesy Davis Museum at Wellesley College, Wellesley, Massachusetts. 1994.89.

phenomena—or at least of one less bound by codes and expectations of aesthetic experience—can occur in King's report as a kind of serial concentration or magnification, analogous to the isolation and schematization of lexically pertinent marks found in Schoolcraft's treatment of American Indian pictography. King's discussion of the expansive Quaternary lakes in the Nevada Basin—Lakes Bonneville and Lahontan, the former the ancestor of what is now the Great Salt Lake—in his chapter on Cenozoic exposures includes a mineralogical analysis pinpointing alternating periods of plentiful and scarce water. The crystal encrustations, or "tufa domes," central to this analysis are first shown emerging from Pyramid Lake (a descendant of Lake Lahontan) in western Nevada in *Pyramid and Tufa Domes, Pyramid Lake* (plate 19); then as a vertical surface in *Tufa Bank, Anaho Island, Pyramid Lake* (figure 67); and finally as a close-up view of crystal structure in *Tufa Details* (figure 68). As this sequence progresses, the more familiar recessional space of the first print (where

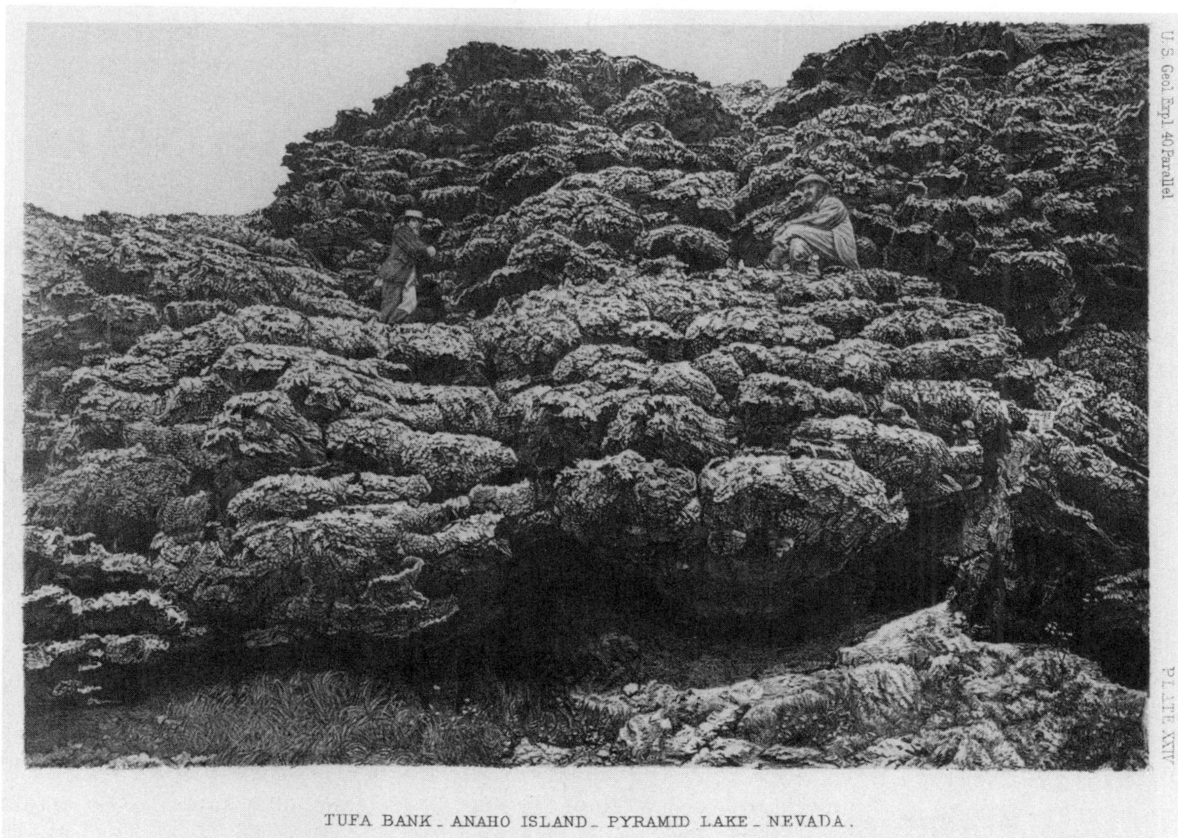

FIGURE 67. Timothy O'Sullivan, *Tufa Bank, Anaho Island, Pyramid Lake, Nevada.* Illustration from Clarence King, *Systematic Geology,* vol. 1 of *Report of the Geological Exploration of the Fortieth Parallel* (Washington, DC: Government Printing Office, 1878). Courtesy Sandel Library, Northeast Louisiana University.

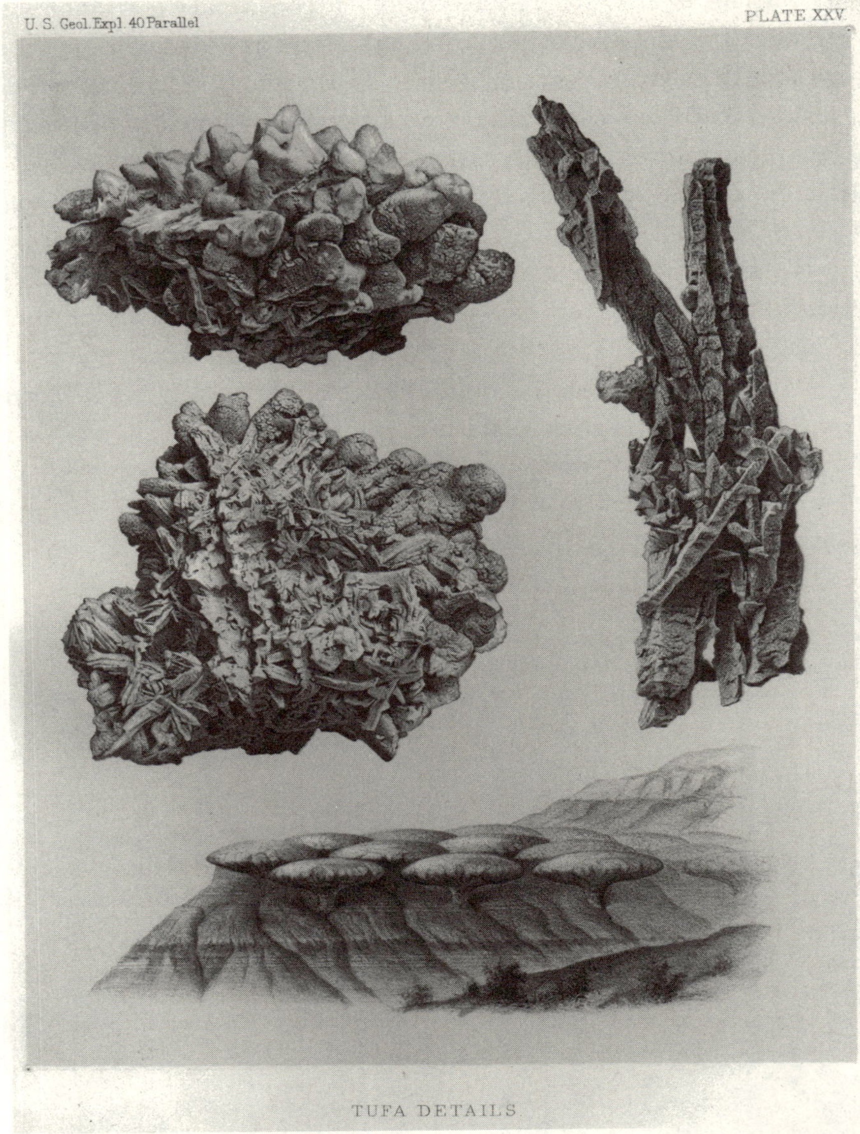

FIGURE 68. Timothy O'Sullivan, *Tufa Details.* Illustration from Clarence King, *Systematic Geology,* vol. 1 of *Report of the Geological Exploration of the Fortieth Parallel* (Washington, DC: Government Printing Office, 1878). Courtesy Sandel Library, Northeast Louisiana University.

the domes still register the upwelling of mineral solution that formed them) is followed by an image that more forcefully orients the viewer along the direction of tufa accumulation (the vertical variations of the Quaternary lake shoreline) and then finally by an image that zeroes in on the aspects of crystal structure that enable King to reconstruct successive periods of inundation and dessication.[72] Attaining scientific perspective and the understanding it produces requires the significant features of the terrain to be wrested away from more familiar images of landscape.

Although, as previously noted, the description of geological exposures in the first chapters is unmarked by a human story line of any kind, certain locales (such as Pyramid Lake) do emerge as focal points in terms of the

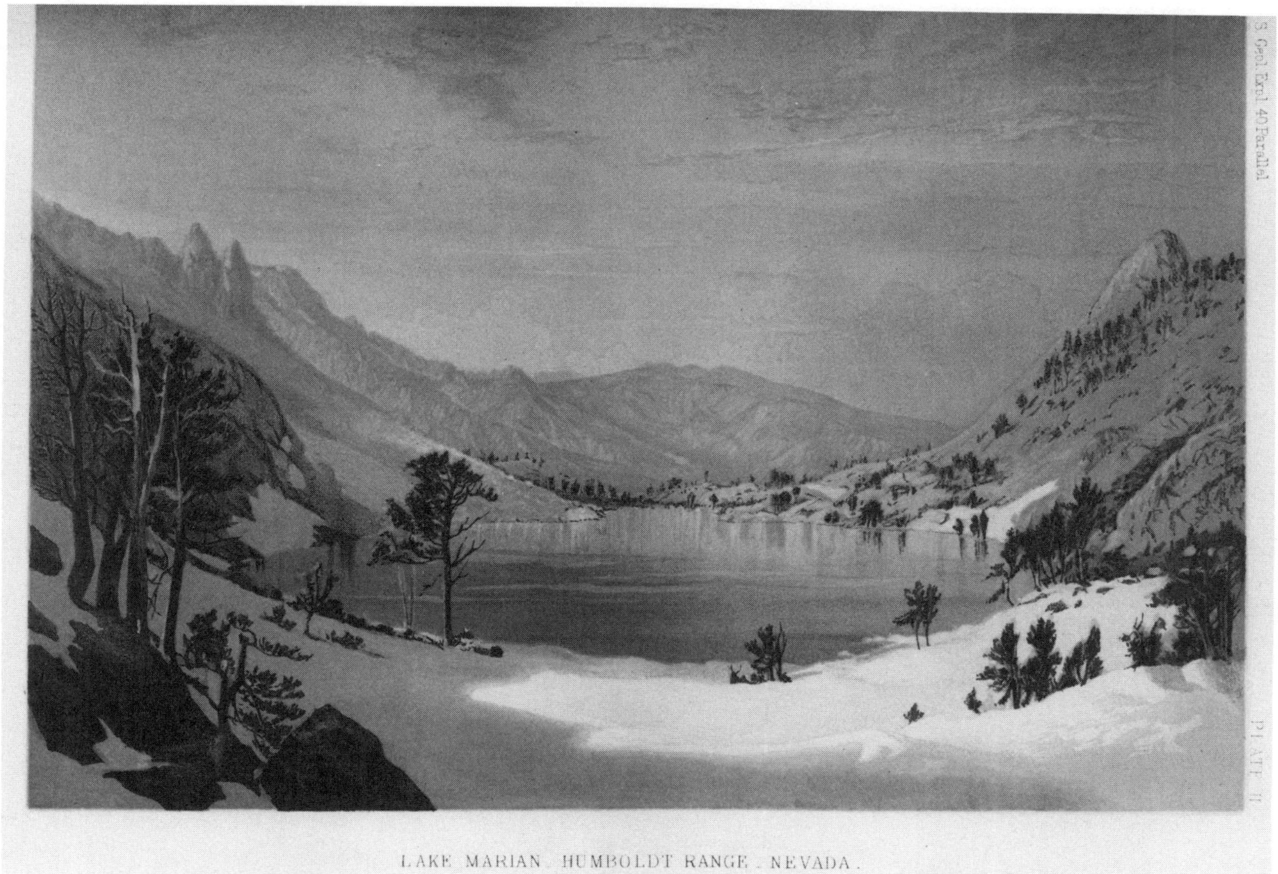

FIGURE 69. Gilbert Munger, *Lake Marian, Humboldt Range, Nevada.* Illustration from Clarence King, *Systematic Geology,* vol. 1 of *Report of the Geological Exploration of the Fortieth Parallel* (Washington, DC: Government Printing Office, 1878). Courtesy Sandel Library, Northeast Louisiana University.

clarity with which they show the details of geological history, and these locales are magnets for illustrations.[73] Quite aside from merely presenting picturesque views of the surveyed territory, illustrations are clustered to depict areas of greatest scientific interest. These clusters of illustrations can concentrate or magnify visual data, but they also often move upward as they purge landscape views of familiar pictorial conventions, imitating the upward movement of King's narrative. This sequencing of illustrations simultaneously evokes the attainment of a geologically sensitive perspective while recording and constituting it. *Archaean Quartzite, Humboldt Range* is the culmination of one such sequence, which begins with a fairly routine picturesque view of *Lake Marian, Humboldt Range, Nevada,* based on a color drawing by Munger, in turn based on a photograph by O'Sullivan (figures 65 and 69). In this chapter King is searching out exposures of Archean rock, which are generally found at the summits of mountains, distant from the effects of successive periods of accumulation and sedimentation. Munger's print of a view from beneath the mountains accordingly offers a geologically uninformative image in the context of

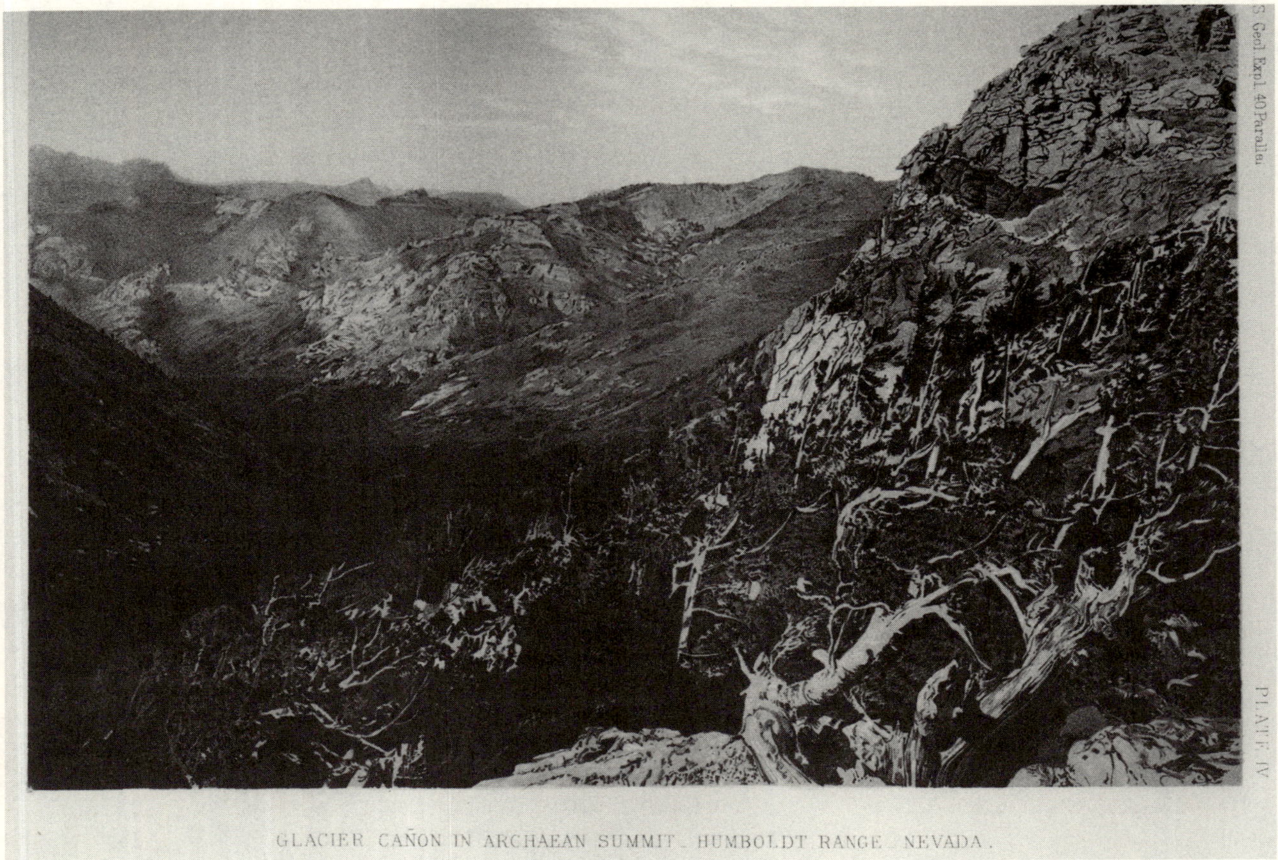

FIGURE 70. Timothy O'Sullivan, *Glacier Cañon in Archaean Summit, Humboldt Range, Nevada.* Illustration from Clarence King, *Systematic Geology,* vol. 1 of *Report of the Geological Exploration of the Fortieth Parallel* (Washington, DC: Government Printing Office, 1878). Courtesy Sandel Library, Northeast Louisiana University

King's surveying and narrative strategies. Nor does the text describe a specific ascent of the Humboldt Mountains. Nonetheless, the report moves to higher and higher elevations in its descriptions of terrain, first encountering evidence of glacial action in the vicinity of the summits, depicted in *Glacier Cañon in Archaean Summit, Humboldt Range, Nevada* (figure 70). This view, somewhat vertiginous in comparison with the stability and serpentine path into depth depicted in Munger's print, also displays to great effect the past agency of glaciers in carving the valley. The last print in the sequence, *Archaean Quartzite, Humboldt Range, Nevada*, marks the discovery of Archaean rocks, presenting them in a manner calculated to make perceptible the history of their upheaval.

A similar upward movement toward a more perspicacious view by the standards of the geological objectives shaping the narrative occurs elsewhere, as in the chapter on Paleozoic exposures, which focuses on an ascent of Mount Agassiz in the Uinta Range. Yet again a conventional print by Munger, *Upper Valley of Bear River, Uinta Range*, situates the viewer below the summit, in front of a stream winding lazily through a meadow toward the mountains in the background. Closer to these mountains, a second print by Munger, *Lake Lal and Mount Agassiz, Uinta Range*, lessens the effect of picturesque access: there is no repoussoir because the viewer is situated on the lake; the receding line of trees is abruptly terminated by the ridge of Mount Agassiz; and greater attention is paid to depicting the horizontal bedding and effects of erosion on that ridge. Finally, just below the summit, in the presence of Paleozoic strata and their sequence of deposition, the reader encounters the lithograph *Mount Agassiz, Uinta Range*, in which the face of the ridge is brought closer, almost parallel to the picture plane. Geological relevance thus literally becomes a function of altitude and of orientation along a vertical plane.

The compelling strangeness of these final, more highly elevated landscape prints based on O'Sullivan's photographs is a function of the intrinsic qualities of the photographs, so often noted by scholars, but also of what the reader expects to encounter in the pairing of narrative and print in a survey report. The landscape in his pictures has been described as "a boundless place of isolation, of contrasts of blinding light and impenetrable shadow. It is astonishing, often alienating, rarely benign," eerie qualities that have continued to attract modern viewers and photographers.[74] Photographs like *Tufa Domes, Pyramid Lake, Nevada,* and *Ridge of Columnar Trachyte, Nevada,* certainly bear this view out (plate 18 and figure 66). Part of what makes his pictures so strange is that while they depict a locale (the West) so deeply associated with American cultural identity, they portray that landscape in a distinctly otherworldly fashion. In comparison, King's text, as an example of nineteenth-century science writing—replete with its quaint terminology and old-fashioned locutions—can only seem prosaic. But that contrast, between celebrated image and disregardable text, has obscured an important aspect of the images' novelty, the way the illustrations based on them were used in conjunction with King's text as part of a narrative ensemble of words and pictures that really was novel in comparison with earlier nineteenth-century geological publications. In moving up "the geological column," King's geological narrative, including O'Sullivan's pictures, disassembles the linear travel account into instances of strata across a band of territory, which are to be reassembled in the conclusion as a narrative of the earth's history. Recalling the breakdown of the picturesque landscape view in Schoolcraft's opus, these manifold shifts—in the construction of pictured space, but also in narrative form and in the way illustrations are connected with text—are both symptomatic and constitutive of evolving geological scientific practice.

Conclusion

IT IS COMMONPLACE for Americans today to largely ignore much of nineteenth-century American history (except for the Civil War), as obscure as the moth-eaten names of forgotten presidents (except for Abraham Lincoln). Much of this cultural amnesia derives from the monumental changes of industrialization, urbanization, and the emergence of a mass-market economy, changes that gained a socially transformational momentum in the second half of the century, effectively erasing the culture that brought these things into being. As no doubt others have observed in relation to other times and places, it is ironic that a society so fascinated with progress would thus forecast its own erasure. In *Present Past,* Richard Terdiman describes how French writers registered these same changes in France explicitly as a collective loss of memory, establishing a break from the past that accorded a distinct identity to modernity.[1] In the United States, the abiding association of land and history characteristically influenced the location for the arrival of modernity, not in a mnemonic disorder affecting the collective social mind, but in a loss of place. The most influential articulation of this location is Frederick Jackson Turner's "The Significance of the Frontier in American History," which essentially carried the programs of Manifest Destiny to its inevitable conclusion, identifying the end of premodern society in the quiet elimination of the "frontier" as a land category in the most recent results of the U.S. Land Survey.[2]

While not contesting this association of land and history, this book seeks to recover other kinds of time and history embedded in constructions of landscape. In some instances, as with certain aspects of the new geological history that Powell and King tried to articulate, such notions of time seem to have survived well into the twentieth century, although comparatively recent scientific breakthroughs, such as plate tectonic theory, have restored a more horizontal perspective in grasping the flow of geological time through views of terrain.[3] The railroad narrative is likewise a form of temporality associated with space that seems appropriate for the modern situation (with its pervasive promise of immediate access to commercial goods). In contrast, Schoolcraft's archaeologizing approach to studying American Indian civilization may have resonated with widespread perceptions of Indians as prehistoric peoples for some time, but the field of anthropology was shifting at the turn of the century from related notions of "cultural evolution" toward the more modern methods of Franz Boas and his followers.[4] In all these cases, though, textual and pictorial narrative forms emerged out of older formulations connecting land and history (such as notions about the progress of civilization that would have been familiar to Turner), but not so much through an inevitable deadline programmed within those formulations as by a liberating contradiction of them.

What I have uncovered here, however, is not a definitive emergence of a visual narrative form or forms somehow essentially constitutive of modernity; rather, these forms substantially contributed to its arrival. The shifting away from picturesque models of viewing within these illustrated books was an important component in what was still an early stage in the evolution of commercial culture and professionalized science. This shift was a movement away from a shared visual literacy, however constrained by the requirements of education and taste, which looked for and was rewarded by a legitimating sense of historical continuity. Accompanying the arrival of big industry, big cities, and stepped-up commercialization was a fragmentation of both narrative and social order, occurring within different discourses that had previously been aligned on the basis of that common visual literacy. In the beginning of the century, an artist like Charles Willson Peale could legitimately make contributions in the sphere of natural history. He established a museum that included portraits of famous citizens, stuffed birds and mammals, and recently uncovered fossil remains; he organized the arrangement of its specimens and exhibits in such a way as to illuminate their significance and correlate human and natural history; and he did so in the public interest.[5] By the end of that same century, artists, let alone any citizen, could no longer act on such civic-minded polymathic impulses on such a scale.

In both tourism and science, over the course of the period 1825–1875, fragmentation in visual narrative order (as evidenced by the illustrated books I have examined here) reflects a similar fragmentation in their audience. In tourism, this sundering corresponded with a new class structure, with a new set of priorities and criteria for making class distinctions, and most of all, with a newly potent apparatus of commercialization and commodification that did not rely on a shared sense of being embedded in a common and purposeful trajectory of history. Instead, the promise of easily accessed goods and services presented itself as a unifying network that could organize and draw together the disparate members of the nation (indeed, this promise no longer addressed the criterion of national unity as explicitly as earlier paintings had in their evocation of nation and history). As I have shown, this realignment occurred across a range of proto-advertising print materials, but its appearance within post-midcentury tourist material especially points to its displacement of that earlier social order (and the picturesque visual narrative forms that helped enable it). What this new narrative order insists on is sameness, an interchangeability among objects, which requires the negation of cause-and-effect ordering (simultaneity rather than temporal progression). Consequently, then, instead of fostering an illusion of mastery over the unfolding of history and one's place in it, this new order increasingly nurtured an illusion of material possession (and an identification with objects, with commodities).[6]

The stepped-up expansion of industry and commercial culture in the second half of the century was assisted by a greater degree of professionalization within the scientific establishment. Here, too, fragmentation occurs on the levels of both narrative order and audience. Both Schoolcraft and King strived to detach observed phenomena from one context (or order) and establish them as data within a more rigorously scientific realm. Among other things, this operation characteristically involved negating a habitual picturesque way of apprehending objects—in other words, establishing that which is viewed or examined. In Schoolcraft's case, this shift involved moving from veduta-like images of Indian ruins to a protolinguistic grid of pictographic signs; in King's, from a horizontal, linear traversal through landscape to a vertical, all-over assimilation of strata that tracked the earth's history. But these early stages in professionalized ethnology and geology also pointed to the more modern specialization and isolation of scientific disciplines and audiences. For example, unlike earlier corps reports, which drew together all the survey observations into more or less a single narrative, later surveys were much more specialized and required multiple separate volumes for reports on geology, mineralogy, meteorology, paleontology, botany, and zoology. Within King's report, this movement toward specialization accounts for the strangeness of the report's first section: it is both a dry and impersonal rehearsal of stratigraphical observations (and thereby more "scientific") and a modified version of the more personal corps travel narrative.

More broadly, though, I have sought to retrieve an entire mode of expression spanning both tourism and science, based on the narrative structuring of landscape views, one that underlies and enables the very association of land and history assumed by Turner. I arrived at this mode of expression via recent art historical interest in narrative and spectatorship, which has demonstrated that the encoding of historical allegories within the perusal of depicted space was a compelling visual rhetoric in painting for conveying ideas about the nation and its place in history. This pictorial rhetoric was especially compelling because vision occupied a middle ground between physicality and substance, on the one hand, and the apparent ephemerality and lack of fixity pertaining to time, on the other. It was a way of providing both a fixed scheme of history's progression and a visceral experience of moving forward in time, of mapping out vaster sequences in human time, but also giving the viewer an immediate and confirming sensation of that mapping. In the range of temporalities (the different kinds of time and history), the variety of strategies for connecting narrative text with imagery, and the multitude of audiences reached in this manner, this pictorial rhetoric both permeated and was critically shaped and then transcended by print culture. Painting had claimed a more extensive or democratic audience at different times in the nineteenth century, and art historical scholarship has characteristically backed up this claim by yoking print culture to a wagon driven by the conventions and concerns of painting. Instead, I have focused on the development of this pictorial rhetoric, not as a simple popularization of painting, but as a representational strategy modified in different ways for different audiences uniquely constituted through print (namely, in the emerging discourses of modern tourism and science). At the beginning of the century, Peale as a painter could legitimately move within the sphere of natural history *as a painter,* and Cole could do the same within the nascent sphere of scenic tourism, but the characteristic modes for bringing stories and pictures together within these spheres after midcentury was through print.

The notion of print culture often presupposes a monumental and homogenous entity that extends beyond a sense of a unitary audience to a unitary language as well. Although related by a similar concern for narrating encounters with places (and a similar process of moving away from earlier picturesque viewing models), the illustration schemes developed in tourism and science are distinct. Though historians of visual culture have explored the nineteenth-century experimentation with narrative and imagery in relation to such entertainments as the moving panorama, illustrated books have not been accorded a similar inventiveness. But as I have shown, the proliferation of print culture in the United States during this time also carried with it experimentation in juxtaposing texts and illustrations analogous to these evolving technologies of representation. The establishment of film and television in the twentieth century as the preeminent formats for marrying words and pictures has, I think, occluded a time when printing inventions held out a similar potential for narrated visual experiences.[7] If I have shed light on the initial stages of modern tourism and science, it is important also to recognize that their syncretic use of narrative text and landscape imagery was also an initial stage in the evolution of appropriate and effective discursive forms within them, especially discursive forms in print. Later print materials would come to dominate the travel and tourist industry, and later scientific publications would instate different rules for categories of illustrations and ways of determining their evidentiary value.[8] Ultimately, film and television would prove to be a more seductive and profitable visual narrative format overall (witness the cost of Super Bowl commercials or the opening weekend take of a new summer blockbuster movie), but before these media emerged, visual narrative forms in print were developed to suit leisure- and knowledge-based enterprises.

Aspects of these earlier print forms of simulation—specifically of conditioning and shaping encounters with places—endured for some time in the new century (for example, guidebooks for automobile tours, especially those first published after the construction of the national highway system, or similar automobile guides published for national parks like Yellowstone). Overall, though, as a corollary to the entrenchment of film and television, the activities of reading and looking that underlie and organize these experiences in print culture have been obscured. Without these activities, many of the separate narrative forms and key concepts present in the books I have examined are either denuded of significance or are meaningless verbal aggregates (like a child learning to speak): railroad narrative, narrating the geological column, "indigenous mental geognosy." I have tried here to resuscitate these forgotten narrative forms, which were so important to and constitutive of the society that preceded our own, but which are otherwise additional casualties of modernity's amnesia.

Notes

Introduction

1. William Guild, *A Chart and Description of the Boston and Worcester and Western Railroads* (Boston, MA: Bradbury and Guild, 1847).
2. Ibid., 4.
3. Classic studies in what is a vast literature include Vivien Green Fryd, *Art and Empire: The Politics of Ethnicity in the United States Capitol, 1815–1860* (New Haven, CT: Yale University Press, 1992); Leo Marx, *The Machine in the Garden: Technology and the Pastoral Ideal in America* (New York: Oxford University Press, 1964); Barbara Novak, *Nature and Culture: American Landscape and Painting, 1825–1875* (New York: Oxford University Press, 1980); and Henry Nash Smith, *Virgin Land: The West as Symbol and Myth* (Cambridge, MA: Harvard University Press, 1950).
4. Not that landscape painting served this function exclusively—paintings might strive for religious or spiritual ends, for example, although these ends were often bound up with themes of progress. The present study, however, focuses on the thread of scholarship concerned with national expansion. All of the aforementioned authors touch on landscape painting. Studies of the relationship between landscape painting specifically and an aggressive American nationalism include Albert Boime, *The Magisterial Gaze: Manifest Destiny and American Landscape Painting, c. 1830–1865* (Washington, DC: Smithsonian Institution Press, 1991); Angela Miller, *The Empire of the Eye: Landscape Representation and American Cultural Politics, 1825–1875* (Ithaca, NY: Cornell University Press, 1993); and William H. Truettner and Alan Wallach, eds., *Thomas Cole: Landscape into History* (New Haven, CT: Yale University Press, 1994). For more recent discussions, see Roger Cushing Aikin, "Paintings of Manifest Destiny: Mapping the Nation," *American Art* 14, no. 3 (Autumn 2000): 78–89; David Bjelajac, "Thomas Cole's *Oxbow* and the American Zion Divided," *American Art* 20, no. 1 (Spring 2006): 60–83; and Andrew Wilton and Tim Barringer, *American Sublime: Landscape Painting in the United States, 1820–1880* (Princeton, NJ: Princeton University Press, 2002).
5. See Neil Harris, *The Artist in American Society: The Formative Years, 1790–1860* (Chicago: University of Chicago Press, 1966); and Lillian B. Miller, *Patrons and Patriotism: The Encouragement of the Fine Arts in America, 1790–1860* (Chicago: University of Chicago Press, 1966). Georgia Barnhill, Diana Korzenik, and Caroline F. Sloat, eds., *The Cultivation of Artists in Nineteenth-Century America* (Worcester, MA: American Antiquarian Society, 1997), complicates a top-down class view of arts education, especially earlier in the century. Regarding the persistence of fine art's elite associations in the first half of the nineteenth century, see, for example, my discussion of Thomas Cole and his artistic legacy in chapter 1. Russ Castronovo, in *Beautiful Democracy: Aesthetics and Anarchy in a Global Era* (Chicago: University of Chicago Press, 2007), examines debates throughout the nineteenth century about the possibility of art serving as a democratizing agent in the wider culture.
6. The North American Print Conference in particular, inaugurated in 1970, has spurred several publications on prints from different regions and depicting different subjects, many only appearing in the last few decades. *American Periodicals*, established in 1991, is increasingly devoting space to articles on illustration practices. Scholarship on political cartoons is especially noteworthy in terms of detailed pictorial analysis of satiric content and inventive reinterpretations of relationships between prints and paintings. See Jennifer Greenhill, "Winslow Homer and the Mechanics of the Visual Deadpan," *Art History* 32, no. 2 (April 2009): 351–86; and Baird Jarman, "The Graphic Art of Thomas Nast: Politics and Propriety in Postbellum Publishing," *American Periodicals* 20, no. 2 (2010): 156–89.

7. Georgia Barnhill, review of *Beyond the Lines: Pictorial Reporting, Everyday Life, and the Crisis of Gilded America*, by Joshua Brown, *Winterthur Portfolio* 38, no. 4 (Winter 2003): 269–71.
8. Miller, *Empire of the Eye*. I cite Miller's study here because it has been influential for subsequent scholarship on American landscape painting and its promotion of expansionist beliefs.
9. Ibid., 7–8. Miller is referring here to Benedict Anderson, *Imagined Communities: Reflections on the Origin and Spread of Nationalism* (London: Verso Editions, 1983).
10. Richard Gassan, *The Birth of American Tourism: New York, the Hudson Valley, and American Culture, 1790–1830* (Amherst: University of Massachusetts Press, 2008).
11. Ibid. 58.
12. I too foreground the British picturesque tradition in early guidebooks in what follows, but I also want to examine how the viewing possibilities of the steamboat and the train, as mediated by the guidebook, condition landscape perception. In contrast to Gassan is the way Jennifer Roberts connects the unusual format of Asher B. Durand's midcentury landscape "sketches" (namely their tendency to ignore spatial depth in favor of close-up views) to his background as an engraver, in the last chapter of *Transporting Visions: The Movement of Images in Early America* (Berkeley: University of California Press, 2014). The point is that this influence is examined via characteristics unique to engraving—as mark, as foreground or background, as multiple—which she brings out precisely in engraving "works" seemingly far removed from landscape painting, namely banknotes. For a different account of Durand's "sketches," see Karen Georgi, "Defining Landscape Painting in Nineteenth-Century American Critical Discourse. Or, Should Art 'Deal in Wares the Age Has Need of'?" *Oxford Art Journal* 29, no. 2 (2006): 227–45.
13. For example, some book-length studies of Winslow Homer note how the hard-edged drawing style and use of high contrast in his print illustration work affected his later paintings; see, in particular, David Tatham, *Winslow Homer and the Illustrated Book* (Syracuse, NY: Syracuse University Press, 1992).
14. There is really no single source for nineteenth-century American book illustration, something like a book illustration version of the Bartsch catalog of Old Master prints; instead, there are separate reference works devoted to individual collections, such as J. R. Abbey, *Travel in Aquatint and Lithography, 1770–1860*, 2 vols. (San Francisco: Alan Wofsy Fine Arts, 1991); Sinclair Hamilton, *Early American Book Illustrators and Wood Engravers, 1670–1870* (Princeton, NJ: Princeton University Press, 1958); and somewhat more comprehensive, David Stauffer, *American Engravers upon Copper and Steel*, 2 vols. (New Castle, DE: Oak Knoll Books, 1994). An example of general scholarship that deviates from a connoisseurly approach is Gerald Ward, ed., *The American Illustrated Book in the Nineteenth Century* (Winterthur, DE: Winterthur Museum, 1987). See also Georgia Barnhill, "Transformations in Pictorial Printing," in *A History of the Book in America*, vol. 2, *An Extensive Republic: Print, Culture, and Society in the New Nation, 1790–1840*, ed. Robert A. Gross and Mary Kelley, 422–39 (Chapel Hill: University of North Carolina Press, 2010). Whereas Barnhill examines illustration practices in the period 1790–1830, no clear chapter is devoted to the subject in volume 3, which covers the period 1840–1880. The series was sponsored by the American Antiquarian Society, which continues to be an institution notably active in supporting print culture research through its Program in the History of the Book in American Culture, as well as its Center for Historic American Visual Culture.
15. Cynthia Patterson, in "'Illustration of a Picture': Nineteenth-Century Writers and the Philadelphia Pictorials," *American Periodicals* 19, no. 2 (2009): 136–64, examines the practice of commissioning writing to accompany already acquired print imagery (textual "illustrations"), reversing the accustomed relationships between text and image in nineteenth-century publishing. A significant body of scholarship on Victorian book illustration also looks at inventive practices for pairing text and illustration; see Richard Maxwell, ed., *The Victorian Illustrated Book* (Charlottesville: University of Virginia Press, 2002); and Gerard Curtis, *Visual Words: Art and the Material Book in Victorian England* (Burlington, VT: Ashgate Publishing, 2002).
16. Nancy Bentley, *Frantic Panoramas: American Literature and Mass Culture, 1870–1920* (Philadelphia: University of Pennsylvania Press, 2009), 5. Related scholarship on nineteenth- and early twentieth-century American literature includes Martha Banta, *Taylored Lives: Narrative Productions in the Age of Taylor, Veblen, and Ford* (Chicago: University of Chicago Press, 1993); Castronovo, *Beautiful Democracy*; and Edward S. Cutler, *Recovering the New: Transatlantic Roots of Modernism* (Hanover: University of New Hampshire Press, 2003). In contrast, Randall Knoper, "Writing, American Literature, and Media Ecologies," *American Literary History* 23, no. 2 (Summer 2011): 362–79, describes a resurgence in recent literary studies of the sort of technological determinism advanced by Marshall McLuhan.
17. Bentley, *Frantic Panoramas*, 5.

18. William Dean Howells, *A Hazard of New Fortunes* (1890; repr., New York: Modern Library, 2002), 139. The journal's publisher is quick to remind March of the profit motive: "Like the society beauties on the stage: people go in for the beauty so much that they don't know what the play is. But the box office gets there all the same" (139).
19. Bill Brown, *A Sense of Things: The Object Matter of American Literature* (Chicago: University of Chicago Press, 2003), 4.
20. Ibid., 5. John Plotz provides an overview of "thing theory" in "Can the Sofa Speak? A Look at Thing Theory," *Criticism* 47, no. 1 (Winter 2005): 109–18, in which he lauds those studies that move beyond "simple symbolic objects . . . pieces of the material world that come to us already marked up as signifiers, with a definite human meaning attached to them by way of representation" (112). I appreciate the appeal of supposing that a "thing" somehow conveys its own meaning, independent of values associated with it in the art or literature of the period ("by way of representation"), but I also think that the process of attaching meanings to objects within nineteenth-century print culture is definitely not "simple," if only because print materials seem to vacillate between being a "thing" and a "representation."
21. Miller's *Empire of the Eye* is the most thorough instance of this kind of analysis, but other studies include Boime, *Magisterial Gaze*, and Truettner and Wallach, *Thomas Cole*. The close relationship between writers and artists at this time, especially those involved in the transcendentalist movement, has long been a component in histories of both art and literature, but examinations of textual and visual hybridity tended to remain on the level of shared content. Such earlier scholarship, which informs the approach of Miller and others, includes James T. Callow, *Kindred Spirits: Knickerbocker Writers and American Artists, 1807–1855* (Chapel Hill: University of North Carolina Press, 1967); Novak, *Nature and Culture*; and Donald Ringe, *The Pictorial Mode: Space and Time in the Art of Irving, Bryant, and Cooper* (Lexington: University of Kentucky Press, 1971). See also, more recently, H. Peck, "Unlikely Kindred Spirits: A New Vision of Landscape in the Works of Henry David Thoreau and Asher B. Durand," *American Literary History*, 17, no. 4 (Winter 2005): 687–713; and David Schuyler, *Sanctified Landscape: Writers, Artists, and the Hudson River Valley, 1820–1909* (Ithaca, NY: Cornell University Press, 2012).
22. I use the term Hudson River school recognizing its origin in subsequent art historical scholarship. See Kevin Avery, "A Historiography of the Hudson River School," in *American Paradise: The World of the Hudson River School*, by Kevin J. Avery, Oswaldo Rodriguez Roque, John K. Howat, Doreen Bolger Burke, and Catherine Hoover Voorsanger (New York: Metropolitan Museum of Art, 1987), for the history of the term. I have specifically in mind those painters, like Durand and Cole, whose works have been enlisted in discussions of the role of landscape painting in promulgating expansionist beliefs.
23. Miller, *Empire of the Eye*, 4. Durand's *Progress* is more self-consciously allegorical than is typical of his oeuvre, but the correlation between spatial and historical depth is a device often adopted in his (and other artists') works. Iconic western images, such as Emanuel Leutze's *Westward the Course of Empire Takes Its Way* (1861), connected the imagined traversal of space (in this case right to left) with prevailing ideas about Manifest Destiny and the progress of civilization.
24. The hierarchy is (in order of decreasing significance): history painting, portraiture, landscape painting, and still life. This system was part of the institutionalization of the fine arts in the English Royal Academy and the French Académie Royale de Peinture, both of which were important models for emerging art institutions in the United States, like New York's National Academy of Design.
25. Photography is the exception. As my chapter on geological survey reports shows, however, discussions of the landscape photographs used within them often problematically carve out a discursive space distinct from painting (see chapter 4, this volume). Stressing the autonomy of the photograph, they end up minimizing or obscuring its role in those reports.
26. Kevin Avery shows how the exhibition of Church's *Heart of the Andes* used techniques from the stationary panorama in "*The Heart of the Andes* Exhibited: Frederic E. Church's Window on the Equatorial World," *American Art Journal* 18 (1986): 52–72. Angela Miller, in "Space as Destiny: The Panorama Vogue in Mid-Nineteenth Century America," in *World Art: Themes of Unity and Diversity*, ed. Irving Lavin (University Park: Pennsylvania State University, 1989), focuses on how painting adopts the viewing possibilities of the panorama. A more recent exception is Stephan Oettermann's *The Panorama: History of a Mass Medium* (New York: Zone Books, 1997), which more fully develops an analysis of the specific characteristics of the panorama experience. Oettermann's subject is panoramic representation as a whole, however, and consequently his examples are weighted toward European countries (England, France, and Germany) as opposed to the United States. See also John Brewer, "Sensibility and the Urban Panorama," *Huntington Library Quarterly*, 70, no. 2 (June 2007): 229–49; and Bernard Comment,

The Painted Panorama (London: Reaktion Books, 1999). In addition, Erkki Huhtamo discusses the specific viewing conditions of the moving panorama in "Global Glimpses for Local Realities: The Moving Panorama, a Forgotten Mass Medium of the 19th Century," *Art Inquiry* 4 (2002): 193–228. Notably, he speculates that the affinity between the stationary wrap-around panorama and traditional painting partially explains the lack of recent scholarly interest in the moving panorama: "Whatever its artistic merits, panorama painting continued the traditions of perspectival and illusionistic painting . . . the circular panorama is a perfect topic for mildly revisionist art historians—not too radically different but not too conventional either" (196).

27. Oettermann, *Panorama*, explains how this preference for the moving panorama reflected Americans' belief in Manifest Destiny. Like the divinely sanctioned settlement of the continent, the viewer of the moving panorama travels forward in both space and time.
28. These three inventions could at best simulate only a few components of a movement or action (a horse running, a person jumping, and so on) and so did not incorporate lengthy narratives, but this constraint does not make them irrelevant here, as I discuss further in this introduction.
29. In fact, most of the panoramas in Oettermann's book are lost and are reconstructed largely through these kinds of guidebooks.
30. Robert Burford, *Description of a View of the Falls of Niagara, Now Exhibiting at the Panorama, Leicester Square* (London: Brettell, 1833). Burford was one of England's most successful panorama entrepreneurs.
31. George Harvey, *Harvey's Illustrations of the Scenery, Resources, and Progress of Our Country* (Boston, MA: Dutton and Wentworth, 1851), 3. Harvey was a struggling portraitist in Boston who later turned to landscape painting. Like many landscapists at this time, such as Cole and Church, Harvey tried to make the exhibition of his work into a quasi-theatrical event, in this case an illustrated lecture. He also produced at least one engraved set of landscape views accompanied by short textual commentaries: *Harvey's Scenes of the Primitive Forest of America, at the Four Seasons of the Year, Spring, Summer, Autumn and Winter*, which is described in Walter Karp, "The American Land As It Was," *American Heritage Magazine* 21, no. 1 (December 1969): 16–21.
32. An example is Theodore Winthrop's critique of Church's *Heart of the Andes*, later published in *Life in the Open Air, and Other Papers* (Boston, MA: Ticknor and Fields, 1863). The interpretive attraction of narratively organized space even extended to works of art, such as figural sculpture, that contained no spatial markers. Thus, an anonymous review of Erastus Dow Palmer's *White Captive* (1859), "Palmer's White Captive," *Atlantic Monthly* 5, no. 27 (January 1860): 108–109, relates the story of the subject's enslavement in part by inferring the invisible features of her wilderness prison.
33. An influential study of debates about the commensurability of linguistic and pictorial signifying systems is W. J. T. Mitchell's *Iconology: Image, Text, Ideology* (Chicago: University of Chicago Press, 1987). Mitchell focuses on the efforts of writers and philosophers to answer this question in absolute terms; the illustration schemes I analyze here are efforts in practice to use these sign systems syncretically.
34. The nineteenth century's investigations into the temporal dimensions of vision and the optical toys that this research enabled are the subjects of Jonathan Crary's *Techniques of the Observer: On Vision and Modernity in the Nineteenth Century* (Cambridge, MA: MIT Press, 1990).
35. I focus here on the work of Paul Ricoeur, but related scholarship on the time of the reader and the time of the text can be found earlier in the work of Wolfgang Iser. See, for example, "The Reading Process: A Phenomenological Approach," in *The Implied Reader: Patterns of Communication in Prose from Bunyan to Beckett* (Baltimore, MD: Johns Hopkins University Press, 1974). Also influential for thinking about this dual perception of time by the reader, the active time of reading the text versus the time it describes, is Gérard Genette, *Narrative Discourse: An Essay in Method*, trans. Jane E. Lewin (Ithaca, NY: Cornell University Press, 1980), taken up in chapter 1 of this volume.
36. Paul Ricoeur, *Time and Narrative*, 3 vols. (Chicago: University of Chicago Press, 1984–1988), in particular volume 3, chapters 1 and 7. Ricoeur locates two basic and essentially irresolvable conceptualizations of time in Augustine's *Confessions* and Aristotle's *Physics*. Whereas Augustine "attempts [and fails] to derive from the distension of the mind alone the very principle of the extension and the measurement of time" (3:12), Aristotle defines time by way of its external manifestations (that is, movement), which likewise fails because although this definition "does not contain an explicit reference to the soul, [it still] draw[s] upon, at each phase of the definition, the operations of perception, discrimination, and comparison, which can only be those of the soul" (3:16). This irreconcilability is a confrontation between the time of the "soul, mind, consciousness" and the time of "nature, the universe, the world" (3:14).
37. History "stands-for" or "takes-the-place-of" the "'real' past," while fiction (or "every temporal fictive experience") implies a "world of the text" (ibid.,

3:157–58). Both the "'real' past" and the "world of the text" are external manifestations of time relative to the reader; therefore, to realize or experience them is to revisit the irresolvable conflict in conceptualizing time laid out in his reading of Augustine and Aristotle. For Ricoeur, in very brief terms, an understanding of the act of reading provides the essential bridge. "Considered apart from reading, the world of the text remains a transcendence in immanence" (3:158). "Yet we are readers of history just as much as we are readers of novels. All forms of writing, including historiography, take their place within an extended theory of reading" (3:180).

38. However, not only is Europe, and specifically England, the source for many of the (primarily picturesque) models for viewing landscape that are used at an early stage by the print materials I discuss in this study, but often, too, motives to alter these viewing models ultimately originate in Europe, such as new theories of geological change in relation to the survey reports I examine in chapter 4.
39. This is the time frame in Boime, Marx, Miller, and Novak; for all four of these canonical writers, the "decline" of landscape painting correlates with the closing of the frontier.
40. See especially the introduction to W. J. T. Mitchell, *Picture Theory: Essays on Verbal and Visual Representation* (Chicago: University of Chicago Press, 1994). Mitchell presents Crary as a victim of the lure of iconology's possibilities, asking "Could it be . . . that 'iconology, in the end, has not proved an especially useful hermeneutic of culture' precisely because its *object* (the visual image) entraps its discourse and method in tautological 'likenesses' between visual images and historical totalities?" (23). The interior quotation is Christopher S. Wood's translation of Erwin Panofsky's *Perspective as Symbolic Form* (Cambridge, MA: Zone Books, 1991).
41. David C. Miller, "The Iconology of Wrecked or Stranded Boats in Mid to Late Nineteenth-Century American Culture," in *American Iconology: New Approaches to Nineteenth-Century Art and Literature*, ed. David C. Miller (New Haven, CT: Yale University Press, 1993), 196. I offer my own reading of luminist works, and particularly their relation to popular representations of beach scenery, in chapter 2.
42. Ibid., 195.
43. Ibid., 196.
44. I return to the issue of mass culture, modernity, and the significance of perceptions of sameness, fragmentation, and instantaneity in chapter 1.

Chapter 1. Reading the Past outside the Window

1. Alan Wallach, "Thomas Cole's *River in the Catskills* as Antipastoral," *Art Bulletin* 84, no. 2 (June 2002): 334–50.
2. Ibid., 334–39. Much of the scholarship on Cole has focused on his ambivalent or negative attitude toward land development, technological innovation, and the nation's historical progress generally. See Bjelajac, "Thomas Cole's *Oxbow*"; Miller, *Empire of the Eye*; Ellwood C. Parry III, *The Art of Thomas Cole: Ambition and Imagination* (Newark: University of Delaware Press, 1988), and more recently, "Overlooking the Oxbow: Thomas Cole's *View from Mount Holyoke* Revisited," *American Art Journal* 34/35 (2003/2004): 6–61; Earl A. Powell, *Thomas Cole* (New York: Abrams, 1990); and Truettner and Wallach, *Thomas Cole.*
3. Wallach, "Thomas Cole's *River in the Catskills*," 343.
4. Ibid., 343–44.
5. Ibid., 343. Again, "Given the artistic means at Cole's disposal."
6. Henry T. Williams, *The Pacific Tourist: Williams' Illustrated Trans-Continental Guide of Travel, from the Atlantic to the Pacific Ocean,* 2nd ed. (New York: Williams, 1876).
7. For a discussion of unusual or eye-catching illustrations and the success of the new illustrated journals, see Kevin G. Barnhurst and John Nerone, "Civic Picturing vs. Realist Photojournalism: The Regime of Illustrated News, 1856–1901," *Design Issues* 16, no. 1 (Spring 2000): 59–79; Sue Rainey, *Creating Picturesque America: Monument to the Natural and Cultural Landscape* (Nashville, TN: Vanderbilt University Press, 1994), part one, "Fighting the Illustration Wars"; and Vanessa Meikle Schulman, "'Making the Magazine': Visuality, Managerial Capitalism, and the Mass Production of Periodicals," *American Periodicals* 22, no. 1 (2012): 1–28.
8. "Sunnyside, The Home of Washington Irving," *Harper's New Monthly Magazine* 14, no. 79 (December 1856): 1–21; and T. Addison Richards, "Idlewild, The Home of N. P. Willis," *Harper's New Monthly Magazine* 16, no. 92 (January 1858): 145–66. Although not specified in the text, I think the prints in figure 3 replicate the view from a Claude glass because of the increasing distortion and darkness near the perimeter. Moreover, the author emphasizes a painterly perspective throughout the article (which the Claude glass imitates), lauding the picturesque merits of the Hudson River and identifying the artists who were Irving's neighbors (Samuel F. B. Morse, Durand, Robert W. Weir, the sculptors Henry Kirke Brown and Palmer, and the art historian Gulian C. Verplanck). Figure 4 looks like a binocular view, but the left and right scenes are actually a sequence of views walking along the path to the Hudson River villa of N. P. Willis.
9. See especially "History and Landscape in Railroad Guidebooks," later in this chapter, for a discussion of

the connections made by guidebook authors between progress and the experience of train travel.

10. Not that significant variations do not occur, notably in luminist paintings near the end of this time frame. See the discussion of luminist works in chapter 2.
11. These aspects of the experience of train travel, and how they and other aspects compromised commonplace categories of time and space, are discussed at length by Wolfgang Schivelbusch in *The Railway Journey: The Industrialization of Time and Space in the 19th Century* (Berkeley: University of California Press, 1977).
12. Other scholars who have followed Marx's characterization of this ambivalent sense of the train include most of the contributors to Susan Danly and Leo Marx, eds., *The Railroad in American Art: Representations of Technological Change* (Cambridge, MA: MIT Press, 1988); Kenneth Maddox, "Thomas Cole and the Railroad: Gentle Maledictions," *Archives of American Art* 26, no. 1 (1986): 2–10; Patricia Hills, "Picturing Progress in the Era of Westward Expansion," in *The West as America: Reinterpreting Images of the Frontier, 1820–1920*, ed. William H. Truettner (Washington, DC: Smithsonian Institution Press, 1991), 126–31; and Novak, *Nature and Culture.* These discussions parallel similar debates about the railroad (and other signs of industry) in impressionist landscape, as in T. J. Clark, *The Painting of Modern Life: Paris in the Art of Manet and His Followers* (New York: Knopf, 1985); and more recently, James Rubin, *Impressionism and the Modern Landscape: Productivity, Technology, and Urbanization from Manet to Van Gogh* (Berkeley: University of California Press, 2008).
13. In the view of the train as a kind of imaging machine, this sense of confinement corresponds with Crary's emphasis on how the use of new optical devices required the immobility of the observer. Crary writes of the stereoscope, the centerpiece in his discussion of the new observer, as follows: "In order to view images with this device, an observer placed his eyes directly in front of two plane mirrors set ninety degrees to one another. . . . Like the phenakistiscope and other nonprojective optical devices, the stereoscope also required the corporeal adjacency and immobility of the observer" (*Techniques of the Observer,* 129).
14. Thomas Cole, *The Collected Essays and Prose Sketches,* ed. Marshall Tymn (St. Paul, MN: Colet Press, 1980), 42. Ruskin is quoted in Schivelbusch, *Railway Journey,* 54.
15. Henry David Thoreau, *Walden* (Boston, MA: Ticknor and Fields, 1854; repr., New York: Random House, 1981), 107.
16. Ibid., 106.
17. Ibid., 109 and 111.
18. Leo Marx, "The Railroad-in-the-Landscape: An Iconological Reading of a Theme in American Art," in Danly and Marx, *The Railroad in American Art,* 198–99.
19. A major railroad patron was Charles Gould, treasurer of the Ohio and Mississippi Railroad, who owned Durand's *Progress* and works by John F. Kensett. Other patrons benefited indirectly from the growth of the railroad, such as Charles Stetson, owner of New York's Astor House, who commissioned work from Thomas Doughty. In 1858 the Baltimore and Ohio Railroad invited Kensett and other artists on a scenic tour of the line, and William Trost Richards was similarly invited in 1885 by the Northern Pacific Railroad.
20. For example, Marx, "Railroad-in-the-Landscape," 202–203.
21. In depicting these deer, Melrose actually seems to anticipate Eadweard Muybridge's famous 1878 photograph proving that a galloping horse's hooves are all off the ground at some point in its cycle of movement. Instantaneity (imminent disaster) would then be captured at an interval too rapid for the human eye to register. The possibility of Melrose visually alluding to photography might also be seen in the bright light of the locomotive striking the deer and casting an equally transient shadow on the tracks.
22. On *vedute* and the European picturesque tradition, see Malcolm Arnold, ed., *The Picturesque: Literary Sources and Documents,* 3 vols. (East Sussex: Helm Information, 1994), especially volume 2, on the United States; Timothy M. Castelloe, *The British Aesthetic Tradition: From Shaftesbury to Wittgenstein* (Cambridge: Cambridge University Press, 2013), parts 1 and 2, "The Age of Taste" and "The Age of Romanticism"; Maurizio Fagiolo Dell'Arco, *The Grand Tour: Landscape and Veduta Paintings, Venice and Rome in the 18th Century* (Atlanta, GA: Oglethorpe University Museum, 1997); Renzo Dubbini, *Geography of the Gaze: Urban and Rural Vision in Early Modern Europe* (Chicago: University of Chicago Press, 2002); Kim Sloan, *Alexander and John Robert Cozens: The Poetry of Landscape* (London: Victoria and Albert Museum, 1986–1987); and Greg Smith, *Thomas Girtin: The Art of Watercolor* (London: Tate Gallery, 2002). On the influence of that tradition on American art and practices of scenic tourism, see Gassan, *Birth of American Tourism*; Harris, *Artist in American Society*; Daniel Huntington, *Art and the Excited Spirit: America in the Romantic Mood* (Ann Arbor: University of Michigan Press, 1972); Novak, *Nature and Culture*; and Bryan Jay Wolf, *Romantic Re-Vision: Culture and Consciousness in Nineteenth-Century American Painting and Literature* (Chicago: University of Chicago Press, 1982).

23. See John Barrell, *The Dark Side of the Landscape: The Rural Poor in English Painting, 1730–1840* (New York: Cambridge University Press, 1980); James Buzard, *The Beaten Track: European Tourism, Literature, and the Ways to Culture, 1800–1918* (New York: Oxford University Press, 1993); Eric Hobsbawm, *The Age of Empire, 1875–1914* (New York: Random House, 1987), especially chapter 7, "Who's Who or the Uncertainties of the Bourgeoisie"; and Angela Miller, "Landscape Taste as an Indicator of Class Identity in Antebellum America," in *Art in Bourgeois Society, 1790–1850*, ed. Andrew Hemingway and William Vaughan (Cambridge: Cambridge University Press, 1998), 340–61. I discuss the effects of cheaper forms of transportation and more popular scenic guides on conceptions of class identity in chapter 2.
24. Early British picturesque painters like J. R. Cozens and Thomas Girtin specialized in watercolors, but some of their paintings were reproduced as prints. Later landscape painters like J. M. W. Turner often produced drawings specifically for print reproduction, such as his *Liber Studiorum* (1807; repr., New York: Stokes, 1911) and *Picturesque Views on the Southern Coast of England* (London: Arch, 1826). For an American audience, access to picturesque views of European sites was often gained through the medium of print.
25. Certainly many of the first widely recognized American writers also contributed to the goals and defining experiences of scenic tourism, such as William Cullen Bryant, Washington Irving, Nathaniel Hawthorne, and James Fenimore Cooper. The works of Irving and Cooper especially provided quasi-historical material that augmented the touristic interest of specific sites in the Hudson River Valley; Cooper's *Last of the Mohicans* is sprinkled with footnotes inviting the reader to visit the locales that are the settings for specific episodes in the novel.
26. For example, Cole, *Collected Essays,* 128–32 and 143–53.
27. Ibid., 129–30. The blindness of the material minded to the aesthetic and spiritual bounty of nature was a refrain of transcendentalist as well as genteel travel writing. See, for example, Callow, *Kindred Spirits,* and Ringe, *Pictorial Mode.* More recently, Jerome Tharaud, in "Evangelical Space," *American Art* 28, no. 3 (Fall 2014): 52–75, discusses the intersection between nature imagery employed during the Second Great Awakening and understandings of the spiritual in nature articulated by transcendentalist writers and painters like Cole. The foibles of ignorant tourists and the pretentiousness of nature aesthetes were staple subjects of literary satire. Hawthorne lampooned both types in a number of stories; compare Cole's comment with Hawthorne's assessment of Niagara Falls, from "My visit to Niagara": "Oh, that I had never heard of Niagara till I beheld it! . . . Had its own mysterious voice been the first to warn me of its existence, then, indeed, I might have knelt down and worshipped. But I had come thither, haunted with a vision of foam and fury, and dizzy cliffs, and an ocean tumbling down out of the sky—a scene, in short, which nature had too much good taste and calm simplicity to realize . . . a wretched sense of disappointment weighed me down." This story and other travel pieces are collected in Alfred Weber, ed., *Hawthorne's American Travel Sketches* (Hanover, NH: University Press of New England, 1989).
28. The most frequently cited source defending American landscape beauty despite the absence of ruins is Cole's "Essay on American Scenery," *American Monthly Magazine* 1 (1836), reprinted in John McCoubrey, ed., *American Art, 1700–1960: Sources and Documents* (Englewood Cliffs, NJ: Prentice Hall, 1965). A convenient overview of this debate is provided by Stephen Fender, "American Landscape and the Figure of Anticipation," in *Views of American Landscape*, ed. Mick Gidley and Robert Lawson-Peebles (New York: Cambridge University Press, 1989), 51–63. The importance of historical meanings, or "associations," in landscape perception derives from Archibald Alison's picturesque treatise *Essays on the Nature and Principles of Taste,* 5th ed. (1790; repr., London: Murray, 1879). See also the writings of his contemporary William Gilpin, such as *Observations on the Wye, and Several Parts of South Wales, &c. Relative Chiefly to Picturesque Beauty* (London: Blamire, 1782).
29. Dona Brown, *Inventing New England: Regional Tourism in the Nineteenth Century* (Washington: Smithsonian Institution Press, 1995), 17–19. Brown discusses the confusion of class affiliation caused by the increasing affordability of recreational travel along the Hudson River at this time. Such confusion is a smaller version of what would occur at midcentury and afterward when the dramatic increase in railroad routes and decrease in ticket prices rendered destinations throughout the East and much of the Midwest accessible to members of the lower middle class. The effects of new modes of transportation on American scenic tourism are also discussed by Gassan, *Birth of American Tourism*; David Schuyler, "The Mid-Hudson Valley as Iconic Landscape: Tourism, Economic Development, and the Beginnings of a Preservationist Impulse," in *Within the Landscape: Essays on Nineteenth-Century American Art and Culture*, ed. Phillip Earenfight and Nancy Siegel (Carlisle, PA: Trout Gallery, 2005), 11–42; and John Sears, *Sacred Places: American Tourist Attractions in the Nineteenth Century* (New York: Oxford University Press, 1989).

30. This study concentrates on American print materials, but American guidebook publishers were certainly looking at European models, as well as producing their own guides to scenic destinations in Europe. Appleton's guidebooks are an example. The guides produced by Baedeker and Murray do not seem to have incorporated scenery viewed from steamboats or trains. But the tendency of later European guides "to use an unmediated language in which 'referential proliferation' was all but impossible," in Rudy Koshar's words, resembles features of the railroad narrative that I describe in this chapter. Rudy Koshar, "'What Ought to Be Seen': Tourists' Guidebooks and National Identity in Modern Germany and Europe," *Journal of Contemporary History,* 33, no. 3 (1998): 323–40.
31. Jon Sterngass, *First Resorts: Pursuing Pleasure at Saratoga Springs, Newport, and Coney Island* (Baltimore, MD: Johns Hopkins University Press, 2001), notes that "railroad mileage leaped from 23 in 1830 to 30,000 in 1860 and 166,000 in 1890" (17). He also estimates that before railroad connections to New York and Boston, "Saratoga had probably never hosted more than six thousand guests in any season"; by 1859 this number increased to forty thousand (21–22). Sterngass also discusses the business connections between railroads and hotels.
32. Such institutions also attempted to cultivate a broader socioeconomic membership through lotteries of paintings and sponsorship of print editions of notable works featured in its annual exhibits.
33. I do not address the literature devoted to canalboats, which vied with the steamboat as the first major engineering marvel in transportation in the nineteenth century. Scenic guides for trips on canals were not as common as those for steamboat excursions. Canal terminals tended to be located away from the big cities where printers were concentrated, and canal carriers were by and large smaller companies than steamboat lines, so they may have had smaller budgets for promotions. Travel by canal was also typically perceived as utilitarian, and its course was necessarily restricted to the canal channel. In "The Canal-Boat," Hawthorne describes the Erie Canal as "an interminable mud-puddle . . . hold[ing] its way through all the dismal swamps and unimpressive scenery that could be found between the great lakes and the sea-coast" (Weber, *Hawthorne's American Travel Sketches*, 36). Also see Carter Goodrich, *Government Promotion of American Canals, 1800–1890* (New York: Columbia University Press, 1992); and Gassan, *Birth of American Tourism,* chapter 5.
34. William Cullen Bryant and Asher B. Durand, eds., *American Landscape,* no. 1 (New York: E. Bliss, 1830). Bryant wrote the preface, while Durand wrote the "Prospectus" that followed. James Smillie produced the engravings. Durand was later an editor and major contributor to the *Crayon,* a more successful journal devoted to American landscape beauty, which appeared in the 1850s. Although abortive, *American Landscape* had several successors in the form of collections of isolated picturesque landmarks sketched by prominent artists paired with brief textual descriptions intended to cultivate a taste for natural beauty. These successors include Elias Magoon, ed., *The Home-Book of the Picturesque: Or, American Scenery, Art, and Literature* (New York: Putnam, 1852); and Nathaniel P. Willis, *American Scenery; Or, Land, Lake, and River Illustrations of Transatlantic Nature* (London: Virtue, 1840). Other collections were organized as sequences of views correlated with a route of travel, almost like a steamboat guide. An early example is William Guy Wall's *The Hudson River Portfolio* (New York: Megarey and Gilley, 1821–1825), discussed in detail by Gassan, in *Birth of American Tourism*, chapter 3. Both Bryant and Durand were also members of the Art-Union.
35. Bryant and Durand, *American Landscape*, 6.
36. Although as scholars of American landscape painting have noted, images of the western landscape encourage the viewer to "enter the picture" more than European works do. As Roger Cushing Aikin writes in "Paintings of Manifest Destiny," "They invite the viewer physically into the picture to the divinely inspired completion of the American destiny, the progressive westward occupation of the land. We are magically transported into the place depicted, and walk into and through it in our mind's eye" (84). Part of the discrepancy here has to do with the intention of Bryant and Durand to foreground these (eastern) scenes as picture-like. A distinction could be made, though, between encouraging viewers to participate in "history" and encouraging them to see "history" itself.
37. See Kathryn Hume, "Narrative Speed in Contemporary Fiction," *Narrative* 13, no. 2 (2005): 105–24; and Jan Baetens and Kathryn Hume, "Speed, Rhythm, Movement: A Dialogue on K. Hume's Article 'Narrative Speed,'" *Narrative* 14, no. 3 (2006): 349–55.
38. Genette, *Narrative Discourse*, 86.
39. Ibid., 88.
40. Bryant and Durand, *American Landscape*, 11–12.
41. Ibid., 12. This imagining of the past is a reversal of Cole's famous view of the future found near of the end of his "Essay on American Scenery": "And in looking over the yet uncultivated scene, the mind's eye may see far into futurity. Where the wolf roams, the plough shall glisten; on the gray crag shall rise temple and tower—mighty deeds shall be done in the now pathless wilderness; and poets yet unborn shall sanctify the soil" (McCoubrey, *American Art,*

109). Characteristically, Cole immediately follows this optimistic view of the future by deploring the present-day despoiling of pristine natural beauty.

42. Bryant and Durand, *American Landscape*, 6.
43. Ibid., 16.
44. Ibid., 15.
45. Ibid., 15–16.
46. Cole is an exception. As many scholars have pointed out, Cole frequently produced works, such as *The Oxbow* (1836), in which leisurely movement into depth is somehow threatened—in this case by a rainstorm that may or may not be approaching from the left side of the canvas. Nonetheless the unobtrusive guiding of the eye's movement into distance continues to function here as a basic pictorial language for structuring landscape.
47. Boime, *Magisterial Gaze*, further equates the elevated vantage point with the proprietary gaze of the landowner surveying property and the perspective of the surveyor mapping terrain, who most often took observations for triangulating distance and position from the highest elevations in a given area. See especially chapter 2, "The View from Above."
48. Ibid. Boime's analysis stresses the gratification of latent (or not so latent) desires for ownership on the part of the viewer. Other studies do not place such an emphasis on the individual pleasures of viewing, but they still acknowledge its role. Although chiefly concerned with the formation of national identity, Miller registers the more blatantly selfish appeal of paintings like Durand's *Progress,* which exemplify a "displaced language of visual mastery . . . in which the eye was the stand-in for the actual human presence, vicariously enacting the rituals of power, property, and custodianship by which Americans defined their relationship to the natural world" (*Empire of the Eye,* 150).
49. Thomas Nelson, *Nelson's Illustrated Guide to the Hudson and Its Tributaries* (New York: Nelson and Sons, 1860).
50. There were Nelson guides for the Hudson River, Lakes George and Champlain (1858), New England seaside destinations (*Our Summer Retreats,* 1858), New York City (1858), Niagara Falls (1870), and Newport, Rhode Island (1870); later, there were also guides for points west, such as Salt Lake City (1870) and the Central Pacific and Union Pacific Railroads (both 1870).
51. Notably, the Taintor guides, produced around the same time and covering steam routes for the Hudson (1869) and Connecticut (1876) Rivers and rail routes such as the Long Island line (1871).
52. Nelson, *Illustrated Guide to the Hudson*, iv-v.
53. Ibid., iii.
54. Ibid.
55. Banvard's moving panorama influenced the production of several other river-based ones. See John Francis McDermott, *The Lost Panoramas of the Mississippi* (Chicago: University of Chicago Press, 1958). Another well-known and almost contemporary panorama is John Egan's *Panorama of the Monumental Grandeur of the Mississippi Valley* (ca. 1850). Nenette Luarca-Shoaf, "Excavating a Nineteenth-Century Medium," *American Art* 27, no. 2 (Summer 2013): 15–20, complicates an understanding of the moving panorama as a protocinematic form of visual entertainment by drawing out the "diagrammatic" character of the individual scenes and their spatial construction as illustrating new scientific findings in archaeology and geology (in other words, new kinds of "history" that can be differentiated from the models of history discussed here).
56. Reader sympathy for Major Andre was not nonexistent; indeed, in the early nineteenth century, conservatives identified with certain aspects of earlier colonial society in contrast to perceived upheavals in the social order resulting from increasingly aggressive expansionist policies. This identification in part accounted for the popularity of Cooper's novels among a particular class of readers; see Larzer Ziff, *Writing in the New Nation: Prose, Print, and Politics in the Early Republic* (New Haven, CT: Yale University Press, 1991).
57. Charles Newhall Taintor, *The Hudson River Route: New York to Albany* (New York: Taintor Brothers, Merrill, 1869). This mapping apparatus was used in the earliest guidebooks covering the Hudson River, such as Theodore Dwight, *The Northern Traveller: Containing the Routes to Niagara, Quebec, and the Springs* (New York: Carvill, 1828).
58. See especially chapters 2 and 3, "The Machine Ensemble" and "Railroad Space and Railroad Time," in Schivelbusch, *Railway Journey.*
59. Ibid., 38.
60. Ibid., 55 and 56.
61. Williams, *Pacific Tourist*, 9. In "Scenery on the Erie Railroad," *Harper's New Monthly Magazine* 1, no. 2 (July 1850): 215–18, the author discusses the ability of the train to frame distinctive views of the landscape. Although this is an earlier document, prone to describe landscape beauty in more familiar picturesque terms, the author essentially alerts the potential rider as to when such-and-such a view will be "presented," while there is also a competing interest in modern engineering as a contrast to such scenes: "There is certainly [no railroad] that can present to the traveler such a succession of triumphs of art over the formidable obstacles which nature has, at almost every step, raised against the iron-clad intruder into her loveliest recesses" (215).

62. Williams, *Pacific Tourist*, 9–10.
63. In Rachael DeLue's introductory essay to Rachael Delue and James Elkins, eds., *Landscape Theory* (New York: Routledge, 2008), she discusses a similar comparison between shifting sights and recent imaging technologies in Thoreau's 1849 *A Week on the Concord and Merrimack Rivers.* Thoreau writes of seeing a distant ship seemingly pass over a cornfield (because the ocean was below the horizon): "The effect was similar, since I had no means of measuring distances, to seeing a painted ship passed backwards and forwards through a magic lantern" (8). DeLue focuses on the disjunction between expectations about renowned scenic destinations and actual sites but likewise notes a shift to more discontinuous narrative forms (and correspondingly discontinuous landscape views) at this time.
64. William Guild, *A Chart and Description of the Boston and Worcester and Western Railroads* (Boston, MA: Bradbury and Guild, 1847). Chesapeake and Ohio Railway, *Route and Resorts of the Chesapeake and Ohio Railway* (Richmond, VA: Baughman Brothers, 1878), does not contain a route line and has more images (some of them provided by Moran), but it contains a similar amount of scenic and historical explanation. C. R. Chisholm, *Chisholm's All-Round Route and Panoramic Guide of the St. Lawrence: Hudson River; Saratoga . . . and Western Tourist's Guide to the Famous Summer Resorts of the Great Far West* (Chicago: Chisholm, 1881); and Alfred A. Hart, *The Traveler's Own Book, A Souvenir of Overland Travel, via the Great and Attractive Route* (Chicago: Horton and Leonard, 1870), forego the extensive illustrations of Guild's book, but their texts are equally fragmented and condensed. Other railroad guides, like Williams's *Pacific Tourist,* correlate the amount of text and illustrations with the speed of travel in a general but still noticeable way. Filler material—the history of the railroad's construction, travel tips, and the like—appears in the long gaps between striking sights, measurable as distances in miles, at which point the text reverts to a discussion of directly visible points of interest.
65. In light of its dramatic suturing of text and image sections, compared with some other railroad guidebooks, it is tempting to compare Guild's guidebook also with the beginnings of the moving panorama "craze" initiated by Banvard. Banvard's own work toured widely, and print descriptions of it were also produced, accompanied by illustrations. However, the succession of "images" orchestrated by Guild's *Chart and Description* was evidently much more rapid.
66. One of the most frequently painted landscapes was the view from the summit of Mount Holyoke (as in Cole's *The Oxbow*), but in the Guild illustration the mountain appears as a distant hump on the horizon, rising above an uninteresting plain dotted with solitary trees. Without its identifying caption, the mountain might be entirely ignored by the passing traveler.
67. This effect is also discussed by Schivelbusch, *Railway Journey*, chapter 3.
68. Guild, *Chart and Description*, 13, 27.
69. More so than the steamboat guides, railroad guidebook text and illustration are circumscribed by the speed of travel. Certainly the guide can be discarded at will, but the perception of continuity would be reinforced more noticeably by factors external to the reader/viewer, such as the rapidly passing scenery, that make the guide more like Genette's "isochronous narrative."
70. This capacity to shift between orders of representation also affects how users of Guild's book would "locate" themselves: at a point on the route line, at a place on the opposite page, at an actual (but rapidly changing) position relative to physical features in the passing landscape. This slippery awareness of "location" might alternatively be configured in terms of forward- versus backward-looking temporal perspectives, anticipatory versus retrospective: one could look forward to a view based on one's location on the route line or look backward in reading about a notable sight that one has passed.
71. Schivelbusch, *Railway Journey*, 68.
72. The pacing of textual explication as it accompanied a succession of images is one of the technical aspects of the moving panorama discussed by Huhtamo in "Global Glimpses for Local Realities": "The continuity across the temporal ellipses between the views was no doubt partly provided by the narrator, who guided the spectators' gazes, but also by visual and perhaps even auditive means" (208). The special challenge for the maker and exhibitor of the moving panorama was to maintain a sense of continuity as one scene was slowly replaced by another in conjunction with the voice-over narration; in the case of Guild's *Chart and Description,* this challenge would be amplified, with some stretches of trip relatively devoid of incident and others relatively crammed. Huhtamo's book-length study of the moving panorama is *Illusions in Motion: Media Archaeology of the Moving Panorama and Related Spectacles* (Cambridge, MA: MIT Press, 2013).
73. For example, Samuel T. Eastman, in the nearly contemporary *The White Mountain Guide Book,* 2nd ed. (Concord, MA: Eastman, 1859), describes the railroad route from Boston to the White Mountains as follows: "Boston to Concord, N. H., by Boston

& Maine, and Concord, Manchester, & Lawrence Railroads (Haymarket Square), passing through Lawrence, Mass., and Manchester, N. H." (vii). This verbal shorthand is comparable to so-called telegraphic style, abbreviating text in the manner of telegraphic messages, seen as influential for some modernist writing styles. See David Hochfelder, *The Telegraph in America, 1832–1920* (Baltimore, MD: John Hopkins University Press, 2012), chapter 3; and Stephen Kern, *The Culture of Time and Space, 1880–1918* (Boston, MA: Harvard University Press, 1983).

74. Guild, *Chart and Description*, 7.
75. See Koshar, "'What Ought to Be Seen.'" These condensed descriptions are especially characteristic of Baedeker guides; they are called "Baedeker 'parentheses.'" Koshar, "'What Ought to Be Seen,'" 330.
76. This is in clear contrast with the Nelson guidebook, *Illustrated Guide to the Hudson*, which promised to "transport [the reader] to grand and glorious scenes, rendered more dear to each free-born American as the theatre of the most thrilling episodes of that glorious war" (iii).
77. Guild, *Chart and Description*, 4.
78. Disconnection, speed, and superficiality are all qualities associated with the problems of modern life and its attendant processes of urbanization, industrialization, and commercialization. Accounts of negative reactions to the city or technology are numerous, but see, for example, Jean Baudrillard, *Simulacra and Simulation*, trans. Sheila Glaser (Ann Arbor: University of Michigan Press, 1981); Clark, *Painting of Modern Life*; Guy Debord, *The Society of the Spectacle* (New York: Zone Books, 1994); and Raymond Williams, *The English Novel from Dickens to Lawrence* (New York: Oxford University Press, 1970). Earlier key texts include Walter Benjamin, "On Some Motifs in Baudelaire" and "The Work of Art in the Age of Mechanical Reproduction," in *Illuminations*, ed. Hannah Arendt (New York: Harcourt, Brace, and World, 1968), 155–200, 217–52; Georg Simmel, "The Metropolis and Mental Life," in *Simmel on Culture: Selected Writings*, ed. David Frisby and Mike Featherstone (1903; repr., London: Sage, 1971), 174–85; and ultimately, Karl Marx, *Capital,* 1867, especially volume 1, selections in *Karl Marx: Selected Writings*, ed. Lawrence Simon (Indianapolis, IN: Hackett Publishing, 1994).
79. Koshar, "'What Ought to Be Seen,'" 324–25. A similar, more empowering account of spectatorship in relation to turn-of-the-century mass culture entertainments is Michael Leja's *Looking Askance: Skepticism and American Art from Eakins to Duchamp* (Berkeley: University of California Press, 2004). Leja characterizes the appeal of amusements like Barnum's American Museum as a knowing participation in the experience of being duped (not unlike the appeal of horror movies, for example), which he then relates to concerns about truth in advertising, among other topics.
80. Other views of this midcentury period see a connection between market expansion through print and a threatened sense of national unity, such as Trish Loughran's *The Republic in Print: Print Culture in the Age of U.S. Nation Building, 1770–1870* (New York: Columbia University Press, 2007), which attempts to answer the question "how do we account for the profound cultural fragmentation that accompanied the eventual emergence of national print networks between 1820 and 1860?" (3). Loughran focuses on how sectional tensions became more pronounced through increasingly nationwide print circulation, but the establishment of a shared experience of consumer desire through modes of advertising, modes of juxtaposing words and pictures in print, acted as both a counterforce and a further source of tension in that the industrial producers it largely served could be associated with the North.
81. Lynne Kirby, *Parallel Tracks: The Railroad and Silent Cinema* (Durham, NC: Duke University Press, 1997), 3. Kirby notes that one of the first silent films was the Lumière Brothers' 1895 short of a train arriving at a station; in *Looking Askance,* Leja questions whether early spectators were as alarmed by this sight as traditional film histories would have it. Nonetheless, the absence of a measured and continuous narrative characteristic of guidebooks like Guild's bears some similarity to the nonnarrative quality of many of the first films, as described by Tom Gunning in "The Cinema of Attraction: Early Film, Its Spectator, and the Avant-Garde," *Wide Angle* 8, nos. 3 and 4 (Fall 1986): 63–70; such films were "less a way of telling stories than . . . a way of presenting a series of views to an audience, fascinating because of their illusory power" (64).
82. Schivelbusch, *Railway Journey*, 57.
83. Once again, as in Williams's *Pacific Tourist,* the view from the train is described by von Eichendorff as a kind of optical toy (the kaleidoscope).
84. Schivelbusch, *Railway Journey*, 60, quoting Matthew E. Ward's 1853 *English Items; Or, Microcosmic Views of England and Englishmen.* Guild's book similarly fosters a dreamlike perception on the part of the viewer, as in his description of the view of Boston from the train car window: "The whole city seems to rise like a vast temple" (Guild, *Chart and Description*, 13).
85. Not that the railroad guidebook per se is a direct vehicle for consumer activity (beyond the way it promotes train travel), but its presentation of content is similar to print publications in which consumer

activity is a more overt goal. Even so, the railroad guidebook does encourage a quantification of touristic experience, the price of the ticket spread out over the discrete segments of the route line. Also, obviously, in its mediation of rapid transportation it foregrounds access.

86. See Oettermann's *Panorama,* chapter 6, for a history of (stationary, wrap-around) panoramas in the United States, and, for a particular city, Hans Bergmann, "Panoramas of New York, 1845–1860," *Prospects* 10 (1985): 119–37. An early American print panorama is James Smillie's *A Panoramic View from Bunker Hill Monument* (1848), although print versions of British painted panoramas (essentially keys to them)—especially those created by Robert Barker—were circulating previously in the United States. Smillie was also active producing engraved versions of landscape paintings by leading artists, such as Kensett's *The White Mountains—From North Conway* (plate 7). Another early American example of the print panorama is J. T. Bowen, *Panorama and Views of Philadelphia and Its Vicinity* (Philadelphia, PA: Bowen, 1838), which consisted of a panoramic view (four separate sheets showing the north, east, south, and west sides of the city viewed from the state capitol) with numbers identifying significant buildings, followed by a pamphlet containing two- or three-page explications of these sites.

87. Julio H. Rae, *Rae's Philadelphia Pictorial Directory and Panoramic Advertiser* (Philadelphia, PA: Rae, 1851); DeWitt C. Baxter, *The Baxter Panoramic Business Directory* (Philadelphia, PA: Baxter, 1859). The web page "Places in Time: Historical Documentation of Place in Greater Philadelphia" (www.brynmawr.edu/iconog/frdr.html) posts excerpts from both city directories, images as well as text, which I am using here. Discussions of Rae and Baxter's work include Stuart Blumin, *The Emergence of the Middle Class: Social Experience in the American City, 1760–1900* (New York: Cambridge University Press, 1989); and, recently published, Louisa Iarocci, *The Urban Department Store in America, 1850–1930* (Farnham, Surrey: Ashgate, 2014), which looks closely at the visual impact of print advertising forms in ways that intersect with my analysis. In *Illusions in Motion,* Huhtamo focuses on print versions of moving panoramas; the works discussed in the following pages were conceived entirely as print publications. Earlier business directories took the form of more prosaic lists of businesses (either alphabetically or by street number); like Guild's guidebook, the works of Rae and Baxter coincide with a midcentury enthusiasm for the moving panorama.

88. The emphasis on typography in city storefront designs is conspicuous in the years following the Civil War, resulting in a sea of signage along commercial avenues, as noted in "A Novelty in Sign-Making," *Manufacturer and Builder* 4, no. 3 (March 1872): "It is hardly possible for any one to stroll down our great thoroughfares without being impressed by the almost endless variety of styles and patterns of signs that meet his eye. Human ingenuity appears to have strained itself to the utmost to invent striking combinations of letters, colors, and gilding by which to attract public attention, and direct the passer-by to special localities" (56). See also David M. Henkin, "City Streets and the Urban World of Print," in *A History of the Book in America,* vol. 3, *The Industrial Book, 1840–1880,* ed. Scott E. Casper et al. (Chapel Hill: University of North Carolina Press, 2007), 331–45.

89. This dual format, combining business cards with pictorial representation, is adopted in railroad guidebooks, such as Chisholm, *All-Round Route and Panoramic Guide,* that are prefaced by a lengthy section of advertisements. Looked at another way, it is as if the preliminary maps that opened the Taintor guide, which organized the rest of the guidebook, are effectively replaced by an arrangement of advertisements. The tendency toward flatness characteristic of both depicted storefront and business card has a further, if somewhat unexpected, analog in the flattened frontal view of businesses in many stereoscopic images produced at this time. In fact the stereoscopic view in general, while allowing the perception of depth in its replication of bifocal vision, also characteristically transforms elements within the image into flat planes. As Crary notes in *Techniques of the Observer,* "We perceive individual elements as flat, cutout forms. . . . Certain planes or surfaces, even though composed of indications of light or shade that normally designate volume, are perceived as flat" (125). See also Peter Hales, *Silver Cities: Photographing American Urbanization, 1839–1939* (Philadelphia, PA: Temple University Press, 1984), on photographic representations of commercial establishments.

90. In a sense, Rae's directory is a more concrete and more commercial version of Benjamin's sense of impressionist painting as training for the unique sights of the modern city, in "On Some Motifs in Baudelaire": "The technique of Impressionist painting, whereby the picture is garnered in a riot of dabs of color, would be a reflection of experiences with which the eyes of the big-city dweller have become familiar" (*Illuminations,* 197).

91. Rae, *Philadelphia Pictorial Directory*; Baxter, *Panoramic Business Directory.*

92. On the nineteenth-century commercialization of American city centers, see Gunther Barth, *City People: The Rise of the Modern City in Nineteenth-*

Century America (New York: Oxford University Press, 1980). Nick Yablon, *Untimely Ruins: An Archaeology of American Modernity, 1819–1919* (Chicago: University of Chicago Press, 2009), examines how the kinds of urban ruins that predominate in nineteenth-century American culture differ from the typical Roman or Renaissance monument that is the focus of the European picturesque tradition: "These vernacular ruins . . . would neither memorialize epoch-defining events and individuals nor embody the period's highest aesthetic standards. On the contrary, they were banal, ambiguous, or obscure in origin, unmediated by well-known legends or preeminent visual or literary representations, and thus unassimilable to the grand historical narratives concretized by the classical and Gothic ruins of Europe" (8). Rae and Baxter disclose a similar kind of history without an accustomed historical content.

93. Solyman Brown, *The Citizen and Strangers' Pictorial and Business Directory for the City of New-York and Its Vicinity* (New York: Charles Spalding, 1853). A comparable city directory is Camille N. Dry, *Pictorial Guide to St. Louis* (St. Louis, MO: Shultz and McDonald, 1877), produced on the occasion of the Centennial Exposition in St. Louis.
94. Brown, *Citizen and Strangers' Pictorial*, 11. It is by no means clear that "greed" is viewed negatively here.
95. Ibid., 278.
96. Ibid., 11.

Chapter 2. The Anatomy of Greed

1. Later in this chapter I discuss Veblen's sociological ideas in relation to how print materials mediate commercial activity and class identity.
2. On the history of tourist development in the Northeast, particularly in Newport, Rhode Island, see Brown, *Inventing New England*, and Sterngass, *First Resorts*. David Scobey, in "Anatomy of the Promenade: The Politics of Bourgeois Sociability in Nineteenth-Century New York," *Social History* 17, no. 2 (May 1992): 203–27, dissects the rituals of class status in sites devoted to leisure activity; in fact, he argues that such sites were particularly charged locations for negotiating class difference (in part because of their semipublic nature).
3. Miller, "Landscape Taste," argues that the themes of national unity contained in Hudson River school paintings reinforced a middle-class identity that was likewise "national" because of growing connections among urban market centers, over and against localized and enclosed rural communities (342–43). The "middle class" I refer to here is less wealthy, professional, and educated than hers; my point is that as scenic tourism became more widely accessible and the railroad narrative came to dominate scenic literature, the picturesque tradition lost its capacity, or rather its intention, to construct a coherent national identity. Instead, it increasingly operated after midcentury to reinforce a sense of class superiority over and against a lower commercial and urban class that was itself increasingly numerous and national. In *The Emergence of the Middle Class*, Blumin provides a detailed historical account of this conjunction of urban growth, new markets, and evolving middle-class identities.
4. Like the Hudson River school, this term is a twentieth-century art historical label, and I use it here with reference specifically to Kensett, Richards, and other "luminist" painters who depicted East Coast tourist destinations. John I. H. Baur first used the term in "American Luminism, A Neglected Aspect of the Realist Movement in Nineteenth-Century American Painting," *Perspectives USA*, 9 (Fall 1954): 90–98. Later studies, such as Barbara Novak's *American Painting of the Nineteenth Century: Realism, Idealism, and the American Experience* (New York: Oxford University Press, 1969), specified the characteristics of luminist style and identified artists who could be classed as luminists, helping to further install the term in American art history. See the introduction to John Wilmerding, ed., *American Light: The Luminist Movement, 1850–1875* (New York: Harper and Row, 1980); and more recently, J. Gray Sweeney, "Inventing Luminism: 'Labels Are the Dickens,'" *Oxford Art Journal* 26, no. 2 (2003): 95–120, which examines how the term's currency affected the art market. I review the various stylistic and interpretive analyses of luminism later in this chapter.
5. George William Curtis, *Lotus-Eating: A Summer Book* (New York: Harper and Brothers, 1852). Although he discusses various popular tourist locales in some detail, the book is less concerned with practical matters such as train timetables and accommodations, concentrating instead on evoking proper modes of aesthetic experience and critiquing the crass habits of most vacationers.
6. At various times in the 1850s, when his career as a writer first started, Curtis wrote columns or did editing work for the *New York Tribune, Putnam's Magazine,* and *Harper's Weekly.* Comparable literary figures were Bayard Taylor, Nathaniel Parker Willis, and Theodore Winthrop.
7. Melissa Grafton, in "'It Is a Joint Venture': John Frederick Kensett's Images for *Lotus-Eating*" *American Art* 25, no. 2 (Summer 2011): 104–19, reconstructs the working arrangements of Curtis and Kensett and analyzes the innovations of Kensett's illustrations, such as using unusually shaped printing blocks, employing a more vertical format, and incorporating the white space of the page within the picture. She

makes many similar observations on the way text and image are integrated, but overall she refrains from stressing the class-defining aspects of Curtis's text or Kensett's illustrations.

8. Curtis, *Lotus-Eating*, 12–13. Generally, earlier travel writers were more absorbed by the idiosyncrasies of local inhabitants or bemused by the odd collection of types of fellow travelers—for example, in Hawthorne's description of Crawford's Notch in the White Mountains in "Sketches from Memory" (Weber, *Hawthorne's American Travel Sketches*, 27–30). Cole could be outraged by the aesthetic ignorance of vacationers in his trips to the Catskills, but as his diary indicates, there was still ample scope for aesthetic discovery. As scenic tourism became more accessible around midcentury, the exclusive tone in travel writing became more strident. Thus, in *Life in the Open Air*, Winthrop dismisses the steamboat passengers as a "Cockney tribe" and can only charitably describe them via their "negative virtues" (3–4). See also "Lyell's Travels in North America," *Living Age* 66, no. 6 (August 16, 1845): 340–43, which aligns class with travelers' observations: "His book is rather a transcript of the results which the journey has left upon his mind, than the waste-book in which common tourists or travelling bookmakers enter their daily rough memorandums of everything that occurs" (340). James Buzard addresses this development in European travel writing in *Beaten Track*, chapter 2, "Tourism and Anti-Tourism: Conventions and Strategies." John Urry, in *The Tourist Gaze: Leisure and Travel in Contemporary Societies* (London: Sage, 1990), notes that with increased access to transportation, "status distinctions then came to be drawn between different classes of traveller" as opposed to the earlier distinction "between those who could and those who could not travel" (18).
9. Curtis, *Lotus-Eating*, 167 and 172–73.
10. Ibid., 166. A later genteel guidebook to Newport comparable to Curtis's work, by Thomas Wentworth Higginson, is actually called *Oldport Days* (Boston, MA: Osgood, 1873).
11. Curtis, *Lotus-Eating*, 165.
12. Brown, *Inventing New England*, 85–86. Newport remained much more elite than Brown's primary example of lower-middle-class "cottage heaven," Wesleyan Grove, on Martha's Vineyard, but working-class incursions had already begun. Curtis writes prophetically that "fashion dwells in cottages now, and the hotel season is brief and not brilliant. The cottagers will come" (*Lotus-Eating*, 164).
13. Alfred Lord Tennyson, "The Lotos-Eaters," in *English Poetry III: From Tennyson to Whitman*, ed. Charles W. Eliot (1832; New York: Collier and Son, 1909), 1026–37. Also relevant is Tennyson's implicit critique of industrialization and rationalized labor in his adaptation of an incident in book 9 of Homer's *Odyssey*. See David Lubin, "Deconstructing Duncanson," in *Picturing a Nation: Art and Social Change in Nineteenth-Century America* (New Haven, CT: Yale University Press, 1996). Grafton too notes that Curtis's "personal form of address engages the reader yet implies a removal from those people the author criticizes" ("'It Is a Joint Venture,'" 107).
14. See chapter 1 in this volume for a more complete discussion of the literature on the American adaptation of European canons of landscape taste, including the dilemma of the absence of ruins.
15. Cole, "Essay on American Scenery," 109.
16. At this time Venice was becoming one of the more popular destinations for Americans able to travel overseas, as well as a frequent subject for painting commissions. Margaretta Lovell, *A Visitable Past: Views of Venice by American Artists, 1860–1915* (Chicago: University of Chicago Press, 1989), explains that "The American enthusiasm for images of Venice . . . seems to be one aspect of a deep interest in exploration of the past, and especially those aspects of the past that were seemingly absent from (or antithetical to) contemporary American political, moral, and aesthetic life" (1).
17. Curtis, *Lotus-Eating*, 194–95.
18. Ibid., 199–200.
19. The Century Association's members also included important writers on nature and art, notably William Cullen Bryant and Henry B. Tuckerman, with whom Curtis was familiar. In addition to the Century Association and the National Academy of Design, Kensett was also a longtime member of the American Art-Union, which became defunct in 1852. See John K. Howat, "Kensett's World," in *John Frederick Kensett: An American Master*, ed. John Paul Driscoll and John K. Howat (New York: Worcester Art Museum, 1985), 12–47.
20. Ibid., 34–35.
21. John Paul Driscoll writes in "From Burin to Brush: The Development of a Painter," in Driscoll and Howat, *John Frederick Kensett* (48–135), that *Camel's Hump from the Western Shore of Lake Champlain* "cogently summarizes Kensett's ideas about landscape painting, in particular the consonant relationship between man and nature" and that his subsequent development as an artist involved "step[ping] from the sphere of influence of . . . Cole and Durand" (63).
22. Curtis, *Lotus-Eating*, 23–24.
23. Ibid., 24. Grafton, "'It Is a Joint Venture,'" also discusses how Kensett's illustrations "echo Curtis' language," in particular in terms of lines of text functioning as landscape forms in relation to the image, whether as rock formations or as flowing water (113).

24. Curtis, *Lotus-Eating*, 192.
25. Ibid., 23.
26. Ibid., 181–82.
27. Ibid., 182.
28. The function of Kensett's illustrations as illuminated letters is one of the principal ways Grafton, "'It Is a Joint Venture,'" sees text and illustration as being especially integrated in *Lotus-Eating*.
29. Thomas Starr King, *The White Hills: Their Legends, Landscape, and Poetry* (Boston, MA: Crosby, Nichols, 1860). Probably the best-known example of scenic literature in the nineteenth century is the mammoth gift book *Picturesque America*, first published as two entire volumes between 1872 and 1874 and edited by William Cullen Bryant, which contains familiar picturesque views, as well as images of fashionable types promenading stylishly in various locales; *Picturesque America: Or, The Land We Live In*, 2 vols. (New York: Appleton, 1872–1874). Such images cater to the interest in ostentatious display and people watching so shunned by Curtis. They may offer evidence that touristic activities were not so rigidly class specific as his book implies (or, conversely, they may testify to the something-for-everyone approach of *Picturesque America*).
30. See Brown, *Inventing New England*. Other recent examinations of King include Rebecca Bailey Bedell, *The Anatomy of Nature: Geology and American Landscape Painting, 1825–1875* (Princeton, NJ: Princeton University Press, 2001), in her chapter on John F. Kensett.
31. King, *White Hills*, vii.
32. King writes that this view of Mount Madison is surrounded by "a *frame* [that] is gracefully carved out of two nearer hills, to seclude it from any neighboring roughness around the Peabody valley" (ibid., 9).
33. Ibid., 2. King's "map" contrasts with illustrated maps of routes and destinations, designed to facilitate travel, as described in David Tatham, "Frank Leavitt's Pictorial Maps of the White Mountains," in *Prints of New England*, ed. Georgia Barnhill (Worcester, MA: American Antiquarian Society, 1991), 105–34.
34. King, *White Hills*, 7. A more humorous rendering of this extended search for distinctive views can be found in Lucia Pychowska, "Sketches of American Life and Scenery," *Continental Monthly* 5, nos. 1–5 (January–April 1864): 9–13, 270–73, 425–31. Functioning as a distraction from the concluding events of the Civil War, it describes the efforts of two young women to locate picturesque scenes in various locales without the benefit of the kind of guidebook published by King, attesting to their disposable time and lack of concern about national events, but also to a recent freedom of movement and ability to explore the country without male protection.
35. King, *White Hills*, 17. This passage is routinely cited in discussions of King and the class stratification implicit in landscape viewing.
36. Ibid., 7.
37. I acknowledge that I have no direct empirical evidence of the economic status of the tourists who actually used the guidebooks I examine in this section. I am basing my sense of class identity on various factors: cost (of the guidebook but also recommended modes of transportation, lodging, and recreational activities), an admittedly subjective assessment of the appearance of figures depicted within the guidebooks, and the inclusive, everyman tone the guidebooks adopt in a variety of ways (which I see as distinct from the exclusive quality of Curtis's book, which is explicitly addressed to an upper class).
38. James H. Bowditch, *"The City by the Sea": Newport* (Providence, RI: Reid, 1870), preface. Bowditch's guide went through several editions, each with modifications to the text and illustration scheme. I examine his 1870 and 1884 editions.
39. George Champlin Mason, *Newport Illustrated in a Series of Pen and Pencil Sketches* (Providence, RI: Appleton, 1854), 9. The alignment of the Mason guide with the middle-class visitor targeted by the developing mass-market tourist industry comes through in its egalitarian tone; its publisher, D. Appleton and Company, was also one of the dominant producers of guidebooks in the second half of the nineteenth century.
40. The transformations that I trace here have parallels in the development of guidebook literature in European tourism (see Koshar, "'What Ought to Be Seen,'" especially). Based on Koshar's descriptions of earlier Murray and later Baedeker guides, the guidebooks I discuss in this section have more in common with the latter, in terms of a lower-middle-class orientation, greater emphasis on access, and condensed treatment of narrative text. Koshar does not really address patterns of organizing text and illustration.
41. "Awkward" in the sense that objects and features within the print are not organized along a clear path into depth but are spread out across the width of the print within planes parallel to the picture plane and at different distances from it. Transitions between planes into depth (for example, along a path) are not made a priority. This arrangement also encourages reading across the image as opposed to into depth.
42. "Hot! Isn't it?" [asks Ned]

    Jack laughs. "I tell you what, Ned, let's go down on the Providence boat to Newport, to-morrow, and make a day of it. The moon is nearly full, and the weather must be fine."

"All right, agreed; I'm with you, hand and glove. Let's see, first boat leaves the wharf, corner of Dyer and Hay streets, at 9.25 a.m. I'll meet you there."

The text then moves on to a point-by-point description of their boat journey, interspersed with dialogue aimed solely at identifying passing places of interest:

"What light is this on our right—stone foundation and white top?"

"Sassafras Point." (Bowditch, 1884, 36)

43. This mapping is efficient to the degree that it eliminates extraneous space, removing an expansive spatial environment in favor of a focus on the thing itself.
44. Thorstein Veblen, *The Theory of the Leisure Class* (New York: MacMillan, 1899). For a discussion of Veblen's impact on sociological thought, see Christopher Shannon, *Conspicuous Criticism: Tradition, the Individual, and Culture in American Social Thought, from Veblen to Mills* (Baltimore, MD: Johns Hopkins University Press, 1996); T. J. Jackson Lears, "Beyond Veblen: Rethinking Consumer Culture in America," in *Consuming Visions: Accumulation and Display of Goods in America, 1880–1920*, ed. Simon J. Bronner (New York: Norton, 1989), 73–97; and Rick Tilman, *Thorstein Veblen, John Dewey, C. Wright Mills and the Generic Ends of Life* (Lanham, MD: Rowman and Littlefield, 2003). Veblen's work was first published in 1899, but it describes a society whose class structure had been in place in previous decades. The increasing class-defining valences of scenic guides and paintings that I describe here in a sense anticipate or lead up to that class structure.
45. Veblen, *Theory of the Leisure Class*, 34.
46. Ibid., 29.
47. Veblen's theories of the psychology of class affiliation have generally not been applied to nineteenth-century painting. Scholarship that addresses self-perception and class affiliation, especially the notion of "aesthetic disinterest," generally concentrates on the eighteenth century. See Barrell, *Dark Side of the Landscape*, and Ann Birmingham, *Landscape and Ideology: The English Rustic Tradition, 1740–1860* (Berkeley: University of California Press, 1986). On the other hand, scholarship often restricts the class valences of viewing to the performance of class-significant behaviors (carrying a Claude glass, for example). See Scobey, "Anatomy of the Promenade."
48. See Driscoll, "From Burin to Brush"; Kathleen Motes Bennewitz, "John F. Kensett at Beverly, Massachusetts," *American Art Journal* 21, no. 4 (1989): 46–65; and Bedell, *Anatomy of Nature,* chapter 4, "John Kensett, Geology, and Landscape Tourism." Bennewitz's article reidentifies the sites depicted in a number of Kensett's late works (as locations near Beverly, as opposed to Newport), convincingly juxtaposing paintings with modern-day photographs of the shoreline, but her detective work also testifies to Kensett's elusive intentions. More than other scholars, Bedell acknowledges the close connections between Kensett and scenic tourism, writing that the "literary correlatives" to his paintings were scenic guides, but her analysis of this correlation boils down to the idea that the "images [guidebook authors] had in mind were preeminently those by American landscape painters like Kensett" (85 and 92).
49. Linda S. Ferber, *Tokens of a Friendship: Miniature Watercolors by William T. Richards* (New York: Metropolitan Museum of Art, 1982), 32 and 37.
50. Linda S. Ferber, *William Trost Richards (1833–1905): American Landscape and Marine Painter* (New York: Garland, 1980).
51. Ibid., 346.
52. See in particular Philip C. Beam, *Winslow Homer in the 1890s: Prout's Neck Observed* (New York: Hudson Hills Press, 1990).
53. Driscoll, "From Burin to Brush," 99; and Oswaldo Rodriguez Roque, "The Last Summer's Work," in Driscoll and Howat, *John Frederick Kensett*, 148.
54. See, for example, Earl A. Powell, "Luminism and the American Sublime," in Wilmerding, *American Light*, 69–94; Lisa Fellows Andrus, "Design and Measurement in Luminist Art," in Wilmerding, *American Light*, 30–56; and Linda S. Ferber, "Luminist Drawings," in Wilmerding, *American Light*, 237–65. In "From Burin to Brush," Driscoll also notes that "Many of the elements of Kensett's new style were deeply rooted in his . . . early grounding in the graphic arts" (99).
55. Ferber relates the development of Richards's earlier style to an interest in Pre-Raphaelite precision and the innovation of his own techniques in watercolor (producing larger-scale works on carpet paper). By the time he began summering in Newport, however, these detailed forest scenes were no longer selling, prompting a search for new subject matter and a new style. See Ferber, *William Trost Richards*, chapter 7, "Watercolors, 1860–1879." On the influence of Ruskin's writings on American art, see Roger Stein, *John Ruskin and Aesthetic Thought in America* (Boston, MA: Harvard University Press, 1967); and Linda S. Ferber and William H. Gerdts, eds. *The New Path: Ruskin and the Pre-Raphaelites* (Brooklyn, NY: Schocken Books, 1985).
56. Richards's modern biographer writes that his "most Ruskinian or Pre-Raphaelite landscapes" are those in which there is a "sharp division between the highly detailed foreground, which presses forward to the surface of the canvas, and the more broadly painted background" (Ferber, *William Trost Richards*, 83).

Allen Staley, in *The Pre-Raphaelite Landscape* (New York: Oxford University Press, 1973), observes that, in terms of landscape painting, the Pre-Raphaelites "avoid[ed] carrying the sharp focus of the foreground into [the] depth of the picture, but had no better way of achieving breadth than to leave [their] work unfinished" (12).

57. Ferber, *William Trost Richards*, 242, 247. Ferber quotes one of Richards's letters to Whitney, remarking that "Richards himself sought out such places; places 'very lonely, rarely visited' because . . . 'there you seem to get a little closer to the heart of the sea than else where'" (248). A more recent assessment of Kensett's work and its tendency toward abstraction is Herbert Hartel, "Luminism, Transcendentalism, and Abstraction in the Landscape Paintings of John F. Kensett," *Source: Notes in the History of Art* 21, no. 4 (Summer 2002): 23–30.
58. David C. Huntington, "Church and Luminism: Light for America's Elect," in Wilmerding, *American Light*, 166.
59. Miller, *Empire of the Eye*, 243–44.
60. Mark Mitchell, "First Light: John I. H. Baur, James Suydam, and Luminism," *Archives of American Art Journal* 46, no. 1 (2006): 24–35, argues that John I. H. Baur's notion of luminism already stressed a "cool-headed appreciation of nature, not moral themes" (30). Mitchell's essay was occasioned by an exhibition of James Suydam's work at New York's National Academy Museum; see Katherine Manthorne, *Luminist Horizons: The Art and Collection of James A. Suydam* (New York: Braziller, 2006).
61. Miller closes *Empire of the Eye*, her history of landscape painting's role in bolstering national identity, with this sentence: "Yet in the end [luminism's] attempt to revalorize nature, to posit a purely unconscious mechanism of reform, foundered on the hard rock of national conflict, one more failed effort to give nature an authoritative voice in the formation of cultural identity" (288).
62. To track this development and decline, histories of American landscape painting routinely bracket the years 1825–1875. In *American Light*, Theodore E. Stebbins, Jr., remarks that "Luminism may better be seen as a last-ditch attempt to make the Hudson River school style of Asher B. Durand and Church serve the complex psychic and aesthetic needs of post–Civil War America" ("Luminism in Context: A New View," 213).
63. As it turns out, the Crane Estate is also the devil's home in the 1987 film *The Witches of Eastwick*.
64. For example, in *American Light*, Barbara Novak refers to "luminist eternity" and "what Gaston Bachelard has called 'intimate immensity'" ("On Defining Luminism," 25 and 28). The interior quote is from Bachelard, *The Poetics of Space*, trans. Maria Jolas (New York: Orion Press, 1964).
65. Bedell, *Anatomy of Nature*, notes this same tendency of Kensett to remove the signs of recent development. In relation to his 1863 *View from Cozzens Hotel near West Point*, she explains, "These omissions were almost certainly calculated to enhance that sense of intimacy with nature" (90). In relation to *Lake George*, she notes that similar erasures evoke the past (98). My point is that "intimacy," or rather exclusivity, is based on a supposed ability to see the past.
66. In *American Light*, see Andrus, "Design and Measurement in Luminist Art," and Ferber, "Luminist Drawings." Kensett and Richards often used rules or straight edges to mark the horizon. The absence of movement in luminist work has also been ascribed to the use of the camera obscura as a drawing aid.
67. See Ferber, *Tokens of a Friendship*, 33, 37. Whitney promoted Richards to increase the value of the works he owned but also to establish his collection as an important civic asset.
68. Collections of drawings were usually motivated by a simple desire to own works by multiple favorite artists. An example is the album owned by John Mackie Falconer, containing landscape sketches, but also figure studies, genre scenes, and so forth. See *M. and M. Karolik Collection of American Water Colors and Drawings* (Boston, MA: Museum of Fine Arts, 1962), 154–55.
69. Ferber, *Tokens of a Friendship*, 44. See Turner, *Liber Studiorum* and *Southern Coast*. In fact, several sites in England that Richards records in the coupons match locales depicted in the *Southern Coast*.
70. The invention of the modern consumer coupon is generally assigned to Asa Candler, co-owner of the Coca-Cola Company, who in 1888 issued paper tickets redeemable for his new soft drink. The older meaning of the term relates to the payment of interest on bonds; presumably the buyer would purchase the coupon and later exchange it for the finished painting.
71. "The canon of expensiveness also affects our tastes in such a way as to inextricably blend the marks of expensiveness, in our appreciation, with the beautiful features of the object, and to subsume the resultant effect under the head of an appreciation of beauty simply" (Veblen, *Theory of the Leisure Class*, 94). Richards's coupons "blend" landscape beauty and the expensiveness of jewelry.

Chapter 3. "Living Statues"

1. William H. Goetzmann's *Army Exploration of the American West, 1803–1863* (New Haven, CT: Yale University Press, 1959) and *Exploration and Empire: The Explorer and the Scientist in the Winning of the*

American West (New York: Knopf, 1966) are the most extensive histories of survey expeditions and their role in western expansion and settlement; see also Bonnie Skell Hardwick, *Science and Art: The Travel Writings of the Great Surveys of the American West after the Civil War* (Ann Arbor, MI: University Microfilms International, 1980). Although not as comprehensive a study, the effects of different ethnographic and ethnological studies on U.S. Indian policy are described in Robert E. Bieder, *Science Encounters the Indian, 1820–1880* (Norman: University of Oklahoma Press, 1986). See also Brian W. Dippie, *The Vanishing American: White Attitudes and U.S. Indian Policy* (Middleton, CT: Wesleyan University Press, 1982), chapter 2, "A New Order of Things"; and Curtis M. Hinsley, Jr., *Savages and Scientists: The Smithsonian Institution and the Development of American Anthropology, 1846–1910* (Washington: Smithsonian Institution Press, 1981), chapter 6, "Toward an Anthropological Survey."

2. Bedell explores the close connections between geology, tourism, and art in *Anatomy of Nature,* especially in her chapter on John Frederick Kensett, although she does not focus specifically on the relationship between texts and illustrations.
3. Most studies of American landscape painting acknowledge this dynamic, but see especially Boime, *Magisterial Gaze.* Specific studies of the depiction of Natives in American art that also address this aspect of landscape painting include Robert F. Berkhofer, *The White Man's Indian: Images of the American Indian from Columbus to the Present* (New York: Knopf, 1978); Karen Jones and John Wills, *The American West: Competing Visions* (Edinburgh: University of Edinburgh Press, 2009), specifically the section on the "New West"; Ellwood C. Parry III, *The Image of the Indian and the Black Man in American Art, 1590–1900* (New York: Braziller, 1974); and Julie Schimmel, "Inventing the 'Indian,'" in Truettner, *West as America*, 149–89. Fryd, in *Art and Empire*, discusses similar representational strategies in decorations for the U.S. Capitol. Related depictions of the Indian in American literature are treated at greater length in Richard Drinnon, *Facing West: The Metaphysics of Indian-Hating and Empire Building* (Minneapolis: University of Minnesota Press, 1980); Richard Slotkin, *Regeneration through Violence: The Mythology of the American Frontier, 1600–1860* (Middletown, CT: Wesleyan University Press, 1973); and Smith, *Virgin Land.*
4. Both Boime and Miller are sensitive to this reading of *Progress.* See Boime, *Magisterial Gaze*; Miller, *Empire of the Eye*, 154–65. Miller also sees a disjunction between the viewer's self-distancing from the group of Indians and the potential of the foregrounded wilderness zone to appear "nurturing and maternal, appealing to the atavistic desire to see without being seen," drawing on Jay Appleton's analysis of the repoussoir in *The Experience of Landscape* (London: Wiley, 1975). I am not sure, however, that the atavistic attraction of this zone as a redoubt would outweigh its dark, rocky, and unstable appearance.
5. Ephraim G. Squier and Edwin H. Davis, *Ancient Monuments of the Mississippi Valley* (New York: Bartlett and Welford, 1848; repr., Washington, DC: Smithsonian Institution Press, 1998). I am using the modern division of anthropology into physical and cultural anthropology, and the subdivision of the latter into archaeology, ethnology, and linguistics. In the nineteenth century, however, these three subdisciplines were often imperfectly differentiated along epistemological and methodological lines.
6. David J. Meltzer notes this double exclusion in his introduction to the Smithsonian reprint of *Ancient Monuments:* "The Indians are no more a part of the archaeological complex than the small log cabin in the foreground or Marietta's 'Old Stockade'" (Squier and Davis, 45). This frontispiece image also appeared later as the initial scene in Egan's *Panorama of the Monumental Grandeur of the Mississippi Valley.*
7. Samuel Morton, *Crania Americana, or, A Comparative View of the Skulls of Various Aboriginal Nations of North and South America* (Philadelphia, PA: Dobson, 1839); and Josiah Nott, *Types of Mankind: or, Ethnological Researches, Based upon the Ancient Monuments, Paintings, Sculptures, and Crania of Races* (London: Trübner, 1854). See also Brian W. Dippie, *Catlin and His Contemporaries: The Politics of Patronage* (Lincoln: University of Nebraska Press, 1990), chapter 5, "Mastodons among Our Books"; and Meltzer's introduction to *Ancient Monuments,* detailing Squier's involvement in polygenism.
8. Hinsley, *Savages and Scientists*, notes that "Morton's school, and physical anthropology generally, fell into disrepute in the second half of the century," and that during the 1850s, the secretary of the Smithsonian Institution "consistently steered [it] away from racial debates" (27). The work of later anthropologists, like Edward Tylor, Lewis Henry Morgan, and John Wesley Powell, focused on evolutionary models of human development. These denied coevalness in another way: the Indian occupied an earlier evolutionary stage.
9. This perception is the subject of Dippie's *Vanishing American.*
10. Henry Rowe Schoolcraft, *An Address, Delivered before the Was-Ah Ho-De-No-Son-Ne, or New Confederacy of the Iroquois, at Its Third Annual Council* (Rochester, NY: Jerome and Brothers, 1846), 3–7 and 29. Hinsley opens his thoughtful history of Smithsonian-

sponsored anthropological science, *Savages and Scientists*, with these unusually worded excerpts from Schoolcraft's speech.

11. Ibid., 7.
12. George Catlin, *Illustrations of the Manners, Customs, and Condition of the North American Indians* (London: Bohn, 1851; first published in 1841 as *Letters and Notes on the Manners, Customs, and Condition of the North American Indians*); and Henry Rowe Schoolcraft, *Historical and Statistical Information Respecting the History, Condition, and Prospects of the Indian Tribes of the United States,* 6 vols. (Philadelphia, PA: Lippincott, Grambo, 1851–1857). The difference between the 1851 and 1841 editions of Catlin's work are slight. In addition, the argument made here with regard to Catlin applies specifically to these smaller publications that included a lengthy narrative account, not the large-scale, largely pictorial lithographed *North American Indian Portfolio.*
13. Hinsley, *Savages and Scientists*, 9–10; see also Kathryn S. Hight, "'Doomed to Perish': George Catlin's Depictions of the Mandan," *Art Journal* 49, no. 2 (Summer 1990): 119–24. Other important ethnographic/ethnological texts produced in the United States in the first half of the nineteenth century include John Gottlieb Heckewelder, *History, Manners and Customs of the Indian Nations who once Inhabited Pennsylvania and the Neighboring States* (1818; rev. ed. Philadelphia: Historical Society of Pennsylvania, 1876); Thomas McKenney and Edwin Hall, *History of the Indian Tribes of North America: With Biographical Sketches and Anecdotes of the Principal Chiefs* (Philadelphia, PA: Greenough, 1838); and Squier and Davis's *Ancient Monuments.*
14. For the history of U.S.–American Indian relations, see Francis Paul Prucha, *The Great Father: The United States Government and the American Indians* (Lincoln: University of Nebraska Press, 1984), and *American Indian Policy in the Formative Years: The Indian Trade and Intercourse Acts, 1780–1834* (Lincoln: University of Nebraska Press, 1964). More recently, Mark Rifkin, *Manifesting America: The Imperial Construction of U.S. National Space* (New York: Oxford University Press, 2009), investigates the legalistic framework enabling Indian removal, and Cathleen Cahill, *Federal Fathers and Mothers: A Social History of the United States Indian Service, 1869–1933* (Chapel Hill: University of North Carolina Press, 2011), uses local case studies to examine the later shift to assimilation policies.
15. Schoolcraft's position is thus a modification of the advocacy of Indian removal espoused by his mentor, Lewis Cass; see Cass, "Indian Treaties, and Laws and Regulations Relating to Indian Affairs," *North American Review,* vol. 24 (1827): 365–442, and "Documents and Proceedings Relating to the Formation and Progress of a Board in the City of New York, for the Emigration, Preservation, and Improvement of the Aborigines of America," *North American Review* 30 (1830): 62–121.
16. Catlin, *Illustrations of the Manners*, 3. Although Catlin stresses the inevitable demise of American Indian civilization, his descriptions of the tribes of the upper Missouri and Mississippi still rely on the equation of Indian and ahistoric nature, as opposed to Schoolcraft's "archaeologizing" approach.
17. Ibid., 16.
18. Although Catlin wanted the government specifically to purchase his Indian Gallery as a monument to American Indian civilization, his published works functioned in a similar role, as substitutes for the Indian Gallery.
19. Mary Louise Pratt, *Imperial Eyes: Travel Writing and Transculturation* (New York: Routledge, 1992), 134. See Alexander von Humboldt, *Ansichten der Kordilleran und Monumente der eingeboren Völker Amerikas* (1810; repr., Frankfort am Main: Eichborn Verlag, 2004). Johannes Fabian, in *Time and the Other: How Anthropology Makes Its Object* (New York: Columbia University Press, 1983), describes how anthropological knowledge risks posing as a substitute for a culture, chiefly in forms of investigation and writing that impose a temporal distance relative to that culture, with similar effects of removal from the present. See also James Clifford, *The Predicament of Culture: Twentieth-Century Ethnography, Literature, and Art* (Cambridge, MA: Harvard University Press, 1988); Clifford Geertz, *The Interpretation of Cultures: Selected Essays* (New York: Basic Books, 1973); and Bruce Trigger, *A History of Archaeological Thought* (New York: Cambridge University Press, 1989).
20. Pratt focuses on Europeans' depictions of foreign lands as ahistoric, so Catlin would be a late example of this approach. Michael Gaudio, *Engraving the Savage: The New World and Techniques of Civilization* (Minneapolis: University of Minnesota Press, 2008), argues against a dismissive assessment of print representations of American Indians in the period he covers (up to the end of the nineteenth century), as if "the deep structure and thus the true significance of [such prints] lies beyond visual surfaces, beyond the deceiving 'hieroglyphics of the image'" (xiv). The interior quote is from Bernadette Bucher, *Icon and Conquest: A Structural Analysis of the Illustrations of De Bry's Great Voyages,* trans. Basia Miller Gulati (Chicago: University of Chicago Press, 1981). As Gaudio notes, the fact that prints are reproductions of other images often discourages looking closely at them, a topic I take up in more detail in chapter 4 but that is applicable to Catlin's illustrations here.

21. This framing of Native civilization may be the ultimate effect of their works, but it is certainly also true that both Catlin and Schoolcraft considered their projects to be sympathetic undertakings.
22. Clifford, *Predicament of Culture*, 220. Clifford is summarizing Susan Stewart's argument in *On Longing: Narratives of the Miniature, the Gigantic, the Souvenir, the Collection* (Baltimore, MD: Johns Hopkins Press, 1984). Also see Brian Durrans, "The Future of the Other: Changing Cultures on Display in Ethnographic Museums," in *Museum Time-Machine: Putting Cultures on Display*, ed. Robert Lumley (New York: Routledge, 1988), 144–69.
23. In *Catlin and His Contemporaries*, Dippie writes, "We see the Indian past through Catlin's eyes" and "imagine that green land and its red peoples exactly as he showed them" (xvi and 434). Truettner, *The Natural Man Observed: A Study of Catlin's Indian Gallery* (Washington, DC: Smithsonian Institution Press, 1979), notes that although "deeply concerned over the condition of North American Indians and committed to the task of rescuing them . . . [Catlin's] most significant contribution [was] the beguiling veil of primitivism that he cast across the American West" (9). More recently, see John Hausdoerffer's similarly qualified sympathy in *Catlin's Lament: Indians, Manifest Destiny, and the Ethics of Nature* (Lawrence: University of Kansas Press, 2009); regarding Catlin's enlistment of ideas about Manifest Destiny in his work, Hausdoerffer writes, "Ideology, then, is *not a conscious justification* of particular social practices like slavery or environmental devastation. Ideology is *the tacit base of assumptions* regarding what is 'natural' about a society" (9).
24. Both Dippie, *Catlin and His Contemporaries*, xvi, and Truettner, *Natural Man Observed*, 9, attempt to reconcile Catlin's impressive "conscious calculation" and ability to "shape his image and to define his mission with dramatic flair" with nagging doubts about his artistic contributions and his evident lack of success in marketing himself to Congress. Robert Lewis, "Wild American Savages and the Civilized English," *European Journal of American Studies* 1 (2008): 2–18, examines the reception of Catlin's dual role as showman and scientist by English audiences.
25. Hinsley, *Savages and Scientists*, 21.
26. This is Dippie's focus in *Catlin and His Contemporaries,* to recount Catlin's efforts to establish a career as "an authority on the West" in competition with other proto-ethnographers like Schoolcraft and Squier.
27. Catlin's various strategies for inducing Congress to purchase his gallery are recounted in detail in Dippie's *Catlin and His Contemporaries* (especially chapters 3 and 8, "My *Grateful* Country" and "Who Doth But Patient Wait"); members of Congress would often read excerpts from *Letters and Notes* in support of legislation to purchase the gallery. Hausdoerffer, *Catlin's Lament,* also traces this process of self-promotion but accords more weight to Catlin's active criticism of the government's expansionist policies, even as he recognizes Catlin's complicity in perpetuating the ideology that underwrote those policies. Truettner's connoisseur-like project sifts through the various print forms of Catlin's paintings to separate the original corpus of paintings from later painted compositions based in part on printed illustrations, adopting a perspective of primary and secondary representations similar to Catlin's view of his gallery and his published works.
28. Catlin, *Illustrations of the Manners*, 1.
29. Ibid., 3.
30. Ibid., 4.
31. This representational loop is also a feature of the main body of *Letters and Notes,* in references that cast the gallery as a future realization of his portrait making: "Of these three tribes [Knistenaux or Cree, Ojibway or Chippewa, and Assinneboin], I have also lined my painting-room with a number of very interesting portraits . . . which will be found in my INDIAN GALLERY, if I live, and they can be preserved" (Catlin, *Illustrations of the Manners*, 54).
32. Ibid., 1.
33. Ibid., 42 and 49.
34. Ibid., 3 and 23.
35. Ibid., 5. Again there is a confusion of writing and picture making, a common trope, but in the absence of a parallel visual record (the gallery), it still directs the reader's attention outside the text.
36. For example, when discussing the numerous tribes trading at the American Fur Company's fort at the mouth of the Yellowstone, Catlin writes that direct observation "would do away the idea which many learned gentlemen entertain, that the Indian languages of North America can all be traced to two or three roots," a theory promulgated by, among others, Albert Gallatin, probably the most eminent American Indian linguist in the early nineteenth century (*Illustrations of the Manners*, 52–53). Later Catlin chides those who go "to Washington City to gaze on the poor embarrassed Indian. . . . There is not the proper place to study the Indian character; yet it is the place where the sycophant and the scribbler go to gaze and frown upon him—to learn his character, and write his history!" (85). Charles Byrd King's portraits of Native delegates to Washington were frequently reproduced in histories of famous chiefs and sachems, such as McKenney and Hall's volume, *History of the Indian Tribes of North America.*

37. "The writer who would undertake to embody the whole history of such a people . . . must needs begin . . . with those who are *living,* or he would be very apt to dwell upon the preamble of his work, until the present living remnants of the race should have passed away" (Catlin, *Illustrations of the Manners*, 5). The writer's account of the past cannot catch up with the present.
38. "I said that I was here in the midst of a strange people, which is literally true; and I find myself surrounded by subjects and scenes worthy the pens of Irving or Cooper . . . rich in legends and romances, which would require no aid of the imagination for a book or a picture" (ibid., 80).
39. "There is no difficulty in approaching the Indian and getting acquainted with him in his wild and unsophisticated state. . . . So the world *may* see him and smoke his friendly pipe . . . But so the mass of the world, most assuredly, will *not* see these people; for they are too far off, and approachable to those only whose avarice or cupidity alone lead them to those remote regions" (ibid., 8–9).
40. Johann Joachim Winckelmann, *Reflections on the Painting and Sculpture of the Greeks: With Instructions for the Connoisseur, and an Essay on Grace in Works of Art,* trans. Henry Fuseli (1755; repr., London: A. Millar, 1765); and *History of Ancient Art,* 4 vols. (1764; repr., New York: Ungar, 1968–1969). Catlin was by no means the first American writer to make this comparison; it was a common American literary motif in novels by James Fenimore Cooper and poems by Henry Wadsworth Longfellow. Catlin does, however, self-consciously act on it.
41. Catlin, *Illustrations of the Manners*, 14–15. Catlin's biographers generally regard this articulation of his artistic motives as both a disingenuous response to his lack of success in eastern artistic centers such as Philadelphia and a genuine effort, shared by many artists and authors at this time, to appropriate Native culture in order to establish a distinctly American cultural heritage; see Truettner, *Natural Man Observed*, 14 and 69. Dippie, *Catlin and His Contemporaries*, writes, "In painting Indians, [Catlin] was answering the call that had echoed since the end of the War of 1812 for a distinctive American culture drawing its inspiration from the land itself," while also noting that, as an artist, Catlin's "limitations are self-evident. Some of his portraits are perfunctory, slipshod. He was capable of compressing the torso and limbs absurdly" (11 and 435–36).
42. Catlin, *Illustrations of the Manners*, 15. David Irwin notes in his introduction to *Winckelmann: Writings on Art* (London: Phaidon, 1972) that "Winckelmann held a particularly blinkered view of contemporary art" (45). Irwin further identifies this distaste as Winckelmann's motivation in persuading Anton Raphael Mengs to leave behind his previous rococo style and adopt what would be early neoclassicism.
43. Catlin, *Illustrations of the Manners*, 15. In *History of Ancient Art,* Winckelmann writes that the climate (as well as the form of government) produced the beautiful Greek body and the disposition to exhibit it (including via works of art): "[In Greece, Nature] chose her central point; and the nigher she approaches it, the more genial and joyous does she become, and the more general is her influence in producing conformations full of spirit and wit, and features strongly marked and rich in promise . . . beauty was thus desired and prized by the Greeks, nothing was concealed which could enhance it. Every beautiful person sought to become known to the whole nation by this endowment, and especially to please the artists" (176–77). He later prefaces his discussion of "the essential of art" by imaginatively inserting himself "in the Olympic Stadium, where I seem to see countless statues of young, manly heroes, and two-horse and four-horse chariots of bronze . . . and other wonders of art" (190).
44. Truettner discusses Catlin's interest in these aspects of personal appearance in *Natural Man Observed,* chapter 5, "The Artist and His Work." Catlin's approach emerges as being purely descriptive, unlike that of the McKenney and Hall volume, *History of the Indian Tribes of North America*, in which prints taken from Charles Byrd King's portraits are followed by colorful historical sketches or fanciful visions of an idyllic though doomed sylvan existence.
45. Catlin, *Illustrations of the Manners*, 29.
46. See Dippie's discussion of vice and virtue (*Vanishing American*), which associates vice with the bastardization of Native culture (25–29). Here too the polluting effect of white American influence is most often dramatized and visualized in terms of clothing, gesture, and other aspects of personal appearance, as in Catlin's comical portrayal of Wi-jun-jon (Pigeon's Egg Head), who returns from an embassy to Washington "with a complete suit *en militaire,* a colonel's uniform of blue . . . a beaver hat and feather, with epaulettes of gold . . . [and] a keg of whiskey under his arm" and is subsequently shunned by his tribe (*Illustrations of the Manners*, 56).
47. For example, Catlin describes his participation in a buffalo hunt by agents of the American Fur Company as a way of experiencing "the mode in which these Indians kill this noble animal . . . spirited and thrilling in the extreme" (*Illustrations of the Manners*, 23–28). Similarly, Karl Bodmer's paintings of Plains Indians focus on different aspects of buffalo hunting and were commissioned by a Scottish nobleman who, like many other wealthy Europeans at this time, traveled

to the American West explicitly to hunt; see Ron Tyler and Brandon K. Ruud, *Karl Bodmer's North American Prints* (Lincoln: University of Nebraska Press, 2004). Catlin's dramatic descriptions of rituals, feasts, and dances are a primary reason for the continued popularity of his text.

48. See *The Iliad of Homer Engraved from the Compositions of John Flaxman R. A.* (London: Parker, 1805). Sarah Symmons, *Flaxman and Europe: The Outline Illustrations and Their Influence* (New York: Garland, 1984), traces Flaxman's stylistic adoption of outline illustrations in archaeological works, such as the sketches of Roman monuments and statues by Henry Fuseli. Numerous artists throughout Europe experimented with this neoclassical graphic style and with various intentions. I am not claiming that Catlin specifically copied Flaxman, but his illustrations fit within a general neoclassical allusiveness to the art of ancient Greece and Rome.
49. Catlin, *Illustrations of the Manners*, 15–16.
50. For example, he conjectures that the bows of the Blackfeet, as well as of neighboring Plains Indian tribes, are made of whalebone, arriving in the upper Missouri region through a series of trades that obscures their identity and origin (ibid., 32). Similarly, in his seventh letter he discusses the art of treating animal skins in a way that suggests the dissemination and alteration of techniques over time (45–46). Although his account of the "Mandan religious ceremony" (the culmination of his visit there) focuses on the bizarre and the brutal, he is also intrigued by its partial significance as the commemoration of a great deluge; nevertheless, he is continually frustrated by "the inefficiency of Indian traditions" (155–84).
51. Ibid., 36. Here too he speculates on the origin of the term "medicine" and notes how its meaning has changed over time and among different speakers, whether Plains Indian or white trapper.
52. Ibid., 84–85. See Truettner, *Natural Man Observed*, chapter 3, "Plains Indians as the Primitive Ideal." As Dippie points out, Catlin's sympathetic, even antiexpansionist description of the Mandans triggered numerous negative reviews of his book in the American press (*Catlin and His Contemporaries*, 71–72). In *Catlin's Lament,* Hausdoerffer more closely identifies such reviews with his competitors for government patronage, including Schoolcraft; see chapter 1, "Catlin's Epiphany." Dippie's discussion of Catlin's theory of virtues and vices (*Vanishing American*) also foregrounds the pollution of natural, and thereby virtuous, Native customs by civilized vices undeterred by religion—a common assessment of the perceived failure of Natives to successfully adopt "white ways." Catlin's description echoes Jean-Jacques Rousseau: "It is neither the development of their understanding nor the restraint of law that hinders [savages] from doing ill; but the peacefulness of their passions and their ignorance of vice," *A Discourse on Inequality,* trans. Maurice Cranston (1755; repr., New York: Penguin Classics, 1984). Elliott West, "Reconstructing Race," *Western Historical Quarterly* 34, no. 1 (Spring 2003): 6–26, situates views of Indians as "incapable of settling down to the useful arts of farming and industry"—to impose a more permanent or lasting mark on the landscape—to changes in the larger discourse on race brought about the acquisition of western territories, changes which have typically been examined primarily in terms of sectional conflict (9).
53. Catlin, *Illustrations of the Manners*, 85.
54. Ibid., 261–62. David Mazel, "'A Beautiful and Thrilling Specimen': George Catlin, the Death of the Wilderness, and the Birth of the National Subject," in *Reading the Earth: New Directions in the Study of Literature and Environment*, ed. Michael B. Branch (Moscow: University of Idaho Press, 1998), 129–43, contrarily considers the possibility that this linkage of Indian and nature "disguises an otherwise purely environmentalist sensibility in an imperialist rhetoric cleverly designed to appeal to the prejudices of his contemporary readership" (130).
55. This is the sense of the frontier depicted in landscape paintings by Durand and others, as discussed in Boime, *Magisterial Gaze,* and Miller, *Empire of the Eye.*
56. To some degree this passing glance is comparable in its effect ("to withhold meaning") to how Kenneth Haltman, in *Looking Close, Seeing Far: Samuel Seymour, Titian Ramsay Peale, and the Art of the Long Expedition, 1818–1823* (University Park: Pennsylvania State University Press, 2008), has described the viewing conditions of paintings by another eastern artist visiting the West, Samuel Seymour, which "keep that distant scenery, that distance, at a distance" (44). Haltman has continued to delineate other connotations of viewing in other artists' depictions of western subjects, as in "Flight and Predation: The Anti-Documentary Poetics of Alfred Jacob Miller," *American Art* 28, no. 1 (Spring 2014): 32–55. In *Catlin's Lament,* Hausdoerffer devotes a chapter to "Catlin's Gaze"; this perspective is not what I describe here, but rather the kind of privileged position of mastery associated with the elevated view, as discussed by Boime, *Magisterial Gaze*, and Miller, *Empire of the Eye.*
57. Catlin, *Illustrations of the Manners*, 60 and 62.
58. Ibid., 58.
59. Ibid., 18, 19, and 67.

60. Note that this is a gaze that moves quickly toward the distance, passing rapidly over landscape features; it is not frozen and focused on the distance, as in luminist paintings.
61. Catlin, *Illustrations of the Manners*, 76.
62. Ibid., 80–81.
63. "The reader, then, to understand me rightly, and draw from these Letters the information which they are intended to give, must follow me a vast way from the civilized world" (ibid., 7), and "I must hastily travel with you over the tedious journey of 2000 miles, from St. Louis to this spot [the American Fur Company fort]; over which distance one is obliged to pass, before he can reach this wild and lovely spot" (17).
64. Ibid., 87.
65. These figures relate negatively to the substitute spectator found in Cole's *River in the Catskills* and so many paintings produced by the Hudson River school; the viewer passes them by instead of identifying with them and engaging in distanced contemplation. The presence of an Indian spectator (discussed especially in Boime, *Magisterial Gaze,* in terms of the works of DeWitt Clinton Boutelle) could be said to accelerate the process of improvements laid out in landscapes like Durand's *Progress,* so that the viewer's disinclination to identify with the Indian, and subsequent immersion into spatial depth, figure the rapidity and inevitability of Manifest Destiny. I am suggesting that Catlin connected this viewing ensemble with the two different kinds of writing, descriptive and narrative, found in his book.
66. Schoolcraft, *History, Condition, and Prospects of the Indian Tribes*, 1:viii–ix. In *Science Encounters the Indian,* Bieder quotes Schoolcraft's intent and concern in a letter to Francis Lieber of March 10, 1857: "The real problem of what is to become of the Race [American Indians] . . . lies at the bottom of the inquiry; and furnished the principal reason, why Congress has authorized it" (185).
67. See Prucha, *Great Father,* chapter 12, "The Indian Office: Men and Policies." Schoolcraft, in positioning his report within this new orientation, is prompted to defend it, as he also does in his dedicatory letter to President Franklin Pierce, in the fourth volume of *History, Condition, and Prospects of the Indian Tribes*: "Too feeble in themselves to exert a prudent or wise use of their power without legal tutorage, yet having had, at all periods, large superfluous territories to cede and alienate, thereby rising to the rank of independent communities, they occupy an anomalous position in our relations. On the one hand, being deemed as wards of the government; and, on the other, as *quasi* foreign nations" (4:v).
68. Schoolcraft, *History, Condition, and Prospects of the Indian Tribes*, 1:ix, 44; 3:62.
69. Schoolcraft is concerned to present knowledge about the Indian, but his effort is also performative, not least because "anthropological knowledge" is relatively new. He essentially attempts to give substance to this kind of knowledge by placing temporal limits on his subject, retroactively transforming that subject into an object, an artifact. In *Time and the Other,* Fabian observes that "it is not difficult to transpose from physics to politics one of the most ancient rules which states that it is impossible for two bodies to occupy the same space at the same time. . . . With the help of various devices of sequencing and distancing one assigns to the conquered populations a *different* Time" (30–31). Schoolcraft is engaging with "devices" of this sort, but I think his motivation is not simply political: rather, it is also necessitated by his particular aspirations for the capacity of the study of language to shed light on the past.
70. Important primary documents on the subject of archaeological remains include Thomas Jefferson's *Notes on the State of Virginia* (1781; repr. edited by William Peden, Chapel Hill: University of North Carolina Press, 1982); and Caleb Atwater, "Descriptions of the Antiquities Discovered in the State of Ohio and Other Western States," *Archaeologica Americana* 1 (1820): 105–267. This early literature also covers Central American ruins; see notably Frederick Catherwood, *Views of Ancient Monuments in Central America: Chiapas and Yucatan* (London: Catherwood, 1844); and Antonio Leon y Gama, *An Historical and Chronological Description of Two Stones Found under Ground, in the Great Square of the City of Mexico*, trans. William E. Huling (Philadelphia, PA: American Philosophical Society, 1818). How the discovery of substantial architectural remains in North and South America affected American perceptions of the Indian's past is addressed in Steven Conn, *History's Shadow: Native Americans and Historical Consciousness in the Nineteenth Century* (Chicago: University of Chicago Press, 2004); and R. Tripp Evans, *Romancing the Maya: Mexican Antiquity in the American Imagination, 1820–1915* (Austin: University of Texas Press, 2004). Archaeological remains were also a recurring theme in fiction, such as Cornelius Mathews's *Behemoth: A Legend of the Mound-Builders* (1839; repr., New York: Garrett Press, 1970), which explained the disappearance of the Mound Builders through the depredations of another extinct creature, the mammoth.
71. The Boundary Survey was headed by John Russell Bartlett, a key colleague of Schoolcraft's and a rival for government patronage. His popular account of the expedition was self-published; the money used for

Schoolcraft's report may have depleted the budget set aside for federally funded scientific publications that would otherwise have financed Bartlett's report. On the other hand, Schoolcraft's principal artist was briefly reassigned to provide watercolors for Bartlett's work, although they were not used in the published account. See Robert V. Hine, *Bartlett's West: Drawing the Mexican Boundary* (New Haven, CT: Yale University Press, 1968).

72. The popularity and effectiveness of American gothic fiction (Charles Brockden Brown, Edgar Allan Poe, etc.) is often traced to this condition of endangered "wishful thinking" (the belief in such a teleological advance that is threatened by the discovery of Native artifacts and monuments). The Indian does not just disappear but can "come back" as a ghost associated with some monument or burial site; as D. H. Lawrence writes in his influential *Studies in Classic American Literature* (1923; repr., New York: Viking Press, 1964), "[America] is full of grinning, unappeased aboriginal demons [and] ghosts, and it persecutes the white men" (51). Also see Roderick Nash, *Wilderness and the American Mind* (1967; repr., New Haven, CT: Yale University Press, 1983).
73. In Schoolcraft's second volume of *History, Condition, and Prospects of the Indian Tribes*, the new policy of more intensely managing Native populations through education and the encouragement of agriculture is defended by carefully interpreting the demonstrable decline in the size of those populations, since 1764, as a consequence not of the failure of past Indian policy, but of "a hunter-population." The "progress of deterioration is seen to have been linked, as by an indissoluble chain, with their scanty means of subsistence and non-industrial habits" (2:viii–ix). In the fourth volume, Schoolcraft notes, "They have occupied this peculiar position ['wards of the government' and '*quasi* foreign nations'] from the days of Washington. Nor have the most timely and persevering efforts been wanting to fulfil these diverse duties faithfully" (4:v).
74. It is worth mentioning, on a personal note, that Schoolcraft's first wife, Jane Johnston, was half-Chippewa. During his tenure as Indian agent in Sault Ste. Marie and superintendent of Indian affairs for Michigan in Michilimackinac (1822–1840), her Chippewa relations were a constant aspect of their domestic life. Jane contributed significantly to the translations of Native tales and legends that helped establish him as an Indian authority, as well as many of the translations used in his report.
75. Richard White, *The Middle Ground: Indians, Empires, and Republics in the Great Lakes Region, 1650–1815* (New York: Cambridge University Press, 1991), charts the successive migrations of Great Lakes tribes under pressure from French and British trappers and colonists and, later, the incursions of American settlers. Schoolcraft turns this narrative in reverse by avoiding the retelling of the history of successive land treaties concluded between the United States and various tribes, even though such a history would have greatly facilitated the task of sorting out current tribal distributions, one of the principal tasks of his report. As a point of comparison, political maps produced in Mexico at this time evoke a shared history through the display of famous pre-Columbian sites in marginal vignettes, however culturally disconnected those sites might have been; see Raymond Craib, "A Nationalist Metaphysics: State Fixations, National Maps, and the Geo-Historical Imagination in Nineteenth-Century Mexico," *Hispanic American Historical Review* 82, no. 1 (February 2002): 33–68.
76. Among these, notably, was a generally positive assessment of Catlin's *Letters and Notes* in "The Red Man of America," *North American Review* 54 (1842): 283–95. In fact, Schoolcraft had been interested in using some of Catlin's material in his report; Catlin had declined, still hoping to secure the government's purchase of his gallery (see Dippie, *Catlin and His Contemporaries*, 80–96).
77. Dippie provides a thorough and entertaining account of their feud and the reasons for suspecting Squier as the article's author (see *Catlin and His Contemporaries*, chapter 5, "Mastodons among Our Books"). Other negative reviews are summarized by Richard G. Bremer, *Indian Agent and Wilderness Scholar: The Life of Henry Rowe Schoolcraft* (Mount Pleasant: Clarke Historical Library, Central Michigan University, 1987).
78. Quoted in Dippie, *Catlin and His Contemporaries*, 224.
79. Schoolcraft, *History, Condition, and Prospects of the Indian Tribes*, 4:vii.
80. Ibid., 1:41 (in this volume the second section is titled "The Mental Type of the Indian Race") and 2:341. Schoolcraft's conclusions about pictography and mythology are arrived at by comparing ancient examples in different parts of the world. The idea that the study of Native languages was the best method for illuminating their past was first systematically articulated and pursued by Albert Gallatin and later taken up by Lewis Cass, Schoolcraft's mentor.
81. Again, see Dippie, *Catlin and His Contemporaries*, chapter 5, "Mastodons among Our Books." To illustrate, Schoolcraft mentions *Ancient Monuments of the Mississippi Valley* but credits Edwin Davis as the principal author ("assisted by Mr. Squier"), and he consistently downplays the significance of monumental remains: "There is little in the history of

the hunter state of man, that can be dignified with the name of monuments" (Schoolcraft, *History, Condition, and Prospects of the Indian Tribes*, 1:47, 44).

82. "Throughout his official career he constantly employed interpreters despite his contempt for their command of the language beyond the narrow rudiments necessary in trade jargon. . . . There are also certain indications that Schoolcraft did not feel entirely at ease in philology. In the 1830s the study of philology demanded a knowledge of more than one language; for comparative purposes it demanded a grasp of several. Schoolcraft did not have such a linguistic foundation" and "He lacked an inclination for [linguistic] theory" (Bieder, *Science Encounters the Indian*, 158–59).
83. Clifford, *Predicament of Culture*, 220.
84. Schoolcraft, *History, Condition, and Prospects of the Indian Tribes*, 4:437.
85. Ibid., 4:435.
86. Ibid., 4:121.
87. Quoted in Sarah E. Boehme, Christian F. Feest, and Patricia Condon Johnston, *Seth Eastman: A Portfolio of North American Indians* (Afton, MN: Afton Historical Society Press, 1995), 109.
88. Francis Bowen (Ephraim Squier?), review of *Historical and Statistical Information Respecting the History, Condition, and Prospects of the Indian Tribes of the United States*, by Henry Rowe Schoolcraft, *North American Review* 77 (1853): 256–57.
89. Schoolcraft, *History, Condition, and Prospects of the Indian Tribes*, 3:22.
90. Ibid., 2:55. Though sugar making was a common practice in many Native communities, clearly the intention is to gloss over differences between tribes and to foster the perception of a unitary Indian. The historical prints imitated extant history paintings, many of which were intended as decoration for government buildings; in a reversal of this arrangement, Eastman's sketches of Dakotas were later used as the basis for paintings adorning the Capitol. See Boehme, Feest, and Johnston, *Seth Eastman*; and Fryd, *Art and Empire* (173–75).
91. Of course, this perspective of the Indian as unfamiliar is depicted using familiar pictorial conventions (that of history and genre painting). To a certain extent, though, those conventions were already enlisted to assert difference between viewer and subject, for example, between the urban patron and viewer of rustic genre scenes and the often lampooned rural subject portrayed in them.
92. In terms of illustration practices, there were not many American precedents. Most contributions to scholarly journals, like *Archaeologica Americana* and *Transactions of the American Philosophical Society,* were not illustrated, and neither was Heckewelder's work. McKenney and Hall's *History of the Indian Tribes of North America* contained only portraits. The illustrations of rituals, buffalo hunts, and so forth in Catlin's *Letters and Notes* come close to the kind of genre scenes found in Schoolcraft's report, which explains Schoolcraft's interest in using Catlin's material. I am thinking of precedents in European illustrated books, especially from the period of exploration and early colonization, such as Thomas Hariot's *A Briefe and True Report of the New Found Land of Virginia* (London: R. Robinson, 1588), with later editions featuring prints by Theodore de Bry starting in 1590. Schoolcraft cites de Bry in particular on many occasions.
93. Schoolcraft, *History, Condition, and Prospects of the Indian Tribes*, 1:109.
94. Ibid., 1:340. This assertion is then immediately followed by a subsection on the "Extreme Antiquity of Pictorial Notation," which includes a comparison with Egyptian hieroglyphics. Schoolcraft acknowledges the essentially nonphonetic character of pictography (it is described as a mnemonic aid for "wabenos," or shamans, requiring the transmission of symbolic meaning from one generation to the next), but he nonetheless still looks for a system underlying its practice using a method of decipherment similar to Champollion's—he wants to be an American Champollion.
95. Richard Parkinson details this process in *Cracking Codes: The Rosetta Stone and Decipherment* (Berkeley: University of California Press, 1999).
96. William M. Clements, "Schoolcraft as Textmaker," *Journal of American Folklore* 103, no. 408 (April–June, 1990): 177–92. Clements calls the Chippewa members of Schoolcraft's family Ojibwa, the Canadian term for the same tribe. The Chippewas call themselves Anishinabe.
97. Ibid., 189.
98. Schoolcraft, *The Myth of Hiawatha, and Other Oral Legends, Mythologic and Allegoric, of the North American Indians* (Philadelphia, PA: Lippincott, 1856), 11.
99. The vedute painted by Cole and Sanford Robinson Gifford, another artist who traveled to Europe and painted landscapes for American patrons, are detailed in Powell, *Thomas Cole*; and Kevin Avery and Franklin Kelly, eds., *Hudson River School Visions: The Landscapes of Sanford R. Gifford* (New York: Metropolitan Museum of Art, 2003).
100. Similar to Peter J. Halliday's argument about scenic photographs of Greek ruins in "Early Photography and the Reception of Classical Antiquity: The Case of the Temple of Athena Nike," in *Periklean Athens and Its Legacy: Problems and Perspectives*, ed. Judith M. Barringer and Jeffrey M. Hurwit (Austin: University

of Texas Press, 2005), the pictograph is also framed in such a way as to remove signs of contemporary Native communities.

101. In the case of Dighton Rock, Schoolcraft provides a translation by way of Chigwauk's interpretation, but more often such a translation is lacking. More important is the arrangement of signs within the grid, both in its adoption of Champollion's procedure and its schematization of language.

Chapter 4. The Figuration of Time in the Geological Surveys of the West

1. Despite the widespread awareness of financial corruption connected with the railroad's construction, which was finally blown open in the Crédit Mobilier scandal, railroad boosters continued to point out the timely return on the government's investment in the project. In *Pacific Tourist,* Henry T. Williams asserts, "The Pacific Railroad is the right-hand saving power of the United States" and calculates a net profit of $42,320,094 for the government (6–7).
2. Quoted in May Castleberry, ed., *Perpetual Mirage: Photographic Narratives of the Desert West* (New York: Whitney Museum of American Art, 1996), 37.
3. Determining a viable route to the Pacific Coast had always motivated western exploration, going back to the Lewis and Clark expedition of 1804–1806. The corps itself was established in 1838; following the accession of what is now the Southwest during the 1840s by treaty or warfare, the corps was employed in establishing boundaries, mapping uncharted lands, ascertaining the extent and navigability of rivers, and, especially in the 1850s, locating the optimal route for a transcontinental railroad. William Goetzmann has written extensively on the history of the Topographical Corps. See *Army Exploration* and *Exploration and Empire*. Another useful source are the essays by Vincent Ponko, Jr. ("The Military Explorers of the American West, 1838–1860") and Richard Bartlett ("Scientific Exploration of the American West, 1865–1900") in *A Continent Comprehended,* vol. 3, *North American Exploration*, ed. John Logan Allen (Lincoln: University of Nebraska Press, 1997), 332–411, 461–520.
4. The parallels and differences between the military and civilian surveys are a contentious issue for modern historians. Here I wish to emphasize their similarities for the purposes of outlining the methods and objectives of the western surveys as a whole. Generally speaking, though, the earlier military expeditions were more narrowly focused on mapping, assaying, and locating transportation routes, while the later civilian ones amassed a broader range of data and were more concerned to enlist those data in comprehensive scientific theories explaining various aspects of the environment of the West.
5. As Goetzmann notes, the curriculum and pedagogy at West Point were heavily influenced by the French École Polytechnique (see *Army Exploration,* chapter 1). Many of the more prominent survey leaders, such as John Charles Frémont and Lieutenant William Helmsley Emory, regularly corresponded with authorities in European geological science, including Alexander von Humboldt, Charles Lyell, and Louis Agassiz. The geology departments at Yale and Harvard were established in the late 1840s and built on European advances in the field. Agassiz himself became a professor at Harvard's Lawrence School in 1848.
6. Georges Cuvier, *Discours sur les révolutions du globe* (Paris: G. Dufour et Ed. D'Ocagne, 1825); Charles Lyell, *Principles of Geology: Being an Attempt to Explain the Former Changes to the Earth's Surface, by Reference to Causes Now in Operation* (London: Murray, 1830–1833); and Louis Agassiz, *Études sur les glaciers* (Neuchâtel: Jent et Gassmann, 1840). For an overview of the nineteenth-century history of geological theory in Europe and its incorporation in the western surveys, see Stephen Jay Gould, *Time's Arrow, Time's Cycle: Myth and Metaphor in the Discovery of Geological Time* (Cambridge, MA: Harvard University Press, 1987); and John McPhee, *Basin and Range* (New York: Farrar, Straus, Giroux, 1980).
7. Robin E. Kelsey, "Viewing the Archive: Timothy O'Sullivan's Photographs for the Wheeler Survey, 1871–1874," *Art Bulletin* 85, no. 4 (December 2003): 702–23, provides a detailed schematization of the process by which data, specimen collections, and written and pictorial descriptions assembled on one of the later surveys were prepared for publication, breaking it down into four distinct phases: collection, preparation, compilation, and distribution. Joni Louise Kinsey, *Thomas Moran and the Surveying of the American West* (Washington, DC: Smithsonian Institution Press, 1992), also describes at considerable length how Moran's sketches, watercolors, and paintings, produced in connection with two other later surveys (Hayden and Powell), were disseminated in print form, especially in commercial journals and railroad promotions. Questions of preparation, dissemination, and audience also permeate studies of images from the Powell and King surveys, the focus of this chapter. On Powell, see Bedell, *Anatomy of Nature,* chapter 6, "Thomas Moran and the Western Surveys"; Elizabeth Childs, "Time's Profile: John Wesley Powell, Art, and Geology at the Grand Canyon," *American Art* 10 (Spring 1996): 6–35; and Rick Van Noy, *Surveying*

the Interior: Literary Cartographers and the Sense of Place (Reno: University of Nevada Press, 2003), chapter 4, "Surveying the Sublime: John Wesley Powell's Representations of Place." The literature on King is more extensive; see François Brunet, "Revisiting the Enigmas of Timothy O'Sullivan: Notes on the William Ashburner Collection of King Survey Photographs at the Bancroft Library," *History of Photography* 31, no. 2 (2007): 97–133; Rick Dingus, *The Photographic Artifacts of Timothy O'Sullivan* (Albuquerque: University of New Mexico Press, 1982); Toby Jurovics et al., *Framing the West: The Survey Photographs of Timothy O'Sullivan* (New Haven, CT: Yale University Press, 2010); Rosalind Krauss, *The Originality of the Avant-Garde and Other Modernist Myths* (Cambridge, MA: MIT Press, 1985), chapter 6, "Photography's Discursive Spaces"; Joel Snyder, *American Frontiers: The Photographs of Timothy H. O'Sullivan, 1867–1874* (Philadelphia, PA: Philadelphia Museum of Art, 1981), and "Territorial Photography," in *Landscape and Power*, ed. W. J. T. Mitchell (Chicago: University of Chicago Press, 1994), 175–207; and Alan Trachtenberg, *Reading American Photographs: Images as History, Mathew Brady to Walker Evans* (New York: Hill and Wang, 1989), chapter 3, "Naming the View."

8. For example, Trachtenberg, *Reading American Photographs*: "With a change of title or caption the survey photographs were freely adopted to sundry uses. This flexibility confounds the question of their precise role within the surveys" (127). On the weighted significance of the survey itself, he quotes Henry Adams's *The Education of Henry Adams* (1918): "Topographers and geologists . . . 'held under their hammers a thousand miles of mineral country with all its riddles to solve, and its stores of possible wealth to mark. They felt the future in their hands'" (124).
9. John Wesley Powell, *Exploration of the Colorado River of the West and Its Tributaries* (Washington, DC: Government Printing Office, 1875); Clarence King, *Systematic Geology,* vol. 1 of *Report of the Geological Exploration of the Fortieth Parallel* (Washington, DC: Government Printing Office, 1878).
10. Kinsey, *Thomas Moran and the Surveying of the American West*; for Powell, see chapters 6 and 7, "The John Wesley Powell Expedition" and "Popularizing the Grand Canyon." In *Anatomy of Nature,* Bedell follows a similar, albeit condensed arrangement. She also avoids discussion of Moran's illustration work for Powell, an omission that for both Kinsey and Bedell may have to do with the fact that many of these prints were based on photographs (Moran produced wood engravings based primarily on the photographs of E. O. Beaman and Jack Hillers). In other words, besides the inclination to view the paintings as the most finished and definitive expressions of Moran's understanding of geological theory, discussion of his illustrations is precluded by an added layer of interference between artist and image. Neither author addresses the illustration work of H. H. Nichols that predominates in the second half of Powell's report. More recently, see Barbara Bloemink et al., *Frederic Church, Winslow Homer, and Thomas Moran: Tourism and the American Landscape* (New York: Bulfinch Press, 2006), which situates Moran's paintings within the emerging tourist industry of the West; and Kinsey's *Thomas Moran's West: Chromolithography, High Art, and Popular Taste* (Lawrence: University of Kansas Press, 2006), which examines the chromolithograph as substitute for Moran's Yellowstone paintings.
11. This is not to say that Kinsey or Bedell ignore the influence of Powell on Moran; Kinsey, especially, carefully documents Moran's activities and interactions with survey members on the expeditions, as well as any input by Powell in preparing *The Chasm of the Colorado.* Nonetheless, these contributions remain critically (and justifiably) filtered through the artist's mind.
12. Childs, "Time's Profile," 27. I do not contest Childs's assessment of Moran's impact on Powell's writing, especially her attention to how Moran's prints intensify the drama of Powell's account. As I argue later, however, I think Moran's prints relate even more closely to Powell's essential project of creating a new kind of narrative—not just a tale of descending the Colorado River, but one of the reconstruction of a history of geological development.
13. Instead of, that is, as mere illustrations of that story, already formulated. For example, Childs reads a photograph of the Grand Canyon taken from the top of one of its sides and showing the river below proceeding into distance (a view that includes a tiny human figure likewise perched on the top) as an illustration of "man's recent arrival in the geological domain—a human cipher that tops both the stratigraphic column and the conceptual map of geological time" (ibid., 17). At the same time, though, such a view reveals "geological time," pointing toward the process by which the geologist recognizes temporal markers in an act of viewing. The human figure connects the present with the vast scale of time evidenced by the strata exposed on the canyon walls, but also invites us to experience the passing of that time through the contemplation of a landscape view. The view makes visible the story of "geological time."
14. Ibid., 19.
15. Kelsey, "Viewing the Archive," 702. Krauss, *Originality of the Avant-Garde*, and Snyder, "Territorial Photography," offer the most nuanced critique

of the assimilation of these photographs within a history of modernist photographic practice, famously beginning with Beaumont Newhall's 1937 exhibition *Photography, 1839–1937,* at the Museum of Modern Art, and continuing with Peter Galassi's 1981 exhibition *Before Photography,* also at the Museum of Modern Art.

16. Krauss, *Originality of the Avant-Garde*, reduces the role of the lithographed versions of O'Sullivan's pictures found in King's report to displaying "the ordinary elements of topographical description" (essentially confirming space as "grounded, coordinated, mapped") and relegates the photographs themselves to the discursive space of commercial stereo views (132). Snyder argues convincingly that the photographs are not merely topographical records but vehicles for aspects of King's geological theories. Nevertheless, he tends to keep the photographs separate from the process of articulating those theories, finding that only "a sympathetic resonance connects King's beliefs about the interior to O'Sullivan's photographs" (*American Frontiers,* 48). Later Snyder reads the photographs as helping to demonstrate the need for specifically civilian scientific surveys of a hostile terrain ("Territorial Photography," 199–200). More recently, Jurovics's opening essay in *Framing the West* accords more independence to O'Sullivan within the survey, but in terms of highlighting features that were the most significant in geological science; Jurovics argues for the pictures' artistry while also recognizing that they spoke primarily to a survey-oriented audience. Also recently, Brunet, in "Revisiting the Enigmas of Timothy O'Sullivan," considers narrative order in particular but (similarly to Jurovics) primarily in terms of sequences of photographs having more personal meaning for the members of the expedition.
17. See especially Kelsey, "Viewing the Archive," 703–10. Kelsey addresses the use of photography in mapping surveys more broadly in *Archive Style: Photographs and Illustrations for U.S. Surveys, 1850–1890* (Berkeley: University of California Press, 2007). His chapter on O'Sullivan concentrates on the Wheeler survey; in stressing O'Sullivan's responsiveness to more "modern modes of representing geological features on a taut graphic surface," Kelsey focuses on the ideological work of O'Sullivan's pictures (108). In terms of their instrumentality relative to the articulation of geological theory, he generally adheres to Snyder's later reading, stating, "His photographs for King depicted the West as a land of geological curiosities . . . odd terrestrial features requir[ing] the expertise of professional geologists such as King and his assistants" (108). Indeed, Kelsey regards the translation of the photographs into print as primarily negative, that it "dampened [their] innovative effects": "By and large, these lithographs and chromolithographs ran counter to the rapidly changing circumstances of survey work and represented illustration that soon disappeared from reports" (116–18). I would argue that one could regard the toned lithographs in the King report as up-to-date technologies in the era immediately preceding photomechanical reproduction of photographs, even if they would be superseded shortly. The same could also be said for the narrative structure of King's report and how the text is related to illustrations—that is, they are transitional forms.
18. I make no claim as to the "correctness" of these theories or whether they shaped geological theory in the long term, although both Powell and King did move on to influential positions within government-sponsored scientific institutions: King was the first director of the U.S. Geological Survey (albeit briefly, 1879–1881), while Powell was its second director (1881–1894) and also director of the Bureau of Ethnology. My principal point is to situate the newness of their theories in relation to previous geological survey reports.
19. This summary of corps practice comes from Goetzmann, *Army Exploration* and *Exploration and Empire.*
20. Some expeditions included a greater number of scientists, included officers with a greater degree of scientific training, pursued a larger number of branch routes, availed themselves more of information from Native tribes, or attempted to arrive at a more complete environmental assessment. Nonetheless, the dominant restriction of these expeditions to a linear course of travel necessarily limited the range of that assessment. See Goetzmann, *Exploration and Empire,* chapter 9, "The Great Reconnaissance."
21. Joseph Christmas Ives, *Report upon the Colorado River of the West, Explored in 1857 and 1858* (Washington, DC: Government Printing Office, 1861). Roughly contemporary and comparable corps reports include those made on the U.S.-Mexican Boundary Survey, such as William H. Emory's *Report on the United States and Mexican Boundary Survey* (Washington, DC: Government Printing Office, 1857–1859), and the reports of the Pacific Railroad surveys, principally *Reports of Explorations and Surveys, to Ascertain the Most Practicable and Economical Route for a Railroad from the Mississippi River to the Pacific Ocean,* 13 vols. (Washington, DC: Government Printing Office, 1855–1861).
22. Ives, *Report upon the Colorado River,* 21.
23. Goetzmann, *Exploration and Empire,* 73.
24. Ibid., 289 and 308. Additional information on Egloffstein and Möllhausen can be found in Ben Huseman, *Wild River, Timeless Canyons: Balduin*

Möllhausen's Watercolors of the Colorado (Fort Worth, TX: Amon Carter Museum, 1995); and Ron Tyler, *Prints of the West* (Golden, CO: Fulcrum, 1994).

25. A similar practice can be found in Emory's report, in this case encompassing the terrain between boundary markers, as discussed in Kelsey, *Archive Style,* chapter 1.
26. This is not to say that the corps reports always followed this organizational format; in fact, the Ives report is fairly exceptional in its introductory panoramas. These prints only make more conspicuous the kind of narrative reading innate to the views of landscape found in the corps reports.
27. Ives, *Report upon the Colorado River*, 48.
28. Ibid., 50. This recognition of resemblance to the human body relates to the widespread practice in the corps expeditions of naming peaks and other landscape features after specific individuals. The subject of naming, and its role in the cartographic erasure of, especially, the history of Native presence in the West, is a frequent topic in studies of the surveys, as in Wallace Stegner, "Powell and the Names on the Plateau," *Western Humanities Review* 50, no. 4–51, no. 1 (Winter 1996–Spring 1997): 105–10; Trachtenberg, *Reading American Photographs*; and Van Noy, "Surveying the Sublime."
29. Ives, *Report upon the Colorado River*, 47.
30. For example, Childs remarks that "Von Egloffstein's illustrations [of the Grand Canyon], wildly exaggerating the vertical dimensions of geological features, reinforced . . . sublime notions" ("Time's Profile," 8). Significantly she identifies these features as "geological," even though the report itself does not attempt to describe them in any consistent or comprehensive geological manner. The print is based on a sketch by Ives, modified later by Egloffstein.
31. They routinely get lost, "wandering astray somewhere in the labyrinth"; Ives, *Report upon the Colorado River,* 109.
32. Ibid., 110.
33. This geological section is tentative and incomplete. Newberry speculates that strata range from the Upper Carboniferous to the Silurian epochs of the Paleozoic era, but he often places question marks beside epochs and strata or merely indicates a stratum's mineralogical composition.
34. John Strong Newberry, *Geological Report from Santa Fe to the Junction of the Grand and Green Rivers* (Washington, DC: Government Printing Office, 1876), 11. Newberry wanted to retroactively compose a more thorough account of the geological history of the Colorado River, stating that this report, although it does not incorporate the contributions of later writers, "is a fair exponent of the state of our geographical and geological knowledge of the West at the date of its preparation [1859]" (11).
35. Apart from Powell's report itself, information about the circumstances and progress of the surveys comes from Goetzmann, *Exploration and Empire,* and Wallace Stegner, *Beyond the Hundredth Meridian: John Wesley Powell and the Second Opening of the West* (Boston, MA: Houghton Mifflin, 1953). Goetzmann and Stegner, as well as later writers, describe Powell's contributions to shaping environmental and federal Indian policy over the course of his life. The articulation of the history of uplift and erosion in the Colorado River Basin in Powell's report is by no means his primary achievement as a scientist, but it is nonetheless my focus in this chapter.
36. Powell did receive rations and limited escorts from the army, instruments from the Smithsonian Institution, and free transport from various railroads.
37. Childs, "Time's Profile," 27; and Stegner, *Beyond the Hundredth Meridian*, 147. Stegner observes that the writing of the report coincided with Powell's progressive relegation of geological duties on the surveys to assistants as well as with his increasing involvement with ethnology and the formation of government policies regarding American Indians and land usage.
38. John Wesley Powell, "The Cañons of the Colorado," pts. 1–3, *Scribner's Monthly* 9, nos. 3–5 (January–March 1875): 293–310, 394–409, 523–37. Also see William H. Truettner, "'Scenes of Majesty and Enduring Interest': Thomas Moran Goes West," *Art Bulletin* 58, no. 2 (June 1976): 241–59.
39. Childs, "Time's Profile," 29.
40. Powell, *Exploration of the Colorado River*, 70.
41. Ibid., 73, 77.
42. Ibid., 64–65.
43. For example, just before the attempt to climb Gypsum Canyon, Powell recounts walking out on a lower bluff overlooking the river: "Out on this we walk, crossing a great number of deep crevices. Usually, the smooth rock slopes down to a fissure on either side. Sometimes it is an interesting question to us whether the slope is not so steep that we cannot stand on it. Sometimes, starting down, we are compelled to go on, and we are not always sure that the crevice is not too wide for a jump, when we measure it with our eye from above. . . . Climbing the face of a cliff, a man will walk along a step or shelf, but a few inches wide, without hesitancy, if the landing is but ten feet below, should he fall; but if the foot of the cliff is a thousand feet down, he will crawl" (*Exploration of the Colorado River*, 59).
44. Ibid., 5. Later he reflects, "The stream is still quiet, and we glide along, through a strange, weird, grand region. The landscape everywhere, away from the river, is of rock—cliffs of rock; tables of rock; plateaus of rock; terraces of rock; crags of rock—ten thousand strangely carved forms. Rocks everywhere, and no vegetation; no soil; no sand. In long, gentle

curves, the river winds about these rocks. When speaking of these rocks, we must not conceive of piles of boulders, or heaps of fragments, but a whole land of naked rock, with giant forms carved on it: cathedral-shaped buttes, towering hundreds or thousands of feet; cliffs that cannot be scaled, and cañon walls that shrink the river into insignificance . . . buff, gray, red, brown, and chocolate; never lichened; never moss-covered; but bare, and often polished" (55).

45. The difficulty of physically accessing the canyons of the Colorado River is related to the difficulty of accessing the story of geological time that they encode. That "story" is also physical, it pertains to an environment that impedes human movement, perhaps especially movement undertaken to uncover that story (the necessity and difficulty of climbing cliff walls for observations). To be sure, this experience of rushing and halting movements is not intrinsic to the articulation of that story but evocative of its reconstruction.
46. Powell, *Exploration of the Colorado River*, 47.
47. In studies of both Powell and King, the instrumentality of sketches and photographs in the survey process is a frequent topic of debate. Generally, both sketches and photographs are ascribed purely aesthetic functions, since even photography cannot produce measurable representations of terrain. I am concentrating on how survey images can record the recognition of geologically pertinent aspects of terrain, especially pertinent in relation to the articulation of a geological history, even prior to the task of measurement. What do the surveyors measure? Something that they see to be significant.
48. Powell, *Exploration of the Colorado River*, 193–94.
49. Ibid., 23.
50. Ibid., 29.
51. Ibid., 16 and 83.
52. Powell's understanding runs contrary to the catastrophic view that the Grand Canyon and other canyon networks are essentially fissures, the results of sudden cleavages in the earth's crust. He reflects on the river's course through the Uinta Mountains: "Again, the question returns to us, why did not the stream turn around this great obstruction, rather than pass through it? The answer is that the river had the right of way; in other words, it was running ere the mountains were formed; not before the rocks of which the mountains are composed, were deposited, but the before the formations were folded, so as to make a mountain range" (*Exploration of the Colorado River*, 152). And later: "The primary agency in the production of these features is upheaval, *i.e.,* upheaval in relation to the level of the sea. . . . The second great agency is erosion, and the action of this agency is conditioned on the character of the displacements above mentioned, the texture and constitution of the rocks, and the amount and relative distribution of the rains. . . . The story we have told is a history of the war of the elements to beat back the march of the lands from the ocean depths" (202–203, 208).
53. Kinsey, *Thomas Moran*, 112. She goes on to cite Powell's appreciation of the painting as an accurate visualization of the processes of erosion occurring in the Grand Canyon, as well as his involvement in its composition (Moran solicited his criticism on a number of occasions). For both Kinsey and Bedell, however, the primary correspondence between the painting and Powell's writing is an aesthetic and emotional one, a shared recognition of the sublime character of geological change.
54. Details of the survey's sponsorship, financing, and organization of observation and data collection come from the report and from Goetzmann, *Exploration and Empire.*
55. King, *Systematic Geology*, 2.
56. This volume was actually published after most of the other reports, in 1878. King's *Systematic Geology* is followed by a more detailed enumeration of the mineralogical and morphological characteristics of the region, *Descriptive Geology,* by Samuel F. Emmons and Arnold Hague, vol. 2 of *Report of the Geological Exploration of the Fortieth Parallel* (Washington, DC: Government Printing Office, 1877). The survey was certainly motivated by an interest in the mining possibilities of the West. Existing mines were visited, and assays over the course of the survey helped locate future mines. One of the survey's major achievements was uncovering the so-called Great Diamond Hoax. King's report, however, presents itself as a disinterested history of Cordilleran geology. See also Goetzmann, *Exploration and Empire*, 438–66.
57. King, *Systematic Geology*, 3.
58. This effect is misleading and may explain why subsequent maps only include the strata described in those chapters. The equation of strata with vertical height (Archean exposures at the top, Paleozoic exposures farther down, etc.) suggests an erroneous correlation between the shape of mountains and the history of their formation as one of gradual uplift of a series of mountains that resemble the current Cordilleran chain. For example, the map of *Archaean and Granitic Exposures* includes a cross-section, below it, of an Archean mountain chain more or less identical with the relative elevations of mountains today (from east to west, the Rockies, the Uintas, the Wasatch, etc.). King is cognizant of the speculative nature of this reconstructed Archean range, and his summation of geological change at the end of his book is more nuanced, embracing multiple periods

of uplift and subsidence. Nonetheless, this vertical and cumulative orientation shapes that summation, setting limits on the kinds of conclusions he can make about geological history.

59. King, *Systematic Geology*, 10.
60. King does speculate that the major driving forces of crustal change are "the statics of the revolving sphere" (specifically, the physics of a rotating planet composed of a solid crust on top of some "critical shell," not unlike the contemporary understanding of crust and mantle) and "the dissipation of energy from its original and existing inner temperatures" (the cooling of the planet). Ibid., 728–29. He determines the presence of land above or below water by analyzing the composition of strata (missing strata from a particular era or epoch indicates presence of land above water at that time, etc.), and estimates the timing and duration of folding by effects on mineralogical structure (although this analysis is more tentative).
61. This transformation between divisions of space and time in the service of assembling a summary of geological history is still problematic. Most notably, there is a tendency for the narrative of progress across horizontal space to reassert itself. The leading events of different eras tend to be localized in areas moving east to west: the first stage, the story of the great Archean range, emerges in a discussion of the Rockies; the third stage, the story of Paleozoic uplift, in the Wasatch; the fourth stage, the story of late Mesozoic compression and folding, in the Sierra Nevada, etc.).
62. In particular, King was unaware of continental drift. Landmasses essentially only move up and down over time in his account, leading to his conclusion that the distribution of mountain chains in ancient times affected the distribution of present-day mountain systems. J. W. H. Monger and G. A. Davis, in "Evolving Concepts of the Tectonics of the North American Cordillera," in *Frontiers of Geological Exploration of Western North America*, ed. Alan E. Leviton et al. (Fresno, CA: Pacific Division of the American Association for the Advancement of Science, 1982), write that "King felt the greatest episode of all was between the metamorphic 'Archean' and the Paleozoic divisions and, perhaps influenced by then current theories, suggested that the resulting Archean mountains strongly influenced later mountain-building; where there was flat Archean country, subsequently there were broad (epirogenic uplifts); where there were ancient mountains, so later terranes were highly deformed" (216). It should be pointed out, though, that Monger and Davis generally regard King's contributions to geological science as more substantive than is generally recognized.
63. Dingus writes that, for his project of rephotography (attempting to take pictures of the same sites as O'Sullivan and other survey photographers, at the same time of day, same season, same point of view and framing), "It was almost as easy to rephotograph a site using the lithograph as it was to use the photographs" (*Photographic Artifacts*, 47).
64. See ibid., 45–51, and Krauss, *Originality of the Avant-Garde*, 131–32. In *American Frontiers,* Snyder provides a thorough discussion of the capabilities and limits of nineteenth-century photography to record landscape features. Some of these are technical (the inability to capture moving water, the overexposure of the sky in detailed photographs of terrain) and some are aesthetic (the variable influence of ideas about landscape beauty).
65. Dingus views these lithographs as transforming O'Sullivan's pictures into scenic and picturesque counterparts (*Photographic Artifacts*, 46–48). Comparing the lithograph of *Tufa Domes, Pyramid Lake* with its photographic original, Krauss writes that the lithograph "is an object of insistent visual banality. Everything mysterious in the photograph has been explained with supplemental, chatty detail" (*Originality of the Avant-Garde*, 131). Relegated to an established practice of "topographical description," it promptly drops out of her discussion.
66. See especially Snyder, *American Frontiers.* This evocation operates in the lithographs as well and becomes one of the principal means of persuading the reader of King's geological theories, allowing the reader to experience them on a visceral level.
67. "Discursive space" is Krauss's principal theoretical tool in assessing the meaning and function of survey photographs; see *Originality of the Avant-Garde.* Snyder, *American Frontiers*, and Kelsey investigate in detail the day-to-day activity of photography within the surveys and precisely how photographic prints were made available to different audiences. If there is little direct evidence of photographs being made with specific intentions for King's (as yet unwritten) report and few documented descriptions (on the photographs themselves or elsewhere) to indicate how they should be reproduced as lithographs, that might discourage an investigation of the illustrations from the standpoint of O'Sullivan's intentions as a photographer, but not from the standpoint of how they in fact function within the report. In *Framing the West,* Jurovics quotes the King geologists Samuel Franklin Emmons and Arnold Hague that, in writing their own report (*Descriptive Geology*), "it was the general bearing of *the leading geological facts* that was most constantly in our minds," observing that "Like the survey itself, O'Sullivan's photographs were to provide the highlights, . . . His images are not a seamless narrative but concentrate in areas of greatest geological and pictorial interest" (18).

I am interested in how the reproduced versions of O'Sullivan's photographs draw the reader's attention to those "leading geological facts" within the report and how the report necessarily acts as a "narrative" framing them.

68. See also *Mount Agassiz, Uinta Range, Utah*; *Provo Falls, Wahsatch Range, Utah*; *Cañon in Wahsatch Limestone, Humboldt Range, Nevada*; and *Devil's Slide, Weber Cañon, Nevada*.
69. For example, "To represent terrain, topographers routinely preferred the delineation of slopes flat to the notebook page to depictions of atmospheric or perspectival recession, and O'Sullivan's emphasis on the crisp planes and morphological outlines of the West suggest that he may have adopted this preference" (Kelsey, "Viewing the Archive," 704). It should be noted that the medium of lithography allows for a heightened level of representation of certain textured surfaces. The grain of the lithographic stone corresponds with the grain of strata, suggesting or perhaps even indexing mineralogical characteristics, the other principal means by which King reconstructs geological history.
70. This practice of tilting the camera is well documented in Dingus, *Photographic Artifacts*, and in Snyder, *American Frontiers*. Its evocation of geological forces is also noted by both authors.
71. Again, see Snyder's conclusions in "Territorial Photography."
72. King proposes the idea of upwelling mineral solutions as the cause of the domes in an earlier exploration of a desert lake near Ragtown, Nevada (*Systematic Geology*, 510–13). His crystal analysis in the vicinity of Pyramid Lake reveals two basic crystal forms, thinolite and gaylussite, with gaylussite forming as a precipitate in a dense carbonate solution (dense because the lakes have evaporated), then, with the influx of fresh water, forming thinolite (514–18).
73. This clustering of illustrations recalls Jurovics's observation that "O'Sullivan's photographs . . . concentrate in areas of greatest geological and pictorial interest" (*Framing the West*, 18).
74. Snyder, *American Frontiers*, 7.

Conclusion

1. Richard Terdiman, *Present Past: Modernity and the Memory Crisis* (Ithaca, NY: Cornell University Press, 1993).
2. Frederick Jackson Turner, "The Significance of the Frontier in American History," *Annual Report of the American Historical Association* (1893). Turner's report thus coincided with the sense of having arrived in a new era, a sense cultivated by Chicago's Columbian Exposition. The persistence of Turner's "frontier thesis" is ubiquitous in American historiography, but see, for example, Allan Bogue, *Frederick Jackson Turner: Strange Roads Going Down* (Norman: University of Oklahoma Press, 1998); and Patricia Limerick, *Legacy of Conquest: The Unbroken Past of the American West* (New York: Norton, 1987).
3. McPhee addresses this revolution and its alteration of practices of observation and synthesis in *Basin and Range*. His *In Suspect Terrain* (New York: Farrar, Straus, Giroux, 1983), however, discusses how these practices have been adopted too extensively, prompting unwarranted searches for the horizontal meanderings of continental fragments when older, more vertically oriented lines of analysis are called for in the explanation of geological phenomena.
4. The framework of "cultural evolution" used in the study of American Indian civilization after midcentury (in particular as articulated by Lewis Henry Morgan) was institutionally embodied in the Bureau of American Ethnology, headed for many years by John Wesley Powell. The BAE was the next step in the growing professionalization of ethnology after Schoolcraft and his contemporaries, but it would be likewise reshaped by Boas's newer conceptualization of anthropology.
5. Peale's museum was the Philadelphia Museum, which had several locations, including the State House from 1802 to 1827. The museum was dismantled and its collections sold in the 1850s (to, among other people, P. T. Barnum). See Laura Rigal, *The American Manufactory: Art, Labor, and the World of Things* (Princeton, NJ: Princeton University Press, 1998); and David Ward, *Charles Willson Peale: Art and Selfhood in the Early Republic* (Berkeley: University of California Press, 2004).
6. This is the essence of Veblen's subject in *Theory of the Leisure Class*, as well as being a major component in Marx's earlier critique of capitalism in *Capital*. See also discussions of "commodity fetishism" and the images (such as advertising) that perpetuate it in Jean Baudrillard, *For a Critique of the Political Economy of the Sign*, trans. Charles Levin (St. Louis, MO: Telos Press, 1981); and Debord, *The Society of the Spectacle*.
7. The experimentation with web pages on the Internet is a kind of return to this awareness of potential in juxtaposing words and pictures.
8. This process was already at play in King's time. Besides taking photographs that reinforced King's new narrative form, describing geological history, O'Sullivan, and other photographers, tried to imitate the characteristics of more accurate diagrams and precisely scaled flat images that could be measured (see Kelsey, "Viewing the Archive").

Bibliography

Primary Sources Published before 1900

Agassiz, Louis. *Études sur les glaciers*. Neuchâtel: Jent et Gassmann, 1840.

Alison, Archibald. *Essays on the Nature and Principles of Taste*. 1790. 5th ed. London: Murray, 1879.

Atwater, Caleb. "Descriptions of the Antiquities Discovered in the State of Ohio and Other Western States." *Archaeologica Americana* 1 (1820): 105–267.

Banvard, John. *Description of Banvard's Panorama of the Mississippi River, Painted on Three Miles of Canvas*. Boston, MA: Putnam, 1847.

Bartlett, John Russell. *Personal Narrative of Explorations and Incidents in Texas, New Mexico, California, Sonora, and Chihuahua, Connected with the United States and Mexican Boundary Survey*, 2 vols. New York: D. Appleton, 1854.

Baxter, DeWitt C. *The Baxter Panoramic Business Directory*. Philadelphia, PA: Baxter, 1859.

Bowditch, James H. *"The City by the Sea": Newport*. Providence, RI: Reid, 1870.

———. *"The City by the Sea": Newport*. Providence, RI: Reid, 1884.

Bowen, Francis. Review of *Historical and Statistical Information Respecting the History, Condition, and Prospects of the Indian Tribes of the United States*, by Henry Rowe Schoolcraft. *North American Review* 77 (1853): 245–62.

Bowen, J. T. *Panorama and Views of Philadelphia and Its Vicinity, Embracing a Collection of 20 Views*. Philadelphia, PA: Bowen, 1838.

Brown, Solyman. *The Citizen and Strangers' Pictorial and Business Directory for the City of New-York and Its Vicinity*. New York: Spalding, 1853.

Bryant, William Cullen, ed. *Picturesque America: Or, The Land We Live In*. 2 vols. New York: Appleton, 1872–1874.

Bryant, William Cullen, and Asher B. Durand, eds. *American Landscape*. No. 1. New York: E. Bliss, 1830.

Burford, Robert. *Description of a View of the Falls of Niagara, Now Exhibiting at the Panorama, Leicester Square*. London: Brettell, 1833.

Cass, Lewis. "Documents and Proceedings Relating to the Formation and Progress of a Board in the City of New York, for the Emigration, Preservation, and Improvement of the Aborigines of America." *North American Review* 30 (1830): 62–121.

———. "Indian Treaties, and Laws and Regulations Relating to Indian Affairs." *North American Review* 24 (1827): 365–442.

Catherwood, Frederick. *Views of Ancient Monuments in Central America: Chiapas and Yucatan*. London: Catherwood, 1844.

Catlin, George. *Illustrations of the Manners, Customs, and Condition of the North American Indians*. London: Bohn, 1851. First published in 1841 as *Letters and Notes on the Manners, Customs, and Condition of the North American Indians*.

Champollion, Jean François. *Lettre à M. Dacier, relatif à l'alphabet des hiéroglyphes phonétiques*. Paris: F. Didot père, 1822.

Chesapeake and Ohio Railway. *Route and Resorts of the Chesapeake and Ohio Railway*. Richmond, VA: Baughman Brothers, 1878.

Chisholm, C. R. *Chisholm's All-Round Route and Panoramic Guide of the St. Lawrence: Hudson River; Saratoga . . . and Western Tourist's Guide to the Famous Summer Resorts of the Great Far West*. Chicago: Chisholm, 1881.

Cole, Thomas. *The Collected Essays and Prose Sketches*, edited by Marshall Tymn. St. Paul, MN: Colet Press, 1980.

———. "Essay on American Scenery." *American Monthly Magazine* 1 (1836).

Cooper, James Fenimore. *The Last of the Mohicans*. 1826. Reprint, New York: Penguin Books, 1986.

Curtis, George William. *Lotus-Eating: A Summer Book*. New York: Harper and Brothers, 1852.

Cuvier, Georges. *Discours sur les révolutions du globe*. Paris: G. Dufour et Ed. D'Ocagne, 1825.

Dry, Camille N. *Pictorial Guide to St. Louis*. St. Louis, MO: Shultz and McDonald, 1877.

Dwight, Theodore. *The Northern Traveller: Containing the Routes to Niagara, Quebec, and the Springs*. New York: Carvill, 1828.

Eastman, Samuel T. *The White Mountain Guide Book*. 2nd ed. Concord, MA: Eastman, 1859.

Emmons, Samuel F., and Arnold Hague. *Descriptive Geology*. Vol. 2 of *Report of the Geological Eploration of the Fortieth Parallel*. Washington, DC: Government Printing Office, 1877.

Emory, William H. *Report of the United States and Mexican Boundary Survey*. Washington, DC: Government Printing Office, 1857–1859.

Gilpin, William. *Observations on the Wye, and Several Parts of South Wales, &c. Relative Chiefly to Picturesque Beauty*. London: Blamire, 1782.

Grand Panorama of London and the R. Thames. London: Azulay, 1849.

Guild, William. *A Chart and Description of the Boston and Worcester and Western Railroads*. Boston, MA: Bradbury and Guild, 1847.

Hariot, Thomas. *A Briefe and True Report of the New Found Land of Virginia*. London: R. Robinson, 1588.

Hart, Alfred A. *The Traveler's Own Book, A Souvenir of Overland Travel, via the Great and Attractive Route*. Chicago: Horton and Leonard, 1870.

Harvey, George. *Harvey's Illustrations of the Scenery, Resources, and Progress of Our Country*. Boston, MA: Dutton and Wentworth, 1851.

Hawthorne, Nathaniel. "My Visit to Niagara." 1835. Reprinted in *Hawthorne's American Travel Sketches*, edited by Alfred Weber, 244–50. Hanover, NH: University Press of New England, 1989.

———. "Sketches from Memory. By a Pedestrian. No. II." 1835. Reprinted in *Hawthorne's American Travel Sketches*, edited by Alfred Weber, 34–35. Hanover, NH: University Press of New England, 1989.

Heckewelder, John Gottlieb. *History, Manners and Customs of the Indian Nations who once Inhabited Pennsylvania and the Neighboring States*. 1818. Rev. ed. Philadelphia: Historical Society of Pennsylvania, 1876.

Higginson, Thomas Wentworth. *Oldport Days*. Boston, MA: Osgood, 1873.

Howells, William Dean. *A Hazard of New Fortunes*. 1890. Reprint, New York: Modern Library, 2002.

Humboldt, Alexander von. *Ansichten der Kordilleran und Monumente der eingeboren Völker Amerikas*. 1810. Reprint, Frankfort am Main: Eichborn Verlag, 2004.

The Iliad of Homer Engraved from the Compositions of John Flaxman R. A. London: Parker, 1805.

Ives, Joseph C. *Report upon the Colorado River of the West, Explored in 1857 and 1858*. Washington, DC: Government Printing Office, 1861.

Jefferson, Thomas. *Notes on the State of Virginia*. 1781. Reprint edited by William Peden. Chapel Hill: University of North Carolina Press, 1982.

King, Clarence. *Systematic Geology*. Vol. 1 of *Report of the Geological Exploration of the Fortieth Parallel*. Washington, DC: Government Printing Office, 1878.

King, Thomas Starr. *The White Hills: Their Legends, Landscape, and Poetry*. Boston, MA: Crosby, Nichols, 1860.

Leon y Gama, Antonio. *An Historical and Chronological Description of Two Stones Found under Ground, in the Great Square of the City of Mexico*. Translated by William E. Huling. Philadelphia, PA: American Philosophical Society, 1818.

Lossing, Benson J. *The Hudson, From the Wilderness to the Sea*. New York: Virtue and Yorston, 1876.

Lyell, Charles. *Principles of Geology: Being an Attempt to Explain the Former Changes to the Earth's Surface, by Reference to Causes Now in Operation*. London: Murray, 1830–1833.

"Lyell's Travels in North America." *Living Age* 66, no. 6 (August 16, 1845): 340–43.

Magoon, Elias, ed. *The Home-Book of the Picturesque: Or, American Scenery, Art, and Literature*. New York: Putnam, 1852.

Marx, Karl. *Capital*. 1867. Selections reprinted in *Karl Marx: Selected Writings*, edited by Lawrence Simon. Indianapolis, IN: Hackett Publishing, 1994.

Mason, George Champlin. *Newport Illustrated in a Series of Pen and Pencil Sketches*. Providence, RI: Appleton, 1854.

Mathews, Cornelius. *Behemoth: A Legend of the Mound-Builders*. 1839. Reprint, New York: Garrett Press, 1970.

McKenney, Thomas, and Edwin Hall. *History of the Indian Tribes of North America: With Biographical Sketches and Anecdotes of the Principal Chiefs*. Philadelphia, PA: Greenough, 1838.

Morton, Samuel. *Crania Americana, or, A Comparative View of the Skulls of Various Aboriginal Nations of North and South America*. Philadelphia, PA: Dobson, 1839.

Nelson, Thomas. *Nelson's Guide to the City of New York and Its Neighborhood*. New York: Nelson and Sons, 1858.

———. *Nelson's Guide to Lake George and Lake Champlain*. New York: Nelson and Sons, 1858.

———. *Nelson's Illustrated Guide to the Hudson and Its Tributaries*. New York: Nelson and Sons, 1860.

———. *Our Summer Retreats: A Handbook to All the Chief Waterfalls, Springs, Mountain and Seaside Resorts*. New York: Nelson and Sons, 1858.

Newberry, John Strong. *Geological Report from Santa Fe to the Junction of the Grand and Green Rivers*. Washington, DC: Government Printing Office, 1876.

Nott, Josiah. *Types of Mankind: or, Ethnological Researches, Based upon the Ancient Monuments, Paintings, Sculptures, and Crania of Races*. London: Trübner, 1854.

"A Novelty in Sign-Making." *Manufacturer and Builder* 4, no. 3 (March 1872): 56.

"Palmer's White Captive." *Atlantic Monthly*, 5, no. 27 (January 1860): 108–109.

Powell, John Wesley. "The Cañons of the Colorado." Pts. 1–3. *Scribner's Monthly* 9, nos. 3–5 (January–March 1875): 293–310, 394–409, 523–37.

———. *Exploration of the Colorado River of the West and Its Tributaries.* Washington, DC: Government Printing Office, 1875.

Pychowska, Lucia. "Sketches of American Life and Scenery." *Continental Monthly* 5, nos. 1–5 (January–April 1864): 9–13, 270–73, 425–31.

Rae, Julio H. *Rae's Philadelphia Pictorial Directory and Panoramic Advertiser.* Philadelphia, PA: Rae, 1851.

Reports of Explorations and Surveys, to Ascertain the Most Practicable and Economical Route for a Railroad from the Mississippi River to the Pacific Ocean. 13 vols. Washington, DC: Government Printing Office, 1855–1861.

Richards, T. Addison. "Idlewild, The Home of N. P. Willis," *Harper's New Monthly Magazine* 16, no. 92 (January 1858): 145–66.

Rousseau, Jean-Jacques. *A Discourse on Inequality.* 1755. Reprinted with translation by Maurice Cranston. New York: Penguin Classics, 1984.

"Scenery on the Erie Railroad." *Harper's New Monthly Magazine* 1, no. 2 (July 1850): 215–18.

Schoolcraft, Henry Rowe. *An Address, Delivered before the Was-ah Ho-De-No-Son-Ne, or New Confederacy of the Iroquois, at Its Third Annual Council.* Rochester, NY: Jerome and Brothers, 1846.

———. *Historical and Statistical Information Respecting the History, Condition, and Prospects of the Indian Tribes of the United States.* 6 vols. Philadelphia, PA: Lippincott, Grambo, 1851–1857.

———. *The Myth of Hiawatha, and Other Oral Legends, Mythologic and Allegoric, of the North American Indians.* Philadelphia, PA: Lippincott, 1856.

———. "The Red Man of America." *North American Review* 54 (1842): 283–95.

Squier, Ephraim G., and Edwin H. Davis. *Ancient Monuments of the Mississippi Valley.* New York: Bartlett and Welford, 1848. Reprint, Washington, DC: Smithsonian Institution Press, 1998.

"Sunnyside, The Home of Washington Irving." *Harper's New Monthly Magazine* 14, no. 79 (December 1856): 1–21.

Taintor, Charles Newhall. *The Connecticut River Route: A Guide of the Most Direct Route from New York to the White Mountains.* New York: Taintor Brothers, Merrill, 1876.

———. *The Hudson River Route: New York to Albany.* New York: Taintor Brothers, Merrill, 1869.

Tennyson, Alfred Lord. "The Lotos-Eaters." 1832. Reprinted in *English Poetry III: From Tennyson to Whitman*, edited by Charles W. Eliot, 1026–37. New York: Collier and Son, 1909.

Thoreau, Henry David. *Walden.* Boston, MA: Ticknor and Fields, 1854. Reprint, New York: Random House, 1981.

Turner, Frederick Jackson. "The Significance of the Frontier in American History." *Report of the American Historical Association* (1893): 199–227.

Turner, J. M. W. *Liber Studiorum.* 1807. Reprint, New York: Stokes, 1911.

———. *Picturesque Views on the Southern Coast of England.* London: Arch, 1826.

Veblen, Thorstein. *The Theory of the Leisure Class.* New York: MacMillan, 1899.

Wall, William Guy. *The Hudson River Portfolio.* New York: Megarey and Gilley, 1821–1825.

Williams, Henry T. *The Pacific Tourist: Williams' Illustrated Trans-Continental Guide of Travel, from the Atlantic to the Pacific Ocean.* 2nd ed. New York: Williams, 1876.

Willis, Nathaniel P. *American Scenery; Or, Land, Lake, and River Illustrations of Transatlantic Nature.* London: Virtue, 1840.

Winckelmann, Johann Joachim. *History of Ancient Art.* 4 vols. 1764. Reprint, New York: Ungar, 1968–1969.

———. *Reflections on the Painting and Sculpture of the Greeks: With Instructions for the Connoisseur, and an Essay on Grace in Works of Art.* Translated by Henry Fuseli. 1755. Reprint, London: Millar, 1765.

Winthrop, Theodore. *Life in the Open Air, and Other Papers.* Boston, MA: Ticknor and Fields, 1863.

Secondary Sources

Abbey, J. R. *Travel in Aquatint and Lithography, 1770–1860.* 2 vols. San Francisco: Alan Wofsy Fine Arts, 1991.

Aikin, Roger Cushing. "Paintings of Manifest Destiny: Mapping the Nation." *American Art* 14, no. 3 (Autumn 2000): 78–89.

Anderson, Benedict. *Imagined Communities: Reflections on the Origin and Spread of Nationalism.* London: Verso Editions, 1983.

Andrus, Lisa Fellows. "Design and Measurement in Luminist Art." In *American Light: The Luminist Movement, 1850–1875*, edited by John Wilmerding, 30–56. New York: Harper and Row, 1980.

Appleton, Jay. *The Experience of Landscape.* London: Wiley, 1975.

Arnold, Malcolm, ed. *The Picturesque: Literary Sources and Documents.* 3 vols. East Sussex: Helm Information, 1994.

Avery, Kevin. "*The Heart of the Andes* Exhibited: Frederic E. Church's Window on the Equatorial World." *American Art Journal* 18 (1986): 52–72.

———. "A Historiography of the Hudson River School." In *American Paradise: The World of the Hudson River School*, by Kevin J. Avery, Oswaldo Rodriguez Roque, John K. Howat, Doreen Bolger Burke, and Catherine Hoover Voorsanger, 3–20. New York: Metropolitan Museum of Art, 1987.

———. "The Reverend E. L. Magoon and the American Drawing Collection." *Magazine Antiques* 157, no. 1 (January 2000): 212–17.

Avery, Kevin, and Franklin Kelly, eds. *Hudson River School Visions: The Landscapes of Sanford R. Gifford*. New York: Metropolitan Museum of Art, 2003.

Bachelard, Gaston. *The Poetics of Space*. Translated by Maria Jolas. New York: Orion Press, 1964.

Baetens, Jan, and Kathryn Hume. "Speed, Rhythm, Movement: A Dialogue on K. Hume's Article 'Narrative Speed.'" *Narrative* 14, no. 3 (2006): 349–55.

Banta, Martha. *Taylored Lives: Narrative Productions in the Age of Taylor, Veblen, and Ford*. Chicago: University of Chicago Press, 1993.

Barnhill, Georgia. Review of *Beyond the Lines: Pictorial Reporting, Everyday Life, and the Crisis of Gilded Age America*, by Joshua Brown. *Winterthur Portfolio* 38, no. 4 (Winter 2003): 269–71.

———. "Transformations in Pictorial Printing." In *A History of the Book in America*, vol. 2, *An Extensive Republic: Print, Culture, and Society in the New Nation, 1790–1840*, edited by Robert A. Gross and Mary Kelley, 422–39. Chapel Hill: University of North Carolina Press, 2010.

Barnhill, Georgia, Diana Korzenik, and Caroline F. Sloat, eds. *The Cultivation of Artists in Nineteenth-Century America*. Worcester, MA: American Antiquarian Society, 1997.

Barnhurst, Kevin G., and John Nerone. "Civic Picturing vs. Realist Photojournalism: The Regime of Illustrated News, 1856–1901." *Design Issues* 16, no. 1 (Spring 2000): 59–79.

Barrell, John. *The Dark Side of the Landscape: The Rural Poor in English Painting, 1730–1840*. New York: Cambridge University Press, 1980.

Barth, Gunther. *City People: The Rise of the Modern City in Nineteenth-Century America*. New York: Oxford University Press, 1980.

Bartlett, Richard. "Scientific Exploration of the American West, 1865–1900." In *A Continent Comprehended*, vol. 3, *North American Exploration*, edited by John Logan Allen, 461–520. Lincoln: University of Nebraska Press, 1997.

Baudrillard, Jean. *For a Critique of the Political Economy of the Sign*. Translated by Charles Levin. St. Louis, MO: Telos Press, 1981.

———. *Simulacra and Simulation*. Translated by Sheila Glaser. Ann Arbor: University of Michigan Press, 1981.

Baur, John I. H. "American Luminism, A Neglected Aspect of the Realist Movement in Nineteenth-Century American Painting." *Perspectives USA* 9 (Fall 1954): 90–98.

Beam, Philip C. *Winslow Homer in the 1890s: Prout's Neck Observed*. New York: Hudson Hills Press, 1990.

Bedell, Rebecca Bailey. *The Anatomy of Nature: Geology and American Landscape Painting, 1825–1875*. Princeton, NJ: Princeton University Press, 2001.

Benjamin, Walter. "On Some Motifs in Baudelaire." 1936. In *Illuminations*, edited by Hannah Arendt, 155–200. Reprint, New York: Harcourt, Brace, and World, 1968.

———. "The Work of Art in the Age of Mechanical Reproduction." 1936. In *Illuminations*, edited by Hannah Arendt, 217–52. Reprint, New York: Harcourt, Brace, and World, 1968.

Bennewitz, Kathleen Motes. "John F. Kensett at Beverly, Massachusetts." *American Art Journal* 21, no. 4 (1989): 46–65.

Bentley, Nancy. *Frantic Panoramas: American Literature and Mass Culture, 1870–1920*. Philadelphia: University of Pennsylvania Press, 2009.

Bergmann, Hans. "Panoramas of New York, 1845–1860." *Prospects* 10 (1985): 119–37.

Berkhofer, Robert E. *The White Man's Indian: Images of the American Indian from Columbus to the Present*. New York: Knopf, 1974.

Bermingham, Ann. *Landscape and Ideology: The English Rustic Tradition, 1740–1860*. Berkeley: University of California Press, 1986.

———. "Landscape-O-Rama: The Exhibition Landscape at Somerset House and the Rise of Popular Landscape Entertainments." In *Art on the Line: The Royal Academy Exhibitions at Somerset House, 1780–1836*, edited by David Solkin, 127–43. New Haven, CT: Yale University Press, 2001.

Bieder, Robert E. *Science Encounters the Indian, 1820–1880*. Norman: University of Oklahoma Press, 1986.

Birmingham, Ann. *Landscape and Ideology: The English Rustic Tradition, 1740–1860*. Berkeley: University of California Press, 1986.

Bjelajac, David. "Thomas Cole's *Oxbow* and the American Zion Divided." *American Art* 20, no. 1 (Spring 2006): 60–83.

Bloemink, Barbara, Sarah Burns, Gail Davidson, and Karal Ann Marling. *Frederic Church, Winslow Homer, and Thomas Moran: Tourism and the American Landscape*. New York: Bulfinch Press, 2006.

Blumin, Stuart M. *The Emergence of the Middle Class: Social Experience in the American City, 1760–1900*. New York: Cambridge University Press, 1989.

Boehme, Sarah E., Christian F. Feest, and Patricia Condon Johnston. *Seth Eastman: A Portfolio of North American Indians*. Afton, MN: Afton Historical Society Press, 1995.

Bogue, Allan. *Frederick Jackson Turner: Strange Roads Going Down*. Norman: University of Oklahoma Press, 1998.

Boime, Albert. *The Magisterial Gaze: Manifest Destiny and American Landscape Painting, c. 1830–1865*. Washington, DC: Smithsonian Institution Press, 1991.

Bremer, Richard G. *Indian Agent and Wilderness Scholar: The Life of Henry Rowe Schoolcraft*. Mount Pleasant: Clarke Historical Library, Central Michigan University, 1987.

Brewer, John. "Sensibility and the Urban Panorama." *Huntington Library Quarterly* 70, no. 2 (June 2007): 229–49.

Brown, Bill. *A Sense of Things: The Object Matter of American Literature*. Chicago: University of Chicago Press, 2003.

Brown, Dona. *Inventing New England: Regional Tourism in the Nineteenth Century*. Washington, DC: Smithsonian Institution Press, 1995.

Brunet, François. "Revisiting the Enigmas of Timothy O'Sullivan: Notes on the William Ashburner Collection of King Survey Photographs at the Bancroft Library." *History of Photography* 31, no. 2 (2007): 97–133.

Bucher, Bernadette. *Icon and Conquest: A Structural Analysis of the Illustrations of De Bry's Great Voyages*. Translated by Basia Miller Gulati. Chicago: University of Chicago Press, 1981.

Buzard, James. *The Beaten Track: European Tourism, Literature, and the Ways to Culture, 1800–1918*. New York: Oxford University Press, 1993.

Cahill, Cathleen. *Federal Fathers and Mothers: A Social History of the United States Indian Service, 1869–1933*. Chapel Hill: University of North Carolina Press, 2011.

Callow, James T. *Kindred Spirits: Knickerbocker Writers and American Artists, 1807–1855*. Chapel Hill: University of North Carolina Press, 1967.

Castelloe, Timothy M. *The British Aesthetic Tradition: From Shaftesbury to Wittgenstein*. Cambridge: Cambridge University Press, 2013.

Castleberry, May, ed. *Perpetual Mirage: Photographic Narratives of the Desert West*. New York: Whitney Museum of American Art, 1996.

Castronovo, Russ. *Beautiful Democracy: Aesthetics and Anarchy in a Global Era*. Chicago: University of Chicago Press, 2007.

Childs, Elizabeth. "Time's Profile: John Wesley Powell, Art, and Geology at the Grand Canyon." *American Art* 10, no. 1 (Spring 1996): 6–35.

Clark, T. J. *The Painting of Modern Life: Paris in the Art of Manet and His Followers*. New York: Knopf, 1985.

Clements, William M. "Schoolcraft as Textmaker." *Journal of American Folklore* 103, no. 408 (April–June 1990): 177–92.

Clifford, James. *The Predicament of Culture: Twentieth-Century Ethnography, Literature, and Art*. Cambridge, MA: Harvard University Press, 1988.

Comment, Bernard. *The Painted Panorama*. London: Reaktion Books, 1999.

Conn, Steven. *History's Shadow: Native Americans and Historical Consciousness in the Nineteenth Century*. Chicago: University of Chicago Press, 2004.

Craib, Raymond. "A Nationalist Metaphysics: State Fixations, National Maps, and the Geo-Historical Imagination in Nineteenth-Century Mexico." *Hispanic American Historical Review* 82, no. 1 (February 2002): 33–68.

Crary, Jonathan. *Techniques of the Observer: On Vision and Modernity in the Nineteenth Century*. Cambridge, MA: MIT Press, 1990.

Cutler, Edward S. *Recovering the New: Transatlantic Roots of Modernism*. Hanover: University of New Hampshire Press, 2003.

Curtis, Gerard. *Visual Words: Art and the Material Book in Victorian England*. Burlington, VT: Ashgate Publishing, 2002.

Danly, Susan, and Leo Marx, eds. *The Railroad in American Art: Representations of Technological Change*. Cambridge, MA: MIT Press, 1988.

Debord, Guy. *The Society of the Spectacle*. New York: Zone Books, 1994.

Dell'Arco, Maurizio Fagiolo, ed. *The Grand Tour: Landscape and Veduta Paintings, Venice and Rome in the 18th Century*. Atlanta, GA: Oglethorpe University Museum, 1997.

DeLue, Rachel, and James Elkins, eds. *Landscape Theory*. New York: Routledge, 2008.

Dingus, Rick. *The Photographic Artifacts of Timothy O'Sullivan*. Albuquerque: University of New Mexico Press, 1982.

Dippie, Brian W. *Catlin and His Contemporaries: The Politics of Patronage*. Lincoln: University of Nebraska Press, 1990.

———. *The Vanishing American: White Attitudes and U.S. Indian Policy*. Middletown, CT: Wesleyan University Press, 1982.

Drinnon, Richard. *Facing West: The Metaphysics of Indian-Hating and Empire Building*. Minneapolis: University of Minnesota Press, 1980.

Driscoll, John Paul. "From Burin to Brush: The Development of a Painter." In *John Frederick Kensett: An American Master*, edited by John Paul Driscoll and John K. Howat, 48–135. New York: Worcester Art Museum, 1985.

Driscoll, John Paul, and John K. Howat, eds. *John Frederick Kensett: An American Master*. New York: Worcester Art Museum, 1985.

Dubbini, Renzo. *Geography of the Gaze: Urban and Rural Vision in Early Modern Europe*. Chicago: University of Chicago Press, 2002.

Durrans, Brian. "The Future of the Other: Changing Cultures on Display in Ethnographic Museums." In *Museum Time-Machine: Putting Cultures on Display*, edited by Robert Lumley, 144–69. New York: Routledge, 1988.

Evans, R. Tripp. *Romancing the Maya: Mexican Antiquity in the American Imagination, 1820–1915*. Austin: University of Texas Press, 2004.

Fabian, Johannes. *Time and the Other: How Anthropology Makes Its Object*. New York: Columbia University Press, 1983.

Fender, Stephen. "American Landscape and the Figure of Anticipation." In *Views of American Landscape*, edited by Mick Gidley and Robert Lawson-Peebles, 51–63. New York: Cambridge University Press, 1989.

Ferber, Linda S. "Luminist Drawings." In *American Light: The Luminist Movement, 1850–1875*, edited by John Wilmerding, 237–65. New York: Harper and Row, 1980.

———. *Tokens of a Friendship: Miniature Watercolors by William T. Richards*. New York: Metropolitan Museum of Art, 1982.

———. *William Trost Richards (1833–1905): American Landscape and Marine Painter.* New York: Garland, 1980.

Ferber, Linda S., and Barbara Dayer Gallati. *Masters of Color and Light: Homer, Sargent, and the American Watercolor Movement.* Washington, DC: Smithsonian Institution Press, 1998.

Ferber, Linda S., and William H. Gerdts, eds. *The New Path: Ruskin and the Pre-Raphaelites*. Brooklyn, NY: Schocken Books, 1985.

Finberg, Alexander J. *The History of Turner's* Liber Studiorum. London: Benn, 1924.

Fryd, Vivien Green. *Art and Empire: The Politics of Ethnicity in the United States Capitol, 1815–1860*. New Haven, CT: Yale University Press, 1992.

Galassi, Peter. *Before Photography: Painting and the Invention of Photography.* New York: Museum of Modern Art, 1981.

Gassan, Richard. *The Birth of American Tourism: New York, the Hudson Valley, and American Culture, 1790–1830.* Amherst: University of Massachusetts Press, 2008.

Gaudio, Michael. *Engraving the Savage: The New World and Techniques of Civilization*. Minneapolis: University of Minnesota Press, 2008.

Geertz, Clifford. *The Interpretation of Cultures: Selected Essays*. New York: Basic Books, 1973.

Genette, Gérard. *Narrative Discourse: An Essay in Method.* Translated by Jane E. Lewin. Ithaca, NY: Cornell University Press, 1980.

Georgi, Karen. "Defining Landscape Painting in Nineteenth-Century American Critical Discourse. Or, Should Art 'Deal in Wares the Age Has Need of'?" *Oxford Art Journal* 29, no. 2 (2006): 227–45.

Goetzmann, William H. *Army Exploration of the American West, 1803–1863*. New Haven, CT: Yale University Press, 1959.

———. *Exploration and Empire: The Explorer and the Scientist in the Winning of the American West.* New York: Knopf, 1966.

Goldman, Paul. *Victorian Illustrated Books, 1850–1870: The Heyday of Wood-Engraving.* London: British Museum Press, 1994.

Goodrich, Carter. *Government Promotion of American Canals, 1800–1890.* New York: Columbia University Press, 1960.

Gould, Stephen Jay. *Time's Arrow, Time's Cycle: Myth and Metaphor in the Discovery of Geological Time.* Cambridge, MA: Harvard University Press, 1987.

Grafton, Melissa. "'It Is a Joint Venture': John Frederick Kensett's Images for *Lotus-Eating*." *American Art* 25, no. 2 (Summer 2011): 104–19.

Greenhill, Jennifer. "Winslow Homer and the Mechanics of the Visual Deadpan." *Art History* 32, no. 2 (April 2009): 351–86.

Gunning, Tom. "The Cinema of Attraction: Early Film, Its Spectator, and the Avant-Garde." *Wide Angle* 8, nos. 3 and 4 (Fall 1986): 63–70.

Hales, Peter. *Silver Cities: Photographing American Urbanization, 1839–1939.* Philadelphia, PA: Temple University Press, 1984.

Halliday, Peter J. "Early Photography and the Reception of Classical Antiquity: The Case of the Temple of Athena Nike." *Periklean Athens and Its Legacy: Problems and Perspectives*, edited by Judith M. Barringer and Jeffrey M. Hurwit, 237–52. Austin: University of Texas Press, 2005.

Haltman, Kenneth. "Flight and Predation: The Anti-Documentary Poetics of Alfred Jacob Miller." *American Art* 28, no. 1 (Spring 2014): 32–55.

———. *Looking Close, Seeing Far: Samuel Seymour, Titian Ramsay Peale, and the Art of the Long Expedition, 1818–1823.* University Park: Pennsylvania State University Press, 2008.

Hamilton, Sinclair. *Early American Book Illustrators and Wood Engravers, 1670–1870.* Princeton, NJ: Princeton University Press, 1958.

Hardwick, Bonnie Skell. *Science and Art: The Travel Writings of the Great Surveys of the American West after the Civil War.* Ann Arbor, MI: University Microfilms International, 1980.

Harris, Neil. *The Artist in American Society: The Formative Years, 1790–1860*. Chicago: University of Chicago Press, 1966.

Hartel, Herbert. "Luminism, Transcendentalism, and Abstraction in the Landscape Paintings of John F. Kensett." *Source: Notes in the History of Art* 21, no. 4 (Summer 2002): 23–30.

Hausdoerffer, John. *Catlin's Lament: Indians, Manifest Destiny, and the Ethics of Nature*. Lawrence: University of Kansas Press, 2009.

Henkin, David M. "City Streets and the Urban World of Print." In *A History of the Book in America*, vol. 3, *The Industrial Book, 1840–1880*, edited by Scott E. Casper, Jeffrey D. Groves, Stephen W. Nissenbaum, and Michael Winship, 331–45. Chapel Hill: University of North Carolina Press, 2007.

Herrmann, Luke. *Turner Prints: The Engraved Work of J. M. W. Turner.* New York: New York University Press, 1990.

Hight, Kathryn S. "'Doomed to Perish': George Catlin's Depictions of the Mandan." *Art Journal* 49, no. 2 (Summer 1990): 119–24.

Hills, Patricia. "Picturing Progress in the Era of Westward Expansion." In *The West as America: Reinterpreting Images of the Frontier, 1820–1920*, edited by William H. Truettner, 126–31. Washington, DC: Smithsonian Institution Press, 1991.

Hine, Robert V. *Bartlett's West: Drawing the Mexican Boundary.* New Haven, CT: Yale University Press, 1968.

Hinsley, Curtis M. *Savages and Scientists: The Smithsonian Institution and the Development of American*

Anthropology, 1846–1910. Washington, DC: Smithsonian Institution Press, 1981.

Hobsbawm, Eric. *The Age of Empire, 1875–1914*. New York: Random House, 1987.

Hochfelder, David. *The Telegraph in America, 1832–1920*. Baltimore, MD: John Hopkins University Press, 2012.

Howat, John K. "Kensett's World." In *John Frederick Kensett: An American Master*, edited by John Paul Driscoll and John K. Howat, 12–47. New York: Worcester Art Museum, 1985.

Huhtamo, Erkki. "Global Glimpses for Local Realities: The Moving Panorama, a Forgotten Mass Medium of the 19th Century." *Art Inquiry* 4 (2002): 193–228.

———. *Illusions in Motion: Media Archaeology of the Moving Panorama and Related Spectacles*. Cambridge, MA: MIT Press, 2013.

Hume, Kathryn. "Narrative Speed in Contemporary Fiction." *Narrative* 13, no. 2 (2005): 105–24.

Huntington, Daniel. *Art and the Excited Spirit: America in the Romantic Mood*. Ann Arbor: University of Michigan Press, 1972.

Huntington, David C. "Church and Luminism: Light for America's Elect." In *American Light: The Luminist Movement, 1850–1875*, edited by John Wilmerding, 155–90. New York: Harper and Row, 1980.

Huseman, Ben. *Wild River, Timeless Canyons: Balduin Möllhausen's Watercolors of the Colorado*. Fort Worth, TX: Amon Carter Museum, 1995.

Iarocci, Louisa. *The Urban Department Store in America, 1850–1930*. Farnham, Surrey: Ashgate, 2014.

Irwin, David, ed. *Winckelmann: Writings on Art*. London: Phaidon, 1972.

Iser, Wolfgang. *The Act of Reading: A Theory of Aesthetic Response*. Baltimore, MD: Johns Hopkins University Press, 1978.

———. *The Implied Reader: Patterns of Communication in Prose from Bunyan to Beckett*. Baltimore, MD: Johns Hopkins University Press, 1974.

Jarman, Baird. "The Graphic Art of Thomas Nast: Politics and Propriety in Postbellum Publishing." *American Periodicals* 20, no. 2 (2010): 156–89.

Jones, Karen, and John Wills. *The American West: Competing Visions*. Edinburgh: University of Edinburgh Press, 2009.

Jurovics, Toby, Carol M. Johnson, Glenn Willumson, and William F. Stapp. *Framing the West: The Survey Photographs of Timothy O'Sullivan*. New Haven, CT: Yale University Press, 2010.

Karp, Walter. "The American Land As It Was." *American Heritage Magazine* 21, no. 1 (December 1969): 16–21.

Kelly, Franklin. *Frederic Edwin Church*. Washington, DC: Smithsonian Institution Press, 1988.

Kelsey, Robin E. *Archive Style: Photographs and Illustrations for U.S. Surveys, 1850–1890*. Berkeley: University of California Press, 2007.

———. "Viewing the Archive: Timothy O'Sullivan's Photographs for the Wheeler Survey, 1871–1874." *Art Bulletin* 85, no. 4 (December 2003): 702–23.

Kern, Stephen. *The Culture of Time and Space, 1880–1918*. Boston, MA: Harvard University Press, 1983.

Kinsey, Joni Louise. *Thomas Moran and the Surveying of the American West*. Washington, DC: Smithsonian Institution Press, 1992.

———. *Thomas Moran's West: Chromolithography, High Art, and Popular Taste*. Lawrence: University of Kansas Press, 2006.

Kirby, Lynne. *Parallel Tracks: The Railroad and Silent Cinema*. Durham, NC: Duke University Press, 1997.

Knoper, Randall. "Writing, American Literature, and Media Ecologies." *American Literary History* 23, no. 2 (Summer 2011): 362–79.

Koshar, Rudy. "'What Ought to Be Seen': Tourists' Guidebooks and National Identity in Modern Germany and Europe." *Journal of Contemporary History* 33, no. 3 (1998): 323–40.

Krauss, Rosalind. *The Originality of the Avant-Garde and Other Modernist Myths*. Cambridge, MA: MIT Press, 1985.

Lawrence, D. H. *Studies in Classic American Literature*. 1923. Reprint, New York: Viking Press, 1964.

Lears, T. J. Jackson. "Beyond Veblen: Rethinking Consumer Culture in America." In *Consuming Visions: Accumulation and Display of Goods in America, 1880–1920*, edited by Simon J. Bronner, 73–97. New York: Norton, 1989.

Leja, Michael. *Looking Askance: Skepticism and American Art from Eakins to Duchamp*. Berkeley: University of California Press, 2004.

Lewis, Robert. "Wild American Savages and the Civilized English." *European Journal of American Studies* 1 (2008): 2–18.

Limerick, Patricia. *Legacy of Conquest: The Unbroken Past of the American West*. New York: Norton, 1987.

Loughran, Trish. *The Republic in Print: Print Culture in the Age of U.S. Nation Building, 1770–1870*. New York: Columbia University Press, 2007.

Lovell, Margaretta. *A Visitable Past: Views of Venice by American Artists, 1860–1915*. Chicago: University of Chicago Press, 1989.

Luarca-Shoaf, Nenette. "Excavating a Nineteenth-Century Medium." *American Art* 27, no. 2 (Summer 2013): 15–20.

Lubin, David. *Picturing a Nation: Art and Social Change in Nineteenth-Century America*. New Haven, CT: Yale University Press, 1996.

Maddox, Kenneth. "Thomas Cole and the Railroad: Gentle Maledictions." *Archives of American Art* 26, no. 1 (1986): 2–10.

M. and M. Karolik Collection of American Water Colors and Drawings. Boston, MA: Museum of Fine Arts, 1962.

Manthorne, Katherine. *Luminist Horizons: The Art and Collection of James A. Suydam*. New York: Braziller, 2006.

Marx, Leo. *The Machine in the Garden: Technology and the Pastoral Ideal in America*. New York: Oxford University Press, 1964.

———. "The Railroad-in-the-Landscape: An Iconological Reading of a Theme in American Art." In *The Railroad in American Art: Representations of Technological Change*, edited by Susan Danly and Leo Marx, 183–208. Cambridge, MA: MIT Press, 1988.

Marzio, Peter. *The Democratic Art: An Exhibition on the History of Chromolithography in America, 1840–1900.* Fort Worth, TX: Amon Carter Museum, 1979.

Maxwell, Richard, ed. *The Victorian Illustrated Book.* Charlottesville: University of Virginia Press, 2002.

Mazel, David. "'A Beautiful and Thrilling Specimen': George Catlin, the Death of the Wilderness, and the Birth of the National Subject." In *Reading the Earth: New Directions in the Study of Literature and Environment*, edited by Michael B. Branch, 129–43. Moscow: University of Idaho Press, 1988.

McCoubrey, John, ed. *American Art, 1700–1960: Sources and Documents.* Englewood Cliffs, NJ: Prentice Hall, 1965.

McDermott, John Francis. *The Lost Panoramas of the Mississippi.* Chicago: University of Chicago Press, 1958.

McPhee, John. *Basin and Range.* New York: Farrar, Straus, Giroux, 1980.

———. *In Suspect Terrain.* New York: Farrar, Straus, Giroux, 1983.

Miller, Angela. *The Empire of the Eye: Landscape Representation and American Cultural Politics, 1825–1875.* Ithaca, NY: Cornell University Press, 1993.

———. "Landscape Taste as an Indicator of Class Identity in Antebellum America." In *Art in Bourgeois Society, 1790–1850*, edited by Andrew Hemingway and William Vaughan, 340–61. Cambridge: Cambridge University Press, 1998.

———. "Space as Destiny: The Panorama Vogue in Mid-Nineteenth-Century America." In *World Art: Themes of Unity and Diversity*, edited by Irving Lavin, 739–44. University Park: Pennsylvania State University Press, 1989.

Miller, David C. "The Iconology of Wrecked or Stranded Boats in Mid to Late Nineteenth-Century American Culture." In *American Iconology: New Approaches to Nineteenth-Century Art and Literature*, edited by David C. Miller, 186–208. New Haven, CT: Yale University Press, 1993.

Miller, Lillian B. *Patrons and Patriotism: The Encouragement of the Fine Arts in America, 1790–1860.* Chicago: University of Chicago Press, 1966.

Mitchell, Mark. "First Light: John I. H. Baur, James Suydam, and Luminism." *Archives of American Art Journal* 46, no. 1 (2006): 24–35.

Mitchell, W. J. T. *Iconology: Image, Text, Ideology.* Chicago: University of Chicago Press, 1987.

———. *Picture Theory: Essays on Verbal and Visual Representation.* Chicago: University of Chicago Press, 1994.

Monger, J. W. H., and G. A. Davis. "Evolving Concepts of the Tectonics of the North American Cordillera." In *Frontiers of Geological Exploration of Western North America*, edited by Alan E. Leviton, Peter U. Rodda, Ellis Yochelson, and Michele L. Aldrich, 215–48. Fresno, CA: Pacific Division of the American Association for the Advancement of Science, 1982.

Naef, Weston. *Era of Exploration: The Rise of Landscape Photography in the American West, 1860–1885.* Buffalo, NY: Albright-Knox Art Gallery, 1975.

Nash, Roderick. *The Wilderness and the American Mind.* 1967. Reprint, New Haven, CT: Yale University Press, 1983.

Newhall, Beaumont. *Photography: A Short Critical History.* New York: Museum of Modern Art, 1938.

Novak, Barbara. *American Painting of the Nineteenth Century: Realism, Idealism, and the American Experience.* New York: Oxford University Press, 1969.

———. *Nature and Culture: American Landscape and Painting, 1825–1875.* New York: Oxford University Press, 1980.

———. "On Defining Luminism." In *American Light: The Luminist Movement, 1850–1875*, edited by John Wilmerding, 23–30. New York: Harper and Row, 1980.

Oettermann, Stephan. *The Panorama: History of a Mass Medium.* New York: Zone Books, 1997.

Panofsky, Erwin. *Perspective as Symbolic Form.* Cambridge, MA: Zone Books, 1991.

Parkinson, Richard. *Cracking Codes: The Rosetta Stone and Decipherment.* Berkeley: University of California Press, 1999.

Parry, Ellwood C., III. *The Art of Thomas Cole: Ambition and Imagination.* Newark: University of Delaware Press, 1988.

———. *The Image of the Indian and the Black Man in American Art, 1590–1900.* New York: Braziller, 1974.

———. "Overlooking the Oxbow: Thomas Cole's *View from Mount Holyoke* Revisited." *American Art Journal* 34–35 (2003–2004): 6–61.

Patterson, Cynthia. "'Illustration of a Picture': Nineteenth-Century Writers and the Philadelphia Pictorials." *American Periodicals* 19, no. 2 (2009): 136–64.

Peck, H. "Unlikely Kindred Spirits: A New Vision of Landscape in the Works of Henry David Thoreau and Asher B. Durand." *American Literary History* 17, no. 4 (Winter 2005): 687–713.

Plotz, John. "Can the Sofa Speak? A Look at Thing Theory." *Criticism* 47, no. 1 (Winter 2005): 109–18.

Ponko, Vincent, Jr. "The Military Explorers of the American West, 1838–1860." In *A Continent Comprehended*, vol. 3, *North American Exploration*, edited by John Logan Allen, 332–411. Lincoln: University of Nebraska Press, 1997.

Powell, Earl A. "Luminism and the American Sublime." In *American Light: The Luminist Movement, 1850–1875*, edited by John Wilmerding, 69–94. New York: Harper and Row, 1980.

———. *Thomas Cole*. New York: Abrams, 1990.

Pratt, Mary Louise. *Imperial Eyes: Travel Writing and Transculturation*. New York: Routledge, 1992.

Prucha, Francis Paul. *American Indian Policy in the Formative Years: The Indian Trade and Intercourse Acts, 1780–1834*. Lincoln: University of Nebraska Press, 1964.

———. *The Great Father: The United States Government and the American Indians*. Lincoln: University of Nebraska Press, 1986.

Rainey, Sue. *Creating Picturesque America: Monument to the Natural and Cultural Landscape*. Nashville, TN: Vanderbilt University Press, 1994.

Ricoeur, Paul. *Time and Narrative*. 3 vols. Chicago: University of Chicago Press, 1984–1988.

Rifkin, Mark. *Manifesting America: The Imperial Construction of U.S. National Space*. New York: Oxford University Press, 2009.

Rigal, Laura. *The American Manufactory: Art, Labor, and the World of Things*. Princeton, NJ: Princeton University Press, 1998.

Ringe, Donald. *The Pictorial Mode: Space and Time in the Art of Irving, Bryant, and Cooper*. Lexington: University of Kentucky Press, 1971.

Roberts, Jennifer. *Transporting Visions: The Movement of Images in Early America*. Berkeley: University of California Press, 2014.

Roque, Oswaldo Rodriguez. "The Last Summer's Work." In *John Frederick Kensett: An American Master*, edited by John Paul Driscoll and John K. Howat, 136–61. New York: Worcester Art Museum, 1985.

Rubin, James. *Impressionism and the Modern Landscape: Productivity, Technology, and Urbanization from Manet to Van Gogh*. Berkeley: University of California Press, 2008.

Schimmel, Julie. "Inventing the 'Indian.'" In *The West as America: Reinterpreting Images of the Frontier, 1820–1920*, edited by William S. Truettner, 149–89. Washington, DC: Smithsonian Institution Press, 1991.

Schivelbusch, Wolfgang. *The Railway Journey: The Industrialization of Time and Space in the 19th Century*. Berkeley: University of California Press, 1977.

Schulman, Vanessa Meikle. "'Making the Magazine': Visuality, Managerial Capitalism, and the Mass Production of Periodicals." *American Periodicals* 22, no. 1 (2012): 1–28.

Schuyler, David. "The Mid-Hudson Valley as Iconic Landscape: Tourism, Economic Development, and the Beginnings of a Preservationist Impulse." In *Within the Landscape: Essays on Nineteenth-Century American Art and Culture*, edited by Phillip Earenfight and Nancy Siegel, 11–42. Carlisle, PA: Trout Gallery, 2005.

———. *Sanctified Landscape: Writers, Artists, and the Hudson River Valley, 1820–1909*. Ithaca, NY: Cornell University Press, 2012.

Scobey, David. "Anatomy of the Promenade: The Politics of Bourgeois Sociability in Nineteenth-Century New York." *Social History* 17, no. 2 (May 1992): 203–27.

Sears, John F. *Sacred Places: American Tourist Attractions in the Nineteenth Century*. New York: Oxford University Press, 1989.

Shank, William H. *Towpaths to Tugboats: A History of American Canal Engineering*. York, PA: American Canal and Transportation Center, 1982.

Shannon, Christopher. *Conspicuous Criticism: Tradition, the Individual, and Culture in American Social Thought, from Veblen to Mills*. Baltimore, MD: Johns Hopkins University Press, 1996.

Simmel, Georg. "The Metropolis and Mental Life." In *Simmel on Culture: Selected Writings*, edited by David Frisby and Mike Featherstone, 174–85. 1903. Reprint, London: Sage, 1997.

Sloan, Kim. *Alexander and John Robert Cozens: The Poetry of Landscape*. London: Victoria and Albert Museum, 1986–1987.

Slotkin, Richard. *Regeneration through Violence: The Mythology of the American Frontier, 1600–1860*. Middletown, CT: Wesleyan University Press, 1973.

Smith, Greg. *Thomas Girtin: The Art of Watercolor*. London: Tate Gallery, 2002.

Smith, Henry Nash. *Virgin Land: The West as Symbol and Myth*. Cambridge, MA: Harvard University Press, 1950.

Snyder, Joel. *American Frontiers: The Photographs of Timothy H. O'Sullivan, 1867–1874*. Philadelphia, PA: Philadelphia Museum of Art, 1981.

———. "Territorial Photography." In *Landscape and Power*, edited by W. J. T. Mitchell, 175–207. Chicago: University of Chicago Press, 1994.

Stafford, Barbara. *Voyage into Substance: Art, Science, Nature, and the Illustrated Travel Account*. Cambridge, MA: MIT Press, 2004.

Staley, Allen. *The Pre-Raphaelite Landscape*. New York: Oxford University Press, 1973.

Stauffer, David M. *American Engravers upon Copper and Steel*. 2 vols. Newcastle, DE: Oak Knoll Books, 1994.

Stebbins, Theodore E., Jr. "Luminism in Context: A New View." In *American Light: The Luminist Movement, 1850–1875*, edited by John Wilmerding, 211–36. New York: Harper and Row, 1980.

Stegner, Wallace. *Beyond the Hundredth Meridian: John Wesley Powell and the Second Opening of the West*. Boston, MA: Houghton Mifflin, 1954.

———. "Powell and the Names on the Plateau." *Western Humanities Review* 50, no. 4 and 51, no. 1 (Winter 1996–Spring 1997): 105–10.

Stein, Roger. *John Ruskin and Aesthetic Thought in America*. Boston, MA: Harvard University Press, 1967.

Sterngass, Jon. *First Resorts: Pursuing Pleasure at Saratoga Springs, Newport, and Coney Island*. Baltimore, MD: Johns Hopkins University Press, 2001.

Stewart, Susan. *On Longing: Narratives of the Miniature, the Gigantic, the Souvenir, the Collection*. Baltimore, MD: Johns Hopkins University Press, 1984.

Sweeney, J. Gray. "Inventing Luminism: 'Labels Are the Dickens.'" *Oxford Art Journal* 26, no. 2 (June 2003): 95–120.

Symmons, Sarah. *Flaxman and Europe: The Outline Illustrations and Their Influence*. New York: Garland, 1984.

Tatham, David. "Frank Leavitt's Pictorial Maps of the White Mountains." In *Prints of New England*, edited by Georgia Barnhill, 105–34. Worcester, MA: American Antiquarian Society, 1991.

———. *Winslow Homer and the Illustrated Book*. Syracuse, NY: Syracuse University Press, 1992.

Terdiman, Richard. *Present Past: Modernity and the Memory Crisis*. Ithaca, NY: Cornell University Press, 1993.

Tharaud, Jerome. "Evangelical Space." *American Art* 28, no. 3 (Fall 2014): 52–75.

Tilman, Rick. *Thorstein Veblen, John Dewey, C. Wright Mills and the Generic Ends of Life*. Lanham, MD: Rowman and Littlefield, 2003.

Trachtenberg, Alan. *Reading American Photographs: Images as History, Mathew Brady to Walker Evans*. New York: Hill and Wang, 1989.

Trigger, Bruce. *A History of Archaeological Thought*. New York: Cambridge University Press, 1989.

Truettner, William H. *The Natural Man Observed: A Study of Catlin's Indian Gallery*. Washington, DC: Smithsonian Institution Press, 1979.

———. "'Scenes of Majesty and Enduring Interest': Thomas Moran Goes West." *Art Bulletin* 58, no. 2 (June 1976): 241–59.

Truettner, William H., and Alan Wallach, eds. *Thomas Cole: Landscape into History*. New Haven, CT: Yale University Press, 1994.

Tyler, Ron. *Prints of the West*. Golden, CO: Fulcrum, 1994.

Tyler, Ron, and Brandon K. Ruud. *Karl Bodmer's North American Prints*. Lincoln: University of Nebraska Press, 2004.

Urry, John. *The Tourist Gaze: Leisure and Travel in Contemporary Societies*. London: Sage, 1990.

Van Noy, Rick. *Surveying the Interior: Literary Cartographers and the Sense of Place*. Reno: University of Nevada Press, 2003.

Wallach, Alan. "Thomas Cole's *River in the Catskills* as Antipastoral." *Art Bulletin* 84, no. 2 (June 2002): 334–50.

Ward, David. *Charles Willson Peale: Art and Selfhood in the Early Republic*. Berkeley: University of California Press, 2004.

Ward, Gerald, ed. *The American Illustrated Book in the Nineteenth Century*. Winterthur, DE: Winterthur Museum, 1987.

Weber, Alfred, ed. *Hawthorne's American Travel Sketches*. Hanover, NH: University Press of New England, 1989.

West, Elliott. "Reconstructing Race." *Western Historical Quarterly* 34, no. 1 (Spring 2003): 6–26.

White, Richard. *The Middle Ground: Indians, Empires, and Republics in the Great Lakes Region, 1650–1815*. New York: Cambridge University Press, 1991.

Williams, Raymond. *The English Novel from Dickens to Lawrence*. New York: Oxford University Press, 1970.

Wilmerding, John, ed. *American Light: The Luminist Movement, 1850–1875*. New York: Harper and Row, 1980.

Wilton, Andrew, and Tim Barringer. *American Sublime: Landscape Painting in the United States, 1820–1880*. Princeton, NJ: Princeton University Press, 2002.

Wolf, Bryan Jay. *Romantic Re-Vision: Culture and Consciousness in Nineteenth-Century American Painting and Literature*. Chicago: University of Chicago Press, 1982.

Yablon, Nick. *Untimely Ruins: An Archaeology of American Urban Modernity, 1819–1919*. Chicago: University of Chicago Press, 2009.

Ziff, Larzer. *Writing in the New Nation: Prose, Print, and Politics in the Early Republic*. New Haven, CT: Yale University Press, 1991.

Illustrations

Figures

Plates

Index

References to illustrations appear in italic type.